Elasticsearch: The Definitive Guide

Clinton Gormley and Zachary Tong

Beijing · Cambridge · Farnham · Köln · Sebastopol · Tokyo

Elasticsearch: The Definitive Guide

by Clinton Gormley and Zachary Tong

Copyright © 2015 Elasticsearch. All rights reserved.

Printed in the United States of America.

Published by O'Reilly Media, Inc. , 1005 Gravenstein Highway North, Sebastopol, CA 95472.

O'Reilly books may be purchased for educational, business, or sales promotional use. Online editions are also available for most titles (*http://safaribooksonline.com*). For more information, contact our corporate/institutional sales department: 800-998-9938 or corporate@oreilly.com.

Editors: Mike Loukides and Brian Anderson
Production Editor: Shiny Kalapurakkel
Proofreader: Sharon Wilkey
Indexer: Ellen Troutman-Zaig

Interior Designer: David Futato
Cover Designer: Ellie Volkhausen
Illustrator: Rebecca Demarest

January 2015: First Edition

Revision History for the First Edition
2015-01-16: First Release

See *http://oreilly.com/catalog/errata.csp?isbn=9781449358549* for release details.

978-1-449-35854-9

[LSI]

Table of Contents

Part I. Getting Started

Part III.   Dealing with Human Language

Part IV.   Aggregations

Part V.   Geolocation

Part VI.   Modeling Your Data

Foreword

One of the most nerve-wracking periods when releasing the first version of an open source project occurs when the IRC channel is created. You are all alone, eagerly hoping and wishing for the first user to come along. I still vividly remember those days.

One of the first users that jumped on IRC was Clint, and how excited was I. Well… for a brief period, until I found out that Clint was actually a Perl user, no less working on a website that dealt with obituaries. I remember asking myself why couldn't we get someone from a more "hyped" community, like Ruby or Python (at the time), and a slightly nicer use case.

How wrong I was. Clint ended up being instrumental to the success of Elasticsearch. He was the first user to roll out Elasticsearch into production (version 0.4 no less!), and the interaction with Clint was pivotal during the early days in shaping Elasticsearch into what it is today. Clint has a unique insight into what is simple, and he is very rarely wrong, which has a huge impact on various usability aspects of Elasticsearch, from management, to API design, to day-to-day usability features. It was a no brainer for us to reach out to Clint and ask if he would join our company immediately after we formed it.

Another one of the first things we did when we formed the company was offer public training. It's hard to express how nervous we were about whether or not people would even sign up for it.

We were wrong.

The trainings were and still are a rave success with waiting lists in all major cities. One of the people who caught our eye was a young fellow, Zach, who came to one of our trainings. We knew about Zach from his blog posts about using Elasticsearch (and secretly envied his ability to explain complex concepts in a very simple manner) and from a PHP client he wrote for the software. What we found out was that Zach had actually paid to attend the Elasticsearch training out of his own pocket! You can't really ask for more than that, and we reached out to Zach and asked if he would join our company as well.

Both Clint and Zach are pivotal to the success of Elasticsearch. They are wonderful communicators who can explain Elasticsearch from its high-level simplicity, to its (and Apache Lucene's) low-level internal complexities. It's a unique skill that we dearly cherish here at Elasticsearch. Clint is also responsible for the Elasticsearch Perl client, while Zach is responsible for the PHP one - both wonderful pieces of code.

And last, both play an instrumental role in most of what happens daily with the Elasticsearch project itself. One of the main reasons why Elasticsearch is so popular is its ability to communicate empathy to its users, and Clint and Zach are both part of the group that makes this a reality.

Preface

The world is swimming in data. For years we have been simply overwhelmed by the quantity of data flowing through and produced by our systems. Existing technology has focused on how to store and structure warehouses full of data. That's all well and good—until you actually need to make decisions in real time informed by that data.

Elasticsearch is a distributed, scalable, real-time search and analytics engine. It enables you to search, analyze, and explore your data, often in ways that you did not anticipate at the start of a project. It exists because raw data sitting on a hard drive is just not useful.

Whether you need full-text search, real-time analytics of structured data, or a combination of the two, this book introduces you to the fundamental concepts required to start working with Elasticsearch at a basic level. With these foundations laid, it will move on to more-advanced search techniques, which you will need to shape the search experience to fit your requirements.

Elasticsearch is not just about full-text search. We explain structured search, analytics, the complexities of dealing with human language, geolocation, and relationships. We will also discuss how best to model your data to take advantage of the horizontal scalability of Elasticsearch, and how to configure and monitor your cluster when moving to production.

Who Should Read This Book

This book is for anybody who wants to put their data to work. It doesn't matter whether you are starting a new project and have the flexibility to design the system from the ground up, or whether you need to give new life to a legacy system. Elasticsearch will help you to solve existing problems and open the way to new features that you haven't yet considered.

This book is suitable for novices and experienced users alike. We expect you to have some programming background and, although not required, it would help to have used SQL and a relational database. We explain concepts from first principles, helping novices to gain a sure footing in the complex world of search.

The reader with a search background will also benefit from this book. Elasticsearch is a new technology that has some familiar concepts. The more experienced user will gain an understanding of how those concepts have been implemented and how they interact in the context of Elasticsearch. Even the early chapters contain nuggets of information that will be useful to the more advanced user.

Finally, maybe you are in DevOps. While the other departments are stuffing data into Elasticsearch as fast as they can, you're the one charged with stopping their servers from bursting into flames. Elasticsearch scales effortlessly, as long as your users play within the rules. You need to know how to set up a stable cluster before going into production, and then be able to recognize the warning signs at three in the morning in order to prevent catastrophe. The earlier chapters may be of less interest to you, but the last part of the book is essential reading—all you need to know to avoid meltdown.

Why We Wrote This Book

We wrote this book because Elasticsearch needs a narrative. The existing reference documentation is excellent—as long as you know what you are looking for. It assumes that you are intimately familiar with information-retrieval concepts, distributed systems, the query DSL, and a host of other topics.

This book makes no such assumptions. It has been written so that a complete beginner—to both search and distributed systems—can pick it up and start building a prototype within a few chapters.

We have taken a problem-based approach: this is the problem, how do I solve it, and what are the trade-offs of the alternative solutions? We start with the basics, and each chapter builds on the preceding ones, providing practical examples and explaining the theory where necessary.

The existing reference documentation explains *how* to use features. We want this book to explain *why* and *when* to use various features.

Elasticsearch Version

The explanations and code examples in this book target the latest version of Elasticsearch available at the time of going to print—version 1.4.0—but Elasticsearch is a rapidly evolving project. The online version of this book will be updated as Elasticsearch changes.

You can find the latest version of this book online (*http://www.elasticsearch.org/guide/*).

You can also track the changes that have been made by visiting the GitHub repository (*https://github.com/elasticsearch/elasticsearch-definitive-guide/*).

How to Read This Book

Elasticsearch tries very hard to make the complex simple, and to a large degree it succeeds in this. That said, search and distributed systems *are* complex, and sooner or later you have to get to grips with some of the complexity in order to take full advantage of Elasticsearch.

Complexity, however, is not the same as magic. We tend to view complex systems as magical black boxes that respond to incantations, but there are usually simple processes at work within. Understanding these processes helps to dispel the magic—instead of hoping that the black box will do what you want, understanding gives you certainty and clarity.

This is a definitive guide: we help you not only to get started with Elasticsearch, but also to tackle the deeper more, interesting topics. These include Chapter 2, Chapter 4, Chapter 9, and Chapter 11, which are not essential reading but do give you a solid understanding of the internals.

The first part of the book should be read in order as each chapter builds on the previous one (although you can skim over the chapters just mentioned). Later chapters such as Chapter 15 and Chapter 16 are more standalone and can be referred to as needed.

Navigating This Book

This book is divided into seven parts:

- Chapters 1 through 11 provide an introduction to Elasticsearch. They explain how to get your data in and out of Elasticsearch, how Elasticsearch interprets the data in your documents, how basic search works, and how to manage indices. By the end of this section, you will already be able to integrate your application with Elasticsearch. Chapters 2, 4, 9, and 11 are supplemental chapters that provide more insight into the distributed processes at work, but are not required reading.

- Chapters 12 through 17 offer a deep dive into search—how to index and query your data to allow you to take advantage of more-advanced concepts such as word proximity, and partial matching. You will understand how relevance works and how to control it to ensure that the best results are on the first page.

- Chapters 18 through 24 tackle the thorny subject of dealing with human language through effective use of analyzers and queries. We start with an easy approach to language analysis before diving into the complexities of language, alphabets, and sorting. We cover stemming, stopwords, synonyms, and fuzzy matching.

- Chapters 25 through 35 discuss aggregations and analytics—ways to summarize and group your data to show overall trends.

- Chapters 36 through 39 present the two approaches to geolocation supported by Elasticsearch: lat/lon geo-points, and complex geo-shapes.

- Chapters 40 through 43 talk about how to model your data to work most efficiently with Elasticsearch. Representing relationships between entities is not as easy in a search engine as it is in a relational database, which has been designed for that purpose. These chapters also explain how to suit your index design to match the flow of data through your system.

- Finally, Chapters 44 through 46 discuss moving to production: the important configurations, what to monitor, and how to diagnose and prevent problems.

There are three topics that we do not cover in this book, because they are evolving rapidly and anything we write will soon be out-of-date:

- Highlighting of result snippets: see Highlighting (*http://bit.ly/151kOhG*).

- *Did-you-mean* and *search-as-you-type* suggesters: see Suggesters (*http://bit.ly/1INTMa9*).

- Percolation—finding queries which match a document: see Percolators (*http://bit.ly/1KNs3du*).

Online Resources

Because this book focuses on problem solving in Elasticsearch rather than syntax, we sometimes reference the existing documentation for a complete list of parameters. The reference documentation can be found here:

http://www.elasticsearch.org/guide/

Conventions Used in This Book

The following typographical conventions are used in this book:

Italic
   Indicates emphasis, and new terms or concepts.

`Constant width`

Used for program listings, as well as within paragraphs to refer to program elements such as variable or function names, databases, data types, environment variables, statements, and keywords.

 This icon signifies a tip, suggestion.

 This icon signifies a general note.

 This icon indicates a warning or caution.

Using Code Examples

This book is here to help you get your job done. In general, if example code is offered with this book, you may use it in your programs and documentation. You do not need to contact us for permission unless you're reproducing a significant portion of the code. For example, writing a program that uses several chunks of code from this book does not require permission. Selling or distributing a CD-ROM of examples from O'Reilly books does require permission. Answering a question by citing this book and quoting example code does not require permission. Incorporating a significant amount of example code from this book into your product's documentation does require permission.

We appreciate, but do not require, attribution. An attribution usually includes the title, author, publisher, and ISBN. For example: *Elasticsearch: The Definitive Guide* by Clinton Gormley and Zachary Tony (O'Reilly). Copyright 2015 Elasticsearch BV, 978-1-449-35854-9.

If you feel your use of code examples falls outside fair use or the permission given above, feel free to contact us at *permissions@oreilly.com*.

Safari® Books Online

 *Safari Books Online* is an on-demand digital library that delivers expert content in both book and video form from the world's leading authors in technology and business.

Technology professionals, software developers, web designers, and business and creative professionals use Safari Books Online as their primary resource for research, problem solving, learning, and certification training.

Safari Books Online offers a range of plans and pricing for enterprise, government, education, and individuals.

Members have access to thousands of books, training videos, and prepublication manuscripts in one fully searchable database from publishers like O'Reilly Media, Prentice Hall Professional, Addison-Wesley Professional, Microsoft Press, Sams, Que, Peachpit Press, Focal Press, Cisco Press, John Wiley & Sons, Syngress, Morgan Kaufmann, IBM Redbooks, Packt, Adobe Press, FT Press, Apress, Manning, New Riders, McGraw-Hill, Jones & Bartlett, Course Technology, and hundreds more. For more information about Safari Books Online, please visit us online.

How to Contact Us

Please address comments and questions concerning this book to the publisher:

O'Reilly Media, Inc.
1005 Gravenstein Highway North
Sebastopol, CA 95472
800-998-9938 (in the United States or Canada)
707-829-0515 (international or local)
707-829-0104 (fax)

We have a web page for this book, where we list errata, examples, and any additional information. You can access this page at *http://oreil.ly/1ylQuK6*.

To comment or ask technical questions about this book, send email to *bookquestions@oreilly.com*.

For more information about our books, courses, conferences, and news, see our website at *http://www.oreilly.com*.

Find us on Facebook: *http://facebook.com/oreilly*

Follow us on Twitter: *http://twitter.com/oreillymedia*

Watch us on YouTube: *http://www.youtube.com/oreillymedia*

Acknowledgments

Why are spouses always relegated to a *last but not least* disclaimer? There is no doubt in our minds that the two people most deserving of our gratitude are Xavi Sánchez Catalán, Clinton's long-suffering husband, and Genevieve Flanders, Zach's fiancée. They have looked after us and loved us, picked up the slack, put up with our absence and our endless moaning about how long the book was taking, and, most importantly, they are still here.

Thank you to Shay Banon for creating Elasticsearch in the first place, and to Elasticsearch the company for supporting our work on the book. Our colleagues at Elasticsearch deserve a big thank you as well. They have helped us pick through the innards of Elasticsearch to really understand how it works, and they have been responsible for adding improvements and fixing inconsistencies that were brought to light by writing about them.

Two colleagues in particular deserve special mention:

- Robert Muir patiently shared his deep knowledge of search in general and Lucene in particular. Several chapters are the direct result of joining his pearls of wisdom into paragraphs.

- Adrien Grand dived deep into the code to answer question after question, and checked our explanations to ensure they make sense.

Thank you to O'Reilly for undertaking this project and working with us to make this book available online for free, to our editor Brian Anderson for cajoling us along gently, and to our kind and gentle reviewers Benjamin Devèze, Ivan Brusic, and Leo Lapworth. Your reassurances kept us hopeful.

Finally, we would like to thank our readers, some of whom we know only by their GitHub identities, who have taken the time to report problems, provide corrections, or suggest improvements:

Adam Canady, Adam Gray, Alexander Kahn, Alexander Reelsen, Alaattin Kahramanlar, Ambrose Ludd, Anna Beyer, Andrew Bramble, Baptiste Cabarrou, Bart Vandewoestyne, Bertrand Dechoux, Brian Wong, Brooke Babcock, Charles Mims, Chris Earle, Chris Gilmore, Christian Burgas, Colin Goodheart-Smithe, Corey Wright, Daniel Wiesmann, David Pilato, Duncan Angus Wilkie, Florian Hopf, Gavin Foo, Gilbert Chang, Grégoire Seux, Gustavo Alberola, Igal Sapir, Iskren Ivov Chernev, Itamar Syn-Hershko, Jan Forrest, Jānis Peisenieks, Japheth Thomson, Jeff Myers, Jeff Patti, Jeremy Falling, Jeremy Nguyen, J.R. Heard, Joe Fleming, Jonathan Page, Joshua Gourneau, Josh Schneier, Jun Ohtani, Keiji Yoshida, Kieren Johnstone, Kim Laplume, Kurt Hurtado, Laszlo Balogh, londocr, losar, Lucian Precup, Lukáš Vlček, Malibu Carl, Margirier Laurent, Martijn Dwars, Matt Ruzicka, Mattias Pfeiffer, Mehdy Amazigh, mhemani, Michael Bonfils, Michael Bruns, Michael Salmon, Michael Scharf , Mitar Milutinović, Mustafa K. Isik, Nathan Peck, Patrick Peschlow, Paul Schwarz, Pieter Coucke, Raphaël Flores, Robert Muir, Ruslan Zavacky, Sanglarsh Boudhh, Santiago Gaviria, Scott Wilkerson, Sebastian Kurfürst, Sergii Golubev, Serkan Kucukbay, Thierry Jossermoz, Thomas Cucchietti, Tom Christie, Ulf Reimers, Venkat Somula, Wei Zhu, Will Kahn-Greene, and Yuri Bakumenko.

PART I

Getting Started

Elasticsearch is a real-time distributed search and analytics engine. It allows you to explore your data at a speed and at a scale never before possible. It is used for full-text search, structured search, analytics, and all three in combination:

- Wikipedia uses Elasticsearch to provide full-text search with highlighted search snippets, and *search-as-you-type* and *did-you-mean* suggestions.
- *The Guardian* uses Elasticsearch to combine visitor logs with social -network data to provide real-time feedback to its editors about the public's response to new articles.
- Stack Overflow combines full-text search with geolocation queries and uses *more-like-this* to find related questions and answers.
- GitHub uses Elasticsearch to query 130 billion lines of code.

But Elasticsearch is not just for mega-corporations. It has enabled many startups like Datadog and Klout to prototype ideas and to turn them into scalable solutions. Elasticsearch can run on your laptop, or scale out to hundreds of servers and petabytes of data.

No individual part of Elasticsearch is new or revolutionary. Full-text search has been done before, as have analytics systems and distributed databases. The revolution is the combination of these individually useful parts into a single, coherent, real-time application. It has a low barrier to entry for the new user, but can keep pace with you as your skills and needs grow.

If you are picking up this book, it is because you have data, and there is no point in having data unless you plan to *do something* with it.

Unfortunately, most databases are astonishingly inept at extracting actionable knowledge from your data. Sure, they can filter by timestamp or exact values, but can they perform full-text search, handle synonyms, and score documents by relevance? Can they generate analytics and aggregations from the same data? Most important, can they do this in real time without big batch-processing jobs?

This is what sets Elasticsearch apart: Elasticsearch encourages you to explore and utilize your data, rather than letting it rot in a warehouse because it is too difficult to query.

Elasticsearch is your new best friend.

CHAPTER 1

You Know, for Search...

Elasticsearch is an open-source search engine built on top of Apache Lucene™ (*https://lucene.apache.org/core/*), a full-text search-engine library. Lucene is arguably the most advanced, high-performance, and fully featured search engine library in existence today—both open source and proprietary.

But Lucene is just a library. To leverage its power, you need to work in Java and to integrate Lucene directly with your application. Worse, you will likely require a degree in information retrieval to understand how it works. Lucene is *very* complex.

Elasticsearch is also written in Java and uses Lucene internally for all of its indexing and searching, but it aims to make full-text search easy by hiding the complexities of Lucene behind a simple, coherent, RESTful API.

However, Elasticsearch is much more than just Lucene and much more than "just" full-text search. It can also be described as follows:

- A distributed real-time document store where *every field* is indexed and searchable
- A distributed search engine with real-time analytics
- Capable of scaling to hundreds of servers and petabytes of structured and unstructured data

And it packages up all this functionality into a standalone server that your application can talk to via a simple RESTful API, using a web client from your favorite programming language, or even from the command line.

It is easy to get started with Elasticsearch. It ships with sensible defaults and hides complicated search theory away from beginners. It *just works*, right out of the box. With minimal understanding, you can soon become productive.

Elasticsearch can be downloaded, used, and modified free of charge. It is available under the Apache 2 license (*http://www.apache.org/licenses/LICENSE-2.0.html*), one of the most flexible open source licenses available.

As your knowledge grows, you can leverage more of Elasticsearch's advanced features. The entire engine is configurable and flexible. Pick and choose from the advanced features to tailor Elasticsearch to your problem domain.

The Mists of Time

Many years ago, a newly married unemployed developer called Shay Banon followed his wife to London, where she was studying to be a chef. While looking for gainful employment, he started playing with an early version of Lucene, with the intent of building his wife a recipe search engine.

Working directly with Lucene can be tricky, so Shay started work on an abstraction layer to make it easier for Java programmers to add search to their applications. He released this as his first open source project, called Compass.

Later Shay took a job working in a high-performance, distributed environment with in-memory data grids. The need for a high-performance, real-time, distributed search engine was obvious, and he decided to rewrite the Compass libraries as a standalone server called Elasticsearch.

The first public release came out in February 2010. Since then, Elasticsearch has become one of the most popular projects on GitHub with commits from over 300 contributors. A company has formed around Elasticsearch to provide commercial support and to develop new features, but Elasticsearch is, and forever will be, open source and available to all.

Shay's wife is still waiting for the recipe search…

Installing Elasticsearch

The easiest way to understand what Elasticsearch can do for you is to play with it, so let's get started!

The only requirement for installing Elasticsearch is a recent version of Java. Preferably, you should install the latest version of the official Java from *www.java.com*.

You can download the latest version of Elasticsearch from *elasticsearch.org/download*.

```
curl -L -O http://download.elasticsearch.org/PATH/TO/VERSION.zip ❶
unzip elasticsearch-$VERSION.zip
cd  elasticsearch-$VERSION
```

❶   Fill in the URL for the latest version available on *elasticsearch.org/download*.

When installing Elasticsearch in production, you can use the method described previously, or the Debian or RPM packages provided on the downloads page (*http://www.elasticsearch.org/downloads*). You can also use the officially supported Puppet module (*https://github.com/elasticsearch/puppet-elasticsearch*) or Chef cookbook (*https://github.com/elasticsearch/cookbook-elasticsearch*).

Installing Marvel

Marvel (*http://www.elasticsearch.com/products/marvel*) is a management and monitoring tool for Elasticsearch, which is free for development use. It comes with an interactive console called Sense, which makes it easy to talk to Elasticsearch directly from your browser.

Many of the code examples in the online version of this book include a View in Sense link. When clicked, it will open up a working example of the code in the Sense console. You do not have to install Marvel, but it will make this book much more interactive by allowing you to experiment with the code samples on your local Elasticsearch cluster.

Marvel is available as a plug-in. To download and install it, run this command in the Elasticsearch directory:

```
./bin/plugin -i elasticsearch/marvel/latest
```

You probably don't want Marvel to monitor your local cluster, so you can disable data collection with this command:

```
echo 'marvel.agent.enabled: false' >> ./config/elasticsearch.yml
```

Running Elasticsearch

Elasticsearch is now ready to run. You can start it up in the foreground with this:

```
./bin/elasticsearch
```

Add -d if you want to run it in the background as a daemon.

Test it out by opening another terminal window and running the following:

```
curl 'http://localhost:9200/?pretty'
```

You should see a response like this:

```
{
   "status": 200,
   "name": "Shrunken Bones",
   "version": {
      "number": "1.4.0",
      "lucene_version": "4.10"
   },
```

```
        "tagline": "You Know, for Search"
    }
```

This means that your Elasticsearch *cluster* is up and running, and we can start experimenting with it.

 A *node* is a running instance of Elasticsearch. A *cluster* is a group of nodes with the same `cluster.name` that are working together to share data and to provide failover and scale, although a single node can form a cluster all by itself.

You should change the default `cluster.name` to something appropriate to you, like your own name, to stop your nodes from trying to join another cluster on the same network with the same name!

You can do this by editing the `elasticsearch.yml` file in the `config/` directory and then restarting Elasticsearch. When Elasticsearch is running in the foreground, you can stop it by pressing Ctrl-C; otherwise, you can shut it down with the `shutdown` API:

```
curl -XPOST 'http://localhost:9200/_shutdown'
```

Viewing Marvel and Sense

If you installed the Marvel management and monitoring tool, you can view it in a web browser by visiting *http://localhost:9200/_plugin/marvel/*.

You can reach the *Sense* developer console either by clicking the "Marvel dashboards" drop-down in Marvel, or by visiting *http://localhost:9200/_plugin/marvel/sense/*.

Talking to Elasticsearch

How you talk to Elasticsearch depends on whether you are using Java.

Java API

If you are using Java, Elasticsearch comes with two built-in clients that you can use in your code:

Node client
> The node client joins a local cluster as a *non data node*. In other words, it doesn't hold any data itself, but it knows what data lives on which node in the cluster, and can forward requests directly to the correct node.

Transport client
> The lighter-weight transport client can be used to send requests to a remote cluster. It doesn't join the cluster itself, but simply forwards requests to a node in the cluster.

Both Java clients talk to the cluster over port *9300*, using the native Elasticsearch *transport* protocol. The nodes in the cluster also communicate with each other over port 9300. If this port is not open, your nodes will not be able to form a cluster.

> The Java client must be from the same version of Elasticsearch as the nodes; otherwise, they may not be able to understand each other.

More information about the Java clients can be found in the Java API section of the Guide (*http://www.elasticsearch.org/guide/*).

RESTful API with JSON over HTTP

All other languages can communicate with Elasticsearch over port *9200* using a RESTful API, accessible with your favorite web client. In fact, as you have seen, you can even talk to Elasticsearch from the command line by using the `curl` command.

> Elasticsearch provides official clients for several languages—Groovy, JavaScript, .NET, PHP, Perl, Python, and Ruby—and there are numerous community-provided clients and integrations, all of which can be found in the Guide (*http://www.elastic search.org/guide/*).

A request to Elasticsearch consists of the same parts as any HTTP request:

```
curl -X<VERB> '<PROTOCOL>://<HOST>/<PATH>?<QUERY_STRING>' -d '<BODY>'
```

The parts marked with < > above are:

VERB
> The appropriate HTTP *method* or *verb*: GET, POST, PUT, HEAD, or DELETE.

PROTOCOL
> Either `http` or `https` (if you have an `https` proxy in front of Elasticsearch.)

HOST
> The hostname of any node in your Elasticsearch cluster, or `localhost` for a node on your local machine.

PORT

> The port running the Elasticsearch HTTP service, which defaults to 9200.

QUERY_STRING

> Any optional query-string parameters (for example ?pretty will *pretty-print* the JSON response to make it easier to read.)

BODY

> A JSON-encoded request body (if the request needs one.)

For instance, to count the number of documents in the cluster, we could use this:

```
curl -XGET 'http://localhost:9200/_count?pretty' -d '
{
    "query": {
        "match_all": {}
    }
}
'
```

Elasticsearch returns an HTTP status code like 200 OK and (except for HEAD requests) a JSON-encoded response body. The preceding curl request would respond with a JSON body like the following:

```
{
    "count" : 0,
    "_shards" : {
        "total" : 5,
        "successful" : 5,
        "failed" : 0
    }
}
```

We don't see the HTTP headers in the response because we didn't ask curl to display them. To see the headers, use the curl command with the -i switch:

```
curl -i -XGET 'localhost:9200/'
```

For the rest of the book, we will show these curl examples using a shorthand format that leaves out all the bits that are the same in every request, like the hostname and port, and the curl command itself. Instead of showing a full request like

```
curl -XGET 'localhost:9200/_count?pretty' -d '
{
    "query": {
        "match_all": {}
    }
}'
```

we will show it in this shorthand format:

```
GET /_count
{
```

```
    "query": {
        "match_all": {}
    }
}
```

In fact, this is the same format that is used by the Sense console that we installed with Marvel. If in the online version of this book, you can open and run this code example in Sense by clicking the View in Sense link above.

Document Oriented

Objects in an application are seldom just a simple list of keys and values. More often than not, they are complex data structures that may contain dates, geo locations, other objects, or arrays of values.

Sooner or later you're going to want to store these objects in a database. Trying to do this with the rows and columns of a relational database is the equivalent of trying to squeeze your rich, expressive objects into a very big spreadsheet: you have to flatten the object to fit the table schema—usually one field per column—and then have to reconstruct it every time you retrieve it.

Elasticsearch is *document oriented*, meaning that it stores entire objects or *documents*. It not only stores them, but also *indexes* the contents of each document in order to make them searchable. In Elasticsearch, you index, search, sort, and filter documents —not rows of columnar data. This is a fundamentally different way of thinking about data and is one of the reasons Elasticsearch can perform complex full-text search.

JSON

Elasticsearch uses JavaScript Object Notation, or *JSON* (*http://en.wikipedia.org/wiki/Json*), as the serialization format for documents. JSON serialization is supported by most programming languages, and has become the standard format used by the NoSQL movement. It is simple, concise, and easy to read.

Consider this JSON document, which represents a user object:

```
{
    "email":      "john@smith.com",
    "first_name": "John",
    "last_name":  "Smith",
    "info": {
        "bio":         "Eco-warrior and defender of the weak",
        "age":         25,
        "interests": [ "dolphins", "whales" ]
    },
    "join_date": "2014/05/01"
}
```

Although the original user object was complex, the structure and meaning of the object has been retained in the JSON version. Converting an object to JSON for indexing in Elasticsearch is much simpler than the equivalent process for a flat table structure.

 Almost all languages have modules that will convert arbitrary data structures or objects into JSON for you, but the details are specific to each language. Look for modules that handle JSON *serialization* or *marshalling*. The official Elasticsearch clients (*http://www.elastic search.org/guide*) all handle conversion to and from JSON for you automatically.

Finding Your Feet

To give you a feel for what is possible in Elasticsearch and how easy it is to use, let's start by walking through a simple tutorial that covers basic concepts such as indexing, search, and aggregations.

We'll introduce some new terminology and basic concepts along the way, but it is OK if you don't understand everything immediately. We'll cover all the concepts introduced here in *much* greater depth throughout the rest of the book.

So, sit back and enjoy a whirlwind tour of what Elasticsearch is capable of.

Let's Build an Employee Directory

We happen to work for *Megacorp*, and as part of HR's new *"We love our drones!"* initiative, we have been tasked with creating an employee directory. The directory is supposed to foster employer empathy and real-time, synergistic, dynamic collaboration, so it has a few business requirements:

- Enable data to contain multi value tags, numbers, and full text.
- Retrieve the full details of any employee.
- Allow structured search, such as finding employees over the age of 30.
- Allow simple full-text search and more-complex *phrase* searches.
- Return highlighted search *snippets* from the text in the matching documents.
- Enable management to build analytic dashboards over the data.

Indexing Employee Documents

The first order of business is storing employee data. This will take the form of an *employee document*: a single document represents a single employee. The act of storing data in Elasticsearch is called *indexing*, but before we can index a document, we need to decide *where* to store it.

In Elasticsearch, a document belongs to a *type*, and those types live inside an *index*. You can draw some (rough) parallels to a traditional relational database:

```
Relational DB  ⇒ Databases ⇒ Tables ⇒ Rows       ⇒ Columns
Elasticsearch  ⇒ Indices   ⇒ Types  ⇒ Documents ⇒ Fields
```

An Elasticsearch cluster can contain multiple *indices* (databases), which in turn contain multiple *types* (tables). These types hold multiple *documents* (rows), and each document has multiple *fields* (columns).

Index Versus Index Versus Index

You may already have noticed that the word *index* is overloaded with several meanings in the context of Elasticsearch. A little clarification is necessary:

Index (noun)
> As explained previously, an *index* is like a *database* in a traditional relational database. It is the place to store related documents. The plural of *index* is *indices* or *indexes*.

Index (verb)
> To *index a document* is to store a document in an *index (noun)* so that it can be retrieved and queried. It is much like the INSERT keyword in SQL except that, if the document already exists, the new document would replace the old.

Inverted index
> Relational databases add an *index*, such as a B-tree index, to specific columns in order to improve the speed of data retrieval. Elasticsearch and Lucene use a structure called an *inverted index* for exactly the same purpose.
>
> By default, every field in a document is *indexed* (has an inverted index) and thus is searchable. A field without an inverted index is not searchable. We discuss inverted indexes in more detail in "Inverted Index" on page 83.

So for our employee directory, we are going to do the following:

- Index a *document* per employee, which contains all the details of a single employee.
- Each document will be of *type* employee.
- That type will live in the megacorp *index*.
- That index will reside within our Elasticsearch cluster.

In practice, this is easy (even though it looks like a lot of steps). We can perform all of those actions in a single command:

```
PUT /megacorp/employee/1
{
    "first_name" : "John",
    "last_name" :  "Smith",
    "age" :        25,
    "about" :       "I love to go rock climbing",
    "interests": [ "sports", "music" ]
}
```

Notice that the path /megacorp/employee/1 contains three pieces of information:

megacorp
> The index name

employee
> The type name

1
> The ID of this particular employee

The request body—the JSON document—contains all the information about this employee. His name is John Smith, he's 25, and enjoys rock climbing.

Simple! There was no need to perform any administrative tasks first, like creating an index or specifying the type of data that each field contains. We could just index a document directly. Elasticsearch ships with defaults for everything, so all the necessary administration tasks were taken care of in the background, using default values.

Before moving on, let's add a few more employees to the directory:

```
PUT /megacorp/employee/2
{
    "first_name" :  "Jane",
    "last_name" :   "Smith",
    "age" :         32,
    "about" :       "I like to collect rock albums",
    "interests":  [ "music" ]
}

PUT /megacorp/employee/3
{
    "first_name" :  "Douglas",
    "last_name" :   "Fir",
    "age" :         35,
    "about":        "I like to build cabinets",
    "interests":  [ "forestry" ]
}
```

Retrieving a Document

Now that we have some data stored in Elasticsearch, we can get to work on the business requirements for this application. The first requirement is the ability to retrieve individual employee data.

This is easy in Elasticsearch. We simply execute an HTTP GET request and specify the *address* of the document—the index, type, and ID. Using those three pieces of information, we can return the original JSON document:

```
GET /megacorp/employee/1
```

And the response contains some metadata about the document, and John Smith's original JSON document as the _source field:

```
{
   "_index" :    "megacorp",
   "_type" :     "employee",
   "_id" :       "1",
   "_version" : 1,
   "found" :     true,
   "_source" :  {
      "first_name" :  "John",
      "last_name" :   "Smith",
      "age" :         25,
      "about" :       "I love to go rock climbing",
      "interests":  [ "sports", "music" ]
   }
}
```

 In the same way that we changed the HTTP verb from PUT to GET in order to retrieve the document, we could use the DELETE verb to delete the document, and the HEAD verb to check whether the document exists. To replace an existing document with an updated version, we just PUT it again.

Search Lite

A GET is fairly simple—you get back the document that you ask for. Let's try something a little more advanced, like a simple search!

The first search we will try is the simplest search possible. We will search for all employees, with this request:

```
GET /megacorp/employee/_search
```

You can see that we're still using index megacorp and type employee, but instead of specifying a document ID, we now use the _search endpoint. The response includes all three of our documents in the `hits` array. By default, a search will return the top 10 results.

```
{
   "took":        6,
   "timed_out": false,
   "_shards": { ... },
   "hits": {
      "total":        3,
      "max_score":   1,
      "hits": [
         {
            "_index":        "megacorp",
            "_type":         "employee",
            "_id":           "3",
            "_score":        1,
            "_source": {
               "first_name": "Douglas",
               "last_name":  "Fir",
               "age":        35,
               "about":      "I like to build cabinets",
               "interests": [ "forestry" ]
            }
         },
         {
            "_index":        "megacorp",
            "_type":         "employee",
            "_id":           "1",
            "_score":        1,
            "_source": {
               "first_name": "John",
               "last_name":  "Smith",
               "age":        25,
               "about":      "I love to go rock climbing",
               "interests": [ "sports", "music" ]
            }
         },
         {
            "_index":        "megacorp",
            "_type":         "employee",
            "_id":           "2",
            "_score":        1,
            "_source": {
               "first_name": "Jane",
               "last_name":  "Smith",
               "age":        32,
               "about":      "I like to collect rock albums",
               "interests": [ "music" ]
            }
         }
      ]
}
```

```
    }
}
```

 The response not only tells us which documents matched, but also includes the whole document itself: all the information that we need in order to display the search results to the user.

Next, let's try searching for employees who have "Smith" in their last name. To do this, we'll use a *lightweight* search method that is easy to use from the command line. This method is often referred to as a *query-string* search, since we pass the search as a URL query-string parameter:

```
GET /megacorp/employee/_search?q=last_name:Smith
```

We use the same _search endpoint in the path, and we add the query itself in the q= parameter. The results that come back show all Smiths:

```
{
    ...
    "hits": {
        "total":     2,
        "max_score": 0.30685282,
        "hits": [
            {
                ...
                "_source": {
                    "first_name":  "John",
                    "last_name":   "Smith",
                    "age":         25,
                    "about":       "I love to go rock climbing",
                    "interests": [ "sports", "music" ]
                }
            },
            {
                ...
                "_source": {
                    "first_name":  "Jane",
                    "last_name":   "Smith",
                    "age":         32,
                    "about":       "I like to collect rock albums",
                    "interests": [ "music" ]
                }
            }
        ]
    }
}
```

Search with Query DSL

Query-string search is handy for ad hoc searches from the command line, but it has its limitations (see "Search *Lite*" on page 78). Elasticsearch provides a rich, flexible, query language called the *query DSL*, which allows us to build much more complicated, robust queries.

The *domain-specific language* (DSL) is specified using a JSON request body. We can represent the previous search for all Smiths like so:

```
GET /megacorp/employee/_search
{
    "query" : {
        "match" : {
            "last_name" : "Smith"
        }
    }
}
```

This will return the same results as the previous query. You can see that a number of things have changed. For one, we are no longer using *query-string* parameters, but instead a request body. This request body is built with JSON, and uses a `match` query (one of several types of queries, which we will learn about later).

More-Complicated Searches

Let's make the search a little more complicated. We still want to find all employees with a last name of Smith, but we want only employees who are older than 30. Our query will change a little to accommodate a *filter*, which allows us to execute structured searches efficiently:

```
GET /megacorp/employee/_search
{
    "query" : {
        "filtered" : {
            "filter" : {
                "range" : {
                    "age" : { "gt" : 30 } ❶
                }
            },
            "query" : {
                "match" : {
                    "last_name" : "smith" ❷
                }
            }
        }
    }
}
```

❶ This portion of the query is a `range` *filter*, which will find all ages older than 30—gt stands for *greater than*.

❷ This portion of the query is the same `match` *query* that we used before.

Don't worry about the syntax too much for now; we will cover it in great detail later. Just recognize that we've added a *filter* that performs a range search, and reused the same `match` query as before. Now our results show only one employee who happens to be 32 and is named Jane Smith:

```
{
   ...
   "hits": {
      "total":        1,
      "max_score":    0.30685282,
      "hits": [
         {
            ...
            "_source": {
               "first_name":    "Jane",
               "last_name":     "Smith",
               "age":           32,
               "about":         "I like to collect rock albums",
               "interests":  [ "music" ]
            }
         }
      ]
   }
}
```

Full-Text Search

The searches so far have been simple: single names, filtered by age. Let's try a more advanced, full-text search—a task that traditional databases would really struggle with.

We are going to search for all employees who enjoy rock climbing:

```
GET /megacorp/employee/_search
{
    "query" : {
        "match" : {
            "about" : "rock climbing"
        }
    }
}
```

You can see that we use the same `match` query as before to search the `about` field for "rock climbing." We get back two matching documents:

```
{
   ...
   "hits": {
      "total":       2,
      "max_score":  0.16273327,
      "hits": [
         {
            ...
            "_score":          0.16273327, ❶
            "_source": {
               "first_name":  "John",
               "last_name":   "Smith",
               "age":         25,
               "about":       "I love to go rock climbing",
               "interests": [ "sports", "music" ]
            }
         },
         {
            ...
            "_score":          0.016878016, ❶
            "_source": {
               "first_name":  "Jane",
               "last_name":   "Smith",
               "age":         32,
               "about":       "I like to collect rock albums",
               "interests": [ "music" ]
            }
         }
      ]
   }
}
```

❶ The relevance scores

By default, Elasticsearch sorts matching results by their relevance score, that is, by how well each document matches the query. The first and highest-scoring result is obvious: John Smith's about field clearly says "rock climbing" in it.

But why did Jane Smith come back as a result? The reason her document was returned is because the word "rock" was mentioned in her about field. Because only "rock" was mentioned, and not "climbing," her _score is lower than John's.

This is a good example of how Elasticsearch can search *within* full-text fields and return the most relevant results first. This concept of *relevance* is important to Elastic-search, and is a concept that is completely foreign to traditional relational databases, in which a record either matches or it doesn't.

Phrase Search

Finding individual words in a field is all well and good, but sometimes you want to match exact sequences of words or *phrases*. For instance, we could perform a query that will match only employee records that contain both "rock" *and* "climbing" *and* that display the words are next to each other in the phrase "rock climbing."

To do this, we use a slight variation of the match query called the match_phrase query:

```
GET /megacorp/employee/_search
{
    "query" : {
        "match_phrase" : {
            "about" : "rock climbing"
        }
    }
}
```

This, to no surprise, returns only John Smith's document:

```
{
    ...
    "hits": {
        "total":        1,
        "max_score":    0.23013961,
        "hits": [
            {
                ...
                "_score":              0.23013961,
                "_source": {
                    "first_name":    "John",
                    "last_name":     "Smith",
                    "age":           25,
                    "about":         "I love to go rock climbing",
                    "interests":  [ "sports", "music" ]
                }
            }
        ]
    }
}
```

Highlighting Our Searches

Many applications like to *highlight* snippets of text from each search result so the user can see *why* the document matched the query. Retrieving highlighted fragments is easy in Elasticsearch.

Let's rerun our previous query, but add a new highlight parameter:

```
GET /megacorp/employee/_search
{
    "query" : {
        "match_phrase" : {
            "about" : "rock climbing"
        }
    },
    "highlight": {
        "fields" : {
            "about" : {}
        }
    }
}
```

When we run this query, the same hit is returned as before, but now we get a new section in the response called highlight. This contains a snippet of text from the about field with the matching words wrapped in <em></em> HTML tags:

```
{
    ...
    "hits": {
        "total":       1,
        "max_score":   0.23013961,
        "hits": [
            {
                ...
                "_score":          0.23013961,
                "_source": {
                    "first_name":  "John",
                    "last_name":   "Smith",
                    "age":         25,
                    "about":       "I love to go rock climbing",
                    "interests": [ "sports", "music" ]
                },
                "highlight": {
                    "about": [
                        "I love to go <em>rock</em> <em>climbing</em>" ❶
                    ]
                }
            }
        ]
    }
}
```

❶ The highlighted fragment from the original text

You can read more about the highlighting of search snippets in the highlighting reference documentation (*http://www.elasticsearch.org/guide/en/elasticsearch/guide/current/highlighting-intro.html*).

Analytics

Finally, we come to our last business requirement: allow managers to run analytics over the employee directory. Elasticsearch has functionality called *aggregations*, which allow you to generate sophisticated analytics over your data. It is similar to `GROUP BY` in SQL, but much more powerful.

For example, let's find the most popular interests enjoyed by our employees:

```
GET /megacorp/employee/_search
{
  "aggs": {
    "all_interests": {
      "terms": { "field": "interests" }
    }
  }
}
```

Ignore the syntax for now and just look at the results:

```
{
   ...
   "hits": { ... },
   "aggregations": {
      "all_interests": {
         "buckets": [
            {
               "key":        "music",
               "doc_count": 2
            },
            {
               "key":        "forestry",
               "doc_count": 1
            },
            {
               "key":        "sports",
               "doc_count": 1
            }
         ]
      }
   }
}
```

We can see that two employees are interested in music, one in forestry, and one in sports. These aggregations are not precalculated; they are generated on the fly from the documents that match the current query. If we want to know the popular interests of people called Smith, we can just add the appropriate query into the mix:

```
GET /megacorp/employee/_search
{
  "query": {
    "match": {
```

```
        "last_name": "smith"
      }
    },
    "aggs": {
      "all_interests": {
        "terms": {
          "field": "interests"
        }
      }
    }
  }
}
```

The `all_interests` aggregation has changed to include only documents matching our query:

```
...
"all_interests": {
  "buckets": [
    {
      "key": "music",
      "doc_count": 2
    },
    {
      "key": "sports",
      "doc_count": 1
    }
  ]
}
```

Aggregations allow hierarchical rollups too. For example, let's find the average age of employees who share a particular interest:

```
GET /megacorp/employee/_search
{
    "aggs" : {
        "all_interests" : {
            "terms" : { "field" : "interests" },
            "aggs" : {
                "avg_age" : {
                    "avg" : { "field" : "age" }
                }
            }
        }
    }
}
```

The aggregations that we get back are a bit more complicated, but still fairly easy to understand:

```
...
"all_interests": {
  "buckets": [
    {
```

```
                      "key": "music",
                      "doc_count": 2,
                      "avg_age": {
                         "value": 28.5
                      }
                  },
                  {
                      "key": "forestry",
                      "doc_count": 1,
                      "avg_age": {
                         "value": 35
                      }
                  },
                  {
                      "key": "sports",
                      "doc_count": 1,
                      "avg_age": {
                         "value": 25
                      }
                  }
              ]
          }
```

The output is basically an enriched version of the first aggregation we ran. We still have a list of interests and their counts, but now each interest has an additional avg_age, which shows the average age for all employees having that interest.

Even if you don't understand the syntax yet, you can easily see how complex aggregations and groupings can be accomplished using this feature. The sky is the limit as to what kind of data you can extract!

Tutorial Conclusion

Hopefully, this little tutorial was a good demonstration about what is possible in Elasticsearch. It is really just scratching the surface, and many features—such as suggestions, geolocation, percolation, fuzzy and partial matching—were omitted to keep the tutorial short. But it did highlight just how easy it is to start building advanced search functionality. No configuration was needed—just add data and start searching!

It's likely that the syntax left you confused in places, and you may have questions about how to tweak and tune various aspects. That's fine! The rest of the book dives into each of these issues in detail, giving you a solid understanding of how Elasticsearch works.

Distributed Nature

At the beginning of this chapter, we said that Elasticsearch can scale out to hundreds (or even thousands) of servers and handle petabytes of data. While our tutorial gave examples of how to use Elasticsearch, it didn't touch on the mechanics at all. Elasticsearch is distributed by nature, and it is designed to hide the complexity that comes with being distributed.

The distributed aspect of Elasticsearch is largely transparent. Nothing in the tutorial required you to know about distributed systems, sharding, cluster discovery, or dozens of other distributed concepts. It happily ran the tutorial on a single node living inside your laptop, but if you were to run the tutorial on a cluster containing 100 nodes, everything would work in exactly the same way.

Elasticsearch tries hard to hide the complexity of distributed systems. Here are some of the operations happening automatically under the hood:

- Partitioning your documents into different containers or *shards*, which can be stored on a single node or on multiple nodes
- Balancing these shards across the nodes in your cluster to spread the indexing and search load
- Duplicating each shard to provide redundant copies of your data, to prevent data loss in case of hardware failure
- Routing requests from any node in the cluster to the nodes that hold the data you're interested in
- Seamlessly integrating new nodes as your cluster grows or redistributing shards to recover from node loss

As you read through this book, you'll encounter supplemental chapters about the distributed nature of Elasticsearch. These chapters will teach you about how the cluster scales and deals with failover (Chapter 2), handles document storage (Chapter 4), executes distributed search (Chapter 9), and what a shard is and how it works (Chapter 11).

These chapters are not required reading—you can use Elasticsearch without understanding these internals—but they will provide insight that will make your knowledge of Elasticsearch more complete. Feel free to skim them and revisit at a later point when you need a more complete understanding.

Next Steps

By now you should have a taste of what you can do with Elasticsearch, and how easy it is to get started. Elasticsearch tries hard to work out of the box with minimal knowledge and configuration. The best way to learn Elasticsearch is by jumping in: just start indexing and searching!

However, the more you know about Elasticsearch, the more productive you can become. The more you can tell Elasticsearch about the domain-specific elements of your application, the more you can fine-tune the output.

The rest of this book will help you move from novice to expert. Each chapter explains the essentials, but also includes expert-level tips. If you're just getting started, these tips are probably not immediately relevant to you; Elasticsearch has sensible defaults and will generally do the right thing without any interference. You can always revisit these chapters later, when you are looking to improve performance by shaving off any wasted milliseconds.

CHAPTER 2

Life Inside a Cluster

Supplemental Chapter

As mentioned earlier, this is the first of several supplemental chapters about how Elasticsearch operates in a distributed environment. In this chapter, we explain commonly used terminology like *cluster*, *node*, and *shard*, the mechanics of how Elasticsearch scales out, and how it deals with hardware failure.

Although this chapter is not required reading—you can use Elasticsearch for a long time without worrying about shards, replication, and failover—it will help you to understand the processes at work inside Elasticsearch. Feel free to skim through the chapter and to refer to it again later.

Elasticsearch is built to be always available, and to scale with your needs. Scale can come from buying bigger servers (*vertical scale*, or *scaling up*) or from buying more servers (*horizontal scale*, or *scaling out*).

While Elasticsearch can benefit from more-powerful hardware, vertical scale has its limits. Real scalability comes from horizontal scale—the ability to add more nodes to the cluster and to spread load and reliability between them.

With most databases, scaling horizontally usually requires a major overhaul of your application to take advantage of these extra boxes. In contrast, Elasticsearch is *distributed* by nature: it knows how to manage multiple nodes to provide scale and high availability. This also means that your application doesn't need to care about it.

In this chapter, we show how you can set up your cluster, nodes, and shards to scale with your needs and to ensure that your data is safe from hardware failure.

An Empty Cluster

If we start a single node, with no data and no indices, our cluster looks like Figure 2-1.

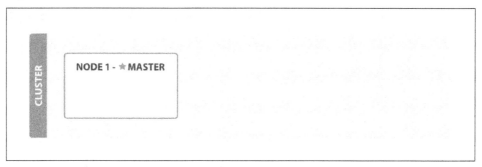

Figure 2-1. A cluster with one empty node

A *node* is a running instance of Elasticsearch, while a *cluster* consists of one or more nodes with the same cluster.name that are working together to share their data and workload. As nodes are added to or removed from the cluster, the cluster reorganizes itself to spread the data evenly.

One node in the cluster is elected to be the *master* node, which is in charge of managing cluster-wide changes like creating or deleting an index, or adding or removing a node from the cluster. The master node does not need to be involved in document-level changes or searches, which means that having just one master node will not become a bottleneck as traffic grows. Any node can become the master. Our example cluster has only one node, so it performs the master role.

As users, we can talk to *any node in the cluster*, including the master node. Every node knows where each document lives and can forward our request directly to the nodes that hold the data we are interested in. Whichever node we talk to manages the process of gathering the response from the node or nodes holding the data and returning the final response to the client. It is all managed transparently by Elasticsearch.

Cluster Health

Many statistics can be monitored in an Elasticsearch cluster, but the single most important one is *cluster health*, which reports a status of either green, yellow, or red:

```
GET /_cluster/health
```

On an empty cluster with no indices, this will return something like the following:

```
{
    "cluster_name":          "elasticsearch",
```

```
"status":               "green", ❶
"timed_out":            false,
"number_of_nodes":      1,
"number_of_data_nodes": 1,
"active_primary_shards": 0,
"active_shards":        0,
"relocating_shards":    0,
"initializing_shards":  0,
"unassigned_shards":    0
}
```

❶ The `status` field is the one we're most interested in.

The `status` field provides an overall indication of how the cluster is functioning. The meanings of the three colors are provided here for reference:

green
:   All primary and replica shards are active.

yellow
:   All primary shards are active, but not all replica shards are active.

red
:   Not all primary shards are active.

In the rest of this chapter, we explain what *primary* and *replica* shards are and explain the practical implications of each of the preceding colors.

Add an Index

To add data to Elasticsearch, we need an *index*—a place to store related data. In reality, an index is just a *logical namespace* that points to one or more physical *shards*.

A *shard* is a low-level *worker unit* that holds just a slice of all the data in the index. In Chapter 11, we explain in detail how a shard works, but for now it is enough to know that a shard is a single instance of Lucene, and is a complete search engine in its own right. Our documents are stored and indexed in shards, but our applications don't talk to them directly. Instead, they talk to an index.

Shards are how Elasticsearch distributes data around your cluster. Think of shards as containers for data. Documents are stored in shards, and shards are allocated to nodes in your cluster. As your cluster grows or shrinks, Elasticsearch will automatically migrate shards between nodes so that the cluster remains balanced.

A shard can be either a *primary* shard or a *replica* shard. Each document in your index belongs to a single primary shard, so the number of primary shards that you have determines the maximum amount of data that your index can hold.

While there is no theoretical limit to the amount of data that a primary shard can hold, there is a practical limit. What constitutes the maximum shard size depends entirely on your use case: the hardware you have, the size and complexity of your documents, how you index and query your documents, and your expected response times.

A replica shard is just a copy of a primary shard. Replicas are used to provide redundant copies of your data to protect against hardware failure, and to serve read requests like searching or retrieving a document.

The number of primary shards in an index is fixed at the time that an index is created, but the number of replica shards can be changed at any time.

Let's create an index called `blogs` in our empty one-node cluster. By default, indices are assigned five primary shards, but for the purpose of this demonstration, we'll assign just three primary shards and one replica (one replica of every primary shard):

```
PUT /blogs
{
   "settings" : {
      "number_of_shards" : 3,
      "number_of_replicas" : 1
   }
}
```

Our cluster now looks like Figure 2-2. All three primary shards have been allocated to Node 1.

Figure 2-2. A single-node cluster with an index

If we were to check the `cluster-health` now, we would see this:

```
{
   "cluster_name":          "elasticsearch",
   "status":                "yellow", ❶
   "timed_out":             false,
   "number_of_nodes":       1,
   "number_of_data_nodes":  1,
```

```
    "active_primary_shards": 3,
    "active_shards":         3,
    "relocating_shards":     0,
    "initializing_shards":   0,
    "unassigned_shards":     3 ❷
}
```

❶ Cluster status is yellow.

❷ Our three replica shards have not been allocated to a node.

A cluster health of yellow means that all *primary* shards are up and running (the cluster is capable of serving any request successfully) but not all *replica* shards are active. In fact, all three of our replica shards are currently unassigned—they haven't been allocated to a node. It doesn't make sense to store copies of the same data on the same node. If we were to lose that node, we would lose all copies of our data.

Currently, our cluster is fully functional but at risk of data loss in case of hardware failure.

Add Failover

Running a single node means that you have a single point of failure—there is no redundancy. Fortunately, all we need to do to protect ourselves from data loss is to start another node.

Starting a Second Node

To test what happens when you add a second node, you can start a new node in exactly the same way as you started the first one (see "Running Elasticsearch" on page 5), and from the same directory. Multiple nodes can share the same directory.

As long as the second node has the same cluster.name as the first node (see the ./config/elasticsearch.yml file), it should automatically discover and join the cluster run by the first node. If it doesn't, check the logs to find out what went wrong. It may be that multicast is disabled on your network, or that a firewall is preventing your nodes from communicating.

If we start a second node, our cluster would look like Figure 2-3.

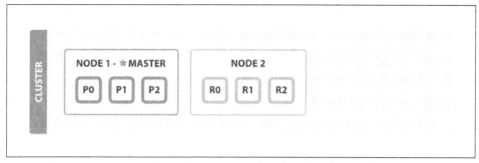

Figure 2-3. A two-node cluster—all primary and replica shards are allocated

The second node has joined the cluster, and three *replica shards* have been allocated to it—one for each primary shard. That means that we can lose either node, and all of our data will be intact.

Any newly indexed document will first be stored on a primary shard, and then copied in parallel to the associated replica shard(s). This ensures that our document can be retrieved from a primary shard or from any of its replicas.

The cluster-health now shows a status of green, which means that all six shards (all three primary shards and all three replica shards) are active:

```
{
    "cluster_name":          "elasticsearch",
    "status":                "green", ❶
    "timed_out":             false,
    "number_of_nodes":       2,
    "number_of_data_nodes":  2,
    "active_primary_shards": 3,
    "active_shards":         6,
    "relocating_shards":     0,
    "initializing_shards":   0,
    "unassigned_shards":     0
}
```

❶   Cluster status is green.

Our cluster is not only fully functional, but also *always available*.

Scale Horizontally

What about scaling as the demand for our application grows? If we start a third node, our cluster reorganizes itself to look like Figure 2-4.

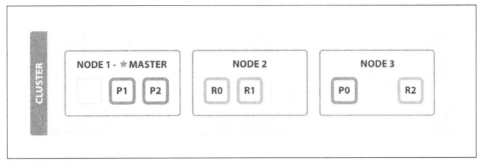

Figure 2-4. A three-node cluster—shards have been reallocated to spread the load

One shard each from `Node` `1` and `Node` `2` have moved to the new `Node` `3`, and we have two shards per node, instead of three. This means that the hardware resources (CPU, RAM, I/O) of each node are being shared among fewer shards, allowing each shard to perform better.

A shard is a fully fledged search engine in its own right, and is capable of using all of the resources of a single node. With our total of six shards (three primaries and three replicas), our index is capable of scaling out to a maximum of six nodes, with one shard on each node and each shard having access to 100% of its node's resources.

Then Scale Some More

But what if we want to scale our search to more than six nodes?

The number of primary shards is fixed at the moment an index is created. Effectively, that number defines the maximum amount of data that can be *stored* in the index. (The actual number depends on your data, your hardware and your use case.) However, read requests—searches or document retrieval—can be handled by a primary *or* a replica shard, so the more copies of data that you have, the more search throughput you can handle.

The number of replica shards can be changed dynamically on a live cluster, allowing us to scale up or down as demand requires. Let's increase the number of replicas from the default of 1 to 2:

```
PUT /blogs/_settings
{
    "number_of_replicas" : 2
}
```

As can be seen in Figure 2-5, the `blogs` index now has nine shards: three primaries and six replicas. This means that we can scale out to a total of nine nodes, again with one shard per node. This would allow us to *triple* search performance compared to our original three-node cluster.

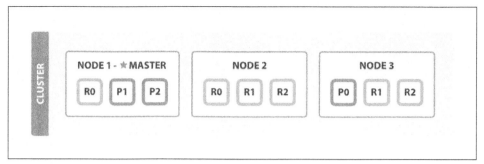

Figure 2-5. Increasing the number_of_replicas *to 2*

Of course, just having more replica shards on the same number of nodes doesn't increase our performance at all because each shard has access to a smaller fraction of its node's resources. You need to add hardware to increase throughput.

But these extra replicas do mean that we have more redundancy: with the node configuration above, we can now afford to lose two nodes without losing any data.

Coping with Failure

We've said that Elasticsearch can cope when nodes fail, so let's go ahead and try it out. If we kill the first node, our cluster looks like Figure 2-6.

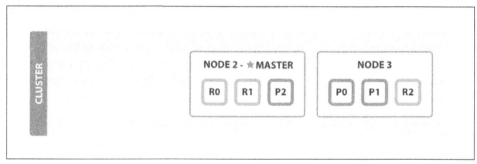

Figure 2-6. Cluster after killing one node

The node we killed was the master node. A cluster must have a master node in order to function correctly, so the first thing that happened was that the nodes elected a new master: Node 2.

Primary shards 1 and 2 were lost when we killed Node 1, and our index cannot function properly if it is missing primary shards. If we had checked the cluster health at this point, we would have seen status red: not all primary shards are active!

Fortunately, a complete copy of the two lost primary shards exists on other nodes, so the first thing that the new master node did was to promote the replicas of these shards on Node 2 and Node 3 to be primaries, putting us back into cluster health yellow. This promotion process was instantaneous, like the flick of a switch.

So why is our cluster health yellow and not green? We have all three primary shards, but we specified that we wanted two replicas of each primary, and currently only one replica is assigned. This prevents us from reaching green, but we're not too worried here: were we to kill Node 2 as well, our application could *still* keep running without data loss, because Node 3 contains a copy of every shard.

If we restart Node 1, the cluster would be able to allocate the missing replica shards, resulting in a state similar to the one described in Figure 2-5. If Node 1 still has copies of the old shards, it will try to reuse them, copying over from the primary shard only the files that have changed in the meantime.

By now, you should have a reasonable idea of how shards allow Elasticsearch to scale horizontally and to ensure that your data is safe. Later we will examine the life cycle of a shard in more detail.

CHAPTER 3

Data In, Data Out

Whatever program we write, the intention is the same: to organize data in a way that serves our purposes. But data doesn't consist of just random bits and bytes. We build relationships between data elements in order to represent entities, or *things* that exist in the real world. A name and an email address have more meaning if we know that they belong to the same person.

In the real world, though, not all entities of the same type look the same. One person might have a home telephone number, while another person has only a cell-phone number, and another might have both. One person might have three email addresses, while another has none. A Spanish person will probably have two last names, while an English person will probably have only one.

One of the reasons that object-oriented programming languages are so popular is that objects help us represent and manipulate real-world entities with potentially complex data structures. So far, so good.

The problem comes when we need to store these entities. Traditionally, we have stored our data in columns and rows in a relational database, the equivalent of using a spreadsheet. All the flexibility gained from using objects is lost because of the inflexibility of our storage medium.

But what if we could store our objects as objects? Instead of modeling our application around the limitations of spreadsheets, we can instead focus on *using* the data. The flexibility of objects is returned to us.

An *object* is a language-specific, in-memory data structure. To send it across the network or store it, we need to be able to represent it in some standard format. JSON (*http://en.wikipedia.org/wiki/Json*) is a way of representing objects in human-readable text. It has become the de facto standard for exchanging data in the NoSQL world. When an object has been serialized into JSON, it is known as a *JSON document*.

Elasticsearch is a distributed *document* store. It can store and retrieve complex data structures—serialized as JSON documents—in *real time*. In other words, as soon as a document has been stored in Elasticsearch, it can be retrieved from any node in the cluster.

Of course, we don't need to only store data; we must also query it, en masse and at speed. While NoSQL solutions exist that allow us to store objects as documents, they still require us to think about how we want to query our data, and which fields require an index in order to make data retrieval fast.

In Elasticsearch, *all data in every field* is *indexed by default*. That is, every field has a dedicated inverted index for fast retrieval. And, unlike most other databases, it can use all of those inverted indices *in the same query*, to return results at breathtaking speed.

In this chapter, we present the APIs that we use to create, retrieve, update, and delete documents. For the moment, we don't care about the data inside our documents or how to query them. All we care about is how to store our documents safely in Elasticsearch and how to get them back again.

What Is a Document?

Most entities or objects in most applications can be serialized into a JSON object, with keys and values. A *key* is the name of a field or property, and a *value* can be a string, a number, a Boolean, another object, an array of values, or some other specialized type such as a string representing a date or an object representing a geolocation:

```
{
    "name":         "John Smith",
    "age":          42,
    "confirmed":    true,
    "join_date":    "2014-06-01",
    "home": {
        "lat":      51.5,
        "lon":      0.1
    },
    "accounts": [
        {
            "type": "facebook",
            "id":   "johnsmith"
        },
        {
            "type": "twitter",
            "id":   "johnsmith"
        }
    ]
}
```

Often, we use the terms *object* and *document* interchangeably. However, there is a distinction. An object is just a JSON object—similar to what is known as a hash, hashmap, dictionary, or associative array. Objects may contain other objects. In Elasticsearch, the term *document* has a specific meaning. It refers to the top-level, or root object that is serialized into JSON and stored in Elasticsearch under a unique ID.

Document Metadata

A document doesn't consist only of its data. It also has *metadata*—information *about* the document. The three required metadata elements are as follows:

_index
> Where the document lives

_type
> The class of object that the document represents

_id
> The unique identifier for the document

_index

An *index* is like a database in a relational database; it's the place we store and index related data.

 Actually, in Elasticsearch, our data is stored and indexed in *shards*, while an index is just a logical namespace that groups together one or more shards. However, this is an internal detail; our application shouldn't care about shards at all. As far as our application is concerned, our documents live in an *index*. Elasticsearch takes care of the details.

We cover how to create and manage indices ourselves in Chapter 10, but for now we will let Elasticsearch create the index for us. All we have to do is choose an index name. This name must be lowercase, cannot begin with an underscore, and cannot contain commas. Let's use website as our index name.

_type

In applications, we use objects to represent *things* such as a user, a blog post, a comment, or an email. Each object belongs to a *class* that defines the properties or data associated with an object. Objects in the user class may have a name, a gender, an age, and an email address.

In a relational database, we usually store objects of the same class in the same table, because they share the same data structure. For the same reason, in Elasticsearch we use the same *type* for documents that represent the same class of *thing*, because they share the same data structure.

Every *type* has its own mapping or schema definition, which defines the data structure for documents of that type, much like the columns in a database table. Documents of all types can be stored in the same index, but the *mapping* for the type tells Elasticsearch how the data in each document should be indexed.

We show how to specify and manage mappings in "Types and Mappings" on page 139, but for now we will rely on Elasticsearch to detect our document's data structure automatically.

A _type name can be lowercase or uppercase, but shouldn't begin with an underscore or contain commas. We will use blog for our type name.

_id

The *ID* is a string that, when combined with the _index and _type, uniquely identifies a document in Elasticsearch. When creating a new document, you can either provide your own _id or let Elasticsearch generate one for you.

Other Metadata

There are several other metadata elements, which are presented in "Types and Mappings" on page 139. With the elements listed previously, we are already able to store a document in Elasticsearch and to retrieve it by ID—in other words, to use Elasticsearch as a document store.

Indexing a Document

Documents are *indexed*—stored and made searchable—by using the index API. But first, we need to decide where the document lives. As we just discussed, a document's _index, _type, and _id uniquely identify the document. We can either provide our own _id value or let the index API generate one for us.

Using Our Own ID

If your document has a natural identifier (for example, a user_account field or some other value that identifies the document), you should provide your own _id, using this form of the index API:

```
PUT /{index}/{type}/{id}
{
  "field": "value",
  ...
}
```

For example, if our index is called website, our type is called blog, and we choose the ID 123, then the index request looks like this:

```
PUT /website/blog/123
{
  "title": "My first blog entry",
  "text":  "Just trying this out...",
  "date":  "2014/01/01"
}
```

Elasticsearch responds as follows:

```
{
  "_index":    "website",
  "_type":     "blog",
  "_id":       "123",
  "_version":  1,
  "created":   true
}
```

The response indicates that the indexing request has been successfully created and includes the _index, _type, and _id metadata, and a new element: _version.

Every document in Elasticsearch has a version number. Every time a change is made to a document (including deleting it), the _version number is incremented. In "Dealing with Conflicts" on page 47, we discuss how to use the _version number to ensure that one part of your application doesn't overwrite changes made by another part.

Autogenerating IDs

If our data doesn't have a natural ID, we can let Elasticsearch autogenerate one for us. The structure of the request changes: instead of using the PUT verb ("store this document at this URL"), we use the POST verb ("store this document *under* this URL").

The URL now contains just the _index and the _type:

```
POST /website/blog/
{
  "title": "My second blog entry",
  "text":  "Still trying this out...",
  "date":  "2014/01/01"
}
```

The response is similar to what we saw before, except that the _id field has been generated for us:

```
{
    "_index":    "website",
    "_type":     "blog",
    "_id":       "wM0OSFhDQXGZAWDf0-drSA",
    "_version":  1,
    "created":   true
}
```

Autogenerated IDs are 22 character long, URL-safe, Base64-encoded string *universally unique identifiers*, or UUIDs (*http://en.wikipedia.org/wiki/Uuid*).

Retrieving a Document

To get the document out of Elasticsearch, we use the same _index, _type, and _id, but the HTTP verb changes to GET:

```
GET /website/blog/123?pretty
```

The response includes the by-now-familiar metadata elements, plus the _source field, which contains the original JSON document that we sent to Elasticsearch when we indexed it:

```
{
    "_index" :    "website",
    "_type" :     "blog",
    "_id" :       "123",
    "_version" :  1,
    "found" :     true,
    "_source" :   {
        "title": "My first blog entry",
        "text":  "Just trying this out...",
        "date":  "2014/01/01"
    }
}
```

> Adding pretty to the query-string parameters for any request, as in the preceding example, causes Elasticsearch to *pretty-print* the JSON response to make it more readable. The _source field, however, isn't pretty-printed. Instead we get back exactly the same JSON string that we passed in.

The response to the GET request includes {"found": true}. This confirms that the document was found. If we were to request a document that doesn't exist, we would still get a JSON response, but found would be set to false.

Also, the HTTP response code would be 404 Not Found instead of 200 OK. We can see this by passing the -i argument to curl, which causes it to display the response headers:

```
curl -i -XGET http://localhost:9200/website/blog/124?pretty
```

The response now looks like this:

```
HTTP/1.1 404 Not Found
Content-Type: application/json; charset=UTF-8
Content-Length: 83

{
  "_index" : "website",
  "_type" :  "blog",
  "_id" :    "124",
  "found" :  false
}
```

Retrieving Part of a Document

By default, a GET request will return the whole document, as stored in the _source
field. But perhaps all you are interested in is the title field. Individual fields can be
requested by using the _source parameter. Multiple fields can be specified in a
comma-separated list:

```
GET /website/blog/123?_source=title,text
```

The _source field now contains just the fields that we requested and has filtered out
the date field:

```
{
  "_index" :   "website",
  "_type" :    "blog",
  "_id" :      "123",
  "_version" : 1,
  "exists" :   true,
  "_source" : {
      "title": "My first blog entry" ,
      "text":  "Just trying this out..."
  }
}
```

Or if you want *just* the _source field without any metadata, you can use the _source
endpoint:

```
GET /website/blog/123/_source
```

which returns just the following:

```
{
   "title": "My first blog entry",
   "text":  "Just trying this out...",
   "date":  "2014/01/01"
}
```

Checking Whether a Document Exists

If all you want to do is to check whether a document exists—you're not interested in the content at all—then use the HEAD method instead of the GET method. HEAD requests don't return a body, just HTTP headers:

```
curl -i -XHEAD http://localhost:9200/website/blog/123
```

Elasticsearch will return a 200 OK status code if the document exists:

```
HTTP/1.1 200 OK
Content-Type: text/plain; charset=UTF-8
Content-Length: 0
```

And a 404 Not Found if it doesn't exist:

```
curl -i -XHEAD http://localhost:9200/website/blog/124

HTTP/1.1 404 Not Found
Content-Type: text/plain; charset=UTF-8
Content-Length: 0
```

Of course, just because a document didn't exist when you checked it, doesn't mean that it won't exist a millisecond later: another process might create the document in the meantime.

Updating a Whole Document

Documents in Elasticsearch are *immutable*; we cannot change them. Instead, if we need to update an existing document, we *reindex* or replace it, which we can do using the same index API that we have already discussed in "Indexing a Document" on page 40.

```
PUT /website/blog/123
{
  "title": "My first blog entry",
  "text":  "I am starting to get the hang of this...",
  "date":  "2014/01/02"
}
```

In the response, we can see that Elasticsearch has incremented the _version number:

```
{
  "_index" :   "website",
  "_type" :    "blog",
  "_id" :      "123",
  "_version" : 2,
  "created":   false ❶
}
```

❶ The `created` flag is set to `false` because a document with the same index, type, and ID already existed.

Internally, Elasticsearch has marked the old document as deleted and added an entirely new document. The old version of the document doesn't disappear immediately, although you won't be able to access it. Elasticsearch cleans up deleted documents in the background as you continue to index more data.

Later in this chapter, we introduce the `update` API, which can be used to make partial updates to a document. This API *appears* to change documents in place, but actually Elasticsearch is following exactly the same process as described previously:

1. Retrieve the JSON from the old document

2. Change it

3. Delete the old document

4. Index a new document

The only difference is that the `update` API achieves this through a single client request, instead of requiring separate `get` and `index` requests.

Creating a New Document

How can we be sure, when we index a document, that we are creating an entirely new document and not overwriting an existing one?

Remember that the combination of `_index`, `_type`, and `_id` uniquely identifies a document. So the easiest way to ensure that our document is new is by letting Elasticsearch autogenerate a new unique `_id`, using the `POST` version of the index request:

```
POST /website/blog/
{ ... }
```

However, if we already have an `_id` that we want to use, then we have to tell Elasticsearch that it should accept our index request only if a document with the same `_index`, `_type`, and `_id` doesn't exist already. There are two ways of doing this, both of which amount to the same thing. Use whichever method is more convenient for you.

The first method uses the `op_type` query-string parameter:

```
PUT /website/blog/123?op_type=create
{ ... }
```

And the second uses the `/_create` endpoint in the URL:

```
PUT /website/blog/123/_create
{ ... }
```

If the request succeeds in creating a new document, Elasticsearch will return the usual metadata and an HTTP response code of `201 Created`.

On the other hand, if a document with the same _index, _type, and _id already exists, Elasticsearch will respond with a `409 Conflict` response code, and an error message like the following:

```
{
   "error" : "DocumentAlreadyExistsException[[website][4] [blog][123]:
              document already exists]",
   "status" : 409
}
```

Deleting a Document

The syntax for deleting a document follows the same pattern that we have seen already, but uses the `DELETE` method :

```
DELETE /website/blog/123
```

If the document is found, Elasticsearch will return an HTTP response code of `200 OK` and a response body like the following. Note that the _version number has been incremented:

```
{
   "found" :      true,
   "_index" :     "website",
   "_type" :      "blog",
   "_id" :        "123",
   "_version" : 3
}
```

If the document isn't found, we get a `404 Not Found` response code and a body like this:

```
{
   "found" :      false,
   "_index" :     "website",
   "_type" :      "blog",
   "_id" :        "123",
   "_version" : 4
}
```

Even though the document doesn't exist (`found` is `false`), the _version number has still been incremented. This is part of the internal bookkeeping, which ensures that changes are applied in the correct order across multiple nodes.

As already mentioned in "Updating a Whole Document" on page 44, deleting a document doesn't immediately remove the document from disk; it just marks it as deleted. Elasticsearch will clean up deleted documents in the background as you continue to index more data.

Dealing with Conflicts

When updating a document with the index API, we read the original document, make our changes, and then reindex the *whole document* in one go. The most recent indexing request wins: whichever document was indexed last is the one stored in Elasticsearch. If somebody else had changed the document in the meantime, their changes would be lost.

Many times, this is not a problem. Perhaps our main data store is a relational database, and we just copy the data into Elasticsearch to make it searchable. Perhaps there is little chance of two people changing the same document at the same time. Or perhaps it doesn't really matter to our business if we lose changes occasionally.

But sometimes losing a change is *very important*. Imagine that we're using Elasticsearch to store the number of widgets that we have in stock in our online store. Every time that we sell a widget, we decrement the stock count in Elasticsearch.

One day, management decides to have a sale. Suddenly, we are selling several widgets every second. Imagine two web processes, running in parallel, both processing the sale of one widget each, as shown in Figure 3-1.

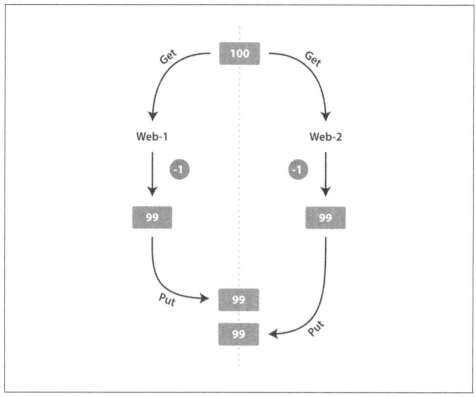

Figure 3-1. Consequence of no concurrency control

The change that web_1 made to the stock_count has been lost because web_2 is unaware that its copy of the stock_count is out-of-date. The result is that we think we have more widgets than we actually do, and we're going to disappoint customers by selling them stock that doesn't exist.

The more frequently that changes are made, or the longer the gap between reading data and updating it, the more likely it is that we will lose changes.

In the database world, two approaches are commonly used to ensure that changes are not lost when making concurrent updates:

Pessimistic concurrency control

Widely used by relational databases, this approach assumes that conflicting changes are likely to happen and so blocks access to a resource in order to prevent conflicts. A typical example is locking a row before reading its data, ensuring that only the thread that placed the lock is able to make changes to the data in that row.

Optimistic concurrency control

Used by Elasticsearch, this approach assumes that conflicts are unlikely to happen and doesn't block operations from being attempted. However, if the underlying data has been modified between reading and writing, the update will fail. It is then up to the application to decide how it should resolve the conflict. For instance, it could reattempt the update, using the fresh data, or it could report the situation to the user.

Optimistic Concurrency Control

Elasticsearch is distributed. When documents are created, updated, or deleted, the new version of the document has to be replicated to other nodes in the cluster. Elasticsearch is also asynchronous and concurrent, meaning that these replication requests are sent in parallel, and may arrive at their destination *out of sequence*. Elasticsearch needs a way of ensuring that an older version of a document never overwrites a newer version.

When we discussed index, get, and delete requests previously, we pointed out that every document has a _version number that is incremented whenever a document is changed. Elasticsearch uses this _version number to ensure that changes are applied in the correct order. If an older version of a document arrives after a new version, it can simply be ignored.

We can take advantage of the _version number to ensure that conflicting changes made by our application do not result in data loss. We do this by specifying the ver sion number of the document that we wish to change. If that version is no longer current, our request fails.

Let's create a new blog post:

```
PUT /website/blog/1/_create
{
  "title": "My first blog entry",
  "text":  "Just trying this out..."
}
```

The response body tells us that this newly created document has _version number 1. Now imagine that we want to edit the document: we load its data into a web form, make our changes, and then save the new version.

First we retrieve the document:

```
GET /website/blog/1
```

The response body includes the same _version number of 1:

```
{
  "_index" :   "website",
```

```
"_type" :      "blog",
"_id" :        "1",
"_version" : 1,
"found" :      true,
"_source" :  {
   "title": "My first blog entry",
   "text":  "Just trying this out..."
}
}
```

Now, when we try to save our changes by reindexing the document, we specify the version to which our changes should be applied:

```
PUT /website/blog/1?version=1 ❶
{
  "title": "My first blog entry",
  "text":  "Starting to get the hang of this..."
}
```

❶   We want this update to succeed only if the current _version of this document in our index is version 1.

This request succeeds, and the response body tells us that the _version has been incremented to 2:

```
{
   "_index":   "website",
   "_type":    "blog",
   "_id":      "1",
   "_version": 2
   "created":  false
}
```

However, if we were to rerun the same index request, still specifying version=1, Elasticsearch would respond with a 409 Conflict HTTP response code, and a body like the following:

```
{
   "error" : "VersionConflictEngineException[[website][2] [blog][1]:
              version conflict, current [2], provided [1]]",
   "status" : 409
}
```

This tells us that the current _version number of the document in Elasticsearch is 2, but that we specified that we were updating version 1.

What we do now depends on our application requirements. We could tell the user that somebody else has already made changes to the document, and to review the changes before trying to save them again. Alternatively, as in the case of the widget stock_count previously, we could retrieve the latest document and try to reapply the change.

All APIs that update or delete a document accept a version parameter, which allows you to apply optimistic concurrency control to just the parts of your code where it makes sense.

Using Versions from an External System

A common setup is to use some other database as the primary data store and Elasticsearch to make the data searchable, which means that all changes to the primary database need to be copied across to Elasticsearch as they happen. If multiple processes are responsible for this data synchronization, you may run into concurrency problems similar to those described previously.

If your main database already has version numbers—or a value such as timestamp that can be used as a version number—then you can reuse these same version numbers in Elasticsearch by adding version_type=external to the query string. Version numbers must be integers greater than zero and less than about 9.2e+18--a positive long value in Java.

The way external version numbers are handled is a bit different from the internal version numbers we discussed previously. Instead of checking that the current _version is *the same* as the one specified in the request, Elasticsearch checks that the current _version is *less than* the specified version. If the request succeeds, the external version number is stored as the document's new _version.

External version numbers can be specified not only on index and delete requests, but also when *creating* new documents.

For instance, to create a new blog post with an external version number of 5, we can do the following:

```
PUT /website/blog/2?version=5&version_type=external
{
  "title": "My first external blog entry",
  "text":  "Starting to get the hang of this..."
}
```

In the response, we can see that the current _version number is 5:

```
{
  "_index":   "website",
  "_type":    "blog",
  "_id":      "2",
  "_version": 5,
  "created":  true
}
```

Now we update this document, specifying a new version number of 10:

```
PUT /website/blog/2?version=10&version_type=external
{
```

```
    "title": "My first external blog entry",
    "text":  "This is a piece of cake..."
}
```

The request succeeds and sets the current _version to 10:

```
{
  "_index":   "website",
  "_type":    "blog",
  "_id":      "2",
  "_version": 10,
  "created":  false
}
```

If you were to rerun this request, it would fail with the same conflict error we saw before, because the specified external version number is not higher than the current version in Elasticsearch.

Partial Updates to Documents

In "Updating a Whole Document" on page 44, we said that the way to update a document is to retrieve it, change it, and then reindex the whole document. This is true. However, using the update API, we can make partial updates like incrementing a counter in a single request.

We also said that documents are immutable: they cannot be changed, only replaced. The update API *must* obey the same rules. Externally, it appears as though we are partially updating a document in place. Internally, however, the update API simply manages the same *retrieve-change-reindex* process that we have already described. The difference is that this process happens within a shard, thus avoiding the network overhead of multiple requests. By reducing the time between the *retrieve* and *reindex* steps, we also reduce the likelihood of there being conflicting changes from other processes.

The simplest form of the update request accepts a partial document as the doc parameter, which just gets merged with the existing document. Objects are merged together, existing scalar fields are overwritten, and new fields are added. For instance, we could add a tags field and a views field to our blog post as follows:

```
POST /website/blog/1/_update
{
   "doc" : {
      "tags" : [ "testing" ],
      "views": 0
   }
}
```

If the request succeeds, we see a response similar to that of the index request:

```
{
   "_index" :    "website",
   "_id" :       "1",
   "_type" :     "blog",
   "_version" : 3
}
```

Retrieving the document shows the updated _source field:

```
{
   "_index":     "website",
   "_type":      "blog",
   "_id":        "1",
   "_version":   3,
   "found":      true,
   "_source": {
      "title":   "My first blog entry",
      "text":    "Starting to get the hang of this...",
      "tags":  [ "testing" ], ❶
      "views":   0 ❶
   }
}
```

❶ Our new fields have been added to the _source.

Using Scripts to Make Partial Updates

Scripts can be used in the update API to change the contents of the _source field, which is referred to inside an update script as ctx._source. For instance, we could use a script to increment the number of views that our blog post has had:

```
POST /website/blog/1/_update
{
   "script" : "ctx._source.views+=1"
}
```

Scripting with Groovy

For those moments when the API just isn't enough, Elasticsearch allows you to write your own custom logic in a script. Scripting is supported in many APIs including search, sorting, aggregations, and document updates. Scripts can be passed in as part of the request, retrieved from the special .scripts index, or loaded from disk.

The default scripting language is a Groovy (*http://groovy.codehaus.org/*), a fast and expressive scripting language, similar in syntax to JavaScript. It runs in a *sandbox* to prevent malicious users from breaking out of Elasticsearch and attacking the server.

You can read more about scripting in the scripting reference documentation (*http://www.elasticsearch.org/guide/en/elasticsearch/reference/current/modules-scripting.html*).

We can also use a script to add a new tag to the `tags` array. In this example we specify the new tag as a parameter rather than hardcoding it in the script itself. This allows Elasticsearch to reuse the script in the future, without having to compile a new script every time we want to add another tag:

```
POST /website/blog/1/_update
{
   "script" : "ctx._source.tags+=new_tag",
   "params" : {
      "new_tag" : "search"
   }
}
```

Fetching the document shows the effect of the last two requests:

```
{
   "_index":      "website",
   "_type":       "blog",
   "_id":         "1",
   "_version":    5,
   "found":       true,
   "_source": {
      "title":   "My first blog entry",
      "text":    "Starting to get the hang of this...",
      "tags":    ["testing", "search"], ❶
      "views":   1 ❷
   }
}
```

❶ The `search` tag has been appended to the `tags` array.

❷ The `views` field has been incremented.

We can even choose to delete a document based on its contents, by setting `ctx.op` to `delete`:

```
POST /website/blog/1/_update
{
   "script" : "ctx.op = ctx._source.views == count ? 'delete' : 'none'",
   "params" : {
      "count": 1
   }
}
```

Updating a Document That May Not Yet Exist

Imagine that we need to store a page view counter in Elasticsearch. Every time that a user views a page, we increment the counter for that page. But if it is a new page, we can't be sure that the counter already exists. If we try to update a nonexistent document, the update will fail.

In cases like these, we can use the upsert parameter to specify the document that should be created if it doesn't already exist:

```
POST /website/pageviews/1/_update
{
   "script" : "ctx._source.views+=1",
   "upsert": {
      "views": 1
   }
}
```

The first time we run this request, the upsert value is indexed as a new document, which initializes the views field to 1. On subsequent runs, the document already exists, so the script update is applied instead, incrementing the views counter.

Updates and Conflicts

In the introduction to this section, we said that the smaller the window between the *retrieve* and *reindex* steps, the smaller the opportunity for conflicting changes. But it doesn't eliminate the possibility completely. It is still possible that a request from another process could change the document before update has managed to reindex it.

To avoid losing data, the update API retrieves the current _version of the document in the *retrieve* step, and passes that to the index request during the *reindex* step. If another process has changed the document between retrieve and reindex, then the _version number won't match and the update request will fail.

For many uses of partial update, it doesn't matter that a document has been changed. For instance, if two processes are both incrementing the page-view counter, it doesn't matter in which order it happens; if a conflict occurs, the only thing we need to do is reattempt the update.

This can be done automatically by setting the retry_on_conflict parameter to the number of times that update should retry before failing; it defaults to 0.

```
POST /website/pageviews/1/_update?retry_on_conflict=5  ❶
{
   "script" : "ctx._source.views+=1",
   "upsert": {
      "views": 0
   }
}
```

❶   Retry this update five times before failing.

This works well for operations such as incrementing a counter, where the order of increments does not matter, but in other situations the order of changes *is* important. Like the index API, the update API adopts a *last-write-wins* approach by default, but it also accepts a version parameter that allows you to use optimistic concurrency control to specify which version of the document you intend to update.

Retrieving Multiple Documents

As fast as Elasticsearch is, it can be faster still. Combining multiple requests into one avoids the network overhead of processing each request individually. If you know that you need to retrieve multiple documents from Elasticsearch, it is faster to retrieve them all in a single request by using the *multi-get*, or mget, API, instead of document by document.

The mget API expects a docs array, each element of which specifies the _index, _type, and _id metadata of the document you wish to retrieve. You can also specify a _source parameter if you just want to retrieve one or more specific fields:

```
GET /_mget
{
   "docs" : [
      {
         "_index" : "website",
         "_type" :  "blog",
         "_id" :       2
      },
      {
         "_index" : "website",
         "_type" :  "pageviews",
         "_id" :       1,
         "_source": "views"
      }
   ]
}
```

The response body also contains a docs array that contains a response per document, in the same order as specified in the request. Each of these responses is the same response body that we would expect from an individual get request:

```
{
   "docs" : [
      {
         "_index" :    "website",
         "_id" :       "2",
         "_type" :     "blog",
         "found" :     true,
         "_source" : {
            "text" :   "This is a piece of cake...",
            "title" : "My first external blog entry"
         },
         "_version" : 10
      },
      {
```

```
            "_index" :    "website",
            "_id" :       "1",
            "_type" :     "pageviews",
            "found" :     true,
            "_version" : 2,
            "_source" : {
               "views" : 2
            }
         }
      ]
   }
```

If the documents you wish to retrieve are all in the same _index (and maybe even of the same _type), you can specify a default /_index or a default /_index/_type in the URL.

You can still override these values in the individual requests:

```
GET /website/blog/_mget
{
   "docs" : [
      { "_id" : 2 },
      { "_type" : "pageviews", "_id" :    1 }
   ]
}
```

In fact, if all the documents have the same _index and _type, you can just pass an array of ids instead of the full docs array:

```
GET /website/blog/_mget
{
   "ids" : [ "2", "1" ]
}
```

Note that the second document that we requested doesn't exist. We specified type blog, but the document with ID 1 is of type pageviews. This nonexistence is reported in the response body:

```
{
   "docs" : [
      {
         "_index" :    "website",
         "_type" :     "blog",
         "_id" :       "2",
         "_version" : 10,
         "found" :     true,
         "_source" : {
            "title":    "My first external blog entry",
            "text":     "This is a piece of cake..."
         }
      },
      {
         "_index" :    "website",
```

```
        "_type" :    "blog",
        "_id" :      "1",
        "found" :    false  ❶
      }
  ]
}
```

❶ This document was not found.

The fact that the second document wasn't found didn't affect the retrieval of the first document. Each doc is retrieved and reported on individually.

 The HTTP status code for the preceding request is 200, even though one document wasn't found. In fact, it would still be 200 if *none* of the requested documents were found—because the mget request itself completed successfully. To determine the success or failure of the individual documents, you need to check the found flag.

Cheaper in Bulk

In the same way that mget allows us to retrieve multiple documents at once, the bulk API allows us to make multiple create, index, update, or delete requests in a single step. This is particularly useful if you need to index a data stream such as log events, which can be queued up and indexed in batches of hundreds or thousands.

The bulk request body has the following, slightly unusual, format:

```
{ action: { metadata }}\n
{ request body        }\n
{ action: { metadata }}\n
{ request body        }\n
...
```

This format is like a *stream* of valid one-line JSON documents joined together by newline (\n) characters. Two important points to note:

- Every line must end with a newline character (\n), *including the last line*. These are used as markers to allow for efficient line separation.

- The lines cannot contain unescaped newline characters, as they would interfere with parsing. This means that the JSON must *not* be pretty-printed.

In "Why the Funny Format?" on page 71, we explain why the bulk API uses this format.

The action/metadata line specifies *what action* to do to *which document*.

The action must be one of the following:

create
> Create a document only if the document does not already exist. See "Creating a New Document" on page 45.

index
> Create a new document or replace an existing document. See "Indexing a Document" on page 40 and "Updating a Whole Document" on page 44.

update
> Do a partial update on a document. See "Partial Updates to Documents" on page 52.

delete
> Delete a document. See "Deleting a Document" on page 46.

The metadata should specify the _index, _type, and _id of the document to be indexed, created, updated, or deleted.

For instance, a delete request could look like this:

```
{ "delete": { "_index": "website", "_type": "blog", "_id": "123" }}
```

The request body line consists of the document _source itself—the fields and values that the document contains. It is required for index and create operations, which makes sense: you must supply the document to index.

It is also required for update operations and should consist of the same request body that you would pass to the update API: doc, upsert, script, and so forth. No request body line is required for a delete.

```
{ "create":  { "_index": "website", "_type": "blog", "_id": "123" }}
{ "title":     "My first blog post" }
```

If no _id is specified, an ID will be autogenerated:

```
{ "index": { "_index": "website", "_type": "blog" }}
{ "title":     "My second blog post" }
```

To put it all together, a complete bulk request has this form:

```
POST /_bulk
{ "delete": { "_index": "website", "_type": "blog", "_id": "123" }} ❶
{ "create": { "_index": "website", "_type": "blog", "_id": "123" }}
{ "title":    "My first blog post" }
{ "index":  { "_index": "website", "_type": "blog" }}
{ "title":    "My second blog post" }
{ "update": { "_index": "website", "_type": "blog", "_id": "123", "_retry_on_conflict" : 3}
{ "doc" : {"title" : "My updated blog post"} } ❷
```

❶ Notice how the delete action does not have a request body; it is followed immediately by another action.

❷ Remember the final newline character.

The Elasticsearch response contains the items array, which lists the result of each
request, in the same order as we requested them:

```
{
    "took": 4,
    "errors": false, ❶
    "items": [
      { "delete": {
            "_index":   "website",
            "_type":    "blog",
            "_id":      "123",
            "_version": 2,
            "status":   200,
            "found":    true
      }},
      { "create": {
            "_index":   "website",
            "_type":    "blog",
            "_id":      "123",
            "_version": 3,
            "status":   201
      }},
      { "create": {
            "_index":   "website",
            "_type":    "blog",
            "_id":      "EiwfApScQiiy7TIKFxRCTw",
            "_version": 1,
            "status":   201
      }},
      { "update": {
            "_index":   "website",
            "_type":    "blog",
            "_id":      "123",
            "_version": 4,
            "status":   200
      }}
    ]
}}
```

❶ All subrequests completed successfully.

Each subrequest is executed independently, so the failure of one subrequest won't affect the success of the others. If any of the requests fail, the top-level error flag is set to true and the error details will be reported under the relevant request:

```
POST /_bulk
{ "create": { "_index": "website", "_type": "blog", "_id": "123" }}
{ "title":    "Cannot create - it already exists" }
{ "index":  { "_index": "website", "_type": "blog", "_id": "123" }}
{ "title":    "But we can update it" }
```

In the response, we can see that it failed to create document 123 because it already exists, but the subsequent index request, also on document 123, succeeded:

```
{
    "took": 3,
    "errors": true, ❶
    "items": [
       { "create": {
              "_index":    "website",
              "_type":     "blog",
              "_id":       "123",
              "status":    409, ❷
              "error":     "DocumentAlreadyExistsException ❸
                           [[website][4] [blog][123]:
                           document already exists]"
       }},
       { "index": {
              "_index":    "website",
              "_type":     "blog",
              "_id":       "123",
              "_version":  5,
              "status":    200 ❹
       }}
    ]
}
```

❶ One or more requests has failed.

❷ The HTTP status code for this request reports 409 CONFLICT.

❸ The error message explaining why the request failed.

❹ The second request succeeded with an HTTP status code of 200 OK.

That also means that bulk requests are not atomic: they cannot be used to implement transactions. Each request is processed separately, so the success or failure of one request will not interfere with the others.

Don't Repeat Yourself

Perhaps you are batch-indexing logging data into the same index, and with the same type. Having to specify the same metadata for every document is a waste. Instead, just as for the mget API, the bulk request accepts a default /_index or /_index/_type in the URL:

```
POST /website/_bulk
{ "index": { "_type": "log" }}
{ "event": "User logged in" }
```

You can still override the _index and _type in the metadata line, but it will use the values in the URL as defaults:

```
POST /website/log/_bulk
{ "index": {}}
{ "event": "User logged in" }
{ "index": { "_type": "blog" }}
{ "title": "Overriding the default type" }
```

How Big Is Too Big?

The entire bulk request needs to be loaded into memory by the node that receives our request, so the bigger the request, the less memory available for other requests. There is an optimal size of bulk request. Above that size, performance no longer improves and may even drop off. The optimal size, however, is not a fixed number. It depends entirely on your hardware, your document size and complexity, and your indexing and search load.

Fortunately, it is easy to find this *sweet spot*: Try indexing typical documents in batches of increasing size. When performance starts to drop off, your batch size is too big. A good place to start is with batches of 1,000 to 5,000 documents or, if your documents are very large, with even smaller batches.

It is often useful to keep an eye on the physical size of your bulk requests. One thousand 1KB documents is very different from one thousand 1MB documents. A good bulk size to start playing with is around 5-15MB in size.

CHAPTER 4

Distributed Document Store

In the preceding chapter, we looked at all the ways to put data into your index and then retrieve it. But we glossed over many technical details surrounding how the data is distributed and fetched from the cluster. This separation is done on purpose; you don't really need to know how data is distributed to work with Elasticsearch. It just works.

In this chapter, we dive into those internal, technical details to help you understand how your data is stored in a distributed system.

Content Warning

The information presented in this chapter is for your interest. You are not required to understand and remember all the detail in order to use Elasticsearch. The options that are discussed are for advanced users only.

Read the section to gain a taste for how things work, and to know where the information is in case you need to refer to it in the future, but don't be overwhelmed by the detail.

Routing a Document to a Shard

When you index a document, it is stored on a single primary shard. How does Elasticsearch know which shard a document belongs to? When we create a new document, how does it know whether it should store that document on shard 1 or shard 2?

The process can't be random, since we may need to retrieve the document in the future. In fact, it is determined by a simple formula:

```
shard = hash(routing) % number_of_primary_shards
```

The `routing` value is an arbitrary string, which defaults to the document's _id but can also be set to a custom value. This `routing` string is passed through a hashing function to generate a number, which is divided by the number of primary shards in the index to return the *remainder*. The remainder will always be in the range 0 to `number_of_primary_shards - 1`, and gives us the number of the shard where a particular document lives.

This explains why the number of primary shards can be set only when an index is created and never changed: if the number of primary shards ever changed in the future, all previous routing values would be invalid and documents would never be found.

 Users sometimes think that having a fixed number of primary shards makes it difficult to scale out an index later. In reality, there are techniques that make it easy to scale out as and when you need. We talk more about these in Chapter 43.

All document APIs (`get`, `index`, `delete`, `bulk`, `update`, and `mget`) accept a `routing` parameter that can be used to customize the document-to- shard mapping. A custom routing value could be used to ensure that all related documents—for instance, all the documents belonging to the same user—are stored on the same shard. We discuss in detail why you may want to do this in Chapter 43.

How Primary and Replica Shards Interact

For explanation purposes, let's imagine that we have a cluster consisting of three nodes. It contains one index called `blogs` that has two primary shards. Each primary shard has two replicas. Copies of the same shard are never allocated to the same node, so our cluster looks something like Figure 4-1.

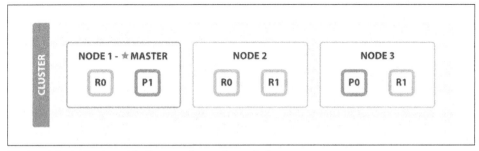

Figure 4-1. A cluster with three nodes and one index

We can send our requests to any node in the cluster. Every node is fully capable of serving any request. Every node knows the location of every document in the cluster and so can forward requests directly to the required node. In the following examples, we will send all of our requests to `Node 1`, which we will refer to as the *requesting node*.

 When sending requests, it is good practice to round-robin through all the nodes in the cluster, in order to spread the load.

Creating, Indexing, and Deleting a Document

Create, index, and delete requests are *write* operations, which must be successfully completed on the primary shard before they can be copied to any associated replica shards, as shown in Figure 4-2.

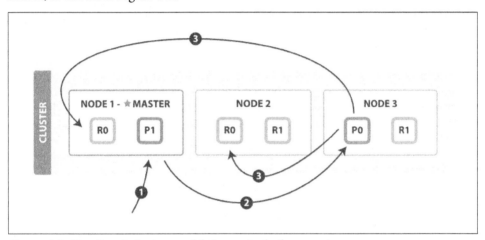

Figure 4-2. Creating, indexing, or deleting a single document

Here is the sequence of steps necessary to successfully create, index, or delete a document on both the primary and any replica shards:

1. The client sends a create, index, or delete request to `Node 1`.

2. The node uses the document's `_id` to determine that the document belongs to shard `0`. It forwards the request to `Node 3`, where the primary copy of shard `0` is currently allocated.

3. `Node 3` executes the request on the primary shard. If it is successful, it forwards the request in parallel to the replica shards on `Node 1` and `Node 2`. Once all of the

replica shards report success, Node 3 reports success to the requesting node, which reports success to the client.

By the time the client receives a successful response, the document change has been executed on the primary shard and on all replica shards. Your change is safe.

There are a number of optional request parameters that allow you to influence this process, possibly increasing performance at the cost of data security. These options are seldom used because Elasticsearch is already fast, but they are explained here for the sake of completeness:

replication

The default value for replication is sync. This causes the primary shard to wait for successful responses from the replica shards before returning.

If you set replication to async, it will return success to the client as soon as the request has been executed on the primary shard. It will still forward the request to the replicas, but you will not know whether the replicas succeeded.

This option is mentioned specifically to advise against using it. The default sync replication allows Elasticsearch to exert back pressure on whatever system is feeding it with data. With async replication, it is possible to overload Elasticsearch by sending too many requests without waiting for their completion.

consistency

By default, the primary shard requires a *quorum*, or majority, of shard copies (where a shard copy can be a primary or a replica shard) to be available before even attempting a write operation. This is to prevent writing data to the "wrong side" of a network partition. A quorum is defined as follows:

```
int( (primary + number_of_replicas) / 2 ) + 1
```

The allowed values for consistency are one (just the primary shard), all (the primary and all replicas), or the default quorum, or majority, of shard copies.

Note that the number_of_replicas is the number of replicas *specified* in the index settings, not the number of replicas that are currently active. If you have specified that an index should have three replicas, a quorum would be as follows:

```
int( (primary + 3 replicas) / 2 ) + 1 = 3
```

But if you start only two nodes, there will be insufficient active shard copies to satisfy the quorum, and you will be unable to index or delete any documents.

timeout

What happens if insufficient shard copies are available? Elasticsearch waits, in the hope that more shards will appear. By default, it will wait up to 1 minute. If you need to, you can use the `timeout` parameter to make it abort sooner: `100` is 100 milliseconds, and `30s` is 30 seconds.

> A new index has 1 replica by default, which means that two active shard copies *should* be required in order to satisfy the need for a quorum. However, these default settings would prevent us from doing anything useful with a single-node cluster. To avoid this problem, the requirement for a quorum is enforced only when `num ber_of_replicas` is greater than 1.

Retrieving a Document

A document can be retrieved from a primary shard or from any of its replicas, as shown in Figure 4-3.

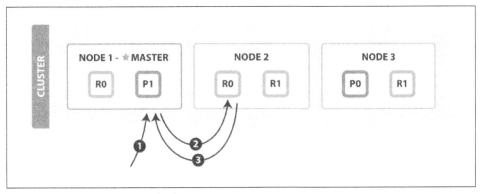

Figure 4-3. Retrieving a single document

Here is the sequence of steps to retrieve a document from either a primary or replica shard:

1. The client sends a get request to `Node 1`.

2. The node uses the document's `_id` to determine that the document belongs to shard `0`. Copies of shard `0` exist on all three nodes. On this occasion, it forwards the request to `Node 2`.

3. `Node 2` returns the document to `Node 1`, which returns the document to the client.

For read requests, the requesting node will choose a different shard copy on every request in order to balance the load; it round-robins through all shard copies.

It is possible that, while a document is being indexed, the document will already be present on the primary shard but not yet copied to the replica shards. In this case, a replica might report that the document doesn't exist, while the primary would have returned the document successfully. Once the indexing request has returned success to the user, the document will be available on the primary and all replica shards.

Partial Updates to a Document

The update API , as shown in Figure 4-4, combines the read and write patterns explained previously.

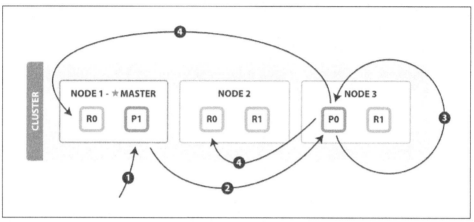

Figure 4-4. Partial updates to a document

Here is the sequence of steps used to perform a partial update on a document:

1. The client sends an update request to Node 1.

2. It forwards the request to Node 3, where the primary shard is allocated.

3. Node 3 retrieves the document from the primary shard, changes the JSON in the _source field, and tries to reindex the document on the primary shard. If the document has already been changed by another process, it retries step 3 up to retry_on_conflict times, before giving up.

4. If Node 3 has managed to update the document successfully, it forwards the new version of the document in parallel to the replica shards on Node 1 and Node 2 to be reindexed. Once all replica shards report success, Node 3 reports success to the requesting node, which reports success to the client.

The update API also accepts the routing, replication, consistency, and timeout parameters that are explained in "Creating, Indexing, and Deleting a Document" on page 65.

Document-Based Replication

When a primary shard forwards changes to its replica shards, it doesn't forward the update request. Instead it forwards the new version of the full document. Remember that these changes are forwarded to the replica shards asynchronously, and there is no guarantee that they will arrive in the same order that they were sent. If Elasticsearch forwarded just the change, it is possible that changes would be applied in the wrong order, resulting in a corrupt document.

Multidocument Patterns

The patterns for the mget and bulk APIs are similar to those for individual documents. The difference is that the requesting node knows in which shard each document lives. It breaks up the multidocument request into a multidocument request *per shard*, and forwards these in parallel to each participating node.

Once it receives answers from each node, it collates their responses into a single response, which it returns to the client, as shown in Figure 4-5.

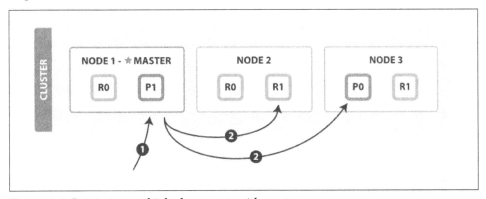

Figure 4-5. Retrieving multiple documents with mget

Here is the sequence of steps necessary to retrieve multiple documents with a single mget request:

1. The client sends an mget request to Node 1.

2. `Node 1` builds a multi-get request per shard, and forwards these requests in parallel to the nodes hosting each required primary or replica shard. Once all replies have been received, `Node 1` builds the response and returns it to the client.

A `routing` parameter can be set for each document in the `docs` array.

The bulk API, as depicted in Figure 4-6, allows the execution of multiple create, index, delete, and update requests within a single bulk request.

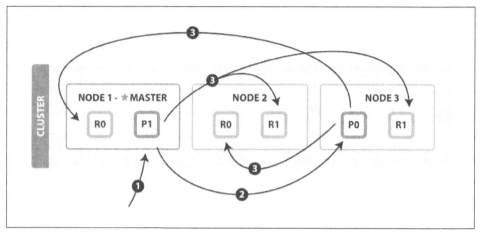

Figure 4-6. Multiple document changes with `bulk`

The sequence of steps followed by the `bulk` API are as follows:

1. The client sends a `bulk` request to `Node 1`.

2. `Node 1` builds a bulk request per shard, and forwards these requests in parallel to the nodes hosting each involved primary shard.

3. The primary shard executes each action serially, one after another. As each action succeeds, the primary forwards the new document (or deletion) to its replica shards in parallel, and then moves on to the next action. Once all replica shards report success for all actions, the node reports success to the requesting node, which collates the responses and returns them to the client.

The `bulk` API also accepts the `replication` and `consistency` parameters at the top level for the whole `bulk` request, and the `routing` parameter in the metadata for each request.

Why the Funny Format?

When we learned about bulk requests earlier in "Cheaper in Bulk" on page 58, you may have asked yourself, "Why does the bulk API require the funny format with the newline characters, instead of just sending the requests wrapped in a JSON array, like the mget API?"

To answer this, we need to explain a little background: Each document referenced in a bulk request may belong to a different primary shard, each of which may be allocated to any of the nodes in the cluster. This means that every *action* inside a bulk request needs to be forwarded to the correct shard on the correct node.

If the individual requests were wrapped up in a JSON array, that would mean that we would need to do the following:

- Parse the JSON into an array (including the document data, which can be very large)
- Look at each request to determine which shard it should go to
- Create an array of requests for each shard
- Serialize these arrays into the internal transport format
- Send the requests to each shard

It would work, but would need a lot of RAM to hold copies of essentially the same data, and would create many more data structures that the Java Virtual Machine (JVM) would have to spend time garbage collecting.

Instead, Elasticsearch reaches up into the networking buffer, where the raw request has been received, and reads the data directly. It uses the newline characters to identify and parse just the small action/metadata lines in order to decide which shard should handle each request.

These raw requests are forwarded directly to the correct shard. There is no redundant copying of data, no wasted data structures. The entire request process is handled in the smallest amount of memory possible.

CHAPTER 5

Searching—The Basic Tools

So far, we have learned how to use Elasticsearch as a simple NoSQL-style distributed document store. We can throw JSON documents at Elasticsearch and retrieve each one by ID. But the real power of Elasticsearch lies in its ability to make sense out of chaos — to turn Big Data into Big Information.

This is the reason that we use structured JSON documents, rather than amorphous blobs of data. Elasticsearch not only *stores* the document, but also *indexes* the content of the document in order to make it searchable.

Every field in a document is indexed and can be queried. And it's not just that. During a single query, Elasticsearch can use *all* of these indices, to return results at breathtaking speed. That's something that you could never consider doing with a traditional database.

A *search* can be any of the following:

- A structured query on concrete fields like gender or age, sorted by a field like join_date, similar to the type of query that you could construct in SQL
- A full-text query, which finds all documents matching the search keywords, and returns them sorted by *relevance*
- A combination of the two

While many searches will just work out of the box, to use Elasticsearch to its full potential, you need to understand three subjects:

Mapping
How the data in each field is interpreted

Analysis
How full text is processed to make it searchable

Query DSL
　　The flexible, powerful query language used by Elasticsearch

Each of these is a big subject in its own right, and we explain them in detail in Part II. The chapters in this section introduce the basic concepts of all three—just enough to help you to get an overall understanding of how search works.

We will start by explaining the `search` API in its simplest form.

Test Data

The documents that we will use for test purposes in this chapter can be found in this gist: *https://gist.github.com/clintongormley/8579281*.

You can copy the commands and paste them into your shell in order to follow along with this chapter.

Alternatively, if you're in the online version of this book, you can click here to open in Sense.

The Empty Search

The most basic form of the search API is the *empty search*, which doesn't specify any query but simply returns all documents in all indices in the cluster:

```
GET /_search
```

The response (edited for brevity) looks something like this:

```
{
   "hits" : {
      "total" :         14,
      "hits" : [
         {
            "_index":    "us",
            "_type":     "tweet",
            "_id":       "7",
            "_score":    1,
            "_source": {
               "date":     "2014-09-17",
               "name":     "John Smith",
               "tweet":    "The Query DSL is really powerful and flexible",
               "user_id": 2
            }
         },
         ... 9 RESULTS REMOVED ...
      ],
      "max_score" :    1
   },
```

```
    "took" :          4,
    "_shards" : {
       "failed" :        0,
       "successful" :   10,
       "total" :        10
    },
    "timed_out" :     false
}
```

hits

The most important section of the response is `hits`, which contains the `total` number of documents that matched our query, and a `hits` array containing the first 10 of those matching documents—the results.

Each result in the `hits` array contains the `_index`, `_type`, and `_id` of the document, plus the `_source` field. This means that the whole document is immediately available to us directly from the search results. This is unlike other search engines, which return just the document ID, requiring you to fetch the document itself in a separate step.

Each element also has a `_score`. This is the *relevance score*, which is a measure of how well the document matches the query. By default, results are returned with the most relevant documents first; that is, in descending order of `_score`. In this case, we didn't specify any query, so all documents are equally relevant, hence the neutral `_score` of 1 for all results.

The `max_score` value is the highest `_score` of any document that matches our query.

took

The `took` value tells us how many milliseconds the entire search request took to execute.

shards

The `_shards` element tells us the `total` number of shards that were involved in the query and, of them, how many were `successful` and how many `failed`. We wouldn't normally expect shards to fail, but it can happen. If we were to suffer a major disaster in which we lost both the primary and the replica copy of the same shard, there would be no copies of that shard available to respond to search requests. In this case, Elasticsearch would report the shard as `failed`, but continue to return results from the remaining shards.

timeout

The `timed_out` value tells us whether the query timed out. By default, search requests do not time out. If low response times are more important to you than complete results, you can specify a `timeout` as `10` or `10ms` (10 milliseconds), or `1s` (1 second):

```
GET /_search?timeout=10ms
```

Elasticsearch will return any results that it has managed to gather from each shard before the requests timed out.

It should be noted that this `timeout` does not halt the execution of the query; it merely tells the coordinating node to return the results collected *so far* and to close the connection. In the background, other shards may still be processing the query even though results have been sent.

Use the time-out because it is important to your SLA, not because you want to abort the execution of long-running queries.

Multi-index, Multitype

Did you notice that the results from the preceding empty search contained documents of different types—user and `tweet`—from two different indices—us and gb?

By not limiting our search to a particular index or type, we have searched across *all* documents in the cluster. Elasticsearch forwarded the search request in parallel to a primary or replica of every shard in the cluster, gathered the results to select the overall top 10, and returned them to us.

Usually, however, you will want to search within one or more specific indices, and probably one or more specific types. We can do this by specifying the index and type in the URL, as follows:

`/_search`
  Search all types in all indices

`/gb/_search`
  Search all types in the gb index

`/gb,us/_search`
  Search all types in the gb and us indices

`/g*,u*/_search`
  Search all types in any indices beginning with g or beginning with u

`/gb/user/_search`
  Search type user in the gb index

`/gb,us/user,tweet/_search`
>   Search types `user` and `tweet` in the `gb` and `us` indices

`/_all/user,tweet/_search`
>   Search types `user` and `tweet` in all indices

When you search within a single index, Elasticsearch forwards the search request to a primary or replica of every shard in that index, and then gathers the results from each shard. Searching within multiple indices works in exactly the same way—there are just more shards involved.

>   Searching one index that has five primary shards is *exactly equivalent* to searching five indices that have one primary shard each.

Later, you will see how this simple fact makes it easy to scale flexibly as your requirements change.

Pagination

Our preceding empty search told us that 14 documents in the cluster match our (empty) query. But there were only 10 documents in the `hits` array. How can we see the other documents?

In the same way as SQL uses the `LIMIT` keyword to return a single "page" of results, Elasticsearch accepts the `from` and `size` parameters:

`size`
>   Indicates the number of results that should be returned, defaults to `10`

`from`
>   Indicates the number of initial results that should be skipped, defaults to `0`

If you wanted to show five results per page, then pages 1 to 3 could be requested as follows:

```
GET /_search?size=5
GET /_search?size=5&from=5
GET /_search?size=5&from=10
```

Beware of paging too deep or requesting too many results at once. Results are sorted before being returned. But remember that a search request usually spans multiple shards. Each shard generates its own sorted results, which then need to be sorted centrally to ensure that the overall order is correct.

Deep Paging in Distributed Systems

To understand why deep paging is problematic, let's imagine that we are searching within a single index with five primary shards. When we request the first page of results (results 1 to 10), each shard produces its own top 10 results and returns them to the *requesting node*, which then sorts all 50 results in order to select the overall top 10.

Now imagine that we ask for page 1,000—results 10,001 to 10,010. Everything works in the same way except that each shard has to produce its top 10,010 results. The requesting node then sorts through all 50,050 results and discards 50,040 of them!

You can see that, in a distributed system, the cost of sorting results grows exponentially the deeper we page. There is a good reason that web search engines don't return more than 1,000 results for any query.

 In "Reindexing Your Data" on page 152 we explain how you *can* retrieve large numbers of documents efficiently.

Search *Lite*

There are two forms of the search API: a "lite" *query-string* version that expects all its parameters to be passed in the query string, and the full *request body* version that expects a JSON request body and uses a rich search language called the query DSL.

The query-string search is useful for running ad hoc queries from the command line. For instance, this query finds all documents of type `tweet` that contain the word `elasticsearch` in the `tweet` field:

```
GET /_all/tweet/_search?q=tweet:elasticsearch
```

The next query looks for `john` in the `name` field and `mary` in the `tweet` field. The actual query is just

```
+name:john +tweet:mary
```

but the *percent encoding* needed for query-string parameters makes it appear more cryptic than it really is:

```
GET /_search?q=%2Bname%3Ajohn+%2Btweet%3Amary
```

The + prefix indicates conditions that *must* be satisfied for our query to match. Similarly a - prefix would indicate conditions that *must not* match. All conditions without a + or - are optional—the more that match, the more relevant the document.

The _all Field

This simple search returns all documents that contain the word mary:

```
GET /_search?q=mary
```

In the previous examples, we searched for words in the tweet or name fields. However, the results from this query mention mary in three fields:

- A user whose name is Mary
- Six tweets by Mary
- One tweet directed at @mary

How has Elasticsearch managed to find results in three different fields?

When you index a document, Elasticsearch takes the string values of all of its fields and concatenates them into one big string, which it indexes as the special _all field. For example, when we index this document:

```
{
    "tweet":    "However did I manage before Elasticsearch?",
    "date":     "2014-09-14",
    "name":     "Mary Jones",
    "user_id":  1
}
```

it's as if we had added an extra field called _all with this value:

```
"However did I manage before Elasticsearch? 2014-09-14 Mary Jones 1"
```

The query-string search uses the _all field unless another field name has been specified.

 The _all field is a useful feature while you are getting started with a new application. Later, you will find that you have more control over your search results if you query specific fields instead of the _all field. When the _all field is no longer useful to you, you can disable it, as explained in "Metadata: _all Field" on page 144.

More Complicated Queries

The next query searches for tweets, using the following criteria:

- The `name` field contains `mary` or `john`
- The `date` is greater than `2014-09-10`
- The `_all` field contains either of the words `aggregations` or `geo`

```
+name:(mary john) +date:>2014-09-10 +(aggregations geo)
```

As a properly encoded query string, this looks like the slightly less readable result:

```
?q=%2Bname%3A(mary+john)+%2Bdate%3A%3E2014-09-10+%2B(aggregations+geo)
```

As you can see from the preceding examples, this *lite* query-string search is surprisingly powerful. Its query syntax, which is explained in detail in the Query String Syntax (*http://www.elasticsearch.org/guide/en/elasticsearch/reference/current/query-dsl-query-string-query.html#query-string-syntax*) reference docs, allows us to express quite complex queries succinctly. This makes it great for throwaway queries from the command line or during development.

However, you can also see that its terseness can make it cryptic and difficult to debug. And it's fragile—a slight syntax error in the query string, such as a misplaced `-`, `:`, `/`, or `"`, and it will return an error instead of results.

Finally, the query-string search allows any user to run potentially slow, heavy queries on any field in your index, possibly exposing private information or even bringing your cluster to its knees!

 For these reasons, we don't recommend exposing query-string searches directly to your users, unless they are power users who can be trusted with your data and with your cluster.

Instead, in production we usually rely on the full-featured *request body* search API, which does all of this, plus a lot more. Before we get there, though, we first need to take a look at how our data is indexed in Elasticsearch.

CHAPTER 6

Mapping and Analysis

While playing around with the data in our index, we notice something odd. Something seems to be broken: we have 12 tweets in our indices, and only one of them contains the date 2014-09-15, but have a look at the total hits for the following queries:

```
GET /_search?q=2014              # 12 results
GET /_search?q=2014-09-15        # 12 results !
GET /_search?q=date:2014-09-15   # 1 result
GET /_search?q=date:2014         # 0 results !
```

Why does querying the _all field for the full date return all tweets, and querying the date field for just the year return no results? Why do our results differ when searching within the _all field or the date field?

Presumably, it is because the way our data has been indexed in the _all field is different from how it has been indexed in the date field. So let's take a look at how Elasticsearch has interpreted our document structure, by requesting the *mapping* (or schema definition) for the tweet type in the gb index:

```
GET /gb/_mapping/tweet
```

This gives us the following:

```
{
   "gb": {
      "mappings": {
         "tweet": {
            "properties": {
               "date": {
                  "type": "date",
                  "format": "dateOptionalTime"
               },
               "name": {
```

```
            "type": "string"
        },
        "tweet": {
            "type": "string"
        },
        "user_id": {
            "type": "long"
        }
    }
  }
 }
}
```

Elasticsearch has dynamically generated a mapping for us, based on what it could guess about our field types. The response shows us that the date field has been recognized as a field of type date. The _all field isn't mentioned because it is a default field, but we know that the _all field is of type string.

So fields of type date and fields of type string are indexed differently, and can thus be searched differently. That's not entirely surprising. You might expect that each of the core data types—strings, numbers, Booleans, and dates—might be indexed slightly differently. And this is true: there are slight differences.

But by far the biggest difference is between fields that represent *exact values* (which can include string fields) and fields that represent *full text*. This distinction is really important—it's the thing that separates a search engine from all other databases.

Exact Values Versus Full Text

Data in Elasticsearch can be broadly divided into two types: exact values and full text.

Exact values are exactly what they sound like. Examples are a date or a user ID, but can also include exact strings such as a username or an email address. The exact value Foo is not the same as the exact value foo. The exact value 2014 is not the same as the exact value 2014-09-15.

Full text, on the other hand, refers to textual data—usually written in some human language — like the text of a tweet or the body of an email.

Full text is often referred to as *unstructured data*, which is a misnomer—natural language is highly structured. The problem is that the rules of natural languages are complex, which makes them difficult for computers to parse correctly. For instance, consider this sentence:

May is fun but June bores me.

Does it refer to months or to people?

Exact values are easy to query. The decision is binary; a value either matches the query, or it doesn't. This kind of query is easy to express with SQL:

```
WHERE name    = "John Smith"
  AND user_id = 2
  AND date    > "2014-09-15"
```

Querying full-text data is much more subtle. We are not just asking, "Does this document match the query" but "How *well* does this document match the query?" In other words, how *relevant* is this document to the given query?

We seldom want to match the whole full-text field exactly. Instead, we want to search *within* text fields. Not only that, but we expect search to understand our *intent*:

- A search for UK should also return documents mentioning the United Kingdom.
- A search for jump should also match jumped, jumps, jumping, and perhaps even leap.
- johnny walker should match Johnnie Walker, and johnnie depp should match Johnny Depp.
- fox news hunting should return stories about hunting on Fox News, while fox hunting news should return news stories about fox hunting.

To facilitate these types of queries on full-text fields, Elasticsearch first *analyzes* the text, and then uses the results to build an *inverted index*. We will discuss the inverted index and the analysis process in the next two sections.

Inverted Index

Elasticsearch uses a structure called an *inverted index*, which is designed to allow very fast full-text searches. An inverted index consists of a list of all the unique words that appear in any document, and for each word, a list of the documents in which it appears.

For example, let's say we have two documents, each with a content field containing the following:

1. The quick brown fox jumped over the lazy dog
2. Quick brown foxes leap over lazy dogs in summer

To create an inverted index, we first split the content field of each document into separate words (which we call *terms*, or *tokens*), create a sorted list of all the unique terms, and then list in which document each term appears. The result looks something like this:

```
Term        Doc_1 Doc_2
-----------------------
Quick    |       |  X
The      |  X    |
brown    |  X    |  X
dog      |  X    |
dogs     |       |  X
fox      |  X    |
foxes    |       |  X
in       |       |  X
jumped   |  X    |
lazy     |  X    |  X
leap     |       |  X
over     |  X    |  X
quick    |  X    |
summer   |       |  X
the      |  X    |
-----------------------
```

Now, if we want to search for quick brown, we just need to find the documents in which each term appears:

```
Term        Doc_1 Doc_2
-----------------------
brown    |  X    |  X
quick    |  X    |
-----------------------
Total    |  2    |  1
```

Both documents match, but the first document has more matches than the second. If we apply a naive *similarity algorithm* that just counts the number of matching terms, then we can say that the first document is a better match—is *more relevant* to our query—than the second document.

But there are a few problems with our current inverted index:

- Quick and quick appear as separate terms, while the user probably thinks of them as the same word.

- fox and foxes are pretty similar, as are dog and dogs; They share the same root word.

- jumped and leap, while not from the same root word, are similar in meaning. They are synonyms.

With the preceding index, a search for +Quick +fox wouldn't match any documents. (Remember, a preceding + means that the word must be present.) Both the term Quick and the term fox have to be in the same document in order to satisfy the query, but the first doc contains quick fox and the second doc contains Quick foxes.

Our user could reasonably expect both documents to match the query. We can do better.

If we normalize the terms into a standard format, then we can find documents that contain terms that are not exactly the same as the user requested, but are similar enough to still be relevant. For instance:

- Quick can be lowercased to become quick.

- foxes can be *stemmed*--reduced to its root form—to become fox. Similarly, dogs could be stemmed to dog.

- jumped and leap are synonyms and can be indexed as just the single term jump.

Now the index looks like this:

```
Term        Doc_1  Doc_2
- - - - - - - - - - - - - - - - - - - - - - - -
brown    |    X    |   X
dog      |    X    |   X
fox      |    X    |   X
in       |         |   X
jump     |    X    |   X
lazy     |    X    |   X
over     |    X    |   X
quick    |    X    |   X
summer   |         |   X
the      |    X    |   X
- - - - - - - - - - - - - - - - - - - - - - - -
```

But we're not there yet. Our search for +Quick +fox would *still* fail, because we no longer have the exact term Quick in our index. However, if we apply the same normalization rules that we used on the content field to our query string, it would become a query for +quick +fox, which would match both documents!

 This is very important. You can find only terms that exist in your index, so *both the indexed text and the query string must be normalized into the same form.*

This process of tokenization and normalization is called *analysis*, which we discuss in the next section.

Analysis and Analyzers

Analysis is a process that consists of the following:

- First, tokenizing a block of text into individual *terms* suitable for use in an inverted index,
- Then normalizing these terms into a standard form to improve their "searchability," or *recall*

This job is performed by analyzers. An *analyzer* is really just a wrapper that combines three functions into a single package:

Character filters
First, the string is passed through any *character filters* in turn. Their job is to tidy up the string before tokenization. A character filter could be used to strip out HTML, or to convert & characters to the word and.

Tokenizer
Next, the string is tokenized into individual terms by a *tokenizer*. A simple tokenizer might split the text into terms whenever it encounters whitespace or punctuation.

Token filters
Last, each term is passed through any *token filters* in turn, which can change terms (for example, lowercasing Quick), remove terms (for example, stopwords such as a, and, the) or add terms (for example, synonyms like jump and leap).

Elasticsearch provides many character filters, tokenizers, and token filters out of the box. These can be combined to create custom analyzers suitable for different purposes. We discuss these in detail in "Custom Analyzers" on page 136.

Built-in Analyzers

However, Elasticsearch also ships with prepackaged analyzers that you can use directly. We list the most important ones next and, to demonstrate the difference in behavior, we show what terms each would produce from this string:

```
"Set the shape to semi-transparent by calling set_trans(5)"
```

Standard analyzer
The standard analyzer is the default analyzer that Elasticsearch uses. It is the best general choice for analyzing text that may be in any language. It splits the text on *word boundaries*, as defined by the Unicode Consortium (*http://www.unicode.org/ reports/tr29/*), and removes most punctuation. Finally, it lowercases all terms. It would produce

```
set, the, shape, to, semi, transparent, by, calling, set_trans, 5
```

Simple analyzer

The simple analyzer splits the text on anything that isn't a letter, and lowercases the terms. It would produce

```
set, the, shape, to, semi, transparent, by, calling, set, trans
```

Whitespace analyzer

The whitespace analyzer splits the text on whitespace. It doesn't lowercase. It would produce

```
Set, the, shape, to, semi-transparent, by, calling, set_trans(5)
```

Language analyzers

Language-specific analyzers are available for many languages (*http://www.elastic search.org/guide/en/elasticsearch/reference/current/analysis-lang-analyzer.html*). They are able to take the peculiarities of the specified language into account. For instance, the `english` analyzer comes with a set of English stopwords (common words like `and` or `the` that don't have much impact on relevance), which it removes. This analyzer also is able to *stem* English words because it understands the rules of English grammar.

The `english` analyzer would produce the following:

```
set, shape, semi, transpar, call, set_tran, 5
```

Note how `transparent`, `calling`, and `set_trans` have been stemmed to their root form.

When Analyzers Are Used

When we *index* a document, its full-text fields are analyzed into terms that are used to create the inverted index. However, when we *search* on a full-text field, we need to pass the query string through the *same analysis process*, to ensure that we are searching for terms in the same form as those that exist in the index.

Full-text queries, which we discuss later, understand how each field is defined, and so they can do the right thing:

- When you query a *full-text* field, the query will apply the same analyzer to the query string to produce the correct list of terms to search for.

- When you query an *exact-value* field, the query will not analyze the query string, but instead search for the exact value that you have specified.

Now you can understand why the queries that we demonstrated at the start of this chapter return what they do:

- The date field contains an exact value: the single term 2014-09-15.

- The _all field is a full-text field, so the analysis process has converted the date into the three terms: 2014, 09, and 15.

When we query the _all field for 2014, it matches all 12 tweets, because all of them contain the term 2014:

```
GET /_search?q=2014          # 12 results
```

When we query the _all field for 2014-09-15, it first analyzes the query string to produce a query that matches *any* of the terms 2014, 09, or 15. This also matches all 12 tweets, because all of them contain the term 2014:

```
GET /_search?q=2014-09-15          # 12 results !
```

When we query the date field for 2014-09-15, it looks for that *exact* date, and finds one tweet only:

```
GET /_search?q=date:2014-09-15  # 1  result
```

When we query the date field for 2014, it finds no documents because none contain that exact date:

```
GET /_search?q=date:2014          # 0  results !
```

Testing Analyzers

Especially when you are new to Elasticsearch, it is sometimes difficult to understand what is actually being tokenized and stored into your index. To better understand what is going on, you can use the analyze API to see how text is analyzed. Specify which analyzer to use in the query-string parameters, and the text to analyze in the body:

```
GET /_analyze?analyzer=standard
Text to analyze
```

Each element in the result represents a single term:

```
{
   "tokens": [
      {
         "token":        "text",
         "start_offset": 0,
         "end_offset":   4,
         "type":         "<ALPHANUM>",
         "position":     1
      },
      {
         "token":        "to",
         "start_offset": 5,
         "end_offset":   7,
```

```
          "type":        "<ALPHANUM>",
          "position":    2
    },
    {
          "token":       "analyze",
          "start_offset": 8,
          "end_offset":  15,
          "type":        "<ALPHANUM>",
          "position":    3
    }
  ]
}
```

The token is the actual term that will be stored in the index. The position indicates
the order in which the terms appeared in the original text. The start_offset and
end_offset indicate the character positions that the original word occupied in the
original string.

 The type values like <ALPHANUM> vary per analyzer and can be
ignored. The only place that they are used in Elasticsearch is in
the keep_types token filter (*http://www.elasticsearch.org/guide/en/
elasticsearch/guide/current/analysis-intro.html#analyze-api*).

The analyze API is a useful tool for understanding what is happening inside Elastic‐
search indices, and we will talk more about it as we progress.

Specifying Analyzers

When Elasticsearch detects a new string field in your documents, it automatically
configures it as a full-text string field and analyzes it with the standard analyzer.

You don't always want this. Perhaps you want to apply a different analyzer that suits
the language your data is in. And sometimes you want a string field to be just a string
field—to index the exact value that you pass in, without any analysis, such as a string
user ID or an internal status field or tag.

To achieve this, we have to configure these fields manually by specifying the mapping.

Mapping

In order to be able to treat date fields as dates, numeric fields as numbers, and string
fields as full-text or exact-value strings, Elasticsearch needs to know what type of data
each field contains. This information is contained in the mapping.

As explained in Chapter 3, each document in an index has a *type*. Every type has its
own *mapping*, or *schema definition*. A mapping defines the fields within a type, the

datatype for each field, and how the field should be handled by Elasticsearch. A mapping is also used to configure metadata associated with the type.

We discuss mappings in detail in "Types and Mappings" on page 139. In this section, we're going to look at just enough to get you started.

Core Simple Field Types

Elasticsearch supports the following simple field types:

- String: `string`
- Whole number: `byte`, `short`, `integer`, `long`
- Floating-point: `float`, `double`
- Boolean: `boolean`
- Date: `date`

When you index a document that contains a new field—one previously not seen—Elasticsearch will use *dynamic mapping* to try to guess the field type from the basic datatypes available in JSON, using the following rules:

JSON type
  Field type

Boolean: `true` *or* `false`
  `boolean`

Whole number: `123`
  `long`

Floating point: `123.45`
  `double`

String, valid date: `2014-09-15`
  `date`

String: `foo bar`
  `string`

 This means that if you index a number in quotes (`"123"`), it will be mapped as type `string`, not type `long`. However, if the field is already mapped as type `long`, then Elasticsearch will try to convert the string into a long, and throw an exception if it can't.

Viewing the Mapping

We can view the mapping that Elasticsearch has for one or more types in one or more indices by using the /_mapping endpoint. At the start of this chapter, we already retrieved the mapping for type tweet in index gb:

```
GET /gb/_mapping/tweet
```

This shows us the mapping for the fields (called *properties*) that Elasticsearch generated dynamically from the documents that we indexed:

```
{
   "gb": {
      "mappings": {
         "tweet": {
            "properties": {
               "date": {
                  "type": "date",
                  "format": "dateOptionalTime"
               },
               "name": {
                  "type": "string"
               },
               "tweet": {
                  "type": "string"
               },
               "user_id": {
                  "type": "long"
               }
            }
         }
      }
   }
}
```

Incorrect mappings, such as having an age field mapped as type string instead of integer, can produce confusing results to your queries.

Instead of assuming that your mapping is correct, check it!

Customizing Field Mappings

While the basic field datatypes are sufficient for many cases, you will often need to customize the mapping for individual fields, especially string fields. Custom mappings allow you to do the following:

- Distinguish between full-text string fields and exact value string fields
- Use language-specific analyzers

- Optimize a field for partial matching

- Specify custom date formats

- And much more

The most important attribute of a field is the `type`. For fields other than `string` fields, you will seldom need to map anything other than `type`:

```
{
    "number_of_clicks": {
        "type": "integer"
    }
}
```

Fields of type `string` are, by default, considered to contain full text. That is, their value will be passed through an analyzer before being indexed, and a full-text query on the field will pass the query string through an analyzer before searching.

The two most important mapping attributes for `string` fields are `index` and `analyzer`.

index

The `index` attribute controls how the string will be indexed. It can contain one of three values:

`analyzed`
: First analyze the string and then index it. In other words, index this field as full text.

`not_analyzed`
: Index this field, so it is searchable, but index the value exactly as specified. Do not analyze it.

`no`
: Don't index this field at all. This field will not be searchable.

The default value of `index` for a `string` field is `analyzed`. If we want to map the field as an exact value, we need to set it to `not_analyzed`:

```
{
    "tag": {
        "type":     "string",
        "index":    "not_analyzed"
    }
}
```

The other simple types (such as `long`, `double`, `date` etc) also accept the `index` parameter, but the only relevant values are `no` and `not_analyzed`, as their values are never analyzed.

analyzer

For `analyzed` string fields, use the `analyzer` attribute to specify which analyzer to apply both at search time and at index time. By default, Elasticsearch uses the `stan dard` analyzer, but you can change this by specifying one of the built-in analyzers, such as `whitespace`, `simple`, or `english`:

```
{
    "tweet": {
        "type":      "string",
        "analyzer": "english"
    }
}
```

In "Custom Analyzers" on page 136, we show you how to define and use custom analyzers as well.

Updating a Mapping

You can specify the mapping for a type when you first create an index. Alternatively, you can add the mapping for a new type (or update the mapping for an existing type) later, using the `/_mapping` endpoint.

 Although you can *add* to an existing mapping, you can't *change* it. If a field already exists in the mapping, the data from that field probably has already been indexed. If you were to change the field mapping, the already indexed data would be wrong and would not be properly searchable.

We can update a mapping to add a new field, but we can't change an existing field from `analyzed` to `not_analyzed`.

To demonstrate both ways of specifying mappings, let's first delete the `gb` index:

```
DELETE /gb
```

Then create a new index, specifying that the `tweet` field should use the `english` analyzer:

```
PUT /gb ❶
{
  "mappings": {
    "tweet" : {
```

```
      "properties" : {
        "tweet" : {
          "type" :     "string",
          "analyzer": "english"
        },
        "date" : {
          "type" :     "date"
        },
        "name" : {
          "type" :     "string"
        },
        "user_id" : {
          "type" :     "long"
        }
      }
    }
  }
}
```

❶ This creates the index with the `mappings` specified in the body.

Later on, we decide to add a new `not_analyzed` text field called `tag` to the `tweet` mapping, using the `_mapping` endpoint:

```
PUT /gb/_mapping/tweet
{
  "properties" : {
    "tag" : {
      "type" :     "string",
      "index":     "not_analyzed"
    }
  }
}
```

Note that we didn't need to list all of the existing fields again, as we can't change them anyway. Our new field has been merged into the existing mapping.

Testing the Mapping

You can use the `analyze` API to test the mapping for string fields by name. Compare the output of these two requests:

```
GET /gb/_analyze?field=tweet
Black-cats ❶
```

```
GET /gb/_analyze?field=tag
Black-cats ❶
```

❶ The text we want to analyze is passed in the body.

The `tweet` field produces the two terms `black` and `cat`, while the `tag` field produces the single term `Black-cats`. In other words, our mapping is working correctly.

Complex Core Field Types

Besides the simple scalar datatypes that we have mentioned, JSON also has `null` values, arrays, and objects, all of which are supported by Elasticsearch.

Multivalue Fields

It is quite possible that we want our `tag` field to contain more than one tag. Instead of a single string, we could index an array of tags:

```
{ "tag": [ "search", "nosql" ]}
```

There is no special mapping required for arrays. Any field can contain zero, one, or more values, in the same way as a full-text field is analyzed to produce multiple terms.

By implication, this means that *all the values of an array must be of the same datatype.* You can't mix dates with strings. If you create a new field by indexing an array, Elasticsearch will use the datatype of the first value in the array to determine the `type` of the new field.

When you get a document back from Elasticsearch, any arrays will be in the same order as when you indexed the document. The `_source` field that you get back contains exactly the same JSON document that you indexed.

However, arrays are *indexed*—made searchable—as multivalue fields, which are unordered. At search time, you can't refer to "the first element" or "the last element." Rather, think of an array as a *bag of values.*

Empty Fields

Arrays can, of course, be empty. This is the equivalent of having zero values. In fact, there is no way of storing a `null` value in Lucene, so a field with a `null` value is also considered to be an empty field.

These four fields would all be considered to be empty, and would not be indexed:

```
"null_value":              null,
"empty_array":             [],
"array_with_null_value":   [ null ]
```

Multilevel Objects

The last native JSON datatype that we need to discuss is the *object* — known in other languages as a hash, hashmap, dictionary or associative array.

Inner objects are often used to embed one entity or object inside another. For instance, instead of having fields called user_name and user_id inside our tweet document, we could write it as follows:

```
{
    "tweet":            "Elasticsearch is very flexible",
    "user": {
        "id":           "@johnsmith",
        "gender":       "male",
        "age":          26,
        "name": {
            "full":     "John Smith",
            "first":    "John",
            "last":     "Smith"
        }
    }
}
```

Mapping for Inner Objects

Elasticsearch will detect new object fields dynamically and map them as type object, with each inner field listed under properties:

```
{
  "gb": {
    "tweet": { ❶
      "properties": {
        "tweet":             { "type": "string" },
        "user": { ❷
          "type":            "object",
          "properties": {
            "id":            { "type": "string" },
            "gender":        { "type": "string" },
            "age":           { "type": "long"   },
            "name":      { ❷
              "type":        "object",
              "properties": {
                "full":      { "type": "string" },
                "first":     { "type": "string" },
                "last":      { "type": "string" }
              }
            }
          }
        }
      }
    }
  }
}
```

```
        }
    }
```

❶ Root object

❷ Inner objects

The mapping for the user and name fields has a similar structure to the mapping for the tweet type itself. In fact, the type mapping is just a special type of object mapping, which we refer to as the *root object*. It is just the same as any other object, except that it has some special top-level fields for document metadata, such as _source, and the _all field.

How Inner Objects are Indexed

Lucene doesn't understand inner objects. A Lucene document consists of a flat list of key-value pairs. In order for Elasticsearch to index inner objects usefully, it converts our document into something like this:

```
{
    "tweet":            [elasticsearch, flexible, very],
    "user.id":          [@johnsmith],
    "user.gender":      [male],
    "user.age":         [26],
    "user.name.full":   [john, smith],
    "user.name.first":  [john],
    "user.name.last":   [smith]
}
```

Inner fields can be referred to by name (for example, first). To distinguish between two fields that have the same name, we can use the full *path* (for example, user.name.first) or even the type name plus the path (tweet.user.name.first).

> In the preceding simple flattened document, there is no field called user and no field called user.name. Lucene indexes only scalar or simple values, not complex data structures.

Arrays of Inner Objects

Finally, consider how an array containing inner objects would be indexed. Let's say we have a followers array that looks like this:

```
{
    "followers": [
        { "age": 35, "name": "Mary White"},
        { "age": 26, "name": "Alex Jones"},
        { "age": 19, "name": "Lisa Smith"}
```

```
        ]
    }
```

This document will be flattened as we described previously, but the result will look like this:

```
{
    "followers.age":     [19, 26, 35],
    "followers.name":    [alex, jones, lisa, smith, mary, white]
}
```

The correlation between {age: 35} and {name: Mary White} has been lost as each multivalue field is just a bag of values, not an ordered array. This is sufficient for us to ask, "Is there a follower who is 26 years old?"

But we can't get an accurate answer to this: "Is there a follower who is 26 years old *and who is called Alex Jones*?"

Correlated inner objects, which are able to answer queries like these, are called *nested* objects, and we cover them later, in Chapter 41.

CHAPTER 7

Full-Body Search

Search *lite*—a query-string search—is useful for ad hoc queries from the command line. To harness the full power of search, however, you should use the *request body search* API, so called because most parameters are passed in the HTTP request body instead of in the query string.

Request body search—henceforth known as *search*—not only handles the query itself, but also allows you to return highlighted snippets from your results, aggregate analytics across all results or subsets of results, and return *did-you-mean* suggestions, which will help guide your users to the best results quickly.

Empty Search

Let's start with the simplest form of the search API, the empty search, which returns all documents in all indices:

```
GET /_search
{} ❶
```

❶ This is an empty request body.

Just as with a query-string search, you can search on one, many, or _all indices, and one, many, or all types:

```
GET /index_2014*/type1,type2/_search
{}
```

And you can use the from and size parameters for pagination:

```
GET /_search
{
  "from": 30,
```

```
    "size": 10
}
```

A GET Request with a Body?

The HTTP libraries of certain languages (notably JavaScript) don't allow `GET` requests to have a request body. In fact, some users are suprised that `GET` requests are ever allowed to have a body.

The truth is that RFC 7231 (*http://tools.ietf.org/html/rfc7231#page-24*)—the RFC that deals with HTTP semantics and content—does not define what should happen to a `GET` request with a body! As a result, some HTTP servers allow it, and some—especially caching proxies—don't.

The authors of Elasticsearch prefer using `GET` for a search request because they feel that it describes the action—retrieving information—better than the `POST` verb. However, because `GET` with a request body is not universally supported, the `search` API also accepts `POST` requests:

```
POST /_search
{
  "from": 30,
  "size": 10
}
```

The same rule applies to any other `GET` API that requires a request body.

We present aggregations in depth in Part IV, but for now, we're going to focus just on the query.

Instead of the cryptic query-string approach, a request body search allows us to write queries by using the *query domain-specific language*, or query DSL.

Query DSL

The query DSL is a flexible, expressive search language that Elasticsearch uses to expose most of the power of Lucene through a simple JSON interface. It is what you should be using to write your queries in production. It makes your queries more flexible, more precise, easier to read, and easier to debug.

To use the Query DSL, pass a query in the `query` parameter:

```
GET /_search
{
    "query": YOUR_QUERY_HERE
}
```

The *empty search*—{}—is functionally equivalent to using the `match_all` query clause, which, as the name suggests, matches all documents:

```
GET /_search
{
    "query": {
        "match_all": {}
    }
}
```

Structure of a Query Clause

A query clause typically has this structure:

```
{
    QUERY_NAME: {
        ARGUMENT: VALUE,
        ARGUMENT: VALUE,...
    }
}
```

If it references one particular field, it has this structure:

```
{
    QUERY_NAME: {
        FIELD_NAME: {
            ARGUMENT: VALUE,
            ARGUMENT: VALUE,...
        }
    }
}
```

For instance, you can use a `match` query clause to find tweets that mention `elastic search` in the `tweet` field:

```
{
    "match": {
        "tweet": "elasticsearch"
    }
}
```

The full search request would look like this:

```
GET /_search
{
    "query": {
        "match": {
            "tweet": "elasticsearch"
        }
    }
}
```

Combining Multiple Clauses

Query clauses are simple building blocks that can be combined with each other to create complex queries. Clauses can be as follows:

- *Leaf clauses* (like the `match` clause) that are used to compare a field (or fields) to a query string.
- *Compound* clauses that are used to combine other query clauses. For instance, a `bool` clause allows you to combine other clauses that either `must` match, `must_not` match, or `should` match if possible:

```
{
    "bool": {
        "must":     { "match": { "tweet": "elasticsearch" }},
        "must_not": { "match": { "name":  "mary" }},
        "should":   { "match": { "tweet": "full text" }}
    }
}
```

It is important to note that a compound clause can combine *any* other query clauses, including other compound clauses. This means that compound clauses can be nested within each other, allowing the expression of very complex logic.

As an example, the following query looks for emails that contain `business opportunity` and should either be starred, or be both in the Inbox and not marked as spam:

```
{
    "bool": {
        "must": { "match":     { "email": "business opportunity" }},
        "should": [
                { "match":      { "starred": true }},
                { "bool": {
                        "must":     { "folder": "inbox" }},
                        "must_not": { "spam": true }}
                }}
        ],
        "minimum_should_match": 1
    }
}
```

Don't worry about the details of this example yet; we will explain in full later. The important thing to take away is that a compound query clause can combine multiple clauses—both leaf clauses and other compound clauses—into a single query.

Queries and Filters

Although we refer to the query DSL, in reality there are two DSLs: the query DSL and the filter DSL. Query clauses and filter clauses are similar in nature, but have slightly different purposes.

A *filter* asks a yes|no question of every document and is used for fields that contain exact values:

- Is the `created` date in the range `2013 - 2014`?
- Does the `status` field contain the term `published`?
- Is the `lat_lon` field within `10km` of a specified point?

A *query* is similar to a filter, but also asks the question: How *well* does this document match?

A typical use for a query is to find documents

- Best matching the words `full text search`
- Containing the word `run`, but maybe also matching `runs`, `running`, `jog`, or `sprint`
- Containing the words `quick`, `brown`, and `fox`—the closer together they are, the more relevant the document
- Tagged with `lucene`, `search`, or `java`—the more tags, the more relevant the document

A query calculates how *relevant* each document is to the query, and assigns it a relevance `_score`, which is later used to sort matching documents by relevance. This concept of relevance is well suited to full-text search, where there is seldom a completely "correct" answer.

Performance Differences

The output from most filter clauses—a simple list of the documents that match the filter—is quick to calculate and easy to cache in memory, using only 1 bit per document. These cached filters can be reused efficiently for subsequent requests.

Queries have to not only find matching documents, but also calculate how relevant each document is, which typically makes queries heavier than filters. Also, query results are not cachable.

Thanks to the inverted index, a simple query that matches just a few documents may perform as well or better than a cached filter that spans millions of documents. In general, however, a cached filter will outperform a query, and will do so consistently.

The goal of filters is to *reduce the number of documents that have to be examined by the query*.

When to Use Which

As a general rule, use query clauses for *full-text* search or for any condition that should affect the *relevance score*, and use filter clauses for everything else.

Most Important Queries and Filters

While Elasticsearch comes with many queries and filters, you will use just a few frequently. We discuss them in much greater detail in Part II but next we give you a quick introduction to the most important queries and filters.

term Filter

The `term` filter is used to filter by exact values, be they numbers, dates, Booleans, or `not_analyzed` exact-value string fields:

```
{ "term": { "age":    26          }}
{ "term": { "date":   "2014-09-01" }}
{ "term": { "public": true        }}
{ "term": { "tag":    "full_text"  }}
```

terms Filter

The `terms` filter is the same as the `term` filter, but allows you to specify multiple values to match. If the field contains any of the specified values, the document matches:

```
{ "terms": { "tag": [ "search", "full_text", "nosql" ] }}
```

range Filter

The `range` filter allows you to find numbers or dates that fall into a specified range:

```
{
    "range": {
        "age": {
            "gte":  20,
            "lt":   30
        }
    }
}
```

The operators that it accepts are as follows:

gt

    Greater than

gte
> Greater than or equal to

lt
> Less than

lte
> Less than or equal to

exists and missing Filters

The `exists` and `missing` filters are used to find documents in which the specified field either has one or more values (`exists`) or doesn't have any values (`missing`). It is similar in nature to IS_NULL (`missing`) and NOT IS_NULL (`exists`)in SQL:

```
{
    "exists":   {
        "field":    "title"
    }
}
```

These filters are frequently used to apply a condition only if a field is present, and to apply a different condition if it is missing.

bool Filter

The `bool` filter is used to combine multiple filter clauses using Boolean logic. It accepts three parameters:

must
> These clauses *must* match, like and.

must_not
> These clauses *must not* match, like not.

should
> At least one of these clauses must match, like or.

Each of these parameters can accept a single filter clause or an array of filter clauses:

```
{
    "bool": {
        "must":     { "term": { "folder": "inbox" }},
        "must_not": { "term": { "tag":     "spam"  }},
        "should": [
                    { "term": { "starred": true   }},
                    { "term": { "unread":  true   }}
        ]
    }
}
```

match_all Query

The match_all query simply matches all documents. It is the default query that is used if no query has been specified:

```
{ "match_all": {}}
```

This query is frequently used in combination with a filter—for instance, to retrieve all emails in the inbox folder. All documents are considered to be equally relevant, so they all receive a neutral _score of 1.

match Query

The match query should be the standard query that you reach for whenever you want to query for a full-text or exact value in almost any field.

If you run a match query against a full-text field, it will analyze the query string by using the correct analyzer for that field before executing the search:

```
{ "match": { "tweet": "About Search" }}
```

If you use it on a field containing an exact value, such as a number, a date, a Boolean, or a not_analyzed string field, then it will search for that exact value:

```
{ "match": { "age":    26          }}
{ "match": { "date":   "2014-09-01" }}
{ "match": { "public": true         }}
{ "match": { "tag":    "full_text"  }}
```

 For exact-value searches, you probably want to use a filter instead of a query, as a filter will be cached.

Unlike the query-string search that we showed in "Search *Lite*" on page 78, the match query does not use a query syntax like +user_id:2 +tweet:search. It just looks for the words that are specified. This means that it is safe to expose to your users via a search field; you control what fields they can query, and it is not prone to throwing syntax errors.

multi_match Query

The multi_match query allows to run the same match query on multiple fields:

```
{
    "multi_match": {
        "query":    "full text search",
        "fields":   [ "title", "body" ]
```

```
        }
    }
```

bool Query

The `bool` query, like the `bool` filter, is used to combine multiple query clauses. However, there are some differences. Remember that while filters give binary yes/no answers, queries calculate a relevance score instead. The `bool` query combines the _score from each `must` or `should` clause that matches. This query accepts the following parameters:

`must`
> Clauses that *must* match for the document to be included.

`must_not`
> Clauses that *must not* match for the document to be included.

`should`
> If these clauses match, they increase the _score; otherwise, they have no effect. They are simply used to refine the relevance score for each document.

The following query finds documents whose `title` field matches the query string how to make millions and that are not marked as spam. If any documents are starred or are from 2014 onward, they will rank higher than they would have otherwise. Documents that match *both* conditions will rank even higher:

```
{
    "bool": {
        "must":     { "match": { "title": "how to make millions" }},
        "must_not": { "match": { "tag":   "spam" }},
        "should": [
            { "match": { "tag": "starred" }},
            { "range": { "date": { "gte": "2014-01-01" }}}
        ]
    }
}
```

 If there are no `must` clauses, at least one `should` clause has to match. However, if there is at least one `must` clause, no `should` clauses are required to match.

Combining Queries with Filters

Queries can be used in *query context*, and filters can be used in *filter context*. Throughout the Elasticsearch API, you will see parameters with `query` or `filter` in the name. These expect a single argument containing either a single query or filter clause respectively. In other words, they establish the outer *context* as query context or filter context.

Compound query clauses can wrap other query clauses, and compound filter clauses can wrap other filter clauses. However, it is often useful to apply a filter to a query or, less frequently, to use a full-text query as a filter.

To do this, there are dedicated query clauses that wrap filter clauses, and vice versa, thus allowing us to switch from one context to another. It is important to choose the correct combination of query and filter clauses to achieve your goal in the most efficient way.

Filtering a Query

Let's say we have this query:

```
{ "match": { "email": "business opportunity" }}
```

We want to combine it with the following `term` filter, which will match only documents that are in our inbox:

```
{ "term": { "folder": "inbox" }}
```

The `search` API accepts only a single `query` parameter, so we need to wrap the query and the filter in another query, called the `filtered` query:

```
{
    "filtered": {
        "query":  { "match": { "email": "business opportunity" }},
        "filter": { "term":  { "folder": "inbox" }}
    }
}
```

We can now pass this query to the `query` parameter of the `search` API:

```
GET /_search
{
    "query": {
        "filtered": {
            "query":  { "match": { "email": "business opportunity" }},
            "filter": { "term": { "folder": "inbox" }}
        }
    }
}
```

Just a Filter

While in query context, if you need to use a filter without a query (for instance, to match all emails in the inbox), you can just omit the query:

```
GET /_search
{
    "query": {
        "filtered": {
            "filter":   { "term": { "folder": "inbox" }}
        }
    }
}
```

If a query is not specified it defaults to using the `match_all` query, so the preceding query is equivalent to the following:

```
GET /_search
{
    "query": {
        "filtered": {
            "query":    { "match_all": {}},
            "filter":   { "term": { "folder": "inbox" }}
        }
    }
}
```

A Query as a Filter

Occasionally, you will want to use a query while you are in filter context. This can be achieved with the query filter, which just wraps a query. The following example shows one way we could exclude emails that look like spam:

```
GET /_search
{
    "query": {
        "filtered": {
            "filter":   {
                "bool": {
                    "must":     { "term":  { "folder": "inbox" }},
                    "must_not": {
                        "query": { ❶
                            "match": { "email": "urgent business proposal" }
                        }
                    }
                }
            }
        }
    }
}
```

❶ Note the query filter, which is allowing us to use the `match` *query* inside a `bool` *filter*.

 You seldom need to use a query as a filter, but we have included it for completeness' sake. The only time you may need it is when you need to use full-text matching while in filter context.

Validating Queries

Queries can become quite complex and, especially when combined with different analyzers and field mappings, can become a bit difficult to follow. The `validate-query` API can be used to check whether a query is valid.

```
GET /gb/tweet/_validate/query
{
   "query": {
      "tweet" : {
         "match" : "really powerful"
      }
   }
}
```

The response to the preceding `validate` request tells us that the query is invalid:

```
{
  "valid" :          false,
  "_shards" : {
     "total" :       1,
     "successful" :  1,
     "failed" :      0
  }
}
```

Understanding Errors

To find out why it is invalid, add the `explain` parameter to the query string:

```
GET /gb/tweet/_validate/query?explain ❶
{
   "query": {
      "tweet" : {
         "match" : "really powerful"
      }
   }
}
```

❶ The `explain` flag provides more information about why a query is invalid.

Apparently, we've mixed up the type of query (`match`) with the name of the field (`tweet`):

```
{
  "valid" :     false,
  "_shards" :   { ... },
  "explanations" : [ {
    "index" :   "gb",
    "valid" :   false,
    "error" :   "org.elasticsearch.index.query.QueryParsingException:
                [gb] No query registered for [tweet]"
  } ]
}
```

Understanding Queries

Using the `explain` parameter has the added advantage of returning a human-readable description of the (valid) query, which can be useful for understanding exactly how your query has been interpreted by Elasticsearch:

```
GET /_validate/query?explain
{
    "query": {
        "match" : {
            "tweet" : "really powerful"
        }
    }
}
```

An `explanation` is returned for each index that we query, because each index can have different mappings and analyzers:

```
{
  "valid" :        true,
  "_shards" :      { ... },
  "explanations" : [ {
    "index" :      "us",
    "valid" :      true,
    "explanation" : "tweet:really tweet:powerful"
  }, {
    "index" :      "gb",
    "valid" :      true,
    "explanation" : "tweet:realli tweet:power"
  } ]
}
```

From the `explanation`, you can see how the `match` query for the query string `really powerful` has been rewritten as two single-term queries against the `tweet` field, one for each term.

Also, for the us index, the two terms are `really` and `powerful`, while for the gb index, the terms are `realli` and `power`. The reason for this is that we changed the `tweet` field in the gb index to use the `english` analyzer.

CHAPTER 8

Sorting and Relevance

By default, results are returned sorted by *relevance*—with the most relevant docs first. Later in this chapter, we explain what we mean by *relevance* and how it is calculated, but let's start by looking at the sort parameter and how to use it.

Sorting

In order to sort by relevance, we need to represent relevance as a value. In Elasticsearch, the *relevance score* is represented by the floating-point number returned in the search results as the _score, so the default sort order is _score descending.

Sometimes, though, you don't have a meaningful relevance score. For instance, the following query just returns all tweets whose user_id field has the value 1:

```
GET /_search
{
    "query" : {
        "filtered" : {
            "filter" : {
                "term" : {
                    "user_id" : 1
                }
            }
        }
    }
}
```

Filters have no bearing on _score, and the missing-but-implied match_all query just sets the _score to a neutral value of 1 for all documents. In other words, all documents are considered to be equally relevant.

Sorting by Field Values

In this case, it probably makes sense to sort tweets by recency, with the most recent tweets first. We can do this with the `sort` parameter:

```
GET /_search
{
    "query" : {
        "filtered" : {
            "filter" : { "term" : { "user_id" : 1 }}
        }
    },
    "sort": { "date": { "order": "desc" }}
}
```

You will notice two differences in the results:

```
"hits" : {
    "total" :           6,
    "max_score" :       null, ❶
    "hits" : [ {
        "_index" :      "us",
        "_type" :       "tweet",
        "_id" :         "14",
        "_score" :      null, ❶
        "_source" :     {
            "date":     "2014-09-24",
            ...
        },
        "sort" :        [ 1411516800000 ] ❷
    },
    ...
}
```

❶ The `_score` is not calculated, because it is not being used for sorting.

❷ The value of the `date` field, expressed as milliseconds since the epoch, is returned in the `sort` values.

The first is that we have a new element in each result called `sort`, which contains the value(s) that was used for sorting. In this case, we sorted on `date`, which internally is indexed as *milliseconds since the epoch*. The long number `1411516800000` is equivalent to the date string `2014-09-24 00:00:00` UTC.

The second is that the `_score` and `max_score` are both `null`. Calculating the `_score` can be quite expensive, and usually its only purpose is for sorting; we're not sorting by relevance, so it doesn't make sense to keep track of the `_score`. If you want the `_score` to be calculated regardless, you can set the `track_scores` parameter to `true`.

As a shortcut, you can specify just the name of the field to sort on:

```
"sort": "number_of_children"
```

Fields will be sorted in ascending order by default, and the _score value in descending order.

Multilevel Sorting

Perhaps we want to combine the _score from a query with the date, and show all matching results sorted first by date, then by relevance:

```
GET /_search
{
    "query" : {
        "filtered" : {
            "query":   { "match": { "tweet": "manage text search" }},
            "filter" : { "term" : { "user_id" : 2 }}
        }
    },
    "sort": [
        { "date":   { "order": "desc" }},
        { "_score": { "order": "desc" }}
    ]
}
```

Order is important. Results are sorted by the first criterion first. Only results whose first sort value is identical will then be sorted by the second criterion, and so on.

Multilevel sorting doesn't have to involve the _score. You could sort by using several different fields, on geo-distance or on a custom value calculated in a script.

Query-string search also supports custom sorting, using the sort parameter in the query string:

```
GET /_search?sort=date:desc&sort=_score&q=search
```

Sorting on Multivalue Fields

When sorting on fields with more than one value, remember that the values do not have any intrinsic order; a multivalue field is just a bag of values. Which one do you choose to sort on?

For numbers and dates, you can reduce a multivalue field to a single value by using the min, max, avg, or sum *sort modes*. For instance, you could sort on the earliest date in each dates field by using the following:

```
"sort": {
    "dates": {
        "order": "asc",
        "mode":  "min"
    }
}
```

String Sorting and Multifields

Analyzed string fields are also multivalue fields, but sorting on them seldom gives you the results you want. If you analyze a string like fine old art, it results in three terms. We probably want to sort alphabetically on the first term, then the second term, and so forth, but Elasticsearch doesn't have this information at its disposal at sort time.

You could use the min and max sort modes (it uses min by default), but that will result in sorting on either art or old, neither of which was the intent.

In order to sort on a string field, that field should contain one term only: the whole not_analyzed string. But of course we still need the field to be analyzed in order to be able to query it as full text.

The naive approach to indexing the same string in two ways would be to include two separate fields in the document: one that is analyzed for searching, and one that is not_analyzed for sorting.

But storing the same string twice in the _source field is waste of space. What we really want to do is to pass in a *single field* but to *index it in two different ways*. All of the *core* field types (strings, numbers, Booleans, dates) accept a fields parameter that allows you to transform a simple mapping like

```
"tweet": {
    "type":     "string",
    "analyzer": "english"
}
```

into a *multifield* mapping like this:

```
"tweet": {                          ❶
    "type":     "string",
    "analyzer": "english",
    "fields": {
        "raw": {                    ❷
            "type":  "string",
            "index": "not_analyzed"
        }
    }
}
```

❶ The main `tweet` field is just the same as before: an `analyzed` full-text field.

❷ The new `tweet.raw` subfield is `not_analyzed`.

Now, or at least as soon as we have reindexed our data, we can use the `tweet` field for search and the `tweet.raw` field for sorting:

```
GET /_search
{
    "query": {
        "match": {
            "tweet": "elasticsearch"
        }
    },
    "sort": "tweet.raw"
}
```

 Sorting on a full-text `analyzed` field can use a lot of memory. See "Fielddata" on page 121 for more information.

What Is Relevance?

We've mentioned that, by default, results are returned in descending order of relevance. But what is relevance? How is it calculated?

The relevance score of each document is represented by a positive floating-point number called the `_score`. The higher the `_score`, the more relevant the document.

A query clause generates a `_score` for each document. How that score is calculated depends on the type of query clause. Different query clauses are used for different purposes: a `fuzzy` query might determine the `_score` by calculating how similar the spelling of the found word is to the original search term; a `terms` query would incorporate the percentage of terms that were found. However, what we usually mean by *relevance* is the algorithm that we use to calculate how similar the contents of a full-text field are to a full-text query string.

The standard *similarity algorithm* used in Elasticsearch is known as *term frequency/inverse document frequency*, or *TF/IDF*, which takes the following factors into account:

Term frequency
How often does the term appear in the field? The more often, the more relevant. A field containing five mentions of the same term is more likely to be relevant than a field containing just one mention.

Inverse document frequency

> How often does each term appear in the index? The more often, the *less* relevant. Terms that appear in many documents have a lower *weight* than more-uncommon terms.

Field-length norm

> How long is the field? The longer it is, the less likely it is that words in the field will be relevant. A term appearing in a short `title` field carries more weight than the same term appearing in a long `content` field.

Individual queries may combine the TF/IDF score with other factors such as the term proximity in phrase queries, or term similarity in fuzzy queries.

Relevance is not just about full-text search, though. It can equally be applied to yes/no clauses, where the more clauses that match, the higher the `_score`.

When multiple query clauses are combined using a compound query like the `bool` query, the `_score` from each of these query clauses is combined to calculate the overall `_score` for the document.

 We have a whole chapter dedicated to relevance calculations and how to bend them to your will: Chapter 17.

Understanding the Score

When debugging a complex query, it can be difficult to understand exactly how a `_score` has been calculated. Elasticsearch has the option of producing an *explanation* with every search result, by setting the `explain` parameter to `true`.

```
GET /_search?explain  ❶
{
   "query"   : { "match" : { "tweet" : "honeymoon" }}
}
```

❶ The `explain` parameter adds an explanation of how the `_score` was calculated to every result.

 Adding `explain` produces a lot of output for every hit, which can look overwhelming, but it is worth taking the time to understand what it all means. Don't worry if it doesn't all make sense now; you can refer to this section when you need it. We'll work through the output for one `hit` bit by bit.

First, we have the metadata that is returned on normal search requests:

```
{
    "_index" :      "us",
    "_type" :       "tweet",
    "_id" :         "12",
    "_score" :      0.076713204,
    "_source" :     { ... trimmed ... },
```

It adds information about the shard and the node that the document came from, which is useful to know because term and document frequencies are calculated per shard, rather than per index:

```
    "_shard" :      1,
    "_node" :       "mzIVYCsqSWCG_M_ZffSs9Q",
```

Then it provides the _explanation. Each entry contains a description that tells you what type of calculation is being performed, a value that gives you the result of the calculation, and the details of any subcalculations that were required:

```
    "_explanation": { ❶
        "description": "weight(tweet:honeymoon in 0)
                        [PerFieldSimilarity], result of:",
        "value":        0.076713204,
        "details": [
            {
                "description": "fieldWeight in 0, product of:",
                "value":        0.076713204,
                "details": [
                    { ❷
                        "description": "tf(freq=1.0), with freq of:",
                        "value":        1,
                        "details": [
                            {
                                "description": "termFreq=1.0",
                                "value":        1
                            }
                        ]
                    },
                    { ❸
                        "description": "idf(docFreq=1, maxDocs=1)",
                        "value":        0.30685282
                    },
                    { ❹
                        "description": "fieldNorm(doc=0)",
                        "value":        0.25,
                    }
                ]
            }
        ]
    }
```

❶ Summary of the score calculation for `honeymoon`

❷ Term frequency

❸ Inverse document frequency

❹ Field-length norm

 Producing the `explain` output is expensive. It is a debugging tool only. Don't leave it turned on in production.

The first part is the summary of the calculation. It tells us that it has calculated the *weight*—the TF/IDF—of the term honeymoon in the field `tweet`, for document 0. (This is an internal document ID and, for our purposes, can be ignored.)

It then provides details of how the weight was calculated:

Term frequency
How many times did the term honeymoon appear in the `tweet` field in this document?

Inverse document frequency
How many times did the term honeymoon appear in the `tweet` field of all documents in the index?

Field-length norm
How long is the `tweet` field in this document? The longer the field, the smaller this number.

Explanations for more-complicated queries can appear to be very complex, but really they just contain more of the same calculations that appear in the preceding example. This information can be invaluable for debugging why search results appear in the order that they do.

 The output from `explain` can be difficult to read in JSON, but it is easier when it is formatted as YAML. Just add `format=yaml` to the query string.

Understanding Why a Document Matched

While the `explain` option adds an explanation for every result, you can use the `explain` API to understand why one particular document matched or, more important, why it *didn't* match.

The path for the request is `/index/type/id/_explain`, as in the following:

```
GET /us/tweet/12/_explain
{
   "query" : {
      "filtered" : {
         "filter" : { "term" :  { "user_id" : 2          }},
         "query" :  { "match" : { "tweet" :   "honeymoon" }}
      }
   }
}
```

Along with the full explanation that we saw previously, we also now have a `description` element, which tells us this:

```
"failure to match filter: cache(user_id:[2 TO 2])"
```

In other words, our `user_id` filter clause is preventing the document from matching.

Fielddata

Our final topic in this chapter is about an internal aspect of Elasticsearch. While we don't demonstrate any new techniques here, fielddata is an important topic that we will refer to repeatedly, and is something that you should be aware of.

When you sort on a field, Elasticsearch needs access to the value of that field for every document that matches the query. The inverted index, which performs very well when searching, is not the ideal structure for sorting on field values:

- When searching, we need to be able to map a term to a list of documents.
- When sorting, we need to map a document to its terms. In other words, we need to "uninvert" the inverted index.

To make sorting efficient, Elasticsearch loads all the values for the field that you want to sort on into memory. This is referred to as *fielddata*.

 Elasticsearch doesn't just load the values for the documents that matched a particular query. It loads the values from *every document in your index*, regardless of the document `type`.

The reason that Elasticsearch loads all values into memory is that uninverting the index from disk is slow. Even though you may need the values for only a few docs for the current request, you will probably need access to the values for other docs on the next request, so it makes sense to load all the values into memory at once, and to keep them there.

Fielddata is used in several places in Elasticsearch:

- Sorting on a field
- Aggregations on a field
- Certain filters (for example, geolocation filters)
- Scripts that refer to fields

Clearly, this can consume a lot of memory, especially for high-cardinality string fields —string fields that have many unique values—like the body of an email. Fortunately, insufficient memory is a problem that can be solved by horizontal scaling, by adding more nodes to your cluster.

For now, all you need to know is what fielddata is, and to be aware that it can be memory hungry. Later, we will show you how to determine the amount of memory that fielddata is using, how to limit the amount of memory that is available to it, and how to preload fielddata to improve the user experience.

CHAPTER 9

Distributed Search Execution

Before moving on, we are going to take a detour and talk about how search is executed in a distributed environment. It is a bit more complicated than the basic *create-read-update-delete* (CRUD) requests that we discussed in Chapter 4.

Content Warning

The information presented in this chapter is for your interest. You are not required to understand and remember all the detail in order to use Elasticsearch.

Read this chapter to gain a taste for how things work, and to know where the information is in case you need to refer to it in the future, but don't be overwhelmed by the detail.

A CRUD operation deals with a single document that has a unique combination of _index, _type, and routing values (which defaults to the document's _id). This means that we know exactly which shard in the cluster holds that document.

Search requires a more complicated execution model because we don't know which documents will match the query: they could be on any shard in the cluster. A search request has to consult a copy of every shard in the index or indices we're interested in to see if they have any matching documents.

But finding all matching documents is only half the story. Results from multiple shards must be combined into a single sorted list before the search API can return a "page" of results. For this reason, search is executed in a two-phase process called *query then fetch*.

Query Phase

During the initial *query phase*, the query is broadcast to a shard copy (a primary or replica shard) of every shard in the index. Each shard executes the search locally and builds a *priority queue* of matching documents.

Priority Queue

A *priority queue* is just a sorted list that holds the *top-n* matching documents. The size of the priority queue depends on the pagination parameters from and size. For example, the following search request would require a priority queue big enough to hold 100 documents:

```
GET /_search
{
    "from": 90,
    "size": 10
}
```

The query phase process is depicted in Figure 9-1.

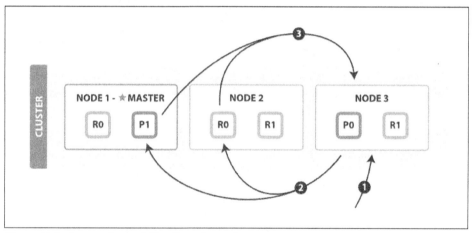

Figure 9-1. Query phase of distributed search

The query phase consists of the following three steps:

1. The client sends a search request to Node 3, which creates an empty priority queue of size from + size.

2. Node 3 forwards the search request to a primary or replica copy of every shard in the index. Each shard executes the query locally and adds the results into a local sorted priority queue of size from + size.

---

3. Each shard returns the doc IDs and sort values of all the docs in its priority queue to the coordinating node, Node 3, which merges these values into its own priority queue to produce a globally sorted list of results.

When a search request is sent to a node, that node becomes the coordinating node. It is the job of this node to broadcast the search request to all involved shards, and to gather their responses into a globally sorted result set that it can return to the client.

The first step is to broadcast the request to a shard copy of every node in the index. Just like document GET requests, search requests can be handled by a primary shard or by any of its replicas. This is how more replicas (when combined with more hardware) can increase search throughput. A coordinating node will round-robin through all shard copies on subsequent requests in order to spread the load.

Each shard executes the query locally and builds a sorted priority queue of length from + size—in other words, enough results to satisfy the global search request all by itself. It returns a lightweight list of results to the coordinating node, which contains just the doc IDs and any values required for sorting, such as the _score.

The coordinating node merges these shard-level results into its own sorted priority queue, which represents the globally sorted result set. Here the query phase ends.

 An index can consist of one or more primary shards, so a search request against a single index needs to be able to combine the results from multiple shards. A search against *multiple* or *all* indices works in exactly the same way—there are just more shards involved.

Fetch Phase

The query phase identifies which documents satisfy the search request, but we still need to retrieve the documents themselves. This is the job of the fetch phase, shown in Figure 9-2.

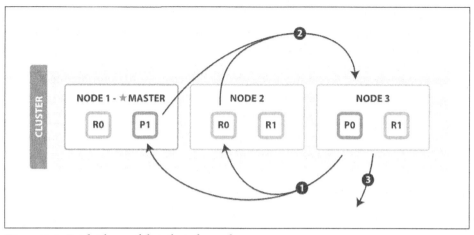

Figure 9-2. Fetch phase of distributed search

The distributed phase consists of the following steps:

1. The coordinating node identifies which documents need to be fetched and issues a multi `GET` request to the relevant shards.

2. Each shard loads the documents and *enriches* them, if required, and then returns the documents to the coordinating node.

3. Once all documents have been fetched, the coordinating node returns the results to the client.

The coordinating node first decides which documents *actually* need to be fetched. For instance, if our query specified { "from": 90, "size": 10 }, the first 90 results would be discarded and only the next 10 results would need to be retrieved. These documents may come from one, some, or all of the shards involved in the original search request.

The coordinating node builds a multi-get request for each shard that holds a pertinent document and sends the request to the same shard copy that handled the query phase.

The shard loads the document bodies—the _source field—and, if requested, enriches the results with metadata and search snippet highlighting. Once the coordinating node receives all results, it assembles them into a single response that it returns to the client.

Deep Pagination

The query-then-fetch process supports pagination with the `from` and `size` parameters, but *within limits*. Remember that each shard must build a priority queue of length `from + size`, all of which need to be passed back to the coordinating node. And the coordinating node needs to sort through `number_of_shards * (from + size)` documents in order to find the correct `size` documents.

Depending on the size of your documents, the number of shards, and the hardware you are using, paging 10,000 to 50,000 results (1,000 to 5,000 pages) deep should be perfectly doable. But with big-enough `from` values, the sorting process can become very heavy indeed, using vast amounts of CPU, memory, and bandwidth. For this reason, we strongly advise against deep paging.

In practice, "deep pagers" are seldom human anyway. A human will stop paging after two or three pages and will change the search criteria. The culprits are usually bots or web spiders that tirelessly keep fetching page after page until your servers crumble at the knees.

If you *do* need to fetch large numbers of docs from your cluster, you can do so efficiently by disabling sorting with the `scan` search type, which we discuss later in this chapter.

Search Options

A few optional query-string parameters can influence the search process.

preference

The `preference` parameter allows you to control which shards or nodes are used to handle the search request. It accepts values such as `_primary`, `_primary_first`, `_local`, `_only_node:xyz`, `_prefer_node:xyz`, and `_shards:2,3`, which are explained in detail on the search `preference` (*http://www.elasticsearch.org/guide/en/elastic search/reference/current/search-request-preference.html*) documentation page.

However, the most generally useful value is some arbitrary string, to avoid the *bouncing results* problem.

Bouncing Results

Imagine that you are sorting your results by a `timestamp` field, and two documents have the same timestamp. Because search requests are round-robined between all available shard copies, these two documents may be returned in one order when the request is served by the primary, and in another order when served by the replica.

This is known as the *bouncing results* problem: every time the user refreshes the page, the results appear in a different order. The problem can be avoided by always using the same shards for the same user, which can be done by setting the `preference` parameter to an arbitrary string like the user's session ID.

---

timeout

By default, the coordinating node waits to receive a response from all shards. If one node is having trouble, it could slow down the response to all search requests.

The `timeout` parameter tells the coordinating node how long it should wait before giving up and just returning the results that it already has. It can be better to return some results than none at all.

The response to a search request will indicate whether the search timed out and how many shards responded successfully:

```
...
"timed_out":     true,   ❶
"_shards": {
   "total":      5,
   "successful": 4,
   "failed":     1 ❷
},
...
```

❶ The search request timed out.

❷ One shard out of five failed to respond in time.

If all copies of a shard fail for other reasons—perhaps because of a hardware failure—this will also be reflected in the `_shards` section of the response.

routing

In "Routing a Document to a Shard" on page 63, we explained how a custom `routing` parameter could be provided at index time to ensure that all related documents, such

---

as the documents belonging to a single user, are stored on a single shard. At search time, instead of searching on all the shards of an index, you can specify one or more `routing` values to limit the search to just those shards:

```
GET /_search?routing=user_1,user2
```

This technique comes in handy when designing very large search systems, and we discuss it in detail in Chapter 43.

search_type

While `query_then_fetch` is the default search type, other search types can be specified for particular purposes, for example:

```
GET /_search?search_type=count
```

count

> The `count` search type has only a `query` phase. It can be used when you don't need search results, just a document count or aggregations on documents matching the query.

query_and_fetch

> The `query_and_fetch` search type combines the query and fetch phases into a single step. This is an internal optimization that is used when a search request targets a single shard only, such as when a `routing` value has been specified. While you can choose to use this search type manually, it is almost never useful to do so.

dfs_query_then_fetch *and* dfs_query_and_fetch

> The `dfs` search types have a prequery phase that fetches the term frequencies from all involved shards in order to calculate global term frequencies. We discuss this further in "Relevance Is Broken!" on page 216.

scan

> The `scan` search type is used in conjunction with the `scroll` API to retrieve large numbers of results efficiently. It does this by disabling sorting. We discuss *scan-and-scroll* in the next section.

scan and scroll

The `scan` search type and the `scroll` API are used together to retrieve large numbers of documents from Elasticsearch efficiently, without paying the penalty of deep pagination.

`scroll`
> A *scrolled search* allows us to do an initial search and to keep pulling batches of results from Elasticsearch until there are no more results left. It's a bit like a *cursor* in a traditional database.
>
> A scrolled search takes a snapshot in time. It doesn't see any changes that are made to the index after the initial search request has been made. It does this by keeping the old data files around, so that it can preserve its "view" on what the index looked like at the time it started.

`scan`
> The costly part of deep pagination is the global sorting of results, but if we disable sorting, then we can return all documents quite cheaply. To do this, we use the `scan` search type. Scan instructs Elasticsearch to do no sorting, but to just return the next batch of results from every shard that still has results to return.

To use *scan-and-scroll*, we execute a search request setting `search_type` to `scan`, and passing a `scroll` parameter telling Elasticsearch how long it should keep the scroll open:

```
GET /old_index/_search?search_type=scan&scroll=1m ❶
{
    "query": { "match_all": {}},
    "size":  1000
}
```

❶ Keep the scroll open for 1 minute.

The response to this request doesn't include any hits, but does include a `_scroll_id`, which is a long Base-64 encoded string. Now we can pass the `_scroll_id` to the `_search/scroll` endpoint to retrieve the first batch of results:

```
GET /_search/scroll?scroll=1m ❶
c2Nhbjs1OzExODpRNV9aY1VyUVM4U0NMd2pWlJ3YWlBOzExOTpRNV9aY1VyUVM4U0 ❷
NMd2pjWlJ3YWlBOzExNjpRNV9aY1VyUVM4U0NMd2pWlJ3YWlBOzExNzpRNV9aY1Vy
UVM4U0NMd2pWlJ3YWlBOzEyMDpRNV9aY1VyUVM4U0NMd2pWlJ3YWlBOzE7dG90YW
xfaGl0czoxOw==
```

❶ Keep the scroll open for another minute.

❷ The `_scroll_id` can be passed in the body, in the URL, or as a query parameter.

Note that we again specify `?scroll=1m`. The scroll expiry time is refreshed every time we run a scroll request, so it needs to give us only enough time to process the current batch of results, not all of the documents that match the query.

The response to this scroll request includes the first batch of results. Although we specified a `size` of 1,000, we get back many more documents. When scanning, the

---

`size` is applied to each shard, so you will get back a maximum of `size` * `num ber_of_primary_shards` documents in each batch.

 The scroll request also returns a *new* `_scroll_id`. Every time we make the next scroll request, we must pass the `_scroll_id` returned by the *previous* scroll request.

When no more hits are returned, we have processed all matching documents.

 Some of the official Elasticsearch clients (*http://www.elastic search.org/guide*) provide *scan-and-scroll* helpers that provide an easy wrapper around this functionality.

CHAPTER 10

Index Management

We have seen how Elasticsearch makes it easy to start developing a new application without requiring any advance planning or setup. However, it doesn't take long before you start wanting to fine-tune the indexing and search process to better suit your particular use case. Almost all of these customizations relate to the index, and the types that it contains. In this chapter, we introduce the APIs for managing indices and type mappings, and the most important settings.

Creating an Index

Until now, we have created a new index by simply indexing a document into it. The index is created with the default settings, and new fields are added to the type mapping by using dynamic mapping. Now we need more control over the process: we want to ensure that the index has been created with the appropriate number of primary shards, and that analyzers and mappings are set up *before* we index any data.

To do this, we have to create the index manually, passing in any settings or type mappings in the request body, as follows:

```
PUT /my_index
{
    "settings": { ... any settings ... },
    "mappings": {
        "type_one": { ... any mappings ... },
        "type_two": { ... any mappings ... },
        ...
    }
}
```

In fact, if you want to, you can prevent the automatic creation of indices by adding the following setting to the config/elasticsearch.yml file on each node:

```
action.auto_create_index: false
```

 Later, we discuss how you can use "Index Templates" on page 597 to preconfigure automatically created indices. This is particularly useful when indexing log data: you log into an index whose name includes the date and, as midnight rolls over, a new properly configured index automatically springs into existence.

Deleting an Index

To delete an index, use the following request:

```
DELETE /my_index
```

You can delete multiple indices with this:

```
DELETE /index_one,index_two
DELETE /index_*
```

You can even delete *all* indices with this:

```
DELETE /_all
```

Index Settings

There are many many knobs that you can twiddle to customize index behavior, which you can read about in the Index Modules reference documentation (*http://www.elas ticsearch.org/guide/en/elasticsearch/guide/current/_index_settings.html#_index_set tings*), but...

 Elasticsearch comes with good defaults. Don't twiddle these knobs until you understand what they do and why you should change them.

Two of the most important settings are as follows:

number_of_shards
> The number of primary shards that an index should have, which defaults to 5. This setting cannot be changed after index creation.

number_of_replicas
> The number of replica shards (copies) that each primary shard should have, which defaults to 1. This setting can be changed at any time on a live index.

For instance, we could create a small index—just one primary shard—and no replica shards with the following request:

```
PUT /my_temp_index
{
    "settings": {
        "number_of_shards" :    1,
        "number_of_replicas" : 0
    }
}
```

Later, we can change the number of replica shards dynamically using the `update-index-settings` API as follows:

```
PUT /my_temp_index/_settings
{
    "number_of_replicas": 1
}
```

Configuring Analyzers

The third important index setting is the `analysis` section, which is used to configure existing analyzers or to create new custom analyzers specific to your index.

In "Analysis and Analyzers" on page 86, we introduced some of the built-in analyzers, which are used to convert full-text strings into an inverted index, suitable for searching.

The `standard` analyzer, which is the default analyzer used for full-text fields, is a good choice for most Western languages. It consists of the following:

- The `standard` tokenizer, which splits the input text on word boundaries
- The `standard` token filter, which is intended to tidy up the tokens emitted by the tokenizer (but currently does nothing)
- The `lowercase` token filter, which converts all tokens into lowercase
- The `stop` token filter, which removes stopwords—common words that have little impact on search relevance, such as `a`, `the`, `and`, `is`.

By default, the stopwords filter is disabled. You can enable it by creating a custom analyzer based on the `standard` analyzer and setting the `stopwords` parameter. Either provide a list of stopwords or tell it to use a predefined stopwords list from a particular language.

In the following example, we create a new analyzer called the `es_std` analyzer, which uses the predefined list of Spanish stopwords:

```
PUT /spanish_docs
{
    "settings": {
        "analysis": {
```

```
        "analyzer": {
            "es_std": {
                "type":      "standard",
                "stopwords": "_spanish_"
            }
        }
      }
    }
  }
```

The `es_std` analyzer is not global—it exists only in the `spanish_docs` index where we have defined it. To test it with the `analyze` API, we must specify the index name:

```
GET /spanish_docs/_analyze?analyzer=es_std
El veloz zorro marrón
```

The abbreviated results show that the Spanish stopword `El` has been removed correctly:

```
{
  "tokens" : [
    { "token" :    "veloz",   "position" : 2 },
    { "token" :    "zorro",   "position" : 3 },
    { "token" :    "marrón",  "position" : 4 }
  ]
}
```

Custom Analyzers

While Elasticsearch comes with a number of analyzers available out of the box, the real power comes from the ability to create your own custom analyzers by combining character filters, tokenizers, and token filters in a configuration that suits your particular data.

In "Analysis and Analyzers" on page 86, we said that an *analyzer* is a wrapper that combines three functions into a single package, which are executed in sequence:

Character filters

Character filters are used to "tidy up" a string before it is tokenized. For instance, if our text is in HTML format, it will contain HTML tags like `<p>` or `<div>` that we don't want to be indexed. We can use the `html_strip` character filter (*http://bit.ly/1B6f4Ay*) to remove all HTML tags and to convert HTML entities like `&Aacute;` into the corresponding Unicode character Á.

An analyzer may have zero or more character filters.

Tokenizers

An analyzer *must* have a single tokenizer. The tokenizer breaks up the string into individual terms or tokens. The `standard` tokenizer (*http://bit.ly/1E3Fd1b*), which is used in the `standard` analyzer, breaks up a string into individual terms on word boundaries, and removes most punctuation, but other tokenizers exist that have different behavior.

For instance, the `keyword` tokenizer (*http://bit.ly/1ICd585*) outputs exactly the same string as it received, without any tokenization. The `whitespace` tokenizer (*http://bit.ly/1xt3t7d*) splits text on whitespace only. The `pattern` tokenizer (*http://bit.ly/1ICdozA*) can be used to split text on a matching regular expression.

Token filters

After tokenization, the resulting *token stream* is passed through any specified token filters, in the order in which they are specified.

Token filters may change, add, or remove tokens. We have already mentioned the `lowercase` (*http://bit.ly/1DIeXvZ*) and `stop` token filters (*http://bit.ly/1INX4tN*), but there are many more available in Elasticsearch. Stemming token filters (*http://bit.ly/1AUfpDN*) "stem" words to their root form. The `ascii_folding` filter (*http://bit.ly/1ylU7Q7*) removes diacritics, converting a term like "très" into "tres". The `ngram` (*http://bit.ly/1CbkmYe*) and `edge_ngram` token filters (*http://bit.ly/1DIf6j5*) can produce tokens suitable for partial matching or autocomplete.

In Part II, we discuss examples of where and how to use these tokenizers and filters. But first, we need to explain how to create a custom analyzer.

Creating a Custom Analyzer

In the same way as we configured the `es_std` analyzer previously, we can configure character filters, tokenizers, and token filters in their respective sections under `analysis`:

```
PUT /my_index
{
    "settings": {
        "analysis": {
            "char_filter": { ... custom character filters ... },
            "tokenizer":   { ...    custom tokenizers    ... },
            "filter":      { ...    custom token filters ... },
            "analyzer":    { ...    custom analyzers     ... }
        }
    }
}
```

As an example, let's set up a custom analyzer that will do the following:

1. Strip out HTML by using the `html_strip` character filter.

2. Replace & characters with " and ", using a custom `mapping` character filter:

```
"char_filter": {
    "&_to_and": {
        "type":        "mapping",
        "mappings": [ "&=> and "]
    }
}
```

3. Tokenize words, using the standard tokenizer.

4. Lowercase terms, using the lowercase token filter.

5. Remove a custom list of stopwords, using a custom stop token filter:

```
"filter": {
    "my_stopwords": {
        "type":        "stop",
        "stopwords": [ "the", "a" ]
    }
}
```

Our analyzer definition combines the predefined tokenizer and filters with the custom filters that we have configured previously:

```
"analyzer": {
    "my_analyzer": {
        "type":         "custom",
        "char_filter":  [ "html_strip", "&_to_and" ],
        "tokenizer":    "standard",
        "filter":       [ "lowercase", "my_stopwords" ]
    }
}
```

To put it all together, the whole create-index request looks like this:

```
PUT /my_index
{
    "settings": {
        "analysis": {
            "char_filter": {
                "&_to_and": {
                    "type":        "mapping",
                    "mappings": [ "&=> and "]
            }},
            "filter": {
                "my_stopwords": {
                    "type":        "stop",
                    "stopwords": [ "the", "a" ]
            }},
            "analyzer": {
                "my_analyzer": {
                    "type":         "custom",
                    "char_filter":  [ "html_strip", "&_to_and" ],
                    "tokenizer":    "standard",
```

```
                    "filter":      [ "lowercase", "my_stopwords" ]
            }}
    }}}
```

After creating the index, use the `analyze` API to test the new analyzer:

```
GET /my_index/_analyze?analyzer=my_analyzer
The quick & brown fox
```

The following abbreviated results show that our analyzer is working correctly:

```
{
  "tokens" : [
      { "token" :   "quick",    "position" : 2 },
      { "token" :   "and",      "position" : 3 },
      { "token" :   "brown",    "position" : 4 },
      { "token" :   "fox",      "position" : 5 }
  ]
}
```

The analyzer is not much use unless we tell Elasticsearch where to use it. We can apply it to a `string` field with a mapping such as the following:

```
PUT /my_index/_mapping/my_type
{
    "properties": {
        "title": {
            "type":      "string",
            "analyzer":  "my_analyzer"
        }
    }
}
```

Types and Mappings

A *type* in Elasticsearch represents a class of similar documents. A type consists of a *name*—such as `user` or `blogpost`—and a *mapping*. The mapping, like a database schema, describes the fields or *properties* that documents of that type may have, the datatype of each field—such as `string`, `integer`, or `date`—and how those fields should be indexed and stored by Lucene.

In "What Is a Document?" on page 38, we said that a type is like a table in a relational database. While this is a useful way to think about types initially, it is worth explaining in more detail exactly what a type is and how they are implemented on top of Lucene.

How Lucene Sees Documents

A document in Lucene consists of a simple list of field-value pairs. A field must have at least one value, but any field can contain multiple values. Similarly, a single string value may be converted into multiple values by the analysis process. Lucene doesn't care if the values are strings or numbers or dates—all values are just treated as *opaque bytes*.

When we index a document in Lucene, the values for each field are added to the inverted index for the associated field. Optionally, the original values may also be *stored* unchanged so that they can be retrieved later.

How Types Are Implemented

Elasticsearch types are implemented on top of this simple foundation. An index may have several types, each with its own mapping, and documents of any of these types may be stored in the same index.

Because Lucene has no concept of document types, the type name of each document is stored with the document in a metadata field called _type. When we search for documents of a particular type, Elasticsearch simply uses a filter on the _type field to restrict results to documents of that type.

Lucene also has no concept of mappings. Mappings are the layer that Elasticsearch uses to *map* complex JSON documents into the simple flat documents that Lucene expects to receive.

For instance, the mapping for the name field in the user type may declare that the field is a string field, and that its value should be analyzed by the whitespace analyzer before being indexed into the inverted index called name:

```
"name": {
    "type":     "string",
    "analyzer": "whitespace"
}
```

Avoiding Type Gotchas

The fact that documents of different types can be added to the same index introduces some unexpected complications.

Imagine that we have two types in our index: blog_en for blog posts in English, and blog_es for blog posts in Spanish. Both types have a title field, but one type uses the english analyzer and the other type uses the spanish analyzer.

The problem is illustrated by the following query:

```
GET /_search
{
    "query": {
        "match": {
            "title": "The quick brown fox"
        }
```

```
        }
    }
```

We are searching in the `title` field in both types. The query string needs to be analyzed, but which analyzer does it use: `spanish` or `english`? It will use the analyzer for the first `title` field that it finds, which will be correct for some docs and incorrect for the others.

We can avoid this problem either by naming the fields differently—for example, `title_en` and `title_es`—or by explicitly including the type name in the field name and querying each field separately:

```
GET /_search
{
    "query": {
        "multi_match": { ❶
            "query":   "The quick brown fox",
            "fields": [ "blog_en.title", "blog_es.title" ]
        }
    }
}
```

❶ The `multi_match` query runs a `match` query on multiple fields and combines the results.

Our new query uses the `english` analyzer for the field `blog_en.title` and the `span ish` analyzer for the field `blog_es.title`, and combines the results from both fields into an overall relevance score.

This solution can help when both fields have the same datatype, but consider what would happen if you indexed these two documents into the same index:

- Type: user

  ```
  { "login": "john_smith" }
  ```

- Type: event

```
{ "login": "2014-06-01" }
```

Lucene doesn't care that one field contains a string and the other field contains a date. It will happily index the byte values from both fields.

However, if we now try to *sort* on the event.login field, Elasticsearch needs to load the values in the login field into memory. As we said in "Fielddata" on page 121, it loads the values for *all documents* in the index regardless of their type.

It will try to load these values either as a string or as a date, depending on which login field it sees first. This will either produce unexpected results or fail outright.

 To ensure that you don't run into these conflicts, it is advisable to ensure that fields with the *same name* are mapped in the *same way* in every type in an index.

The Root Object

The uppermost level of a mapping is known as the *root object*. It may contain the following:

- A *properties* section, which lists the mapping for each field that a document may contain
- Various metadata fields, all of which start with an underscore, such as _type, _id, and _source
- Settings, which control how the dynamic detection of new fields is handled, such as analyzer, dynamic_date_formats, and dynamic_templates
- Other settings, which can be applied both to the root object and to fields of type object, such as enabled, dynamic, and include_in_all

Properties

We have already discussed the three most important settings for document fields or properties in "Core Simple Field Types" on page 90 and "Complex Core Field Types" on page 95:

type
    The datatype that the field contains, such as string or date

index
> Whether a field should be searchable as full text (analyzed), searchable as an exact value (not_analyzed), or not searchable at all (no)

analyzer
> Which analyzer to use for a full-text field, both at index time and at search time

We will discuss other field types such as ip, geo_point, and geo_shape in the appropriate sections later in the book.

Metadata: _source Field

By default, Elasticsearch stores the JSON string representing the document body in the _source field. Like all stored fields, the _source field is compressed before being written to disk.

This is almost always desired functionality because it means the following:

- The full document is available directly from the search results—no need for a separate round-trip to fetch the document from another data store.
- Partial update requests will not function without the _source field.
- When your mapping changes and you need to reindex your data, you can do so directly from Elasticsearch instead of having to retrieve all of your documents from another (usually slower) data store.
- Individual fields can be extracted from the _source field and returned in get or search requests when you don't need to see the whole document.
- It is easier to debug queries, because you can see exactly what each document contains, rather than having to guess their contents from a list of IDs.

That said, storing the _source field does use disk space. If none of the preceding reasons is important to you, you can disable the _source field with the following mapping:

```
PUT /my_index
{
    "mappings": {
        "my_type": {
            "_source": {
                "enabled": false
            }
        }
    }
}
```

In a search request, you can ask for only certain fields by specifying the _source parameter in the request body:

```
GET /_search
{
    "query":    { "match_all": {}},
    "_source": [ "title", "created" ]
}
```

Values for these fields will be extracted from the _source field and returned instead of the full _source.

Stored Fields

Besides indexing the values of a field, you can also choose to store the original field value for later retrieval. Users with a Lucene background use stored fields to choose which fields they would like to be able to return in their search results. In fact, the _source field is a stored field.

In Elasticsearch, setting individual document fields to be stored is usually a false optimization. The whole document is already stored as the _source field. It is almost always better to just extract the fields that you need by using the _source parameter.

Metadata: _all Field

In "Search *Lite*" on page 78, we introduced the _all field: a special field that indexes the values from all other fields as one big string. The query_string query clause (and searches performed as ?q=john) defaults to searching in the _all field if no other field is specified.

The _all field is useful during the exploratory phase of a new application, while you are still unsure about the final structure that your documents will have. You can throw any query string at it and you have a good chance of finding the document you're after:

```
GET /_search
{
    "match": {
        "_all": "john smith marketing"
    }
}
```

As your application evolves and your search requirements become more exacting, you will find yourself using the _all field less and less. The _all field is a shotgun approach to search. By querying individual fields, you have more flexbility, power, and fine-grained control over which results are considered to be most relevant.

One of the important factors taken into account by the relevance algorithm is the length of the field: the shorter the field, the more important. A term that appears in a short title field is likely to be more important than the same term that appears somewhere in a long content field. This distinction between field lengths disappears in the _all field.

If you decide that you no longer need the _all field, you can disable it with this mapping:

```
PUT /my_index/_mapping/my_type
{
    "my_type": {
        "_all": { "enabled": false }
    }
}
```

Inclusion in the _all field can be controlled on a field-by-field basis by using the include_in_all setting, which defaults to true. Setting include_in_all on an object (or on the root object) changes the default for all fields within that object.

You may find that you want to keep the _all field around to use as a catchall full-text field just for specific fields, such as title, overview, summary, and tags. Instead of disabling the _all field completely, disable include_in_all for all fields by default, and enable it only on the fields you choose:

```
PUT /my_index/my_type/_mapping
{
    "my_type": {
        "include_in_all": false,
        "properties": {
            "title": {
                "type":           "string",
                "include_in_all": true
            },
            ...
        }
    }
}
```

Remember that the _all field is just an analyzed string field. It uses the default analyzer to analyze its values, regardless of which analyzer has been set on the fields where the values originate. And like any string field, you can configure which analyzer the _all field should use:

```
PUT /my_index/my_type/_mapping
{
    "my_type": {
        "_all": { "analyzer": "whitespace" }
```

```
        }
    }
```

Metadata: Document Identity

There are four metadata fields associated with document identity:

_id
>   The string ID of the document

_type
>   The type name of the document

_index
>   The index where the document lives

_uid
>   The _type and _id concatenated together as type#id

By default, the _uid field is stored (can be retrieved) and indexed (searchable). The
_type field is indexed but not stored, and the _id and _index fields are neither
indexed nor stored, meaning they don't really exist.

In spite of this, you can query the _id field as though it were a real field. Elasticsearch
uses the _uid field to derive the _id. Although you can change the index and store
settings for these fields, you almost never need to do so.

The _id field does have one setting that you may want to use: the path setting tells
Elasticsearch that it should extract the value for the _id from a field within the document itself.

```
PUT /my_index
{
    "mappings": {
        "my_type": {
            "_id": {
                "path": "doc_id" ❶
            },
            "properties": {
                "doc_id": {
                    "type":    "string",
                    "index":   "not_analyzed"
                }
            }
        }
    }
}
```

❶ Extract the doc _id from the doc_id field.

Then, when you index a document:

```
POST /my_index/my_type
{
    "doc_id": "123"
}
```

the _id value will be extracted from the doc_id field in the document body:

```
{
    "_index":   "my_index",
    "_type":    "my_type",
    "_id":      "123", ❶
    "_version": 1,
    "created":  true
}
```

❶ The _id has been extracted correctly.

 While this is very convenient, be aware that it has a slight performance impact on bulk requests (see "Why the Funny Format?"
on page 71). The node handling the request can no longer use
the optimized bulk format to parse just the metadata line in
order to decide which shard should receive the request. Instead, it has to parse
the document body as well.

Dynamic Mapping

When Elasticsearch encounters a previously unknown field in a document, it uses
dynamic mapping to determine the datatype for the field and automatically adds the
new field to the type mapping.

Sometimes this is the desired behavior and sometimes it isn't. Perhaps you don't know
what fields will be added to your documents later, but you want them to be indexed
automatically. Perhaps you just want to ignore them. Or—especially if you are using
Elasticsearch as a primary data store—perhaps you want unknown fields to throw an
exception to alert you to the problem.

Fortunately, you can control this behavior with the dynamic setting, which accepts the
following options:

true
    Add new fields dynamically—the default

false
    Ignore new fields

```
strict
```
Throw an exception if an unknown field is encountered

The `dynamic` setting may be applied to the root object or to any field of type `object`. You could set `dynamic` to `strict` by default, but enable it just for a specific inner object:

```
PUT /my_index
{
    "mappings": {
        "my_type": {
            "dynamic":       "strict",  ❶
            "properties": {
                "title":  { "type": "string"},
                "stash":  {
                    "type":       "object",
                    "dynamic":   true ❷
                }
            }
        }
    }
}
```

❶ The `my_type` object will throw an exception if an unknown field is encountered.

❷ The `stash` object will create new fields dynamically.

With this mapping, you can add new searchable fields into the `stash` object:

```
PUT /my_index/my_type/1
{
    "title":   "This doc adds a new field",
    "stash": { "new_field": "Success!" }
}
```

But trying to do the same at the top level will fail:

```
PUT /my_index/my_type/1
{
    "title":       "This throws a StrictDynamicMappingException",
    "new_field": "Fail!"
}
```

 Setting `dynamic` to `false` doesn't alter the contents of the `_source` field at all. The `_source` will still contain the whole JSON document that you indexed. However, any unknown fields will not be added to the mapping and will not be searchable.

Customizing Dynamic Mapping

If you know that you are going to be adding new fields on the fly, you probably want to leave dynamic mapping enabled. At times, though, the dynamic mapping "rules" can be a bit blunt. Fortunately, there are settings that you can use to customize these rules to better suit your data.

date_detection

When Elasticsearch encounters a new string field, it checks to see if the string contains a recognizable date, like `2014-01-01`. If it looks like a date, the field is added as type `date`. Otherwise, it is added as type `string`.

Sometimes this behavior can lead to problems. Imagine that you index a document like this:

```
{ "note": "2014-01-01" }
```

Assuming that this is the first time that the `note` field has been seen, it will be added as a `date` field. But what if the next document looks like this:

```
{ "note": "Logged out" }
```

This clearly isn't a date, but it is too late. The field is already a date field and so this "malformed date" will cause an exception to be thrown.

Date detection can be turned off by setting `date_detection` to `false` on the root object:

```
PUT /my_index
{
    "mappings": {
        "my_type": {
            "date_detection": false
        }
    }
}
```

With this mapping in place, a string will always be a `string`. If you need a `date` field, you have to add it manually.

 Elasticsearch's idea of which strings look like dates can be altered with the `dynamic_date_formats` setting (*http://www.elastic search.org/guide/en/elasticsearch/reference/current/mapping-root-object-type.html*).

dynamic_templates

With `dynamic_templates`, you can take complete control over the mapping that is generated for newly detected fields. You can even apply a different mapping depending on the field name or datatype.

Each template has a name, which you can use to describe what the template does, a `mapping` to specify the mapping that should be applied, and at least one parameter (such as `match`) to define which fields the template should apply to.

Templates are checked in order; the first template that matches is applied. For instance, we could specify two templates for `string` fields:

- es: Field names ending in _es should use the `spanish` analyzer.
- en: All others should use the `english` analyzer.

We put the es template first, because it is more specific than the catchall en template, which matches all string fields:

```
PUT /my_index
{
    "mappings": {
        "my_type": {
            "dynamic_templates": [
                { "es": {
                    "match":              "*_es",     ❶
                    "match_mapping_type": "string",
                    "mapping": {
                        "type":           "string",
                        "analyzer":       "spanish"
                    }
                }},
                { "en": {
                    "match":              "*",        ❷
                    "match_mapping_type": "string",
                    "mapping": {
                        "type":           "string",
                        "analyzer":       "english"
                    }
                }}
            ]
}}}
```

❶ Match string fields whose name ends in _es.

❷ Match all other string fields.

The `match_mapping_type` allows you to apply the template only to fields of the specified type, as detected by the standard dynamic mapping rules, (for example `string` or `long`).

The `match` parameter matches just the field name, and the `path_match` parameter matches the full path to a field in an object, so the pattern `address.*.name` would match a field like this:

```
{
    "address": {
        "city": {
            "name": "New York"
        }
    }
}
```

The `unmatch` and `path_unmatch` patterns can be used to exclude fields that would otherwise match.

More configuration options can be found in the reference documentation for the root object (*http://bit.ly/1wdHOzG*).

Default Mapping

Often, all types in an index share similar fields and settings. It can be more convenient to specify these common settings in the `_default_` mapping, instead of having to repeat yourself every time you create a new type. The `_default_` mapping acts as a template for new types. All types created *after* the `_default_` mapping will include all of these default settings, unless explicitly overridden in the type mapping itself.

For instance, we can disable the `_all` field for all types, using the `_default_` mapping, but enable it just for the `blog` type, as follows:

```
PUT /my_index
{
    "mappings": {
        "_default_": {
            "_all": { "enabled":  false }
        },
        "blog": {
            "_all": { "enabled":  true }
        }
    }
}
```

The `_default_` mapping can also be a good place to specify index-wide dynamic templates.

Reindexing Your Data

Although you can add new types to an index, or add new fields to a type, you can't add new analyzers or make changes to existing fields. If you were to do so, the data that had already been indexed would be incorrect and your searches would no longer work as expected.

The simplest way to apply these changes to your existing data is to reindex: create a new index with the new settings and copy all of your documents from the old index to the new index.

One of the advantages of the _source field is that you already have the whole document available to you in Elasticsearch itself. You don't have to rebuild your index from the database, which is usually much slower.

To reindex all of the documents from the old index efficiently, use *scan-and-scroll* to retrieve batches of documents from the old index, and the bulk API to push them into the new index.

Reindexing in Batches

You can run multiple reindexing jobs at the same time, but you obviously don't want their results to overlap. Instead, break a big reindex down into smaller jobs by filtering on a date or timestamp field:

```
GET /old_index/_search?search_type=scan&scroll=1m
{
    "query": {
        "range": {
            "date": {
                "gte":  "2014-01-01",
                "lt":   "2014-02-01"
            }
        }
    },
    "size":  1000
}
```

If you continue making changes to the old index, you will want to make sure that you include the newly added documents in your new index as well. This can be done by rerunning the reindex process, but again filtering on a date field to match only documents that have been added since the last reindex process started.

Index Aliases and Zero Downtime

The problem with the reindexing process described previously is that you need to update your application to use the new index name. Index aliases to the rescue!

An index *alias* is like a shortcut or symbolic link, which can point to one or more indices, and can be used in any API that expects an index name. Aliases give us an enormous amount of flexibility. They allow us to do the following:

- Switch transparently between one index and another on a running cluster
- Group multiple indices (for example, `last_three_months`)
- Create "views" on a subset of the documents in an index

We will talk more about the other uses for aliases later in the book. For now we will explain how to use them to switch from an old index to a new index with zero downtime.

There are two endpoints for managing aliases: `_alias` for single operations, and `_aliases` to perform multiple operations atomically.

In this scenario, we will assume that your application is talking to an index called `my_index`. In reality, `my_index` will be an alias that points to the current real index. We will include a version number in the name of the real index: `my_index_v1`, `my_index_v2`, and so forth.

To start off, create the index `my_index_v1`, and set up the alias `my_index` to point to it:

```
PUT /my_index_v1 ❶
PUT /my_index_v1/_alias/my_index ❷
```

❶ Create the index `my_index_v1`.

❷ Set the `my_index` alias to point to `my_index_v1`.

You can check which index the alias points to:

```
GET /*/_alias/my_index
```

Or which aliases point to the index:

```
GET /my_index_v1/_alias/*
```

Both of these return the following:

```
{
    "my_index_v1" : {
        "aliases" : {
            "my_index" : { }
        }
    }
}
```

```
        }
    }
```

Later, we decide that we want to change the mappings for a field in our index. Of course, we can't change the existing mapping, so we have to reindex our data. To start, we create my_index_v2 with the new mappings:

```
PUT /my_index_v2
{
    "mappings": {
        "my_type": {
            "properties": {
                "tags": {
                    "type":    "string",
                    "index":   "not_analyzed"
                }
            }
        }
    }
}
```

Then we reindex our data from my_index_v1 to my_index_v2, following the process described in "Reindexing Your Data" on page 152. Once we are satisfied that our documents have been reindexed correctly, we switch our alias to point to the new index.

An alias can point to multiple indices, so we need to remove the alias from the old index at the same time as we add it to the new index. The change needs to be atomic, which means that we must use the _aliases endpoint:

```
POST /_aliases
{
    "actions": [
        { "remove": { "index": "my_index_v1", "alias": "my_index" }},
        { "add":    { "index": "my_index_v2", "alias": "my_index" }}
    ]
}
```

Your application has switched from using the old index to the new index transparently, with zero downtime.

Even when you think that your current index design is perfect, it is likely that you will need to make some change later, when your index is already being used in production.

Be prepared: use aliases instead of indices in your application. Then you will be able to reindex whenever you need to. Aliases are cheap and should be used liberally.

CHAPTER 11

Inside a Shard

In Chapter 2, we introduced the *shard*, and described it as a low-level *worker unit*. But what exactly *is* a shard and how does it work? In this chapter, we answer these questions:

- Why is search *near* real-time?
- Why are document CRUD (create-read-update-delete) operations *real-time*?
- How does Elasticsearch ensure that the changes you make are durable, that they won't be lost if there is a power failure?
- Why does deleting documents not free up space immediately?
- What do the `refresh`, `flush`, and `optimize` APIs do, and when should you use them?

The easiest way to understand how a shard functions today is to start with a history lesson. We will look at the problems that needed to be solved in order to provide a distributed durable data store with near real-time search and analytics.

Content Warning

The information presented in this chapter is for your interest. You are not required to understand and remember all the detail in order to use Elasticsearch. Read this chapter to gain a taste for how things work, and to know where the information is in case you need to refer to it in the future, but don't be overwhelmed by the detail.

Making Text Searchable

The first challenge that had to be solved was how to make text searchable. Traditional databases store a single value per field, but this is insufficient for full-text search. Every word in a text field needs to be searchable, which means that the database needs to be able to index multiple values—words, in this case—in a single field.

The data structure that best supports the *multiple-values-per-field* requirement is the *inverted index*, which we introduced in "Inverted Index" on page 83. The inverted index contains a sorted list of all of the unique values, or *terms*, that occur in any document and, for each term, a list of all the documents that contain it.

```
Term  | Doc 1 | Doc 2 | Doc 3 | ...
-------------------------------------
brown |   X   |       |   X   | ...
fox   |   X   |   X   |   X   | ...
quick |   X   |   X   |       | ...
the   |   X   |       |   X   | ...
```

 When discussing inverted indices, we talk about indexing *documents* because, historically, an inverted index was used to index whole unstructured text documents. A *document* in Elasticsearch is a structured JSON document with fields and values. In reality, every indexed field in a JSON document has its own inverted index.

The inverted index may hold a lot more information than the list of documents that contain a particular term. It may store a count of the number of documents that contain each term, the number of times a term appears in a particular document, the order of terms in each document, the length of each document, the average length of all documents, and more. These statistics allow Elasticsearch to determine which terms are more important than others, and which documents are more important than others, as described in "What Is Relevance?" on page 117.

The important thing to realize is that the inverted index needs to know about *all* documents in the collection in order for it to function as intended.

In the early days of full-text search, one big inverted index was built for the entire document collection and written to disk. As soon as the new index was ready, it replaced the old index, and recent changes became searchable.

Immutability

The inverted index that is written to disk is *immutable*: it doesn't change. Ever. This immutability has important benefits:

- There is no need for locking. If you never have to update the index, you never have to worry about multiple processes trying to make changes at the same time.

- Once the index has been read into the kernel's filesystem cache, it stays there, because it never changes. As long as there is enough space in the filesystem cache, most reads will come from memory instead of having to hit disk. This provides a big performance boost.

- Any other caches (like the filter cache) remain valid for the life of the index. They don't need to be rebuilt every time the data changes, because the data doesn't change.

- Writing a single large inverted index allows the data to be compressed, reducing costly disk I/O and the amount of RAM needed to cache the index.

Of course, an immutable index has its downsides too, primarily the fact that it is immutable! You can't change it. If you want to make new documents searchable, you have to rebuild the entire index. This places a significant limitation either on the amount of data that an index can contain, or the frequency with which the index can be updated.

Dynamically Updatable Indices

The next problem that needed to be solved was how to make an inverted index updatable without losing the benefits of immutability? The answer turned out to be: use more than one index.

Instead of rewriting the whole inverted index, add new supplementary indices to reflect more-recent changes. Each inverted index can be queried in turn—starting with the oldest—and the results combined.

Lucene, the Java libraries on which Elasticsearch is based, introduced the concept of *per-segment search*. A *segment* is an inverted index in its own right, but now the word *index* in Lucene came to mean a *collection of segments* plus a *commit point*—a file that lists all known segments, as depicted in Figure 11-1. New documents are first added to an in-memory indexing buffer, as shown in Figure 11-2, before being written to an on-disk segment, as in Figure 11-3

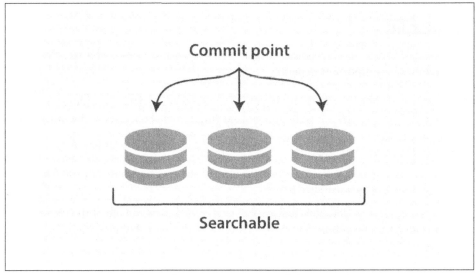

Figure 11-1. A Lucene index with a commit point and three segments

Index Versus Shard

To add to the confusion, a *Lucene index* is what we call a *shard* in Elasticsearch, while an *index* in Elasticsearch is a collection of shards. When Elasticsearch searches an index, it sends the query out to a copy of every shard (Lucene index) that belongs to the index, and then reduces the per-shards results to a global result set, as described in Chapter 9.

A per-segment search works as follows:

1. New documents are collected in an in-memory indexing buffer. See Figure 11-2.

2. Every so often, the buffer is *commited*:

   - A new segment—a supplementary inverted index—is written to disk.

   - A new *commit point* is written to disk, which includes the name of the new segment.

   - The disk is *fsync'ed*—all writes waiting in the filesystem cache are flushed to disk, to ensure that they have been physically written.

3. The new segment is opened, making the documents it contains visible to search.

4. The in-memory buffer is cleared, and is ready to accept new documents.

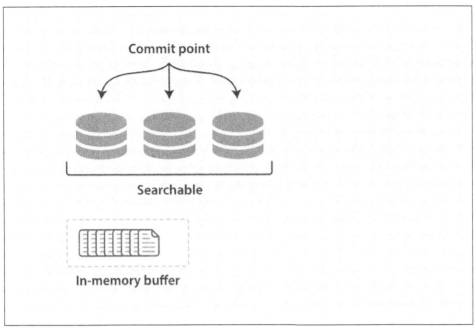

Figure 11-2. A Lucene index with new documents in the in-memory buffer, ready to commit

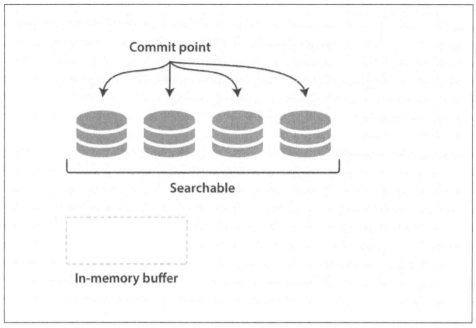

Figure 11-3. After a commit, a new segment is added to the commit point and the buffer is cleared

When a query is issued, all known segments are queried in turn. Term statistics are aggregated across all segments to ensure that the relevance of each term and each document is calculated accurately. In this way, new documents can be added to the index relatively cheaply.

Deletes and Updates

Segments are immutable, so documents cannot be removed from older segments, nor can older segments be updated to reflect a newer version of a document. Instead, every commit point includes a `.del` file that lists which documents in which segments have been deleted.

When a document is "deleted," it is actually just *marked* as deleted in the `.del` file. A document that has been marked as deleted can still match a query, but it is removed from the results list before the final query results are returned.

Document updates work in a similar way: when a document is updated, the old version of the document is marked as deleted, and the new version of the document is indexed in a new segment. Perhaps both versions of the document will match a query, but the older deleted version is removed before the query results are returned.

In "Segment Merging" on page 168, we show how deleted documents are purged from the filesystem.

Near Real-Time Search

With the development of per-segment search, the delay between indexing a document and making it visible to search dropped dramatically. New documents could be made searchable within minutes, but that still isn't fast enough.

The bottleneck is the disk. Commiting a new segment to disk requires an `fsync` (*http://en.wikipedia.org/wiki/Fsync*) to ensure that the segment is physically written to disk and that data will not be lost if there is a power failure. But an `fsync` is costly; it cannot be performed every time a document is indexed without a big performance hit.

What was needed was a more lightweight way to make new documents visible to search, which meant removing `fsync` from the equation.

Sitting between Elasticsearch and the disk is the filesystem cache. As before, documents in the in-memory indexing buffer (Figure 11-4) are written to a new segment (Figure 11-5). But the new segment is written to the filesystem cache first—which is cheap—and only later is it flushed to disk—which is expensive. But once a file is in the cache, it can be opened and read, just like any other file.

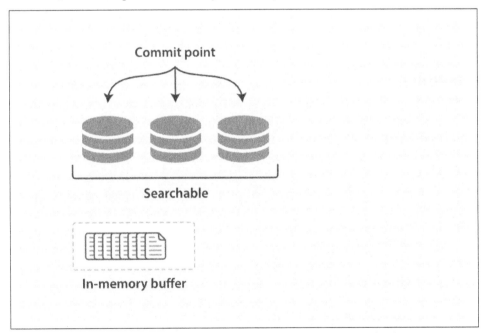

Figure 11-4. A Lucene index with new documents in the in-memory buffer

Lucene allows new segments to be written and opened—making the documents they contain visible to search—without performing a full commit. This is a much lighter process than a commit, and can be done frequently without ruining performance.

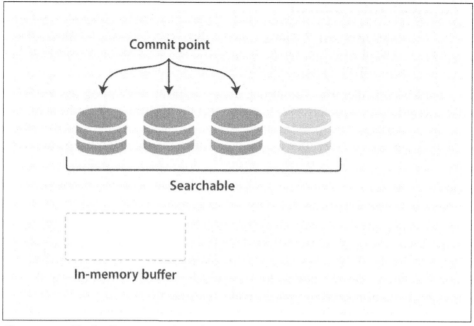

Figure 11-5. The buffer contents have been written to a segment, which is searchable, but is not yet commited

refresh API

In Elasticsearch, this lightweight process of writing and opening a new segment is called a *refresh*. By default, every shard is refreshed automatically once every second. This is why we say that Elasticsearch has *near* real-time search: document changes are not visible to search immediately, but will become visible within 1 second.

This can be confusing for new users: they index a document and try to search for it, and it just isn't there. The way around this is to perform a manual refresh, with the refresh API:

```
POST /_refresh ❶
POST /blogs/_refresh ❷
```

❶ Refresh all indices.

❷ Refresh just the blogs index.

While a refresh is much lighter than a commit, it still has a performance cost. A manual refresh can be useful when writing tests, but don't do a manual refresh every time you index a document in production; it will hurt your performance. Instead, your application needs to be aware of the near real-time nature of Elasticsearch and make allowances for it.

Not all use cases require a refresh every second. Perhaps you are using Elasticsearch to index millions of log files, and you would prefer to optimize for index speed rather than near real-time search. You can reduce the frequency of refreshes on a per-index basis by setting the `refresh_interval`:

```
PUT /my_logs
{
  "settings": {
    "refresh_interval": "30s" ❶
  }
}
```

❶ Refresh the `my_logs` index every 30 seconds.

The `refresh_interval` can be updated dynamically on an existing index. You can turn off automatic refreshes while you are building a big new index, and then turn them back on when you start using the index in production:

```
POST /my_logs/_settings
{ "refresh_interval": -1 } ❶

POST /my_logs/_settings
{ "refresh_interval": "1s" } ❷
```

❶ Disable automatic refreshes.

❷ Refresh automatically every second.

 The `refresh_interval` expects a *duration* such as 1s (1 second) or 2m (2 minutes). An absolute number like 1 means *1 millisecond*--a sure way to bring your cluster to its knees.

Making Changes Persistent

Without an `fsync` to flush data in the filesystem cache to disk, we cannot be sure that the data will still be there after a power failure, or even after exiting the application normally. For Elasticsearch to be reliable, it needs to ensure that changes are persisted to disk.

In "Dynamically Updatable Indices" on page 157, we said that a full commit flushes segments to disk and writes a commit point, which lists all known segments. Elasticsearch uses this commit point during startup or when reopening an index to decide which segments belong to the current shard.

While we refresh once every second to achieve near real-time search, we still need to do full commits regularly to make sure that we can recover from failure. But what about the document changes that happen between commits? We don't want to lose those either.

Elasticsearch added a *translog*, or transaction log, which records every operation in Elasticsearch as it happens. With the translog, the process now looks like this:

1. When a document is indexed, it is added to the in-memory buffer *and* appended to the translog, as shown in Figure 11-6.

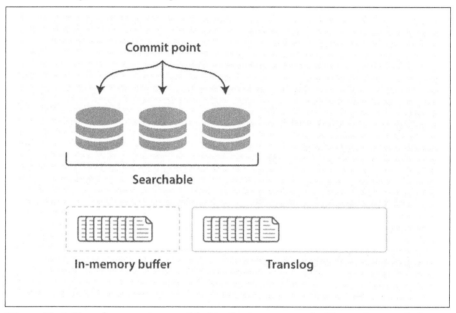

Figure 11-6. New documents are added to the in-memory buffer and appended to the transaction log

2. The refresh leaves the shard in the state depicted in Figure 11-7. Once every second, the shard is refreshed:

   - The docs in the in-memory buffer are written to a new segment, without an fsync.

   - The segment is opened to make it visible to search.

- The in-memory buffer is cleared.

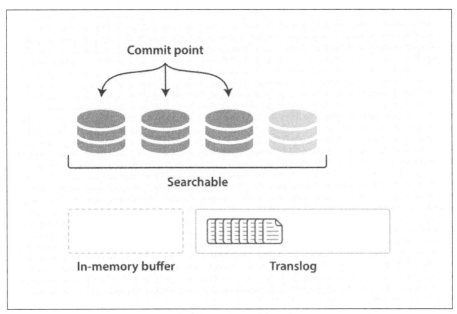

Figure 11-7. After a refresh, the buffer is cleared but the transaction log is not

3. This process continues with more documents being added to the in-memory buffer and appended to the transaction log (see Figure 11-8).

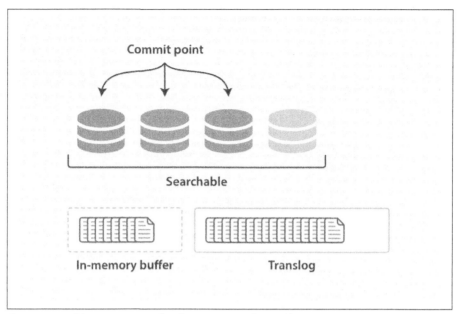

Figure 11-8. The transaction log keeps accumulating documents

4. Every so often—such as when the translog is getting too big—the index is flushed; a new translog is created, and a full commit is performed (see Figure 11-9):

- Any docs in the in-memory buffer are written to a new segment.
- The buffer is cleared.
- A commit point is written to disk.
- The filesystem cache is flushed with an `fsync`.
- The old translog is deleted.

The translog provides a persistent record of all operations that have not yet been flushed to disk. When starting up, Elasticsearch will use the last commit point to recover known segments from disk, and will then replay all operations in the translog to add the changes that happened after the last commit.

The translog is also used to provide real-time CRUD. When you try to retrieve, update, or delete a document by ID, it first checks the translog for any recent changes before trying to retrieve the document from the relevant segment. This means that it always has access to the latest known version of the document, in real-time.

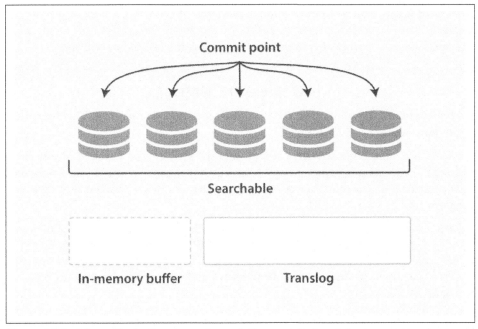

Figure 11-9. After a flush, the segments are fully commited and the transaction log is cleared

flush API

The action of performing a commit and truncating the translog is known in Elasticsearch as a *flush*. Shards are flushed automatically every 30 minutes, or when the translog becomes too big. See the `translog` documentation (*http://bit.ly/1E3HKbD*) for settings that can be used to control these thresholds:

The `flush` API (*http://bit.ly/1ICgxiU*) can be used to perform a manual flush:

```
POST /blogs/_flush ❶

POST /_flush?wait_for_ongoing ❷
```

❶ Flush the `blogs` index.

❷ Flush all indices and wait until all flushes have completed before returning.

You seldom need to issue a manual `flush` yourself; usually, automatic flushing is all that is required.

That said, it is beneficial to flush your indices before restarting a node or closing an index. When Elasticsearch tries to recover or reopen an index, it has to replay all of the operations in the translog, so the shorter the log, the faster the recovery.

How Safe Is the Translog?

The purpose of the translog is to ensure that operations are not lost. This begs the question: how safe is the translog?

Writes to a file will not survive a reboot until the file has been fsync'ed to disk. By default, the translog is fsync'ed every 5 seconds. Potentially, we could lose 5 seconds worth of data—if the translog were the only mechanism that we had for dealing with failure.

Fortunately, the translog is only part of a much bigger system. Remember that an indexing request is considered successful only after it has completed on both the primary shard and all replica shards. Even if the node holding the primary shard were to suffer catastrophic failure, it would be unlikely to affect the nodes holding the replica shards at the same time.

While we could force the translog to fsync more frequently (at the cost of indexing performance), it is unlikely to provide more reliability.

Segment Merging

With the automatic refresh process creating a new segment every second, it doesn't take long for the number of segments to explode. Having too many segments is a problem. Each segment consumes file handles, memory, and CPU cycles. More important, every search request has to check every segment in turn; the more segments there are, the slower the search will be.

Elasticsearch solves this problem by merging segments in the background. Small segments are merged into bigger segments, which, in turn, are merged into even bigger segments.

This is the moment when those old deleted documents are purged from the filesystem. Deleted documents (or old versions of updated documents) are not copied over to the new bigger segment.

There is nothing you need to do to enable merging. It happens automatically while you are indexing and searching. The process works like as depicted in Figure 11-10:

1. While indexing, the refresh process creates new segments and opens them for search.

---

2. The merge process selects a few segments of similar size and merges them into a new bigger segment in the background. This does not interrupt indexing and searching.

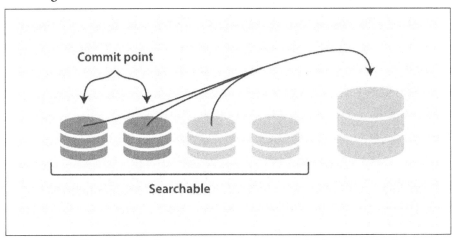

Figure 11-10. Two commited segments and one uncommited segment in the process of being merged into a bigger segment

3. Figure 11-11 illustrates activity as the merge completes:

- The new segment is flushed to disk.
- A new commit point is written that includes the new segment and excludes the old, smaller segments.
- The new segment is opened for search.
- The old segments are deleted.

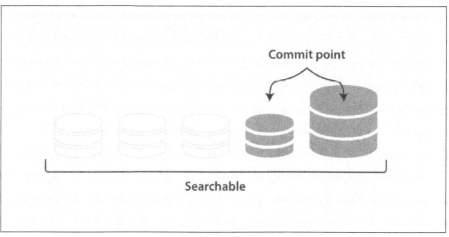

Figure 11-11. Once merging has finished, the old segments are deleted

The merging of big segments can use a lot of I/O and CPU, which can hurt search performance if left unchecked. By default, Elasticsearch throttles the merge process so that search still has enough resources available to perform well.

 See "Segments and Merging" on page 656 for advice about tuning merging for your use case.

optimize API

The `optimize` API is best described as the *forced merge* API. It forces a shard to be merged down to the number of segments specified in the `max_num_segments` parameter. The intention is to reduce the number of segments (usually to one) in order to speed up search performance.

 The `optimize` API should *not* be used on a dynamic index—an index that is being actively updated. The background merge process does a very good job, and optimizing will hinder the process. Don't interfere!

In certain specific circumstances, the `optimize` API can be beneficial. The typical use case is for logging, where logs are stored in an index per day, week, or month. Older indices are essentially read-only; they are unlikely to change.

In this case, it can be useful to optimize the shards of an old index down to a single segment each; it will use fewer resources and searches will be quicker:

```
POST /logstash-2014-10/_optimize?max_num_segments=1 ❶
```

❶ Merges each shard in the index down to a single segment

 Be aware that merges triggered by the `optimize` API are not throttled at all. They can consume all of the I/O on your nodes, leaving nothing for search and potentially making your cluster unresponsive. If you plan on optimizing an index, you should use shard allocation (see "Migrate Old Indices" on page 599) to first move the index to a node where it is safe to run.

PART II

Search in Depth

In Part I we covered the basic tools in just enough detail to allow you to start searching your data with Elasticsearch. It won't take long, though, before you find that you want more: more flexibility when matching user queries, more-accurate ranking of results, more-specific searches to cover different problem domains.

To move to the next level, it is not enough to just use the `match` query. You need to understand your data and how you want to be able to search it. The chapters in this part explain how to index and query your data to allow you to take advantage of word proximity, partial matching, fuzzy matching, and language awareness.

Understanding how each query contributes to the relevance `_score` will help you to tune your queries: to ensure that the documents you consider to be the best results appear on the first page, and to trim the "long tail" of barely relevant results.

Search is not just about full-text search: a large portion of your data will be structured values like dates and numbers. We will start by explaining how to combine structured search with full-text search in the most efficient way.

CHAPTER 12

Structured Search

Structured search is about interrogating data that has inherent structure. Dates, times, and numbers are all structured: they have a precise format that you can perform logical operations on. Common operations include comparing ranges of numbers or dates, or determining which of two values is larger.

Text can be structured too. A box of crayons has a discrete set of colors: red, green, blue. A blog post may be tagged with keywords distributed and search. Products in an ecommerce store have Universal Product Codes (UPCs) or some other identifier that requires strict and structured formatting.

With structured search, the answer to your question is *always* a yes or no; something either belongs in the set or it does not. Structured search does not worry about document relevance or scoring; it simply includes or excludes documents.

This should make sense logically. A number can't be *more* in a range than any other number that falls in the same range. It is either in the range—or it isn't. Similarly, for structured text, a value is either equal or it isn't. There is no concept of *more similar*.

Finding Exact Values

When working with exact values, you will be working with filters. Filters are important because they are very, very fast. Filters do not calculate relevance (avoiding the entire scoring phase) and are easily cached. We'll talk about the performance benefits of filters later in "All About Caching" on page 194, but for now, just keep in mind that you should use filters as often as you can.

term Filter with Numbers

We are going to explore the `term` filter first because you will use it often. This filter is capable of handling numbers, Booleans, dates, and text.

Let's look at an example using numbers first by indexing some products. These documents have a `price` and a `productID`:

```
POST /my_store/products/_bulk
{ "index": { "_id": 1 }}
{ "price" : 10, "productID" : "XHDK-A-1293-#fJ3" }
{ "index": { "_id": 2 }}
{ "price" : 20, "productID" : "KDKE-B-9947-#kL5" }
{ "index": { "_id": 3 }}
{ "price" : 30, "productID" : "JODL-X-1937-#pV7" }
{ "index": { "_id": 4 }}
{ "price" : 30, "productID" : "QQPX-R-3956-#aD8" }
```

Our goal is to find all products with a certain price. You may be familiar with SQL if you are coming from a relational database background. If we expressed this query as an SQL query, it would look like this:

```
SELECT document
FROM   products
WHERE  price = 20
```

In the Elasticsearch query DSL, we use a `term` filter to accomplish the same thing. The `term` filter will look for the exact value that we specify. By itself, a `term` filter is simple. It accepts a field name and the value that we wish to find:

```
{
    "term" : {
        "price" : 20
    }
}
```

The `term` filter isn't very useful on its own, though. As discussed in "Query DSL" on page 100, the `search` API expects a `query`, not a `filter`. To use our `term` filter, we need to wrap it with a `filtered` query:

```
GET /my_store/products/_search
{
    "query" : {
        "filtered" : {   ❶
            "query" : {
                "match_all" : {}   ❷
            },
            "filter" : {
                "term" : {   ❸
                    "price" : 20
                }
            }
```

```
            }
        }
    }
```

❶ The `filtered` query accepts both a `query` and a `filter`.

❷ A `match_all` is used to return all matching documents. This is the default behavior, so in future examples we will simply omit the `query` section.

❸ The `term` filter that we saw previously. Notice how it is placed inside the `filter` clause.

Once executed, the search results from this query are exactly what you would expect: only document 2 is returned as a hit (because only 2 had a price of 20):

```
"hits" : [
    {
        "_index" : "my_store",
        "_type" :  "products",
        "_id" :       "2",
        "_score" : 1.0, ❶
        "_source" : {
          "price" :      20,
          "productID" : "KDKE-B-9947-#kL5"
        }
    }
]
```

❶ Filters do not perform scoring or relevance. The score comes from the `match_all` query, which treats all docs as equal, so all results receive a neutral score of 1.

term Filter with Text

As mentioned at the top of this section, the `term` filter can match strings just as easily as numbers. Instead of price, let's try to find products that have a certain UPC identification code. To do this with SQL, we might use a query like this:

```
SELECT product
FROM   products
WHERE  productID = "XHDK-A-1293-#fJ3"
```

Translated into the query DSL, we can try a similar query with the `term` filter, like so:

```
GET /my_store/products/_search
{
    "query" : {
        "filtered" : {
            "filter" : {
                "term" : {
                    "productID" : "XHDK-A-1293-#fJ3"
```

```
                    }
                }
            }
        }
    }
```

Except there is a little hiccup: we don't get any results back! Why is that? The problem isn't with the the the `term` query; it is with the way the data has been indexed. If we use the `analyze` API ("Testing Analyzers" on page 88), we can see that our UPC has been tokenized into smaller tokens:

```
GET /my_store/_analyze?field=productID
XHDK-A-1293-#fJ3

{
  "tokens" : [ {
    "token" :          "xhdk",
    "start_offset" : 0,
    "end_offset" :     4,
    "type" :           "<ALPHANUM>",
    "position" :       1
  }, {
    "token" :          "a",
    "start_offset" : 5,
    "end_offset" :     6,
    "type" :           "<ALPHANUM>",
    "position" :       2
  }, {
    "token" :          "1293",
    "start_offset" : 7,
    "end_offset" :     11,
    "type" :           "<NUM>",
    "position" :       3
  }, {
    "token" :          "fj3",
    "start_offset" : 13,
    "end_offset" :     16,
    "type" :           "<ALPHANUM>",
    "position" :       4
  } ]
}
```

There are a few important points here:

- We have four distinct tokens instead of a single token representing the UPC.
- All letters have been lowercased.
- We lost the hyphen and the hash (#) sign.

So when our `term` filter looks for the exact value XHDK-A-1293-#fJ3, it doesn't find anything, because that token does not exist in our inverted index. Instead, there are the four tokens listed previously.

Obviously, this is not what we want to happen when dealing with identification codes, or any kind of precise enumeration.

To prevent this from happening, we need to tell Elasticsearch that this field contains an exact value by setting it to be `not_analyzed`. We saw this originally in "Customizing Field Mappings" on page 91. To do this, we need to first delete our old index (because it has the incorrect mapping) and create a new one with the correct mappings:

```
DELETE /my_store ❶

PUT /my_store ❷
{
    "mappings" : {
        "products" : {
            "properties" : {
                "productID" : {
                    "type" : "string",
                    "index" : "not_analyzed" ❸
                }
            }
        }
    }
}
```

❶ Deleting the index first is required, since we cannot change mappings that already exist.

❷ With the index deleted, we can re-create it with our custom mapping.

❸ Here we explicitly say that we don't want `productID` to be analyzed.

Now we can go ahead and reindex our documents:

```
POST /my_store/products/_bulk
{ "index": { "_id": 1 }}
{ "price" : 10, "productID" : "XHDK-A-1293-#fJ3" }
{ "index": { "_id": 2 }}
{ "price" : 20, "productID" : "KDKE-B-9947-#kL5" }
{ "index": { "_id": 3 }}
{ "price" : 30, "productID" : "JODL-X-1937-#pV7" }
{ "index": { "_id": 4 }}
{ "price" : 30, "productID" : "QQPX-R-3956-#aD8" }
```

Only now will our `term` filter work as expected. Let's try it again on the newly indexed data (notice, the query and filter have not changed at all, just how the data is mapped):

```
GET /my_store/products/_search
{
    "query" : {
        "filtered" : {
            "filter" : {
                "term" : {
                    "productID" : "XHDK-A-1293-#fJ3"
                }
            }
        }
    }
}
```

Since the `productID` field is not analyzed, and the `term` filter performs no analysis, the query finds the exact match and returns document 1 as a hit. Success!

Internal Filter Operation

Internally, Elasticsearch is performing several operations when executing a filter:

1. *Find matching docs.*

   The `term` filter looks up the term XHDK-A-1293-#fJ3 in the inverted index and retrieves the list of documents that contain that term. In this case, only document 1 has the term we are looking for.

2. *Build a bitset.*

   The filter then builds a *bitset*--an array of 1s and 0s—that describes which documents contain the term. Matching documents receive a 1 bit. In our example, the bitset would be [1,0,0,0].

3. *Cache the bitset.*

   Last, the bitset is stored in memory, since we can use this in the future and skip steps 1 and 2. This adds a lot of performance and makes filters very fast.

When executing a `filtered` query, the `filter` is executed before the `query`. The resulting bitset is given to the `query`, which uses it to simply skip over any documents that have already been excluded by the filter. This is one of the ways that filters can improve performance. Fewer documents evaluated by the query means faster response times.

Combining Filters

The previous two examples showed a single filter in use. In practice, you will probably need to filter on multiple values or fields. For example, how would you express this SQL in Elasticsearch?

```
SELECT product
FROM   products
WHERE  (price = 20 OR productID = "XHDK-A-1293-#fJ3")
  AND  (price != 30)
```

In these situations, you will need the `bool` filter. This is a *compound filter* that accepts other filters as arguments, combining them in various Boolean combinations.

Bool Filter

The `bool` filter is composed of three sections:

```
{
   "bool" : {
      "must" :      [],
      "should" :    [],
      "must_not" : [],
   }
}
```

must
> All of these clauses *must* match. The equivalent of AND.

must_not
> All of these clauses *must not* match. The equivalent of NOT.

should
> At least one of these clauses must match. The equivalent of OR.

And that's it! When you need multiple filters, simply place them into the different sections of the `bool` filter.

 Each section of the `bool` filter is optional (for example, you can have a `must` clause and nothing else), and each section can contain a single filter or an array of filters.

To replicate the preceding SQL example, we will take the two `term` filters that we used previously and place them inside the `should` clause of a `bool` filter, and add another clause to deal with the NOT condition:

```
GET /my_store/products/_search
{
    "query" : {
        "filtered" : {  ❶
            "filter" : {
                "bool" : {
                    "should" : [
                        { "term" : {"price" : 20}},  ❷
                        { "term" : {"productID" : "XHDK-A-1293-#fJ3"}}  ❷
                    ],
                    "must_not" : {
                        "term" : {"price" : 30}  ❸
                    }
                }
            }
        }
    }
}
```

❶ Note that we still need to use a filtered query to wrap everything.

❷ These two term filters are *children* of the bool filter, and since they are placed inside the should clause, at least one of them needs to match.

❸ If a product has a price of 30, it is automatically excluded because it matches a must_not clause.

Our search results return two hits, each document satisfying a different clause in the bool filter:

```
"hits" : [
    {
        "_id" :       "1",
        "_score" :  1.0,
        "_source" : {
            "price" :      10,
            "productID" : "XHDK-A-1293-#fJ3"  ❶
        }
    },
    {
        "_id" :       "2",
        "_score" :  1.0,
        "_source" : {
            "price" :      20,  ❷
            "productID" : "KDKE-B-9947-#kL5"
        }
    }
]
```

❶ Matches the term filter for productID = "XHDK-A-1293-#fJ3"

❷ Matches the `term` filter for `price = 20`

Nesting Boolean Filters

Even though `bool` is a compound filter and accepts children filters, it is important to understand that `bool` is just a filter itself. This means you can nest `bool` filters inside other `bool` filters, giving you the ability to make arbitrarily complex Boolean logic.

Given this SQL statement:

```
SELECT document
FROM    products
WHERE   productID        = "KDKE-B-9947-#kL5"
  OR (      productID = "JODL-X-1937-#pV7"
        AND price      = 30 )
```

We can translate it into a pair of nested `bool` filters:

```
GET /my_store/products/_search
{
    "query" : {
        "filtered" : {
            "filter" : {
                "bool" : {
                    "should" : [
                        { "term" : {"productID" : "KDKE-B-9947-#kL5"}},  ❶
                        { "bool" : {  ❶
                            "must" : [
                                { "term" : {"productID" : "JODL-X-1937-#pV7"}},  ❷
                                { "term" : {"price" : 30}}  ❷
                            ]
                        }}
                    ]
                }
            }
        }
    }
}
```

❶ Because the `term` and the `bool` are sibling clauses inside the first Boolean `should`, at least one of these filters must match for a document to be a hit.

❷ These two `term` clauses are siblings in a `must` clause, so they both have to match for a document to be returned as a hit.

The results show us two documents, one matching each of the `should` clauses:

```
"hits" : [
    {
        "_id" :      "2",
        "_score" : 1.0,
```

```
            "_source" : {
              "price" :      20,
              "productID" : "KDKE-B-9947-#kL5" ❶
            }
        },
        {
            "_id" :      "3",
            "_score" :  1.0,
            "_source" : {
              "price" :      30, ❷
              "productID" : "JODL-X-1937-#pV7" ❷
            }
        }
    ]
```

❶   This productID matches the term in the first bool.

❷   These two fields match the term filters in the nested bool.

This was a simple example, but it demonstrates how Boolean filters can be used as building blocks to construct complex logical conditions.

Finding Multiple Exact Values

The term filter is useful for finding a single value, but often you'll want to search for multiple values. What if you want to find documents that have a price of $20 or $30?

Rather than using multiple term filters, you can instead use a single terms filter (note the *s* at the end). The terms filter is simply the plural version of the singular term filter.

It looks nearly identical to a vanilla term too. Instead of specifying a single price, we are now specifying an array of values:

```
{
    "terms" : {
        "price" : [20, 30]
    }
}
```

And like the term filter, we will place it inside a filtered query to use it:

```
GET /my_store/products/_search
{
    "query" : {
        "filtered" : {
            "filter" : {
                "terms" : {  ❶
                    "price" : [20, 30]
                }
            }
```

```
            }
        }
    }
```

❶ The `terms` filter as seen previously, but placed inside the `filtered` query

The query will return the second, third, and fourth documents:

```
"hits" : [
    {
        "_id" :      "2",
        "_score" : 1.0,
        "_source" : {
          "price" :      20,
          "productID" : "KDKE-B-9947-#kL5"
        }
    },
    {
        "_id" :      "3",
        "_score" : 1.0,
        "_source" : {
          "price" :      30,
          "productID" : "JODL-X-1937-#pV7"
        }
    },
    {
        "_id":       "4",
        "_score": 1.0,
        "_source": {
            "price":      30,
            "productID": "QQPX-R-3956-#aD8"
        }
    }
]
```

Contains, but Does Not Equal

It is important to understand that `term` and `terms` are *contains* operations, not *equals*.
What does that mean?

If you have a term filter for `{ "term" : { "tags" : "search" } }`, it will match
both of the following documents:

```
{ "tags" : ["search"] }
{ "tags" : ["search", "open_source"] } ❶
```

❶ This document is returned, even though it has terms other than `search`.

Recall how the `term` filter works: it checks the inverted index for all documents that
contain a term, and then constructs a bitset. In our simple example, we have the following inverted index:

Token	DocIDs
open_source	2
search	1,2

When a `term` filter is executed for the token `search`, it goes straight to the corresponding entry in the inverted index and extracts the associated doc IDs. As you can see, both document 1 and document 2 contain the token in the inverted index. Therefore, they are both returned as a result.

 The nature of an inverted index also means that entire field equality is rather difficult to calculate. How would you determine whether a particular document contains *only* your request term? You would have to find the term in the inverted index, extract the document IDs, and then scan *every row in the inverted index*, looking for those IDs to see whether a doc has any other terms.

As you might imagine, that would be tremendously inefficient and expensive. For that reason, `term` and `terms` are *must contain* operations, not *must equal exactly*.

Equals Exactly

If you do want that behavior—entire field equality—the best way to accomplish it involves indexing a secondary field. In this field, you index the number of values that your field contains. Using our two previous documents, we now include a field that maintains the number of tags:

```
{ "tags" : ["search"], "tag_count" : 1 }
{ "tags" : ["search", "open_source"], "tag_count" : 2 }
```

Once you have the count information indexed, you can construct a `bool` filter that enforces the appropriate number of terms:

```
GET /my_index/my_type/_search
{
    "query": {
        "filtered" : {
            "filter" : {
                "bool" : {
                    "must" : [
                        { "term" : { "tags" : "search" } }, ❶
                        { "term" : { "tag_count" : 1 } } ❷
                    ]
                }
            }
        }
    }
```

```
        }
    }
```

❶ Find all documents that have the term search.

❷ But make sure the document has only one tag.

This query will now match only the document that has a single tag that is search, rather than any document that contains search.

Ranges

When dealing with numbers in this chapter, we have so far searched for only exact numbers. In practice, filtering on ranges is often more useful. For example, you might want to find all products with a price greater than $20 and less than $40.

In SQL terms, a range can be expressed as follows:

```
SELECT document
FROM   products
WHERE  price BETWEEN 20 AND 40
```

Elasticsearch has a range filter, which, unsurprisingly, allows you to filter ranges:

```
"range" : {
    "price" : {
        "gt" : 20,
        "lt" : 40
    }
}
```

The range filter supports both inclusive and exclusive ranges, through combinations of the following options:

- gt: > greater than
- lt: < less than
- gte: >= greater than or equal to
- lte: <= less than or equal to

```
GET /my_store/products/_search
{
    "query" : {
        "filtered" : {
            "filter" : {
                "range" : {
                    "price" : {
                        "gte" : 20,
                        "lt"  : 40
                    }
```

```
                    }
                }
            }
        }
    }
```

If you need an unbounded range (for example, just >20), omit one of the boundaries:

```
"range" : {
    "price" : {
        "gt" : 20
    }
}
```

Ranges on Dates

The range filter can be used on date fields too:

```
"range" : {
    "timestamp" : {
        "gt" : "2014-01-01 00:00:00",
        "lt" : "2014-01-07 00:00:00"
    }
}
```

When used on date fields, the range filter supports *date math* operations. For example, if we want to find all documents that have a timestamp sometime in the last hour:

```
"range" : {
    "timestamp" : {
        "gt" : "now-1h"
    }
}
```

This filter will now constantly find all documents with a timestamp greater than the current time minus 1 hour, making the filter a *sliding window* across your documents.

Date math can also be applied to actual dates, rather than a placeholder like now. Just add a double pipe (||) after the date and follow it with a date math expression:

```
"range" : {
    "timestamp" : {
        "gt" : "2014-01-01 00:00:00",
        "lt" : "2014-01-01 00:00:00||+1M"  ❶
    }
}
```

❶ Less than January 1, 2014 plus one month

Date math is *calendar aware*, so it knows the number of days in each month, days in a year, and so forth. More details about working with dates can be found in the date format reference documentation (*http://www.elasticsearch.org/guide/en/elasticsearch/reference/current/mapping-date-format.html*).

Ranges on Strings

The `range` filter can also operate on string fields. String ranges are calculated *lexicographically* or alphabetically. For example, these values are sorted in lexicographic order:

- 5, 50, 6, B, C, a, ab, abb, abc, b

> Terms in the inverted index are sorted in lexicographical order, which is why string ranges use this order.

If we want a range from a up to but not including b, we can use the same `range` filter syntax:

```
"range" : {
    "title" : {
        "gte" : "a",
        "lt" :  "b"
    }
}
```

Be Careful of Cardinality

Numeric and date fields are indexed in such a way that ranges are efficient to calculate. This is not the case for string fields, however. To perform a range on a string field, Elasticsearch is effectively performing a `term` filter for every term that falls in the range. This is much slower than a date or numeric range.

String ranges are fine on a field with *low cardinality*—a small number of unique terms. But the more unique terms you have, the slower the string range will be.

Dealing with Null Values

Think back to our earlier example, where documents have a field named `tags`. This is a multivalue field. A document may have one tag, many tags, or potentially no tags at all. If a field has no values, how is it stored in an inverted index?

That's a trick question, because the answer is, it isn't stored at all. Let's look at that inverted index from the previous section:

Token	DocIDs
open_source	2
search	1,2

How would you store a field that doesn't exist in that data structure? You can't! An inverted index is simply a list of tokens and the documents that contain them. If a field doesn't exist, it doesn't hold any tokens, which means it won't be represented in an inverted index data structure.

Ultimately, this means that a null, [] (an empty array), and [null] are all equivalent. They simply don't exist in the inverted index!

Obviously, the world is not simple, and data is often missing fields, or contains explicit nulls or empty arrays. To deal with these situations, Elasticsearch has a few tools to work with null or missing values.

exists Filter

The first tool in your arsenal is the exists filter. This filter will return documents that have any value in the specified field. Let's use the tagging example and index some example documents:

```
POST /my_index/posts/_bulk
{ "index": { "_id": "1"             }}
{ "tags" : ["search"]               } ❶
{ "index": { "_id": "2"             }}
{ "tags" : ["search", "open_source"] } ❷
{ "index": { "_id": "3"             }}
{ "other_field" : "some data"       } ❸
{ "index": { "_id": "4"             }}
{ "tags" : null                     } ❹
{ "index": { "_id": "5"             }}
{ "tags" : ["search", null]         } ❺
```

❶ The tags field has one value.

❷ The tags field has two values.

❸ The tags field is missing altogether.

❹ The tags field is set to null.

❺ The tags field has one value and a null.

The resulting inverted index for our tags field will look like this:

Token	DocIDs
open_source	2
search	1,2,5

Our objective is to find all documents where a tag is set. We don't care what the tag is, so long as it exists within the document. In SQL parlance, we would use an IS NOT NULL query:

```
SELECT tags
FROM   posts
WHERE  tags IS NOT NULL
```

In Elasticsearch, we use the exists filter:

```
GET /my_index/posts/_search
{
    "query" : {
        "filtered" : {
            "filter" : {
                "exists" : { "field" : "tags" }
            }
        }
    }
}
```

Our query returns three documents:

```
"hits" : [
    {
      "_id" :      "1",
      "_score" :  1.0,
      "_source" : { "tags" : ["search"] }
    },
    {
      "_id" :      "5",
      "_score" :  1.0,
      "_source" : { "tags" : ["search", null] } ❶
    },
    {
      "_id" :      "2",
      "_score" :  1.0,
      "_source" : { "tags" : ["search", "open source"] }
    }
]
```

❶ Document 5 is returned even though it contains a null value. The field exists because a real-value tag was indexed, so the null had no impact on the filter.

The results are easy to understand. Any document that has terms in the tags field was returned as a hit. The only two documents that were excluded were documents 3 and 4.

missing Filter

The missing filter is essentially the inverse of exists: it returns documents where there is *no* value for a particular field, much like this SQL:

```
SELECT tags
FROM   posts
WHERE  tags IS  NULL
```

Let's swap the exists filter for a missing filter from our previous example:

```
GET /my_index/posts/_search
{
    "query" : {
        "filtered" : {
            "filter": {
                "missing" : { "field" : "tags" }
            }
        }
    }
}
```

And, as you would expect, we get back the two docs that have no real values in the tags field—documents 3 and 4:

```
"hits" : [
    {
      "_id" :        "3",
      "_score" :  1.0,
      "_source" : { "other_field" : "some data" }
    },
    {
      "_id" :        "4",
      "_score" :  1.0,
      "_source" : { "tags" : null }
    }
]
```

When null Means null

Sometimes you need to be able to distinguish between a field that doesn't have a value, and a field that has been explicitly set to null. With the default behavior that we saw previously, this is impossible; the data is lost. Luckily, there is an option that we can set that replaces explicit null values with a *placeholder* value of our choosing.

When specifying the mapping for a string, numeric, Boolean, or date field, you can also set a `null_value` that will be used whenever an explicit `null` value is encountered. A field without a value will still be excluded from the inverted index.

When choosing a suitable `null_value`, ensure the following:

- It matches the field's type. You can't use a string `null_value` in a field of type date.
- It is different from the normal values that the field may contain, to avoid confusing real values with `null` values.

exists/missing on Objects

The `exists` and `missing` filters also work on inner objects, not just core types. With the following document

```
{
    "name" : {
        "first" : "John",
        "last" :  "Smith"
    }
}
```

you can check for the existence of `name.first` and `name.last` but also just `name`. However, in "Types and Mappings" on page 139, we said that an object like the preceding one is flattened internally into a simple field-value structure, much like this:

```
{
    "name.first" : "John",
    "name.last"  : "Smith"
}
```

So how can we use an `exists` or `missing` filter on the `name` field, which doesn't really exist in the inverted index?

The reason that it works is that a filter like

```
{
    "exists" : { "field" : "name" }
}
```

is really executed as

```
{
    "bool": {
        "should": [
            { "exists": { "field": { "name.first" }}},
            { "exists": { "field": { "name.last"  }}}
        ]
```

```
        }
    }
```

That also means that if `first` and `last` were both empty, the `name` namespace would not exist.

All About Caching

Earlier in this chapter ("Internal Filter Operation" on page 180), we briefly discussed how filters are calculated. At their heart is a bitset representing which documents match the filter. Elasticsearch aggressively caches these bitsets for later use. Once cached, these bitsets can be reused *wherever* the same filter is used, without having to reevaluate the entire filter again.

These cached bitsets are "smart": they are updated incrementally. As you index new documents, only those new documents need to be added to the existing bitsets, rather than having to recompute the entire cached filter over and over. Filters are real-time like the rest of the system; you don't need to worry about cache expiry.

Independent Filter Caching

Each filter is calculated and cached independently, regardless of where it is used. If two different queries use the same filter, the same filter bitset will be reused. Likewise, if a single query uses the same filter in multiple places, only one bitset is calculated and then reused.

Let's look at this example query, which looks for emails that are either of the following:

- In the inbox and have not been read
- *Not* in the inbox but have been marked as important

```
"bool": {
    "should": [
        { "bool": {
            "must": [
                { "term": { "folder": "inbox" }}, ❶
                { "term": { "read": false }}
            ]
        }},
        { "bool": {
            "must_not": {
                "term": { "folder": "inbox" } ❶
            },
            "must": {
                "term": { "important": true }
            }
        }}
    ]
}
```

```
    ]
  }
```

❶ These two filters are identical and will use the same bitset.

Even though one of the inbox clauses is a must clause and the other is a must_not clause, the two clauses themselves are identical. This means that the bitset is calculated once for the first clause that is executed, and then the cached bitset is used for the other clause. By the time this query is run a second time, the inbox filter is already cached and so both clauses will use the cached bitset.

This ties in nicely with the composability of the query DSL. It is easy to move filters around, or reuse the same filter in multiple places within the same query. This isn't just convenient to the developer—it has direct performance benefits.

Controlling Caching

Most *leaf filters*—those dealing directly with fields like the term filter—are cached, while compound filters, like the bool filter, are not.

 Leaf filters have to consult the inverted index on disk, so it makes sense to cache them. Compound filters, on the other hand, use fast bit logic to combine the bitsets resulting from their inner clauses, so it is efficient to recalculate them every time.

Certain leaf filters, however, are not cached by default, because it doesn't make sense to do so:

Script filters
> The results from script filters (*http://www.elasticsearch.org/guide/en/elastic search/guide/current/filter-caching.html#_controlling_caching*) cannot be cached because the meaning of the script is opaque to Elasticsearch.

Geo-filters
> The geolocation filters, which we cover in more detail in Part V, are usually used to filter results based on the geolocation of a specific user. Since each user has a unique geolocation, it is unlikely that geo-filters will be reused, so it makes no sense to cache them.

Date ranges
> Date ranges that use the now function (for example "now-1h"), result in values accurate to the millisecond. Every time the filter is run, now returns a new time. Older filters will never be reused, so caching is disabled by default. However, when using now with rounding (for example, now/d rounds to the nearest day), caching is enabled by default.

Sometimes the default caching strategy is not correct. Perhaps you have a complicated `bool` expression that is reused several times in the same query. Or you have a filter on a `date` field that will never be reused. The default caching strategy can be overridden on almost any filter by setting the _cache flag:

```
{
    "range" : {
        "timestamp" : {
            "gt" : "2014-01-02 16:15:14" ❶
        },
        "_cache": false ❷
    }
}
```

❶ It is unlikely that we will reuse this exact timestamp.

❷ Disable caching of this filter.

Later chapters provide examples of when it can make sense to override the default caching strategy.

Filter Order

The order of filters in a `bool` clause is important for performance. More-specific filters should be placed before less-specific filters in order to exclude as many documents as possible, as early as possible.

If Clause A could match 10 million documents, and Clause B could match only 100 documents, then Clause B should be placed before Clause A.

Cached filters are very fast, so they should be placed before filters that are not cacheable. Imagine that we have an index that contains one month's worth of log events. However, we're mostly interested only in log events from the previous hour:

```
GET /logs/2014-01/_search
{
    "query" : {
        "filtered" : {
            "filter" : {
                "range" : {
                    "timestamp" : {
                        "gt" : "now-1h"
                    }
                }
            }
        }
    }
}
```

This filter is not cached because it uses the now function, the value of which changes every millisecond. That means that we have to examine one month's worth of log events every time we run this query!

We could make this much more efficient by combining it with a cached filter: we can exclude most of the month's data by adding a filter that uses a fixed point in time, such as midnight last night:

```
"bool": {
    "must": [
        { "range" : {
            "timestamp" : {
                "gt" : "now-1h/d" ❶
            }
        }},
        { "range" : {
            "timestamp" : {
                "gt" : "now-1h" ❷
            }
        }}
    ]
}
```

❶ This filter is cached because it uses now rounded to midnight.

❷ This filter is not cached because it uses now *without* rounding.

The now-1h/d clause rounds to the previous midnight and so excludes all documents created before today. The resulting bitset is cached because now is used with rounding, which means that it is executed only once a day, when the value for *midnight-last-night* changes. The now-1h clause isn't cached because now produces a time accurate to the nearest millisecond. However, thanks to the first filter, this second filter need only check documents that have been created since midnight.

The order of these clauses is important. This approach works only because the *since-midnight* clause comes before the *last-hour* clause. If they were the other way around, then the *last-hour* clause would need to examine all documents in the index, instead of just documents created since midnight.

CHAPTER 13

Full-Text Search

Now that we have covered the simple case of searching for structured data, it is time to explore *full-text search*: how to search within full-text fields in order to find the most relevant documents.

The two most important aspects of full-text search are as follows:

Relevance
> The ability to rank results by how relevant they are to the given query, whether relevance is calculated using TF/IDF (see "What Is Relevance?" on page 117), proximity to a geolocation, fuzzy similarity, or some other algorithm.

Analysis
> The process of converting a block of text into distinct, normalized tokens (see "Analysis and Analyzers" on page 86) in order to (a) create an inverted index and (b) query the inverted index.

As soon as we talk about either relevance or analysis, we are in the territory of queries, rather than filters.

Term-Based Versus Full-Text

While all queries perform some sort of relevance calculation, not all queries have an analysis phase. Besides specialized queries like the `bool` or `function_score` queries, which don't operate on text at all, textual queries can be broken down into two families:

Term-based queries
> Queries like the `term` or `fuzzy` queries are low-level queries that have no analysis phase. They operate on a single term. A `term` query for the term `Foo` looks for

that *exact term* in the inverted index and calculates the TF/IDF relevance `_score` for each document that contains the term.

It is important to remember that the `term` query looks in the inverted index for the exact term only; it won't match any variants like `foo` or `FOO`. It doesn't matter how the term came to be in the index, just that it is. If you were to index `["Foo","Bar"]` into an exact value `not_analyzed` field, or `Foo Bar` into an analyzed field with the `whitespace` analyzer, both would result in having the two terms `Foo` and `Bar` in the inverted index.

Full-text queries

Queries like the `match` or `query_string` queries are high-level queries that understand the mapping of a field:

- If you use them to query a `date` or `integer` field, they will treat the query string as a date or integer, respectively.

- If you query an exact value (`not_analyzed`) string field, they will treat the whole query string as a single term.

- But if you query a full-text (`analyzed`) field, they will first pass the query string through the appropriate analyzer to produce the list of terms to be queried.

Once the query has assembled a list of terms, it executes the appropriate low-level query for each of these terms, and then combines their results to produce the final relevance score for each document.

We will discuss this process in more detail in the following chapters.

You seldom need to use the term-based queries directly. Usually you want to query full text, not individual terms, and this is easier to do with the high-level full-text queries (which end up using term-based queries internally).

If you do find yourself wanting to use a query on an exact value not_analyzed field, think about whether you really want a query or a filter.

Single-term queries usually represent binary yes/no questions and are almost always better expressed as a filter, so that they can benefit from filter caching:

```
GET /_search
{
    "query": {
        "filtered": {
            "filter": {
                "term": { "gender": "female" }
            }
        }
    }
}
```

The match Query

The match query is the *go-to* query—the first query that you should reach for whenever you need to query any field. It is a high-level *full-text query*, meaning that it knows how to deal with both full-text fields and exact-value fields.

That said, the main use case for the match query is for full-text search. So let's take a look at how full-text search works with a simple example.

Index Some Data

First, we'll create a new index and index some documents using the bulk API:

```
DELETE /my_index ❶

PUT /my_index
{ "settings": { "number_of_shards": 1 }} ❷

POST /my_index/my_type/_bulk
{ "index": { "_id": 1 }}
{ "title": "The quick brown fox" }
{ "index": { "_id": 2 }}
{ "title": "The quick brown fox jumps over the lazy dog" }
{ "index": { "_id": 3 }}
{ "title": "The quick brown fox jumps over the quick dog" }
{ "index": { "_id": 4 }}
{ "title": "Brown fox brown dog" }
```

❶   Delete the index in case it already exists.

❷ Later, in "Relevance Is Broken!" on page 216, we explain why we created this index with only one primary shard.

A Single-Word Query

Our first example explains what happens when we use the match query to search within a full-text field for a single word:

```
GET /my_index/my_type/_search
{
    "query": {
        "match": {
            "title": "QUICK!"
        }
    }
}
```

Elasticsearch executes the preceding match query as follows:

1. *Check the field type.*

   The title field is a full-text (analyzed) string field, which means that the query string should be analyzed too.

2. *Analyze the query string.*

   The query string QUICK! is passed through the standard analyzer, which results in the single term quick. Because we have a just a single term, the match query can be executed as a single low-level term query.

3. *Find matching docs.*

   The term query looks up quick in the inverted index and retrieves the list of documents that contain that term—in this case, documents 1, 2, and 3.

4. *Score each doc.*

   The term query calculates the relevance _score for each matching document, by combining the term frequency (how often quick appears in the title field of each document), with the inverse document frequency (how often quick appears in the title field in *all* documents in the index), and the length of each field (shorter fields are considered more relevant). See "What Is Relevance?" on page 117.

This process gives us the following (abbreviated) results:

```
"hits": [
    {
        "_id":      "1",
        "_score":   0.5, ❶
        "_source": {
```

```
            "title": "The quick brown fox"
        }
    },
    {
        "_id":      "3",
        "_score":   0.44194174, ❷
        "_source": {
            "title": "The quick brown fox jumps over the quick dog"
        }
    },
    {
        "_id":      "2",
        "_score":   0.3125, ❷
        "_source": {
            "title": "The quick brown fox jumps over the lazy dog"
        }
    }
]
```

❶ Document 1 is most relevant because its `title` field is short, which means that quick represents a large portion of its content.

❷ Document 3 is more relevant than document 2 because quick appears twice.

Multiword Queries

If we could search for only one word at a time, full-text search would be pretty inflexible. Fortunately, the `match` query makes multiword queries just as simple:

```
GET /my_index/my_type/_search
{
    "query": {
        "match": {
            "title": "BROWN DOG!"
        }
    }
}
```

The preceding query returns all four documents in the results list:

```
{
  "hits": [
    {
        "_id":      "4",
        "_score":   0.73185337, ❶
        "_source": {
            "title": "Brown fox brown dog"
        }
    },
    {
        "_id":      "2",
```

```
      "_score":    0.47486103,  ❷
      "_source": {
         "title": "The quick brown fox jumps over the lazy dog"
      }
   },
   {
      "_id":       "3",
      "_score":    0.47486103,  ❷
      "_source": {
         "title": "The quick brown fox jumps over the quick dog"
      }
   },
   {
      "_id":       "1",
      "_score":    0.11914785,  ❸
      "_source": {
         "title": "The quick brown fox"
      }
   }
  ]
}
```

❶ Document 4 is the most relevant because it contains "brown" twice and "dog" once.

❷ Documents 2 and 3 both contain brown and dog once each, and the title field is the same length in both docs, so they have the same score.

❸ Document 1 matches even though it contains only brown, not dog.

Because the match query has to look for two terms—["brown","dog"]—internally it has to execute two term queries and combine their individual results into the overall result. To do this, it wraps the two term queries in a bool query, which we examine in detail in "Combining Queries" on page 206.

The important thing to take away from this is that any document whose title field contains *at least one of the specified terms* will match the query. The more terms that match, the more relevant the document.

Improving Precision

Matching any document that contains *any* of the query terms may result in a long tail of seemingly irrelevant results. It's a shotgun approach to search. Perhaps we want to show only documents that contain *all* of the query terms. In other words, instead of brown OR dog, we want to return only documents that match brown AND dog.

The match query accepts an operator parameter that defaults to or. You can change it to and to require that all specified terms must match:

```
GET /my_index/my_type/_search
{
    "query": {
        "match": {
            "title": {              ❶
                "query":    "BROWN DOG!",
                "operator": "and"
            }
        }
    }
}
```

❶ The structure of the `match` query has to change slightly in order to accommodate
   the `operator` parameter.

This query would exclude document 1, which contains only one of the two terms.

Controlling Precision

The choice between *all* and *any* is a bit too black-or-white. What if the user specified
five query terms, and a document contains only four of them? Setting `operator` to
and would exclude this document.

Sometimes that is exactly what you want, but for most full-text search use cases, you
want to include documents that may be relevant but exclude those that are unlikely to
be relevant. In other words, we need something in-between.

The `match` query supports the `minimum_should_match` parameter, which allows you
to specify the number of terms that must match for a document to be considered relevant. While you can specify an absolute number of terms, it usually makes sense to
specify a percentage instead, as you have no control over the number of words the
user may enter:

```
GET /my_index/my_type/_search
{
  "query": {
    "match": {
      "title": {
        "query":                "quick brown dog",
        "minimum_should_match": "75%"
      }
    }
  }
}
```

When specified as a percentage, `minimum_should_match` does the right thing: in the
preceding example with three terms, 75% would be rounded down to 66.6%, or two
out of the three terms. No matter what you set it to, at least one term must match for
a document to be considered a match.

The `minimum_should_match` parameter is flexible, and different rules can be applied depending on the number of terms the user enters. For the full documentation see the `minimum_should_match` reference documentation (*http://www.elasticsearch.org/guide/en/ elasticsearch/guide/current/match-multi-word.html#match-precision*).

To fully understand how the `match` query handles multiword queries, we need to look at how to combine multiple queries with the `bool` query.

Combining Queries

In "Combining Filters" on page 181 we discussed how to, use the `bool` filter to combine multiple filter clauses with `and`, `or`, and `not` logic. In query land, the `bool` query does a similar job but with one important difference.

Filters make a binary decision: should this document be included in the results list or not? Queries, however, are more subtle. They decide not only whether to include a document, but also how *relevant* that document is.

Like the filter equivalent, the `bool` query accepts multiple query clauses under the `must`, `must_not`, and `should` parameters. For instance:

```
GET /my_index/my_type/_search
{
  "query": {
    "bool": {
      "must":     { "match": { "title": "quick" }},
      "must_not": { "match": { "title": "lazy"  }},
      "should": [
                  { "match": { "title": "brown" }},
                  { "match": { "title": "dog"   }}
      ]
    }
  }
}
```

The results from the preceding query include any document whose `title` field contains the term `quick`, except for those that also contain `lazy`. So far, this is pretty similar to how the `bool` filter works.

The difference comes in with the two `should` clauses, which say that: a document is *not required* to contain either `brown` or `dog`, but if it does, then it should be considered *more relevant*:

```
{
  "hits": [
    {
```

```
            "_id":       "3",
            "_score":    0.70134366, ❶
            "_source": {
                "title": "The quick brown fox jumps over the quick dog"
            }
        },
        {
            "_id":       "1",
            "_score":    0.3312608,
            "_source": {
                "title": "The quick brown fox"
            }
        }
    ]
}
```

❶ Document 3 scores higher because it contains both brown and dog.

Score Calculation

The bool query calculates the relevance _score for each document by adding together the _score from all of the matching must and should clauses, and then dividing by the total number of must and should clauses.

The must_not clauses do not affect the score; their only purpose is to exclude documents that might otherwise have been included.

Controlling Precision

All the must clauses must match, and all the must_not clauses must not match, but how many should clauses should match? By default, none of the should clauses are required to match, with one exception: if there are no must clauses, then at least one should clause must match.

Just as we can control the precision of the match query, we can control how many should clauses need to match by using the minimum_should_match parameter, either as an absolute number or as a percentage:

```
GET /my_index/my_type/_search
{
  "query": {
    "bool": {
      "should": [
        { "match": { "title": "brown" }},
        { "match": { "title": "fox"   }},
        { "match": { "title": "dog"   }}
      ],
      "minimum_should_match": 2 ❶
    }
```

```
        }
    }
```

❶   This could also be expressed as a percentage.

The results would include only documents whose title field contains "brown" AND
"fox", "brown" AND "dog", or "fox" AND "dog". If a document contains all three, it
would be considered more relevant than those that contain just two of the three.

How match Uses bool

By now, you have probably realized that multiword match queries simply wrap the
generated term queries in a bool query. With the default or operator, each term query
is added as a should clause, so at least one clause must match. These two queries are
equivalent:

```
{
    "match": { "title": "brown fox"}
}

{
  "bool": {
    "should": [
      { "term": { "title": "brown" }},
      { "term": { "title": "fox"   }}
    ]
  }
}
```

With the and operator, all the term queries are added as must clauses, so *all* clauses
must match. These two queries are equivalent:

```
{
    "match": {
        "title": {
            "query":     "brown fox",
            "operator": "and"
        }
    }
}

{
  "bool": {
    "must": [
      { "term": { "title": "brown" }},
      { "term": { "title": "fox"   }}
    ]
  }
}
```

And if the `minimum_should_match` parameter is specified, it is passed directly through to the `bool` query, making these two queries equivalent:

```
{
    "match": {
        "title": {
            "query":                 "quick brown fox",
            "minimum_should_match": "75%"
        }
    }
}
{
  "bool": {
    "should": [
      { "term": { "title": "brown" }},
      { "term": { "title": "fox"   }},
      { "term": { "title": "quick" }}
    ],
    "minimum_should_match": 2 ❶
  }
}
```

❶ Because there are only three clauses, the `minimum_should_match` value of 75% in the `match` query is rounded down to 2. At least two out of the three `should` clauses must match.

Of course, we would normally write these types of queries by using the `match` query, but understanding how the `match` query works internally lets you take control of the process when you need to. Some things can't be done with a single `match` query, such as give more weight to some query terms than to others. We will look at an example of this in the next section.

Boosting Query Clauses

Of course, the `bool` query isn't restricted to combining simple one-word `match` queries. It can combine any other query, including other `bool` queries. It is commonly used to fine-tune the relevance `_score` for each document by combining the scores from several distinct queries.

Imagine that we want to search for documents about "full-text search," but we want to give more *weight* to documents that also mention "Elasticsearch" or "Lucene." By *more weight*, we mean that documents mentioning "Elasticsearch" or "Lucene" will receive a higher relevance `_score` than those that don't, which means that they will appear higher in the list of results.

A simple bool *query* allows us to write this fairly complex logic as follows:

```
GET /_search
{
    "query": {
        "bool": {
            "must": {
                "match": {
                    "content": { ❶
                        "query":    "full text search",
                        "operator": "and"
                    }
                }
            },
            "should": [ ❷
                { "match": { "content": "Elasticsearch" }},
                { "match": { "content": "Lucene"        }}
            ]
        }
    }
}
```

❶ The content field must contain all of the words full, text, and search.

❷ If the content field also contains Elasticsearch or Lucene, the document will receive a higher _score.

The more should clauses that match, the more relevant the document. So far, so good.

But what if we want to give more weight to the docs that contain Lucene and even more weight to the docs containing Elasticsearch?

We can control the relative weight of any query clause by specifying a boost value, which defaults to 1. A boost value greater than 1 increases the relative weight of that clause. So we could rewrite the preceding query as follows:

```
GET /_search
{
    "query": {
        "bool": {
            "must": {
                "match": { ❶
                    "content": {
                        "query":    "full text search",
                        "operator": "and"
                    }
                }
            },
            "should": [
                { "match": {
                    "content": {
                        "query": "Elasticsearch",
```

```
                    "boost": 3 ❷
                }
            }},
            { "match": {
                "content": {
                    "query": "Lucene",
                    "boost": 2 ❸
                }
            }}
        ]
    }
  }
}
```

❶ These clauses use the default boost of 1.

❷ This clause is the most important, as it has the highest boost.

❸ This clause is more important than the default, but not as important as the Elas
    ticsearch clause.

 The boost parameter is used to increase the relative weight of a
clause (with a boost greater than 1) or decrease the relative weight
(with a boost between 0 and 1), but the increase or decrease is not
linear. In other words, a boost of 2 does not result in double the
_score.

Instead, the new _score is *normalized* after the boost is applied.
Each type of query has its own normalization algorithm, and the
details are beyond the scope of this book. Suffice to say that a
higher boost value results in a higher _score.

If you are implementing your own scoring model not based on
TF/IDF and you need more control over the boosting process, you
can use the function_score query to manipulate a document's
boost without the normalization step.

We present other ways of combining queries in the next chapter, Chapter 14. But first,
let's take a look at the other important feature of queries: text analysis.

Controlling Analysis

Queries can find only terms that actually exist in the inverted index, so it is important
to ensure that the same analysis process is applied both to the document at index
time, and to the query string at search time so that the terms in the query match the
terms in the inverted index.

Although we say *document*, analyzers are determined per field. Each field can have a different analyzer, either by configuring a specific analyzer for that field or by falling back on the type, index, or node defaults. At index time, a field's value is analyzed by using the configured or default analyzer for that field.

For instance, let's add a new field to my_index:

```
PUT /my_index/_mapping/my_type
{
    "my_type": {
        "properties": {
            "english_title": {
                "type":     "string",
                "analyzer": "english"
            }
        }
    }
}
```

Now we can compare how values in the english_title field and the title field are analyzed at index time by using the analyze API to analyze the word Foxes:

```
GET /my_index/_analyze?field=my_type.title        ❶
Foxes

GET /my_index/_analyze?field=my_type.english_title ❷
Foxes
```

❶ Field title, which uses the default standard analyzer, will return the term foxes.

❷ Field english_title, which uses the english analyzer, will return the term fox.

This means that, were we to run a low-level term query for the exact term fox, the english_title field would match but the title field would not.

High-level queries like the match query understand field mappings and can apply the correct analyzer for each field being queried. We can see this in action with the validate-query API:

```
GET /my_index/my_type/_validate/query?explain
{
    "query": {
        "bool": {
            "should": [
                { "match": { "title":         "Foxes"}},
                { "match": { "english_title": "Foxes"}}
            ]
        }
    }
}
```

which returns this `explanation`:

```
(title:foxes english_title:fox)
```

The `match` query uses the appropriate analyzer for each field to ensure that it looks for each term in the correct format for that field.

Default Analyzers

While we can specify an analyzer at the field level, how do we determine which analyzer is used for a field if none is specified at the field level?

Analyzers can be specified at several levels. Elasticsearch works through each level until it finds an analyzer that it can use. At index time, the order is as follows:

- The `analyzer` defined in the field mapping, else
- *The analyzer defined in the `_analyzer` field of the document, else*
- The default `analyzer` for the `type`, which defaults to
- The analyzer named `default` in the index settings, which defaults to
- The analyzer named `default` at node level, which defaults to
- The `standard` analyzer

At search time, the sequence is slightly different:

- *The `analyzer` defined in the query itself, else*
- The `analyzer` defined in the field mapping, else
- The default `analyzer` for the `type`, which defaults to
- The analyzer named `default` in the index settings, which defaults to
- The analyzer named `default` at node level, which defaults to
- The `standard` analyzer

The two lines in italics in the preceding lists highlight differences in the index time sequence and the search time sequence. The `_analyzer` field allows you to specify a default analyzer for each document (for example, `english`, `french`, `spanish`) while the `analyzer` parameter in the query specifies which analyzer to use on the query string. However, this is not the best way to handle multiple languages in a single index because of the pitfalls highlighted in Part III.

Occasionally, it makes sense to use a different analyzer at index and search time. For instance, at index time we may want to index synonyms (for example, for every occurrence of `quick`, we also index `fast`, `rapid`, and `speedy`). But at search time, we don't need to search for all of these synonyms. Instead we can just look up the single word that the user has entered, be it `quick`, `fast`, `rapid`, or `speedy`.

To enable this distinction, Elasticsearch also supports the `index_analyzer` and `search_analyzer` parameters, and analyzers named `default_index` and `default_search`.

Taking these extra parameters into account, the *full* sequence at index time really looks like this:

- The `index_analyzer` defined in the field mapping, else
- The `analyzer` defined in the field mapping, else
- The analyzer defined in the `_analyzer` field of the document, else
- The default `index_analyzer` for the `type`, which defaults to
- The default `analyzer` for the `type`, which defaults to
- The analyzer named `default_index` in the index settings, which defaults to
- The analyzer named `default` in the index settings, which defaults to
- The analyzer named `default_index` at node level, which defaults to
- The analyzer named `default` at node level, which defaults to
- The `standard` analyzer

And at search time:

- The `analyzer` defined in the query itself, else
- The `search_analyzer` defined in the field mapping, else
- The `analyzer` defined in the field mapping, else
- The default `search_analyzer` for the `type`, which defaults to
- The default `analyzer` for the `type`, which defaults to
- The analyzer named `default_search` in the index settings, which defaults to
- The analyzer named `default` in the index settings, which defaults to
- The analyzer named `default_search` at node level, which defaults to
- The analyzer named `default` at node level, which defaults to
- The `standard` analyzer

Configuring Analyzers in Practice

The sheer number of places where you can specify an analyzer is quite overwhelming. In practice, though, it is pretty simple.

Use index settings, not config files

The first thing to remember is that, even though you may start out using Elasticsearch for a single purpose or a single application such as logging, chances are that you will find more use cases and end up running several distinct applications on the same cluster. Each index needs to be independent and independently configurable. You don't want to set defaults for one use case, only to have to override them for another use case later.

This rules out configuring analyzers at the node level. Additionally, configuring analyzers at the node level requires changing the config file on every node and restarting every node, which becomes a maintenance nightmare. It's a much better idea to keep Elasticsearch running and to manage settings only via the API.

Keep it simple

Most of the time, you will know what fields your documents will contain ahead of time. The simplest approach is to set the analyzer for each full-text field when you create your index or add type mappings. While this approach is slightly more verbose, it enables you to easily see which analyzer is being applied to each field.

Typically, most of your string fields will be exact-value `not_analyzed` fields such as tags or enums, plus a handful of full-text fields that will use some default analyzer like `standard` or `english` or some other language. Then you may have one or two fields that need custom analysis: perhaps the `title` field needs to be indexed in a way that supports *find-as-you-type*.

You can set the `default` analyzer in the index to the analyzer you want to use for almost all full-text fields, and just configure the specialized analyzer on the one or two fields that need it. If, in your model, you need a different default analyzer per type, then use the type level `analyzer` setting instead.

> A common work flow for time based data like logging is to create a new index per day on the fly by just indexing into it. While this work flow prevents you from creating your index up front, you can still use index templates (*http://bit.ly/1ygczeq*) to specify the settings and mappings that a new index should have.

Relevance Is Broken!

Before we move on to discussing more-complex queries in Chapter 14, let's make a quick detour to explain why we created our test index with just one primary shard.

Every now and again a new user opens an issue claiming that sorting by relevance is broken and offering a short reproduction: the user indexes a few documents, runs a simple query, and finds apparently less-relevant results appearing above more-relevant results.

To understand why this happens, let's imagine that we create an index with two primary shards and we index ten documents, six of which contain the word foo. It may happen that shard 1 contains three of the foo documents and shard 2 contains the other three. In other words, our documents are well distributed.

In "What Is Relevance?" on page 117, we described the default similarity algorithm used in Elasticsearch, called *term frequency / inverse document frequency* or TF/IDF. Term frequency counts the number of times a term appears within the field we are querying in the current document. The more times it appears, the more relevant is this document. The *inverse document frequency* takes into account how often a term appears as a percentage of *all the documents in the index*. The more frequently the term appears, the less weight it has.

However, for performance reasons, Elasticsearch doesn't calculate the IDF across all documents in the index. Instead, each shard calculates a local IDF for the documents contained *in that shard*.

Because our documents are well distributed, the IDF for both shards will be the same. Now imagine instead that five of the foo documents are on shard 1, and the sixth document is on shard 2. In this scenario, the term foo is very common on one shard (and so of little importance), but rare on the other shard (and so much more important). These differences in IDF can produce incorrect results.

In practice, this is not a problem. The differences between local and global IDF diminish the more documents that you add to the index. With real-world volumes of data, the local IDFs soon even out. The problem is not that relevance is broken but that there is too little data.

For testing purposes, there are two ways we can work around this issue. The first is to create an index with one primary shard, as we did in the section introducing the match query. If you have only one shard, then the local IDF *is* the global IDF.

The second workaround is to add ?search_type=dfs_query_then_fetch to your search requests. The dfs stands for *Distributed Frequency Search*, and it tells Elasticsearch to first retrieve the local IDF from each shard in order to calculate the global IDF across the whole index.

Don't use `dfs_query_then_fetch` in production. It really isn't required. Just having enough data will ensure that your term frequencies are well distributed. There is no reason to add this extra DFS step to every query that you run.

CHAPTER 14

Multifield Search

Queries are seldom simple one-clause `match` queries. We frequently need to search for the same or different query strings in one or more fields, which means that we need to be able to combine multiple query clauses and their relevance scores in a way that makes sense.

Perhaps we're looking for a book called *War and Peace* by an author called Leo Tolstoy. Perhaps we're searching the Elasticsearch documentation for "minimum should match," which might be in the title or the body of a page. Or perhaps we're searching for users with first name John and last name Smith.

In this chapter, we present the available tools for constructing multiclause searches and how to figure out which solution you should apply to your particular use case.

Multiple Query Strings

The simplest multifield query to deal with is the one where we can *map search terms to specific fields*. If we know that *War and Peace* is the title, and Leo Tolstoy is the author, it is easy to write each of these conditions as a `match` clause and to combine them with a `bool` query:

```
GET /_search
{
  "query": {
    "bool": {
      "should": [
        { "match": { "title":  "War and Peace" }},
        { "match": { "author": "Leo Tolstoy"   }}
      ]
    }
  }
}
```

The `bool` query takes a *more-matches-is-better* approach, so the score from each `match` clause will be added together to provide the final `_score` for each document. Documents that match both clauses will score higher than documents that match just one clause.

Of course, you're not restricted to using just `match` clauses: the `bool` query can wrap any other query type, including other `bool` queries. We could add a clause to specify that we prefer to see versions of the book that have been translated by specific translators:

```
GET /_search
{
  "query": {
    "bool": {
      "should": [
        { "match": { "title":  "War and Peace" }},
        { "match": { "author": "Leo Tolstoy"   }},
        { "bool":  {
          "should": [
            { "match": { "translator": "Constance Garnett" }},
            { "match": { "translator": "Louise Maude"      }}
          ]
        }}
      ]
    }
  }
}
```

Why did we put the translator clauses inside a separate `bool` query? All four `match` queries are `should` clauses, so why didn't we just put the translator clauses at the same level as the title and author clauses?

The answer lies in how the score is calculated. The `bool` query runs each `match` query, adds their scores together, then multiplies by the number of matching clauses, and divides by the total number of clauses. Each clause at the same level has the same weight. In the preceding query, the `bool` query containing the translator clauses counts for one-third of the total score. If we had put the translator clauses at the same level as title and author, they would have reduced the contribution of the title and author clauses to one-quarter each.

Prioritizing Clauses

It is likely that an even one-third split between clauses is not what we need for the preceding query. Probably we're more interested in the title and author clauses then we are in the translator clauses. We need to tune the query to make the title and author clauses relatively more important.

The simplest weapon in our tuning arsenal is the boost parameter. To increase the weight of the title and author fields, give them a boost value higher than 1:

```
GET /_search
{
  "query": {
    "bool": {
      "should": [
        { "match": {  ❶
            "title":  {
              "query": "War and Peace",
              "boost": 2
        }}},
        { "match": {  ❶
            "author":  {
              "query": "Leo Tolstoy",
              "boost": 2
        }}},
        { "bool":  {  ❷
            "should": [
              { "match": { "translator": "Constance Garnett" }},
              { "match": { "translator": "Louise Maude"       }}
            ]
        }}
      ]
    }
  }
}
```

❶ The title and author clauses have a boost value of 2.

❷ The nested bool clause has the default boost of 1.

The "best" value for the boost parameter is most easily determined by trial and error: set a boost value, run test queries, repeat. A reasonable range for boost lies between 1 and 10, maybe 15. Boosts higher than that have little more impact because scores are normalized.

Single Query String

The bool query is the mainstay of multiclause queries. It works well for many cases, especially when you are able to map different query strings to individual fields.

The problem is that, these days, users expect to be able to type all of their search terms into a single field, and expect that the application will figure out how to give them the right results. It is ironic that the multifield search form is known as *Advanced Search*—it may appear advanced to the user, but it is much simpler to implement.

There is no simple *one-size-fits-all* approach to multiword, multifield queries. To get the best results, you have to *know your data* and know how to use the appropriate tools.

Know Your Data

When your only user input is a single query string, you will encounter three scenarios frequently:

Best fields

When searching for words that represent a concept, such as "brown fox," the words mean more together than they do individually. Fields like the `title` and `body`, while related, can be considered to be in competition with each other. Documents should have as many words as possible in *the same field*, and the score should come from the *best-matching field*.

Most fields

A common technique for fine-tuning relevance is to index the same data into multiple fields, each with its own analysis chain.

The main field may contain words in their stemmed form, synonyms, and words stripped of their *diacritics*, or accents. It is used to match as many documents as possible.

The same text could then be indexed in other fields to provide more-precise matching. One field may contain the unstemmed version, another the original word with accents, and a third might use *shingles* to provide information about word proximity.

These other fields act as *signals* to increase the relevance score of each matching document. The *more fields that match*, the better.

Cross fields

For some entities, the identifying information is spread across multiple fields, each of which contains just a part of the whole:

- Person: `first_name` and `last_name`
- Book: `title`, `author`, and `description`
- Address: `street`, `city`, `country`, and `postcode`

In this case, we want to find as many words as possible in *any* of the listed fields. We need to search across multiple fields as if they were one big field.

All of these are multiword, multifield queries, but each requires a different strategy. We will examine each strategy in turn in the rest of this chapter.

Best Fields

Imagine that we have a website that allows users to search blog posts, such as these two documents:

```
PUT /my_index/my_type/1
{
    "title": "Quick brown rabbits",
    "body":  "Brown rabbits are commonly seen."
}

PUT /my_index/my_type/2
{
    "title": "Keeping pets healthy",
    "body":  "My quick brown fox eats rabbits on a regular basis."
}
```

The user types in the words "Brown fox" and clicks Search. We don't know ahead of time if the user's search terms will be found in the `title` or the body field of the post, but it is likely that the user is searching for related words. To our eyes, document 2 appears to be the better match, as it contains both words that we are looking for.

Now we run the following `bool` query:

```
{
    "query": {
        "bool": {
            "should": [
                { "match": { "title": "Brown fox" }},
                { "match": { "body":  "Brown fox" }}
            ]
        }
    }
}
```

And we find that this query gives document 1 the higher score:

```
{
  "hits": [
     {
        "_id":      "1",
        "_score":   0.14809652,
        "_source": {
           "title": "Quick brown rabbits",
           "body":  "Brown rabbits are commonly seen."
        }
     },
     {
        "_id":      "2",
        "_score":   0.09256032,
        "_source": {
           "title": "Keeping pets healthy",
```

```
            "body":  "My quick brown fox eats rabbits on a regular basis."
        }
    }
  ]
}
```

To understand why, think about how the bool query calculates its score:

1. It runs both of the queries in the should clause.

2. It adds their scores together.

3. It multiplies the total by the number of matching clauses.

4. It divides the result by the total number of clauses (two).

Document 1 contains the word brown in both fields, so both match clauses are successful and have a score. Document 2 contains both brown and fox in the body field but neither word in the title field. The high score from the body query is added to the zero score from the title query, and multiplied by one-half, resulting in a lower overall score than for document 1.

In this example, the title and body fields are competing with each other. We want to find the single *best-matching* field.

What if, instead of combining the scores from each field, we used the score from the *best-matching* field as the overall score for the query? This would give preference to a single field that contains *both* of the words we are looking for, rather than the same word repeated in different fields.

dis_max Query

Instead of the bool query, we can use the dis_max or *Disjunction Max Query*. Disjunction means *or* (while conjunction means *and*) so the Disjunction Max Query simply means *return documents that match any of these queries, and return the score of the best matching query*:

```
{
    "query": {
        "dis_max": {
            "queries": [
                { "match": { "title": "Brown fox" }},
                { "match": { "body":  "Brown fox" }}
            ]
        }
    }
}
```

This produces the results that we want:

```
{
  "hits": [
    {
      "_id":        "2",
      "_score":     0.21509302,
      "_source": {
        "title": "Keeping pets healthy",
        "body":  "My quick brown fox eats rabbits on a regular basis."
      }
    },
    {
      "_id":        "1",
      "_score":     0.12713557,
      "_source": {
        "title": "Quick brown rabbits",
        "body":  "Brown rabbits are commonly seen."
      }
    }
  ]
}
```

Tuning Best Fields Queries

What would happen if the user had searched instead for "quick pets"? Both documents contain the word quick, but only document 2 contains the word pets. Neither document contains *both words* in the *same field*.

A simple dis_max query like the following would choose the single best matching field, and ignore the other:

```
{
    "query": {
        "dis_max": {
            "queries": [
                { "match": { "title": "Quick pets" }},
                { "match": { "body":  "Quick pets" }}
            ]
        }
    }
}
```

```
{
  "hits": [
    {
      "_id": "1",
      "_score": 0.12713557, ❶
      "_source": {
        "title": "Quick brown rabbits",
        "body": "Brown rabbits are commonly seen."
      }
    },
    {
```

```
        "_id": "2",
        "_score": 0.12713557, ❶
        "_source": {
           "title": "Keeping pets healthy",
           "body": "My quick brown fox eats rabbits on a regular basis."
        }
     }
  ]
}
```

❶ Note that the scores are exactly the same.

We would probably expect documents that match on both the `title` field and the body field to rank higher than documents that match on just one field, but this isn't the case. Remember: the `dis_max` query simply uses the `_score` from the *single* best-matching clause.

tie_breaker

It is possible, however, to also take the `_score` from the other matching clauses into account, by specifying the `tie_breaker` parameter:

```
{
    "query": {
        "dis_max": {
            "queries": [
                { "match": { "title": "Quick pets" }},
                { "match": { "body":  "Quick pets" }}
            ],
            "tie_breaker": 0.3
        }
    }
}
```

This gives us the following results:

```
{
  "hits": [
     {
        "_id": "2",
        "_score": 0.14757764, ❶
        "_source": {
           "title": "Keeping pets healthy",
           "body": "My quick brown fox eats rabbits on a regular basis."
        }
     },
     {
        "_id": "1",
        "_score": 0.124275915, ❶
        "_source": {
           "title": "Quick brown rabbits",
```

```
        "body": "Brown rabbits are commonly seen."
      }
    }
  ]
}
```

❶ Document 2 now has a small lead over document 1.

The `tie_breaker` parameter makes the `dis_max` query behave more like a halfway house between `dis_max` and `bool`. It changes the score calculation as follows:

1. Take the `_score` of the best-matching clause.

2. Multiply the score of each of the other matching clauses by the `tie_breaker`.

3. Add them all together and normalize.

With the `tie_breaker`, all matching clauses count, but the best-matching clause counts most.

The `tie_breaker` can be a floating-point value between 0 and 1, where 0 uses just the best-matching clause and 1 counts all matching clauses equally. The exact value can be tuned based on your data and queries, but a reasonable value should be close to zero, (for example, 0.1 - 0.4), in order not to overwhelm the best-matching nature of `dis_max`.

multi_match Query

The `multi_match` query provides a convenient shorthand way of running the same query against multiple fields.

There are several types of `multi_match` query, three of which just happen to coincide with the three scenarios that we listed in "Know Your Data" on page 222: `best_fields`, `most_fields`, and `cross_fields`.

By default, this query runs as type `best_fields`, which means that it generates a `match` query for each field and wraps them in a `dis_max` query. This `dis_max` query

```
{
  "dis_max": {
    "queries": [
      {
        "match": {
          "title": {
            "query": "Quick brown fox",
```

```
                    "minimum_should_match": "30%"
                }
            }
        },
        {
            "match": {
                "body": {
                    "query": "Quick brown fox",
                    "minimum_should_match": "30%"
                }
            }
        },
    ],
    "tie_breaker": 0.3
  }
}
```

could be rewritten more concisely with `multi_match` as follows:

```
{
    "multi_match": {
        "query":                    "Quick brown fox",
        "type":                     "best_fields",  ❶
        "fields":                   [ "title", "body" ],
        "tie_breaker":              0.3,
        "minimum_should_match":     "30%"  ❷
    }
}
```

❶ The `best_fields` type is the default and can be left out.

❷ Parameters like `minimum_should_match` or `operator` are passed through to the generated `match` queries.

Using Wildcards in Field Names

Field names can be specified with wildcards: any field that matches the wildcard pattern will be included in the search. You could match on the `book_title`, `chapter_title`, and `section_title` fields, with the following:

```
{
    "multi_match": {
        "query":  "Quick brown fox",
        "fields": "*_title"
    }
}
```

Boosting Individual Fields

Individual fields can be boosted by using the caret (^) syntax: just add ^boost after the field name, where boost is a floating-point number:

```
{
    "multi_match": {
        "query":  "Quick brown fox",
        "fields": [ "*_title", "chapter_title^2" ] ❶
    }
}
```

❶ The chapter_title field has a boost of 2, while the book_title and sec tion_title fields have a default boost of 1.

Most Fields

Full-text search is a battle between *recall*—returning all the documents that are relevant—and *precision*—not returning irrelevant documents. The goal is to present the user with the most relevant documents on the first page of results.

To improve recall, we cast the net wide—we include not only documents that match the user's search terms exactly, but also documents that we believe to be pertinent to the query. If a user searches for "quick brown fox," a document that contains fast foxes may well be a reasonable result to return.

If the only pertinent document that we have is the one containing fast foxes, it will appear at the top of the results list. But of course, if we have 100 documents that contain the words quick brown fox, then the fast foxes document may be considered less relevant, and we would want to push it further down the list. After including many potential matches, we need to ensure that the best ones rise to the top.

A common technique for fine-tuning full-text relevance is to index the same text in multiple ways, each of which provides a different relevance *signal*. The main field would contain terms in their broadest-matching form to match as many documents as possible. For instance, we could do the following:

- Use a stemmer to index jumps, jumping, and jumped as their root form: jump. Then it doesn't matter if the user searches for jumped; we could still match documents containing jumping.

- Include synonyms like jump, leap, and hop.

- Remove diacritics, or accents: for example, ésta, está, and esta would all be indexed without accents as esta.

However, if we have two documents, one of which contains jumped and the other jumping, the user would probably expect the first document to rank higher, as it contains exactly what was typed in.

We can achieve this by indexing the same text in other fields to provide more-precise matching. One field may contain the unstemmed version, another the original word with diacritics, and a third might use *shingles* to provide information about word proximity. These other fields act as *signals* that increase the relevance score of each matching document. The more fields that match, the better.

A document is included in the results list if it matches the broad-matching main field. If it also matches the *signal* fields, it gets extra points and is pushed up the results list.

We discuss synonyms, word proximity, partial-matching and other potential signals later in the book, but we will use the simple example of stemmed and unstemmed fields to illustrate this technique.

Multifield Mapping

The first thing to do is to set up our field to be indexed twice: once in a stemmed form and once in an unstemmed form. To do this, we will use *multifields*, which we introduced in "String Sorting and Multifields" on page 116:

```
DELETE /my_index

PUT /my_index
{
    "settings": { "number_of_shards": 1 }, ❶
    "mappings": {
        "my_type": {
            "properties": {
                "title": { ❷
                    "type":     "string",
                    "analyzer": "english",
                    "fields": {
                        "std":    { ❸
                            "type":     "string",
                            "analyzer": "standard"
                        }
                    }
                }
            }
        }
    }
}
```

❶   See "Relevance Is Broken!" on page 216.

❷   The title field is stemmed by the english analyzer.

❸ The title.std field uses the standard analyzer and so is not stemmed.

Next we index some documents:

```
PUT /my_index/my_type/1
{ "title": "My rabbit jumps" }

PUT /my_index/my_type/2
{ "title": "Jumping jack rabbits" }
```

Here is a simple match query on the title field for jumping rabbits:

```
GET /my_index/_search
{
    "query": {
        "match": {
            "title": "jumping rabbits"
        }
    }
}
```

This becomes a query for the two stemmed terms jump and rabbit, thanks to the english analyzer. The title field of both documents contains both of those terms, so both documents receive the same score:

```
{
  "hits": [
     {
        "_id": "1",
        "_score": 0.42039964,
        "_source": {
           "title": "My rabbit jumps"
        }
     },
     {
        "_id": "2",
        "_score": 0.42039964,
        "_source": {
           "title": "Jumping jack rabbits"
        }
     }
  ]
}
```

If we were to query just the title.std field, then only document 2 would match. However, if we were to query both fields and to *combine* their scores by using the bool query, then both documents would match (thanks to the title field) and document 2 would score higher (thanks to the title.std field):

```
GET /my_index/_search
{
    "query": {
```

```
            "multi_match": {
                "query":  "jumping rabbits",
                "type":   "most_fields", ❶
                "fields": [ "title", "title.std" ]
            }
        ]
    }
}
```

❶ We want to combine the scores from all matching fields, so we use the most_fields type. This causes the multi_match query to wrap the two field-clauses in a bool query instead of a dis_max query.

```
{
  "hits": [
     {
        "_id": "2",
        "_score": 0.8226396, ❶
        "_source": {
           "title": "Jumping jack rabbits"
        }
     },
     {
        "_id": "1",
        "_score": 0.10741998, ❶
        "_source": {
           "title": "My rabbit jumps"
        }
     }
  ]
}
```

❶ Document 2 now scores much higher than document 1.

We are using the broad-matching title field to include as many documents as possible—to increase recall—but we use the title.std field as a *signal* to push the most relevant results to the top.

The contribution of each field to the final score can be controlled by specifying custom boost values. For instance, we could boost the title field to make it the most important field, thus reducing the effect of any other signal fields:

```
GET /my_index/_search
{
    "query": {
        "multi_match": {
            "query":     "jumping rabbits",
            "type":      "most_fields",
            "fields":    [ "title^10", "title.std" ] ❶
        }
    }
}
```

❶ The `boost` value of `10` on the `title` field makes that field relatively much more important than the `title.std` field.

Cross-fields Entity Search

Now we come to a common pattern: cross-fields entity search. With entities like `person`, `product`, or `address`, the identifying information is spread across several fields. We may have a `person` indexed as follows:

```
{
    "firstname": "Peter",
    "lastname":  "Smith"
}
```

Or an address like this:

```
{
    "street":   "5 Poland Street",
    "city":     "London",
    "country":  "United Kingdom",
    "postcode": "W1V 3DG"
}
```

This sounds a lot like the example we described in "Multiple Query Strings" on page 219, but there is a big difference between these two scenarios. In "Multiple Query Strings" on page 219, we used a separate query string for each field. In this scenario, we want to search across multiple fields with a *single* query string.

Our user might search for the person "Peter Smith" or for the address "Poland Street W1V." Each of those words appears in a different field, so using a `dis_max` / `best_fields` query to find the *single* best-matching field is clearly the wrong approach.

A Naive Approach

Really, we want to query each field in turn and add up the scores of every field that matches, which sounds like a job for the `bool` query:

```
{
  "query": {
    "bool": {
      "should": [
        { "match": { "street":   "Poland Street W1V" }},
        { "match": { "city":     "Poland Street W1V" }},
        { "match": { "country":  "Poland Street W1V" }},
        { "match": { "postcode": "Poland Street W1V" }}
      ]
    }
```

```
      }
    }
```

Repeating the query string for every field soon becomes tedious. We can use the `multi_match` query instead, and set the `type` to `most_fields` to tell it to combine the scores of all matching fields:

```
{
  "query": {
    "multi_match": {
      "query":        "Poland Street W1V",
      "type":         "most_fields",
      "fields":       [ "street", "city", "country", "postcode" ]
    }
  }
}
```

Problems with the most_fields Approach

The `most_fields` approach to entity search has some problems that are not immediately obvious:

- It is designed to find the most fields matching *any* words, rather than to find the most matching words *across all fields*.
- It can't use the `operator` or `minimum_should_match` parameters to reduce the long tail of less-relevant results.
- Term frequencies are different in each field and could interfere with each other to produce badly ordered results.

Field-Centric Queries

All three of the preceding problems stem from `most_fields` being *field-centric* rather than *term-centric*: it looks for the most matching *fields*, when really what we're interested is the most matching *terms*.

 The `best_fields` type is also field-centric and suffers from similar problems.

First we'll look at why these problems exist, and then how we can combat them.

Problem 1: Matching the Same Word in Multiple Fields

Think about how the most_fields query is executed: Elasticsearch generates a separate match query for each field and then wraps these match queries in an outer bool query.

We can see this by passing our query through the validate-query API:

```
GET /_validate/query?explain
{
  "query": {
    "multi_match": {
      "query":   "Poland Street W1V",
      "type":    "most_fields",
      "fields":  [ "street", "city", "country", "postcode" ]
    }
  }
}
```

which yields this explanation:

```
(street:poland    street:street    street:w1v)
(city:poland      city:street      city:w1v)
(country:poland   country:street   country:w1v)
(postcode:poland  postcode:street  postcode:w1v)
```

You can see that a document matching just the word poland in *two* fields could score higher than a document matching poland and street in one field.

Problem 2: Trimming the Long Tail

In "Controlling Precision" on page 205, we talked about using the and operator or the minimum_should_match parameter to trim the long tail of almost irrelevant results. Perhaps we could try this:

```
{
    "query": {
        "multi_match": {
            "query":      "Poland Street W1V",
            "type":       "most_fields",
            "operator":   "and",  ❶
            "fields":     [ "street", "city", "country", "postcode" ]
        }
    }
}
```

❶ All terms must be present.

However, with best_fields or most_fields, these parameters are passed down to the generated match queries. The explanation for this query shows the following:

```
(+street:poland   +street:street   +street:w1v)
(+city:poland     +city:street     +city:w1v)
(+country:poland  +country:street  +country:w1v)
(+postcode:poland +postcode:street +postcode:w1v)
```

In other words, using the and operator means that all words must exist *in the same field*, which is clearly wrong! It is unlikely that any documents would match this query.

Problem 3: Term Frequencies

In "What Is Relevance?" on page 117, we explained that the default similarity algorithm used to calculate the relevance score for each term is TF/IDF:

Term frequency
> The more often a term appears in a field in a single document, the more relevant the document.

Inverse document frequency
> The more often a term appears in a field in all documents in the index, the less relevant is that term.

When searching against multiple fields, TF/IDF can introduce some surprising results.

Consider our example of searching for "Peter Smith" using the first_name and last_name fields. Peter is a common first name and Smith is a common last name— both will have low IDFs. But what if we have another person in the index whose name is Smith Williams? Smith as a first name is very uncommon and so will have a high IDF!

A simple query like the following may well return Smith Williams above Peter Smith in spite of the fact that the second person is a better match than the first.

```
{
    "query": {
        "multi_match": {
            "query":       "Peter Smith",
            "type":        "most_fields",
            "fields":      [ "*_name" ]
        }
    }
}
```

The high IDF of smith in the first name field can overwhelm the two low IDFs of peter as a first name and smith as a last name.

Solution

These problems only exist because we are dealing with multiple fields. If we were to combine all of these fields into a single field, the problems would vanish. We could achieve this by adding a `full_name` field to our `person` document:

```
{
    "first_name":  "Peter",
    "last_name":   "Smith",
    "full_name":   "Peter Smith"
}
```

When querying just the `full_name` field:

- Documents with more matching words would trump documents with the same word repeated.
- The `minimum_should_match` and `operator` parameters would function as expected.
- The inverse document frequencies for first and last names would be combined so it wouldn't matter whether Smith were a first or last name anymore.

While this would work, we don't like having to store redundant data. Instead, Elasticsearch offers us two solutions—one at index time and one at search time—which we discuss next.

Custom _all Fields

In "Metadata: _all Field" on page 144, we explained that the special _all field indexes the values from all other fields as one big string. Having all fields indexed into one field is not terribly flexible, though. It would be nice to have one custom _all field for the person's name, and another custom _all field for the address.

Elasticsearch provides us with this functionality via the `copy_to` parameter in a field mapping:

```
PUT /my_index
{
    "mappings": {
        "person": {
            "properties": {
                "first_name": {
                    "type":     "string",
                    "copy_to":  "full_name" ❶
                },
                "last_name": {
                    "type":     "string",
                    "copy_to":  "full_name" ❶
                },
```

```
                "full_name": {
                    "type":        "string"
                }
            }
        }
    }
}
```

❶ The values in the first_name and last_name fields are also copied to the full_name field.

With this mapping in place, we can query the first_name field for first names, the last_name field for last name, or the full_name field for first and last names.

 Mappings of the first_name and last_name fields have no bearing on how the full_name field is indexed. The full_name field copies the string values from the other two fields, then indexes them according to the mapping of the full_name field only.

cross-fields Queries

The custom _all approach is a good solution, as long as you thought about setting it up before you indexed your documents. However, Elasticsearch also provides a search-time solution to the problem: the multi_match query with type cross_fields. The cross_fields type takes a term-centric approach, quite different from the field-centric approach taken by best_fields and most_fields. It treats all of the fields as one big field, and looks for *each term* in *any field*.

To illustrate the difference between field-centric and term-centric queries, look at the explanation for this field-centric most_fields query:

```
GET /_validate/query?explain
{
    "query": {
        "multi_match": {
            "query":        "peter smith",
            "type":         "most_fields",
            "operator":     "and",  ❶
            "fields":       [ "first_name", "last_name" ]
        }
    }
}
```

❶ All terms are required.

For a document to match, both peter and smith must appear in the same field, either the first_name field or the last_name field:

```
(+first_name:peter +first_name:smith)
(+last_name:peter  +last_name:smith)
```

A *term-centric* approach would use this logic instead:

```
+(first_name:peter last_name:peter)
+(first_name:smith last_name:smith)
```

In other words, the term `peter` must appear in either field, and the term `smith` must appear in either field.

The `cross_fields` type first analyzes the query string to produce a list of terms, and then it searches for each term in any field. That difference alone solves two of the three problems that we listed in "Field-Centric Queries" on page 234, leaving us just with the issue of differing inverse document frequencies.

Fortunately, the `cross_fields` type solves this too, as can be seen from this `validate-query` request:

```
GET /_validate/query?explain
{
    "query": {
        "multi_match": {
            "query":     "peter smith",
            "type":      "cross_fields", ❶
            "operator":  "and",
            "fields":    [ "first_name", "last_name" ]
        }
    }
}
```

❶ Use `cross_fields` term-centric matching.

It solves the term-frequency problem by *blending* inverse document frequencies across fields:

```
+blended("peter", fields: [first_name, last_name])
+blended("smith", fields: [first_name, last_name])
```

In other words, it looks up the IDF of `smith` in both the `first_name` and the `last_name` fields and uses the minimum of the two as the IDF for both fields. The fact that `smith` is a common last name means that it will be treated as a common first name too.

For the `cross_fields` query type to work optimally, all fields should have the same analyzer. Fields that share an analyzer are grouped together as blended fields.

If you include fields with a different analysis chain, they will be added to the query in the same way as for `best_fields`. For instance, if we added the `title` field to the preceding query (assuming it uses a different analyzer), the explanation would be as follows:

```
(+title:peter +title:smith)
(
  +blended("peter", fields: [first_name, last_name])
  +blended("smith", fields: [first_name, last_name])
)
```

This is particularly important when using the `mini mum_should_match` and `operator` parameters.

Per-Field Boosting

One of the advantages of using the `cross_fields` query over custom `_all` fields is that you can boost individual fields at query time.

For fields of equal value like `first_name` and `last_name`, this generally isn't required, but if you were searching for books using the `title` and `description` fields, you might want to give more weight to the `title` field. This can be done as described before with the caret (^) syntax:

```
GET /books/_search
{
    "query": {
        "multi_match": {
            "query":      "peter smith",
            "type":       "cross_fields",
            "fields":     [ "title^2", "description" ] ❶
        }
    }
}
```

❶ The `title` field has a boost of 2, while the `description` field has the default boost of 1.

The advantage of being able to boost individual fields should be weighed against the cost of querying multiple fields instead of querying a single custom `_all` field. Use whichever of the two solutions that delivers the most bang for your buck.

Exact-Value Fields

The final topic that we should touch on before leaving multifield queries is that of exact-value not_analyzed fields. It is not useful to mix not_analyzed fields with analyzed fields in multi_match queries.

The reason for this can be demonstrated easily by looking at a query explanation. Imagine that we have set the title field to be not_analyzed:

```
GET /_validate/query?explain
{
    "query": {
        "multi_match": {
            "query":       "peter smith",
            "type":        "cross_fields",
            "fields":      [ "title", "first_name", "last_name" ]
        }
    }
}
```

Because the title field is not analyzed, it searches that field for a single term consisting of the whole query string!

```
title:peter smith
(
    blended("peter", fields: [first_name, last_name])
    blended("smith", fields: [first_name, last_name])
)
```

That term clearly does not exist in the inverted index of the title field, and can never be found. Avoid using not_analyzed fields in multi_match queries.

CHAPTER 15

Proximity Matching

Standard full-text search with TF/IDF treats documents, or at least each field within a document, as a big *bag of words*. The `match` query can tell us whether that bag contains our search terms, but that is only part of the story. It can't tell us anything about the relationship between words.

Consider the difference between these sentences:

- Sue ate the alligator.
- The alligator ate Sue.
- Sue never goes anywhere without her alligator-skin purse.

A `match` query for `sue alligator` would match all three documents, but it doesn't tell us whether the two words form part of the same idea, or even the same paragraph.

Understanding how words relate to each other is a complicated problem, and we can't solve it by just using another type of query, but we can at least find words that appear to be related because they appear near each other or even right next to each other.

Each document may be much longer than the examples we have presented: `Sue` and `alligator` may be separated by paragraphs of other text. Perhaps we still want to return these documents in which the words are widely separated, but we want to give documents in which the words are close together a higher relevance score.

This is the province of *phrase matching*, or *proximity matching*.

In this chapter, we are using the same example documents that we used for the match query.

Phrase Matching

In the same way that the match query is the go-to query for standard full-text search, the match_phrase query is the one you should reach for when you want to find words that are near each other:

```
GET /my_index/my_type/_search
{
    "query": {
        "match_phrase": {
            "title": "quick brown fox"
        }
    }
}
```

Like the match query, the match_phrase query first analyzes the query string to produce a list of terms. It then searches for all the terms, but keeps only documents that contain *all* of the search terms, in the same *positions* relative to each other. A query for the phrase quick fox would not match any of our documents, because no document contains the word quick immediately followed by fox.

The match_phrase query can also be written as a match query with type phrase:

```
"match": {
    "title": {
        "query": "quick brown fox",
        "type":  "phrase"
    }
}
```

Term Positions

When a string is analyzed, the analyzer returns not only a list of terms, but also the *position*, or order, of each term in the original string:

```
GET /_analyze?analyzer=standard
Quick brown fox
```

This returns the following:

```
{
    "tokens": [
        {
            "token": "quick",
            "start_offset": 0,
            "end_offset": 5,
            "type": "<ALPHANUM>",
            "position": 1 ❶
        },
        {
            "token": "brown",
            "start_offset": 6,
            "end_offset": 11,
            "type": "<ALPHANUM>",
            "position": 2 ❶
        },
        {
            "token": "fox",
            "start_offset": 12,
            "end_offset": 15,
            "type": "<ALPHANUM>",
            "position": 3 ❶
        }
    ]
}
```

❶ The `position` of each term in the original string.

Positions can be stored in the inverted index, and position-aware queries like the `match_phrase` query can use them to match only documents that contain all the words in exactly the order specified, with no words in-between.

What Is a Phrase

For a document to be considered a match for the phrase "quick brown fox," the following must be true:

- `quick`, `brown`, and `fox` must all appear in the field.
- The position of `brown` must be 1 greater than the position of `quick`.
- The position of `fox` must be 2 greater than the position of `quick`.

If any of these conditions is not met, the document is not considered a match.

Internally, the `match_phrase` query uses the low-level `span` query family to do position-aware matching. Span queries are term-level queries, so they have no analysis phase; they search for the exact term specified.

Thankfully, most people never need to use the `span` queries directly, as the `match_phrase` query is usually good enough. However, certain specialized fields, like patent searches, use these low-level queries to perform very specific, carefully constructed positional searches.

Mixing It Up

Requiring exact-phrase matches may be too strict a constraint. Perhaps we *do* want documents that contain "quick brown fox" to be considered a match for the query "quick fox," even though the positions aren't exactly equivalent.

We can introduce a degree of flexibility into phrase matching by using the `slop` parameter:

```
GET /my_index/my_type/_search
{
    "query": {
        "match_phrase": {
            "title": {
             "query": "quick fox",
             "slop":  1
            }
        }
    }
}
```

The `slop` parameter tells the `match_phrase` query how far apart terms are allowed to be while still considering the document a match. By *how far apart* we mean *how many times do you need to move a term in order to make the query and document match?*

We'll start with a simple example. To make the query `quick fox` match a document containing `quick brown fox` we need a `slop` of just 1:

```
               Pos 1        Pos 2        Pos 3
    ------------------------------------------------
    Doc:       quick        brown        fox
    ------------------------------------------------
    Query:     quick        fox
    Slop 1:    quick             ↳  fox
```

Although all words need to be present in phrase matching, even when using `slop`, the words don't necessarily need to be in the same sequence in order to match. With a high enough `slop` value, words can be arranged in any order.

To make the query `fox quick` match our document, we need a `slop` of 3:

```
              Pos 1          Pos 2          Pos 3
-------------------------------------------------
Doc:          quick          brown          fox
-------------------------------------------------
Query:        fox            quick
Slop 1:       fox|quick   ↵  ❶
Slop 2:       quick       ↳  fox
Slop 3:       quick                      ↳   fox
```

❶ Note that `fox` and `quick` occupy the same position in this step. Switching word order from `fox quick` to `quick fox` thus requires two steps, or a `slop` of 2.

Multivalue Fields

A curious thing can happen when you try to use phrase matching on multivalue fields. Imagine that you index this document:

```
PUT /my_index/groups/1
{
    "names": [ "John Abraham", "Lincoln Smith"]
}
```

Then run a phrase query for `Abraham Lincoln`:

```
GET /my_index/groups/_search
{
    "query": {
        "match_phrase": {
            "names": "Abraham Lincoln"
        }
    }
}
```

Surprisingly, our document matches, even though `Abraham` and `Lincoln` belong to two different people in the `names` array. The reason for this comes down to the way arrays are indexed in Elasticsearch.

When `John Abraham` is analyzed, it produces this:

- Position 1: `john`
- Position 2: `abraham`

Then when `Lincoln Smith` is analyzed, it produces this:

- Position 3: `lincoln`
- Position 4: `smith`

In other words, Elasticsearch produces exactly the same list of tokens as it would have for the single string John Abraham Lincoln Smith. Our example query looks for abraham directly followed by lincoln, and these two terms do indeed exist, and they are right next to each other, so the query matches.

Fortunately, there is a simple workaround for cases like these, called the posi tion_offset_gap, which we need to configure in the field mapping:

```
DELETE /my_index/groups/ ❶

PUT /my_index/_mapping/groups ❷
{
    "properties": {
        "names": {
            "type":                "string",
            "position_offset_gap": 100
        }
    }
}
```

❶   First delete the groups mapping and all documents of that type.

❷   Then create a new groups mapping with the correct values.

The position_offset_gap setting tells Elasticsearch that it should increase the current term position by the specified value for every new array element. So now, when we index the array of names, the terms are emitted with the following positions:

- Position 1: john
- Position 2: abraham
- Position 103: lincoln
- Position 104: smith

Our phrase query would no longer match a document like this because abraham and lincoln are now 100 positions apart. You would have to add a slop value of 100 in order for this document to match.

Closer Is Better

Whereas a phrase query simply excludes documents that don't contain the exact query phrase, a *proximity query*—a phrase query where slop is greater than 0—incorporates the proximity of the query terms into the final relevance _score. By setting a high slop value like 50 or 100, you can exclude documents in which the words are really too far apart, but give a higher score to documents in which the words are closer together.

The following proximity query for `quick dog` matches both documents that contain the words `quick` and `dog`, but gives a higher score to the document in which the words are nearer to each other:

```
POST /my_index/my_type/_search
{
    "query": {
        "match_phrase": {
            "title": {
                "query": "quick dog",
                "slop":  50 ❶
            }
        }
    }
}
```

❶ Note the high `slop` value.

```
{
  "hits": [
      {
         "_id":      "3",
         "_score":   0.75, ❶
         "_source": {
            "title": "The quick brown fox jumps over the quick dog"
         }
      },
      {
         "_id":      "2",
         "_score":   0.28347334, ❷
         "_source": {
            "title": "The quick brown fox jumps over the lazy dog"
         }
      }
  ]
}
```

❶ Higher score because `quick` and `dog` are close together

❷ Lower score because `quick` and `dog` are further apart

Proximity for Relevance

Although proximity queries are useful, the fact that they require all terms to be present can make them overly strict. It's the same issue that we discussed in "Controlling Precision" on page 205 in Chapter 13: if six out of seven terms match, a document is probably relevant enough to be worth showing to the user, but the `match_phrase` query would exclude it.

Instead of using proximity matching as an absolute requirement, we can use it as a *signal*—as one of potentially many queries, each of which contributes to the overall score for each document (see "Most Fields" on page 229).

The fact that we want to add together the scores from multiple queries implies that we should combine them by using the bool query.

We can use a simple match query as a must clause. This is the query that will determine which documents are included in our result set. We can trim the long tail with the minimum_should_match parameter. Then we can add other, more specific queries as should clauses. Every one that matches will increase the relevance of the matching docs.

```
GET /my_index/my_type/_search
{
  "query": {
    "bool": {
      "must": {
        "match": {                              ❶
          "title": {
            "query":                "quick brown fox",
            "minimum_should_match": "30%"
          }
        }
      },
      "should": {
        "match_phrase": {                       ❷
          "title": {
            "query": "quick brown fox",
            "slop":  50
          }
        }
      }
    }
  }
}
```

❶ The must clause includes or excludes documents from the result set.

❷ The should clause increases the relevance score of those documents that match.

We could, of course, include other queries in the should clause, where each query targets a specific aspect of relevance.

Improving Performance

Phrase and proximity queries are more expensive than simple match queries. Whereas a match query just has to look up terms in the inverted index, a match_phrase query has to calculate and compare the positions of multiple possibly repeated terms.

The Lucene nightly benchmarks (*http://people.apache.org/~mikemccand/lucene bench/*) show that a simple term query is about 10 times as fast as a phrase query, and about 20 times as fast as a proximity query (a phrase query with slop). And of course, this cost is paid at search time instead of at index time.

Usually the extra cost of phrase queries is not as scary as these numbers suggest. Really, the difference in performance is a testimony to just how fast a simple term query is. Phrase queries on typical full-text data usually complete within a few milliseconds, and are perfectly usable in practice, even on a busy cluster.

In certain pathological cases, phrase queries can be costly, but this is unusual. An example of a pathological case is DNA sequencing, where there are many many identical terms repeated in many positions. Using higher slop values in this case results in a huge growth in the number of position calculations.

So what can we do to limit the performance cost of phrase and proximity queries? One useful approach is to reduce the total number of documents that need to be examined by the phrase query.

Rescoring Results

In the preceding section, we discussed using proximity queries just for relevance purposes, not to include or exclude results from the result set. A query may match millions of results, but chances are that our users are interested in only the first few pages of results.

A simple match query will already have ranked documents that contain all search terms near the top of the list. Really, we just want to rerank the *top results* to give an extra relevance bump to those documents that also match the phrase query.

The search API supports exactly this functionality via *rescoring*. The rescore phase allows you to apply a more expensive scoring algorithm—like a phrase query—to just the top K results from each shard. These top results are then resorted according to their new scores.

The request looks like this:

```
GET /my_index/my_type/_search
{
    "query": {
        "match": {       ❶
            "title": {
                "query":                "quick brown fox",
                "minimum_should_match": "30%"
            }
        }
    },
    "rescore": {
        "window_size": 50, ❷
        "query": {         ❸
            "rescore_query": {
                "match_phrase": {
                    "title": {
                        "query": "quick brown fox",
                        "slop":  50
                    }
                }
            }
        }
    }
}
```

❶ The match query decides which results will be included in the final result set and ranks results according to TF/IDF.

❷ The window_size is the number of top results to rescore, per shard.

❸ The only rescoring algorithm currently supported is another query, but there are plans to add more algorithms later.

Finding Associated Words

As useful as phrase and proximity queries can be, they still have a downside. They are overly strict: all terms must be present for a phrase query to match, even when using slop.

The flexibility in word ordering that you gain with slop also comes at a price, because you lose the association between word pairs. While you can identify documents in which sue, alligator, and ate occur close together, you can't tell whether *Sue ate* or the *alligator ate*.

When words are used in conjunction with each other, they express an idea that is bigger or more meaningful than each word in isolation. The two clauses *I'm not happy*

I'm working and *I'm happy I'm not working* contain the sames words, in close proximity, but have quite different meanings.

If, instead of indexing each word independently, we were to index pairs of words, then we could retain more of the context in which the words were used.

For the sentence `Sue ate the alligator`, we would not only index each word (or *unigram*) as a term

```
["sue", "ate", "the", "alligator"]
```

but also each word *and its neighbor* as single terms:

```
["sue ate", "ate the", "the alligator"]
```

These word pairs (or *bigrams*) are known as *shingles*.

 Shingles are not restricted to being pairs of words; you could index word triplets (*trigrams*) as well:

```
["sue ate the", "ate the alligator"]
```

Trigrams give you a higher degree of precision, but greatly increase the number of unique terms in the index. Bigrams are sufficient for most use cases.

Of course, shingles are useful only if the user enters the query in the same order as in the original document; a query for `sue alligator` would match the individual words but none of our shingles.

Fortunately, users tend to express themselves using constructs similar to those that appear in the data they are searching. But this point is an important one: it is not enough to index just bigrams; we still need unigrams, but we can use matching bigrams as a signal to increase the relevance score.

Producing Shingles

Shingles need to be created at index time as part of the analysis process. We could index both unigrams and bigrams into a single field, but it is cleaner to keep unigrams and bigrams in separate fields that can be queried independently. The unigram field would form the basis of our search, with the bigram field being used to boost relevance.

First, we need to create an analyzer that uses the `shingle` token filter:

```
DELETE /my_index

PUT /my_index
{
    "settings": {
```

```
        "number_of_shards": 1,  ❶
        "analysis": {
            "filter": {
                "my_shingle_filter": {
                    "type":             "shingle",
                    "min_shingle_size": 2,  ❷
                    "max_shingle_size": 2,  ❷
                    "output_unigrams":  false   ❸
                }
            },
            "analyzer": {
                "my_shingle_analyzer": {
                    "type":             "custom",
                    "tokenizer":        "standard",
                    "filter": [
                        "lowercase",
                        "my_shingle_filter"  ❹
                    ]
                }
            }
        }
    }
}
```

❶ See "Relevance Is Broken!" on page 216.

❷ The default min/max shingle size is 2 so we don't really need to set these.

❸ The `shingle` token filter outputs unigrams by default, but we want to keep unigrams and bigrams separate.

❹ The `my_shingle_analyzer` uses our custom `my_shingles_filter` token filter.

First, let's test that our analyzer is working as expected with the `analyze` API:

```
GET /my_index/_analyze?analyzer=my_shingle_analyzer
Sue ate the alligator
```

Sure enough, we get back three terms:

- `sue ate`
- `ate the`
- `the alligator`

Now we can proceed to setting up a field to use the new analyzer.

Multifields

We said that it is cleaner to index unigrams and bigrams separately, so we will create the `title` field as a multifield (see "String Sorting and Multifields" on page 116):

```
PUT /my_index/_mapping/my_type
{
    "my_type": {
        "properties": {
            "title": {
                "type": "string",
                "fields": {
                    "shingles": {
                        "type":     "string",
                        "analyzer": "my_shingle_analyzer"
                    }
                }
            }
        }
    }
}
```

With this mapping, values from our JSON document in the field `title` will be indexed both as unigrams (`title`) and as bigrams (`title.shingles`), meaning that we can query these fields independently.

And finally, we can index our example documents:

```
POST /my_index/my_type/_bulk
{ "index": { "_id": 1 }}
{ "title": "Sue ate the alligator" }
{ "index": { "_id": 2 }}
{ "title": "The alligator ate Sue" }
{ "index": { "_id": 3 }}
{ "title": "Sue never goes anywhere without her alligator skin purse" }
```

Searching for Shingles

To understand the benefit that the `shingles` field adds, let's first look at the results from a simple `match` query for "The hungry alligator ate Sue":

```
GET /my_index/my_type/_search
{
    "query": {
        "match": {
            "title": "the hungry alligator ate sue"
        }
    }
}
```

This query returns all three documents, but note that documents 1 and 2 have the same relevance score because they contain the same words:

```
{
  "hits": [
    {
      "_id": "1",
      "_score": 0.44273707,  ❶
      "_source": {
        "title": "Sue ate the alligator"
      }
    },
    {
      "_id": "2",
      "_score": 0.44273707,  ❶
      "_source": {
        "title": "The alligator ate Sue"
      }
    },
    {
      "_id": "3",  ❷
      "_score": 0.046571054,
      "_source": {
        "title": "Sue never goes anywhere without her alligator skin purse"
      }
    }
  ]
}
```

❶ Both documents contain the, alligator, and ate and so have the same score.

❷ We could have excluded document 3 by setting the minimum_should_match parameter. See "Controlling Precision" on page 205.

Now let's add the shingles field into the query. Remember that we want matches on the shingles field to act as a signal—to increase the relevance score—so we still need to include the query on the main title field:

```
GET /my_index/my_type/_search
{
  "query": {
    "bool": {
      "must": {
        "match": {
          "title": "the hungry alligator ate sue"
        }
      },
      "should": {
        "match": {
          "title.shingles": "the hungry alligator ate sue"
        }
      }
    }
```

We still match all three documents, but document 2 has now been bumped into first place because it matched the shingled term `ate sue`.

```json
{
   "hits": [
      {
         "_id": "2",
         "_score": 0.4883322,
         "_source": {
            "title": "The alligator ate Sue"
         }
      },
      {
         "_id": "1",
         "_score": 0.13422975,
         "_source": {
            "title": "Sue ate the alligator"
         }
      },
      {
         "_id": "3",
         "_score": 0.014119488,
         "_source": {
            "title": "Sue never goes anywhere without her alligator skin purse"
         }
      }
   ]
}
```

Even though our query included the word hungry, which doesn't appear in any of our documents, we still managed to use word proximity to return the most relevant document first.

Performance

Not only are shingles more flexible than phrase queries, but they perform better as well. Instead of paying the price of a phrase query every time you search, queries for shingles are just as efficient as a simple `match` query. A small price is paid at index time, because more terms need to be indexed, which also means that fields with shingles use more disk space. However, most applications write once and read many times, so it makes sense to optimize for fast queries.

This is a theme that you will encounter frequently in Elasticsearch: enables you to achieve a lot at search time, without requiring any up-front setup. Once you understand your requirements more clearly, you can achieve better results with better performance by modeling your data correctly at index time.

CHAPTER 16

Partial Matching

A keen observer will notice that all the queries so far in this book have operated on whole terms. To match something, the smallest unit had to be a single term. You can find only terms that exist in the inverted index.

But what happens if you want to match parts of a term but not the whole thing? *Partial matching* allows users to specify a portion of the term they are looking for and find any words that contain that fragment.

The requirement to match on part of a term is less common in the full-text search-engine world than you might think. If you have come from an SQL background, you likely have, at some stage of your career, implemented a *poor man's full-text search* using SQL constructs like this:

```
WHERE text LIKE "*quick*"
  AND text LIKE "*brown*"
  AND text LIKE "*fox*" ❶
```

❶ *fox* would match "fox" and "foxes."

Of course, with Elasticsearch, we have the analysis process and the inverted index that remove the need for such brute-force techniques. To handle the case of matching both "fox" and "foxes," we could simply use a stemmer to index words in their root form. There is no need to match partial terms.

That said, on some occasions partial matching can be useful. Common use cases include the following:

- Matching postal codes, product serial numbers, or other not_analyzed values that start with a particular prefix or match a wildcard pattern or even a regular expression

- *search-as-you-type*—displaying the most likely results before the user has finished typing the search terms
- Matching in languages like German or Dutch, which contain long compound words, like *Weltgesundheitsorganisation* (World Health Organization)

We will start by examining prefix matching on exact-value `not_analyzed` fields.

Postcodes and Structured Data

We will use United Kingdom postcodes (postal codes in the United States) to illustrate how to use partial matching with structured data. UK postcodes have a well-defined structure. For instance, the postcode W1V 3DG can be broken down as follows:

- W1V: This outer part identifies the postal area and district:
  — W indicates the area (one or two letters)
  — 1V indicates the district (one or two numbers, possibly followed by a letter
- 3DG: This inner part identifies a street or building:
  — 3 indicates the sector (one number)
  — DG indicates the unit (two letters)

Let's assume that we are indexing postcodes as exact-value `not_analyzed` fields, so we could create our index as follows:

```
PUT /my_index
{
    "mappings": {
        "address": {
            "properties": {
                "postcode": {
                    "type":  "string",
                    "index": "not_analyzed"
                }
            }
        }
    }
}
```

And index some postcodes:

```
PUT /my_index/address/1
{ "postcode": "W1V 3DG" }

PUT /my_index/address/2
{ "postcode": "W2F 8HW" }

PUT /my_index/address/3
```

```
{ "postcode": "W1F 7HW" }

PUT /my_index/address/4
{ "postcode": "WC1N 1LZ" }

PUT /my_index/address/5
{ "postcode": "SW5 0BE" }
```

Now our data is ready to be queried.

prefix Query

To find all postcodes beginning with W1, we could use a simple prefix query:

```
GET /my_index/address/_search
{
    "query": {
        "prefix": {
            "postcode": "W1"
        }
    }
}
```

The prefix query is a low-level query that works at the term level. It doesn't analyze the query string before searching. It assumes that you have passed it the exact prefix that you want to find.

By default, the prefix query does no relevance scoring. It just finds matching documents and gives them all a score of 1. Really, it behaves more like a filter than a query. The only practical difference between the prefix query and the prefix filter is that the filter can be cached.

Previously, we said that "you can find only terms that exist in the inverted index," but we haven't done anything special to index these postcodes; each postcode is simply indexed as the exact value specified in each document. So how does the prefix query work?

Remember that the inverted index consists of a sorted list of unique terms (in this case, postcodes). For each term, it lists the IDs of the documents containing that term in the *postings list*. The inverted index for our example documents looks something like this:

```
Term:              Doc IDs:
-------------------------
"SW5 0BE"    |   5
"W1F 7HW"    |   3
"W1V 3DG"    |   1
"W2F 8HW"    |   2
"WC1N 1LZ"   |   4
-------------------------
```

To support prefix matching on the fly, the query does the following:

1. Skips through the terms list to find the first term beginning with `W1`.

2. Collects the associated document IDs.

3. Moves to the next term.

4. If that term also begins with `W1`, the query repeats from step 2; otherwise, we're finished.

While this works fine for our small example, imagine that our inverted index contains a million postcodes beginning with `W1`. The prefix query would need to visit all one million terms in order to calculate the result!

And the shorter the prefix, the more terms need to be visited. If we were to look for the prefix `W` instead of `W1`, perhaps we would match 10 million terms instead of just one million.

 The `prefix` query or filter are useful for ad hoc prefix matching, but should be used with care. They can be used freely on fields with a small number of terms, but they scale poorly and can put your cluster under a lot of strain. Try to limit their impact on your cluster by using a long prefix; this reduces the number of terms that need to be visited.

Later in this chapter, we present an alternative index-time solution that makes prefix matching much more efficient. But first, we'll take a look at two related queries: the `wildcard` and `regexp` queries.

wildcard and regexp Queries

The `wildcard` query is a low-level, term-based query similar in nature to the `prefix` query, but it allows you to specify a pattern instead of just a prefix. It uses the standard shell wildcards: ? matches any character, and * matches zero or more characters.

This query would match the documents containing `W1F 7HW` and `W2F 8HW`:

```
GET /my_index/address/_search
{
    "query": {
        "wildcard": {
            "postcode": "W?F*HW" ❶
        }
    }
}
```

❶ The ? matches the 1 and the 2, while the * matches the space and the 7 and 8.

Imagine now that you want to match all postcodes just in the W area. A prefix match would also include postcodes starting with WC, and you would have a similar problem with a wildcard match. We want to match only postcodes that begin with a W, followed by a number. The regexp query allows you to write these more complicated patterns:

```
GET /my_index/address/_search
{
    "query": {
        "regexp": {
            "postcode": "W[0-9].+" ❶
        }
    }
}
```

❶ The regular expression says that the term must begin with a W, followed by any number from 0 to 9, followed by one or more other characters.

The wildcard and regexp queries work in exactly the same way as the prefix query. They also have to scan the list of terms in the inverted index to find all matching terms, and gather document IDs term by term. The only difference between them and the prefix query is that they support more-complex patterns.

This means that the same caveats apply. Running these queries on a field with many unique terms can be resource intensive indeed. Avoid using a pattern that starts with a wildcard (for example, *foo or, as a regexp, .*foo).

Whereas prefix matching can be made more efficient by preparing your data at index time, wildcard and regular expression matching can be done only at query time. These queries have their place but should be used sparingly.

The `prefix`, `wildcard`, and `regexp` queries operate on terms. If you use them to query an `analyzed` field, they will examine each term in the field, not the field as a whole.

For instance, let's say that our `title` field contains "Quick brown fox" which produces the terms `quick`, `brown`, and `fox`.

This query would match:

```
{ "regexp": { "title": "br.*" }}
```

But neither of these queries would match:

```
{ "regexp": { "title": "Qu.*" }} ❶
{ "regexp": { "title": "quick br*" }} ❷
```

❶ The term in the index is `quick`, not `Quick`.

❷ `quick` and `brown` are separate terms.

Query-Time Search-as-You-Type

Leaving postcodes behind, let's take a look at how prefix matching can help with full-text queries. Users have become accustomed to seeing search results before they have finished typing their query—so-called *instant search*, or *search-as-you-type*. Not only do users receive their search results in less time, but we can guide them toward results that actually exist in our index.

For instance, if a user types in `johnnie walker bl`, we would like to show results for Johnnie Walker Black Label and Johnnie Walker Blue Label before they can finish typing their query.

As always, there are more ways than one to skin a cat! We will start by looking at the way that is simplest to implement. You don't need to prepare your data in any way; you can implement *search-as-you-type* at query time on any full-text field.

In "Phrase Matching" on page 244, we introduced the `match_phrase` query, which matches all the specified words in the same positions relative to each other. For-query time search-as-you-type, we can use a specialization of this query, called the `match_phrase_prefix` query:

```
{
    "match_phrase_prefix" : {
        "brand" : "johnnie walker bl"
    }
}
```

This query behaves in the same way as the `match_phrase` query, except that it treats the last word in the query string as a prefix. In other words, the preceding example would look for the following:

- johnnie
- Followed by `walker`
- Followed by words beginning with `bl`

If you were to run this query through the `validate-query` API, it would produce this explanation:

```
"johnnie walker bl*"
```

Like the `match_phrase` query, it accepts a `slop` parameter (see "Mixing It Up" on page 246) to make the word order and relative positions somewhat less rigid:

```
{
    "match_phrase_prefix" : {
        "brand" : {
            "query": "walker johnnie bl",  ❶
            "slop":  10
        }
    }
}
```

❶ Even though the words are in the wrong order, the query still matches because we have set a high enough `slop` value to allow some flexibility in word positions.

However, it is always only the last word in the query string that is treated as a prefix.

Earlier, in "prefix Query" on page 261, we warned about the perils of the prefix—how `prefix` queries can be resource intensive. The same is true in this case. A prefix of `a` could match hundreds of thousands of terms. Not only would matching on this many terms be resource intensive, but it would also not be useful to the user.

We can limit the impact of the prefix expansion by setting `max_expansions` to a reasonable number, such as 50:

```
{
    "match_phrase_prefix" : {
        "brand" : {
            "query":            "johnnie walker bl",
            "max_expansions": 50
        }
    }
}
```

The `max_expansions` parameter controls how many terms the prefix is allowed to match. It will find the first term starting with `bl` and keep collecting terms (in alphabetical order) until it either runs out of terms with prefix `bl`, or it has more terms than `max_expansions`.

Don't forget that we have to run this query every time the user types another character, so it needs to be fast. If the first set of results isn't what users are after, they'll keep typing until they get the results that they want.

Index-Time Optimizations

All of the solutions we've talked about so far are implemented at *query time*. They don't require any special mappings or indexing patterns; they simply work with the data that you've already indexed.

The flexibility of query-time operations comes at a cost: search performance. Sometimes it may make sense to move the cost away from the query. In a real- time web application, an additional 100ms may be too much latency to tolerate.

By preparing your data at index time, you can make your searches more flexible and improve performance. You still pay a price: increased index size and slightly slower indexing throughput, but it is a price you pay once at index time, instead of paying it on every query.

Your users will thank you.

Ngrams for Partial Matching

As we have said before, "You can find only terms that exist in the inverted index." Although the `prefix`, `wildcard`, and `regexp` queries demonstrated that that is not strictly true, it *is* true that doing a single-term lookup is much faster than iterating through the terms list to find matching terms on the fly. Preparing your data for partial matching ahead of time will increase your search performance.

Preparing your data at index time means choosing the right analysis chain, and the tool that we use for partial matching is the *n-gram*. An n-gram can be best thought of as a *moving window on a word*. The *n* stands for a length. If we were to n-gram the word `quick`, the results would depend on the length we have chosen:

- Length 1 (unigram): [q, u, i, c, k]
- Length 2 (bigram): [qu, ui, ic, ck]
- Length 3 (trigram): [qui, uic, ick]
- Length 4 (four-gram): [quic, uick]
- Length 5 (five-gram): [quick]

Plain n-grams are useful for matching *somewhere within a word*, a technique that we will use in "Ngrams for Compound Words" on page 273. However, for search-as-you-type, we use a specialized form of n-grams called *edge n-grams*. Edge n-grams are anchored to the beginning of the word. Edge n-gramming the word `quick` would result in this:

- q
- qu
- qui
- quic
- quick

You may notice that this conforms exactly to the letters that a user searching for "quick" would type. In other words, these are the perfect terms to use for instant search!

Index-Time Search-as-You-Type

The first step to setting up index-time search-as-you-type is to define our analysis chain, which we discussed in "Configuring Analyzers" on page 135, but we will go over the steps again here.

Preparing the Index

The first step is to configure a custom `edge_ngram` token filter, which we will call the `autocomplete_filter`:

```
{
    "filter": {
        "autocomplete_filter": {
            "type":      "edge_ngram",
            "min_gram": 1,
            "max_gram": 20
        }
    }
}
```

This configuration says that, for any term that this token filter receives, it should produce an n-gram anchored to the start of the word of minimum length 1 and maximum length 20.

Then we need to use this token filter in a custom analyzer, which we will call the `autocomplete` analyzer:

```
{
    "analyzer": {
        "autocomplete": {
            "type":      "custom",
            "tokenizer": "standard",
```

```
            "filter": [
                "lowercase",
                "autocomplete_filter"  ❶
            ]
        }
    }
}
```

❶ Our custom edge-ngram token filter

This analyzer will tokenize a string into individual terms by using the `standard` tokenizer, lowercase each term, and then produce edge n-grams of each term, thanks to our `autocomplete_filter`.

The full request to create the index and instantiate the token filter and analyzer looks like this:

```
PUT /my_index
{
    "settings": {
        "number_of_shards": 1,  ❶
        "analysis": {
            "filter": {
                "autocomplete_filter": {  ❷
                    "type":     "edge_ngram",
                    "min_gram": 1,
                    "max_gram": 20
                }
            },
            "analyzer": {
                "autocomplete": {
                    "type":      "custom",
                    "tokenizer": "standard",
                    "filter": [
                        "lowercase",
                        "autocomplete_filter"  ❸
                    ]
                }
            }
        }
    }
}
```

❶ See "Relevance Is Broken!" on page 216.

❷ First we define our custom token filter.

❸ Then we use it in an analyzer.

You can test this new analyzer to make sure it is behaving correctly by using the `ana lyze` API:

```
GET /my_index/_analyze?analyzer=autocomplete
quick brown
```

The results show us that the analyzer is working correctly. It returns these terms:

- q
- qu
- qui
- quic
- quick
- b
- br
- bro
- brow
- brown

To use the analyzer, we need to apply it to a field, which we can do with the update-mapping API:

```
PUT /my_index/_mapping/my_type
{
    "my_type": {
        "properties": {
            "name": {
                "type":     "string",
                "analyzer": "autocomplete"
            }
        }
    }
}
```

Now, we can index some test documents:

```
POST /my_index/my_type/_bulk
{ "index": { "_id": 1           }}
{ "name": "Brown foxes"    }
{ "index": { "_id": 2           }}
{ "name": "Yellow furballs" }
```

Querying the Field

If you test out a query for "brown fo" by using a simple match query

```
GET /my_index/my_type/_search
{
    "query": {
```

```
            "match": {
                "name": "brown fo"
            }
        }
    }
```

you will see that *both* documents match, even though the Yellow furballs doc contains neither brown nor fo:

```
{
    "hits": [
        {
            "_id": "1",
            "_score": 1.5753809,
            "_source": {
                "name": "Brown foxes"
            }
        },
        {
            "_id": "2",
            "_score": 0.012520773,
            "_source": {
                "name": "Yellow furballs"
            }
        }
    ]
}
```

As always, the validate-query API shines some light:

```
GET /my_index/my_type/_validate/query?explain
{
    "query": {
        "match": {
            "name": "brown fo"
        }
    }
}
```

The explanation shows us that the query is looking for edge n-grams of every word in the query string:

```
name:b name:br name:bro name:brow name:brown name:f name:fo
```

The name:f condition is satisfied by the second document because furballs has been indexed as f, fu, fur, and so forth. In retrospect, this is not surprising. The same autocomplete analyzer is being applied both at index time and at search time, which in most situations is the right thing to do. This is one of the few occasions when it makes sense to break this rule.

We want to ensure that our inverted index contains edge n-grams of every word, but we want to match only the full words that the user has entered (brown and fo). We can do this by using the autocomplete analyzer at index time and the standard analyzer at search time. One way to change the search analyzer is just to specify it in the query:

```
GET /my_index/my_type/_search
{
    "query": {
        "match": {
            "name": {
                "query":    "brown fo",
                "analyzer": "standard" ❶
            }
        }
    }
}
```

❶ This overrides the analyzer setting on the name field.

Alternatively, we can specify the index_analyzer and search_analyzer in the mapping for the name field itself. Because we want to change only the search_analyzer, we can update the existing mapping without having to reindex our data:

```
PUT /my_index/my_type/_mapping
{
    "my_type": {
        "properties": {
            "name": {
                "type":            "string",
                "index_analyzer":  "autocomplete", ❶
                "search_analyzer": "standard" ❷
            }
        }
    }
}
```

❶ Use the autocomplete analyzer at index time to produce edge n-grams of every term.

❷ Use the standard analyzer at search time to search only on the terms that the user has entered.

If we were to repeat the validate-query request, it would now give us this explanation:

```
name:brown name:fo
```

Repeating our query correctly returns just the Brown foxes document.

Because most of the work has been done at index time, all this query needs to do is to look up the two terms brown and fo, which is much more efficient than the match_phrase_prefix approach of having to find all terms beginning with fo.

Completion Suggester

Using edge n-grams for search-as-you-type is easy to set up, flexible, and fast. However, sometimes it is not fast enough. Latency matters, especially when you are trying to provide instant feedback. Sometimes the fastest way of searching is not to search at all.

The completion suggester (*http://bit.ly/1IChV5j*) in Elasticsearch takes a completely different approach. You feed it a list of all possible completions, and it builds them into a *finite state transducer*, an optimized data structure that resembles a big graph. To search for suggestions, Elasticsearch starts at the beginning of the graph and moves character by character along the matching path. Once it has run out of user input, it looks at all possible endings of the current path to produce a list of suggestions.

This data structure lives in memory and makes prefix lookups extremely fast, much faster than any term-based query could be. It is an excellent match for autocompletion of names and brands, whose words are usually organized in a common order: "Johnny Rotten" rather than "Rotten Johnny."

When word order is less predictable, edge n-grams can be a better solution than the completion suggester. This particular cat may be skinned in myriad ways.

Edge n-grams and Postcodes

The edge n-gram approach can also be used for structured data, such as the postcodes example from earlier in this chapter. Of course, the postcode field would need to be analyzed instead of not_analyzed, but you could use the keyword tokenizer to treat the postcodes as if they were not_analyzed.

 The keyword tokenizer is the no-operation tokenizer, the tokenizer that does nothing. Whatever string it receives as input, it emits exactly the same string as a single token. It can therefore be used for values that we would normally treat as not_analyzed but that require some other analysis transformation such as lowercasing.

This example uses the keyword tokenizer to convert the postcode string into a token stream, so that we can use the edge n-gram token filter:

```
{
    "analysis": {
```

```
            "filter": {
                "postcode_filter": {
                    "type":     "edge_ngram",
                    "min_gram": 1,
                    "max_gram": 8
                }
            },
            "analyzer": {
                "postcode_index": {  ❶
                    "tokenizer": "keyword",
                    "filter":    [ "postcode_filter" ]
                },
                "postcode_search": {  ❷
                    "tokenizer": "keyword"
                }
            }
        }
    }
}
```

❶ The `postcode_index` analyzer would use the `postcode_filter` to turn postcodes into edge n-grams.

❷ The `postcode_search` analyzer would treat search terms as if they were `not_indexed`.

Ngrams for Compound Words

Finally, let's take a look at how n-grams can be used to search languages with compound words. German is famous for combining several small words into one massive compound word in order to capture precise or complex meanings. For example:

Aussprachewörterbuch
Pronunciation dictionary

Militärgeschichte
Military history

Weißkopfseeadler
White-headed sea eagle, or bald eagle

Weltgesundheitsorganisation
World Health Organization

Rindfleischetikettierungsüberwachungsaufgabenübertragungsgesetz
The law concerning the delegation of duties for the supervision of cattle marking and the labeling of beef

Somebody searching for "Wörterbuch" (dictionary) would probably expect to see "Aussprachewörtebuch" in the results list. Similarly, a search for "Adler" (eagle) should include "Weißkopfseeadler."

One approach to indexing languages like this is to break compound words into their constituent parts using the compound word token filter (*http://bit.ly/1ygdjjC*). However, the quality of the results depends on how good your compound-word dictionary is.

Another approach is just to break all words into n-grams and to search for any matching fragments—the more fragments that match, the more relevant the document.

Given that an n-gram is a moving window on a word, an n-gram of any length will cover all of the word. We want to choose a length that is long enough to be meaningful, but not so long that we produce far too many unique terms. A *trigram* (length 3) is probably a good starting point:

```
PUT /my_index
{
    "settings": {
        "analysis": {
            "filter": {
                "trigrams_filter": {
                    "type":      "ngram",
                    "min_gram": 3,
                    "max_gram": 3
                }
            },
            "analyzer": {
                "trigrams": {
                    "type":      "custom",
                    "tokenizer": "standard",
                    "filter":    [
                        "lowercase",
                        "trigrams_filter"
                    ]
                }
            }
        }
    },
    "mappings": {
        "my_type": {
            "properties": {
                "text": {
                    "type":      "string",
                    "analyzer": "trigrams" ❶
                }
            }
        }
    }
```

```
    }
}
```

❶ The `text` field uses the `trigrams` analyzer to index its contents as n-grams of length 3.

Testing the trigrams analyzer with the `analyze` API

```
GET /my_index/_analyze?analyzer=trigrams
Weißkopfseeadler
```

returns these terms:

```
wei, eiß, ißk, ßko, kop, opf, pfs, fse, see, eea,ead, adl, dle, ler
```

We can index our example compound words to test this approach:

```
POST /my_index/my_type/_bulk
{ "index": { "_id": 1 }}
{ "text": "Aussprachewörterbuch" }
{ "index": { "_id": 2 }}
{ "text": "Militärgeschichte" }
{ "index": { "_id": 3 }}
{ "text": "Weißkopfseeadler" }
{ "index": { "_id": 4 }}
{ "text": "Weltgesundheitsorganisation" }
{ "index": { "_id": 5 }}
{ "text": "Rindfleischetikettierungsüberwachungsaufgabenübertragungsgesetz" }
```

A search for "Adler" (eagle) becomes a query for the three terms `adl`, `dle`, and `ler`:

```
GET /my_index/my_type/_search
{
    "query": {
        "match": {
            "text": "Adler"
        }
    }
}
```

which correctly matches "Weißkopfsee-*adler*":

```
{
  "hits": [
    {
        "_id": "3",
        "_score": 3.3191128,
        "_source": {
            "text": "Weißkopfseeadler"
        }
    }
  ]
}
```

A similar query for "Gesundheit" (health) correctly matches "Welt-*gesundheit*-sorganisation*," but it also matches "Militär-*ges*-chichte" and "Rindfleischetikettierungsüberwachungsaufgabenübertragungs-*ges*-etz," both of which also contain the trigram ges.

Judicious use of the minimum_should_match parameter can remove these spurious results by requiring that a minimum number of trigrams must be present for a document to be considered a match:

```
GET /my_index/my_type/_search
{
    "query": {
        "match": {
            "text": {
                "query":                "Gesundheit",
                "minimum_should_match": "80%"
            }
        }
    }
}
```

This is a bit of a shotgun approach to full-text search and can result in a large inverted index, but it is an effective generic way of indexing languages that use many compound words or that don't use whitespace between words, such as Thai.

This technique is used to increase *recall*—the number of relevant documents that a search returns. It is usually used in combination with other techniques, such as shingles (see "Finding Associated Words" on page 252) to improve precision and the relevance score of each document.

CHAPTER 17

Controlling Relevance

Databases that deal purely in structured data (such as dates, numbers, and string enums) have it easy: they just have to check whether a document (or a row, in a relational database) matches the query.

While Boolean yes/no matches are an essential part of full-text search, they are not enough by themselves. Instead, we also need to know how relevant each document is to the query. Full-text search engines have to not only find the matching documents, but also sort them by relevance.

Full-text relevance formulae, or *similarity algorithms*, combine several factors to produce a single relevance _score for each document. In this chapter, we examine the various moving parts and discuss how they can be controlled.

Of course, relevance is not just about full-text queries; it may need to take structured data into account as well. Perhaps we are looking for a vacation home with particular features (air-conditioning, sea view, free WiFi). The more features that a property has, the more relevant it is. Or perhaps we want to factor in sliding scales like recency, price, popularity, or distance, while still taking the relevance of a full-text query into account.

All of this is possible thanks to the powerful scoring infrastructure available in Elasticsearch.

We will start by looking at the theoretical side of how Lucene calculates relevance, and then move on to practical examples of how you can control the process.

Theory Behind Relevance Scoring

Lucene (and thus Elasticsearch) uses the *Boolean model* (*http://en.wikipedia.org/wiki/ Standard_Boolean_model*) to find matching documents, and a formula called the *practical scoring function* to calculate relevance. This formula borrows concepts from *term frequency/inverse document frequency* (*http://en.wikipedia.org/wiki/Tfidf*) and the *vector space model* (*http://en.wikipedia.org/wiki/Vector_space_model*) but adds more-modern features like a coordination factor, field length normalization, and term or query clause boosting.

 Don't be alarmed! These concepts are not as complicated as the names make them appear. While this section mentions algorithms, formulae, and mathematical models, it is intended for consumption by mere humans. Understanding the algorithms themselves is not as important as understanding the factors that influence the outcome.

Boolean Model

The *Boolean model* simply applies the AND, OR, and NOT conditions expressed in the query to find all the documents that match. A query for

    full AND text AND search AND (elasticsearch OR lucene)

will include only documents that contain all of the terms full, text, and search, and either elasticsearch or lucene.

This process is simple and fast. It is used to exclude any documents that cannot possibly match the query.

Term Frequency/Inverse Document Frequency (TF/IDF)

Once we have a list of matching documents, they need to be ranked by relevance. Not all documents will contain all the terms, and some terms are more important than others. The relevance score of the whole document depends (in part) on the *weight* of each query term that appears in that document.

The weight of a term is determined by three factors, which we already introduced in "What Is Relevance?" on page 117. The formulae are included for interest's sake, but you are not required to remember them.

Term frequency

How often does the term appear in this document? The more often, the *higher* the weight. A field containing five mentions of the same term is more likely to be relevant than a field containing just one mention. The term frequency is calculated as follows:

    tf(t in d) = √frequency ❶

❶ The term frequency (tf) for term t in document d is the square root of the number of times the term appears in the document.

If you don't care about how often a term appears in a field, and all you care about is that the term is present, then you can disable term frequencies in the field mapping:

```
PUT /my_index
{
  "mappings": {
    "doc": {
      "properties": {
        "text": {
          "type":          "string",
          "index_options": "docs" ❶
        }
      }
    }
  }
}
```

❶ Setting index_options to docs will disable term frequencies and term positions. A field with this mapping will not count how many times a term appears, and will not be usable for phrase or proximity queries. Exact-value not_analyzed string fields use this setting by default.

Inverse document frequency

How often does the term appear in all documents in the collection? The more often, the *lower* the weight. Common terms like and or the contribute little to relevance, as they appear in most documents, while uncommon terms like elastic or hippopota mus help us zoom in on the most interesting documents. The inverse document frequency is calculated as follows:

```
idf(t) = 1 + log ( numDocs / (docFreq + 1)) ❶
```

❶ The inverse document frequency (idf) of term t is the logarithm of the number of documents in the index, divided by the number of documents that contain the term.

Field-length norm

How long is the field? The shorter the field, the *higher* the weight. If a term appears in a short field, such as a title field, it is more likely that the content of that field is *about* the term than if the same term appears in a much bigger body field. The field length norm is calculated as follows:

```
norm(d) = 1 / √numTerms ❶
```

❶ The field-length norm (norm) is the inverse square root of the number of terms in the field.

While the field-length norm is important for full-text search, many other fields don't need norms. Norms consume approximately 1 byte per `string` field per document in the index, whether or not a document contains the field. Exact-value `not_analyzed` string fields have norms disabled by default, but you can use the field mapping to disable norms on `analyzed` fields as well:

```
PUT /my_index
{
  "mappings": {
    "doc": {
      "properties": {
        "text": {
          "type": "string",
          "norms": { "enabled": false } ❶
        }
      }
    }
  }
}
```

❶ This field will not take the field-length norm into account. A long field and a short field will be scored as if they were the same length.

For use cases such as logging, norms are not useful. All you care about is whether a field contains a particular error code or a particular browser identifier. The length of the field does not affect the outcome. Disabling norms can save a significant amount of memory.

Putting it together

These three factors—term frequency, inverse document frequency, and field-length norm—are calculated and stored at index time. Together, they are used to calculate the *weight* of a single term in a particular document.

 When we refer to *documents* in the preceding formulae, we are actually talking about a field within a document. Each field has its own inverted index and thus, for TF/IDF purposes, the value of the field is the value of the document.

When we run a simple `term` query with `explain` set to `true` (see "Understanding the Score" on page 118), you will see that the only factors involved in calculating the score are the ones explained in the preceding sections:

```
PUT /my_index/doc/1
{ "text" : "quick brown fox" }

GET /my_index/doc/_search?explain
{
  "query": {
    "term": {
      "text": "fox"
    }
  }
}
```

The (abbreviated) `explanation` from the preceding request is as follows:

```
weight(text:fox in 0) [PerFieldSimilarity]:  0.15342641  ❶
result of:
    fieldWeight in 0                         0.15342641
    product of:
        tf(freq=1.0), with freq of 1:       1.0  ❷
        idf(docFreq=1, maxDocs=1):          0.30685282  ❸
        fieldNorm(doc=0):                    0.5  ❹
```

❶ The final `score` for term fox in field `text` in the document with internal Lucene doc ID 0.

❷ The term `fox` appears once in the `text` field in this document.

❸ The inverse document frequency of `fox` in the `text` field in all documents in this index.

❹ The field-length normalization factor for this field.

Of course, queries usually consist of more than one term, so we need a way of combining the weights of multiple terms. For this, we turn to the vector space model.

Vector Space Model

The *vector space model* provides a way of comparing a multiterm query against a document. The output is a single score that represents how well the document matches the query. In order to do this, the model represents both the document and the query as *vectors*.

A vector is really just a one-dimensional array containing numbers, for example:

```
[1,2,5,22,3,8]
```

In the vector space model, each number in the vector is the *weight* of a term, as calculated with term frequency/inverse document frequency.

While TF/IDF is the default way of calculating term weights for the vector space model, it is not the only way. Other models like Okapi-BM25 exist and are available in Elasticsearch. TF/IDF is the default because it is a simple, efficient algorithm that produces high-quality search results and has stood the test of time.

Imagine that we have a query for "happy hippopotamus." A common word like happy will have a low weight, while an uncommon term like hippopotamus will have a high weight. Let's assume that happy has a weight of 2 and hippopotamus has a weight of 5. We can plot this simple two-dimensional vector—[2,5]—as a line on a graph starting at point (0,0) and ending at point (2,5), as shown in Figure 17-1.

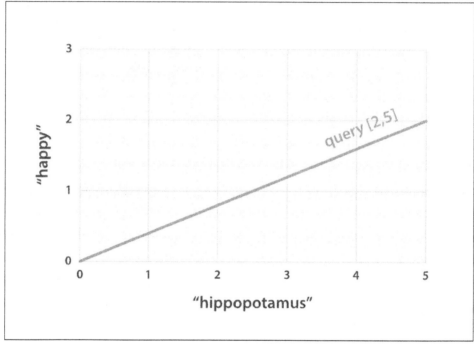

Figure 17-1. A two-dimensional query vector for "happy hippopotamus" represented

Now, imagine we have three documents:

1. I am *happy* in summer.
2. After Christmas I'm a *hippopotamus*.
3. The *happy hippopotamus* helped Harry.

We can create a similar vector for each document, consisting of the weight of each query term—happy and hippopotamus—that appears in the document, and plot these vectors on the same graph, as shown in Figure 17-2:

- Document 1: (happy,_____)—[2,0]
- Document 2: (___ ,hippopotamus)—[0,5]
- Document 3: (happy,hippopotamus)—[2,5]

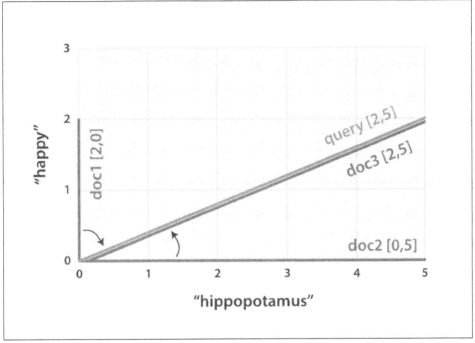

Figure 17-2. Query and document vectors for "happy hippopotamus"

The nice thing about vectors is that they can be compared. By measuring the angle between the query vector and the document vector, it is possible to assign a relevance score to each document. The angle between document 1 and the query is large, so it is of low relevance. Document 2 is closer to the query, meaning that it is reasonably relevant, and document 3 is a perfect match.

In practice, only two-dimensional vectors (queries with two terms) can be plotted easily on a graph. Fortunately, *linear algebra*—the branch of mathematics that deals with vectors—provides tools to compare the angle between multidimensional vectors, which means that we can apply the same principles explained above to queries that consist of many terms.

You can read more about how to compare two vectors by using *cosine similarity (http://en.wikipedia.org/wiki/Cosine_similarity)*.

Now that we have talked about the theoretical basis of scoring, we can move on to see how scoring is implemented in Lucene.

Lucene's Practical Scoring Function

For multiterm queries, Lucene takes the Boolean model, TF/IDF, and the vector space model and combines them in a single efficient package that collects matching documents and scores them as it goes.

A multiterm query like

```
GET /my_index/doc/_search
{
  "query": {
    "match": {
      "text": "quick fox"
    }
  }
}
```

is rewritten internally to look like this:

```
GET /my_index/doc/_search
{
  "query": {
    "bool": {
      "should": [
        {"term": { "text": "quick" }},
        {"term": { "text": "fox"   }}
      ]
    }
  }
}
```

The `bool` query implements the Boolean model and, in this example, will include only documents that contain either the term `quick` or the term `fox` or both.

As soon as a document matches a query, Lucene calculates its score for that query, combining the scores of each matching term. The formula used for scoring is called the *practical scoring function*. It looks intimidating, but don't be put off—most of the components you already know. It introduces a few new elements that we discuss next.

```
score(q,d)  =  ❶
            queryNorm(q)  ❷
        ·  coord(q,d)   ❸
        ·  Σ (           ❹
              tf(t in d)   ❺
          ·  idf(t)²       ❻
          ·  t.getBoost()  ❼
          ·  norm(t,d)     ❽
        ) (t in q)     ❹
```

❶   score(q,d) is the relevance score of document d for query q.

❷   queryNorm(q) is the *query normalization* factor (new).

❸   coord(q,d) is the *coordination* factor (new).

❹   The sum of the weights for each term t in the query q for document d.

❺   tf(t in d) is the term frequency for term t in document d.

❻   idf(t) is the inverse document frequency for term t.

❼   t.getBoost() is the *boost* that has been applied to the query (new).

❽   norm(t,d) is the field-length norm, combined with the index-time field-level boost, if any. (new).

You should recognize score, tf, and idf. The queryNorm, coord, t.getBoost, and norm are new.

We will talk more about query-time boosting later in this chapter, but first let's get query normalization, coordination, and index-time field-level boosting out of the way.

Query Normalization Factor

The *query normalization factor* (queryNorm) is an attempt to *normalize* a query so that the results from one query may be compared with the results of another.

Even though the intent of the query norm is to make results from different queries comparable, it doesn't work very well. The only purpose of the relevance _score is to sort the results of the current query in the correct order. You should not try to compare the relevance scores from different queries.

This factor is calculated at the beginning of the query. The actual calculation depends on the queries involved, but a typical implementation is as follows:

```
queryNorm = 1 / √sumOfSquaredWeights ❶
```

❶ The sumOfSquaredWeights is calculated by adding together the IDF of each term in the query, squared.

The same query normalization factor is applied to every document, and you have no way of changing it. For all intents and purposes, it can be ignored.

Query Coordination

The *coordination factor* (coord) is used to reward documents that contain a higher percentage of the query terms. The more query terms that appear in the document, the greater the chances that the document is a good match for the query.

Imagine that we have a query for quick brown fox, and that the weight for each term is 1.5. Without the coordination factor, the score would just be the sum of the weights of the terms in a document. For instance:

- Document with fox → score: 1.5
- Document with quick fox → score: 3.0
- Document with quick brown fox → score: 4.5

The coordination factor multiplies the score by the number of matching terms in the document, and divides it by the total number of terms in the query. With the coordination factor, the scores would be as follows:

- Document with fox → score: 1.5 * 1 / 3 = 0.5
- Document with quick fox → score: 3.0 * 2 / 3 = 2.0
- Document with quick brown fox → score: 4.5 * 3 / 3 = 4.5

The coordination factor results in the document that contains all three terms being much more relevant than the document that contains just two of them.

Remember that the query for quick brown fox is rewritten into a bool query like this:

```
GET /_search
{
  "query": {
    "bool": {
      "should": [
        { "term": { "text": "quick" }},
        { "term": { "text": "brown" }},
        { "term": { "text": "fox"   }}
      ]
    }
  }
}
```

The bool query uses query coordination by default for all should clauses, but it does allow you to disable coordination. Why might you want to do this? Well, usually the answer is, you don't. Query coordination is usually a good thing. When you use a bool query to wrap several high-level queries like the match query, it also makes sense to leave coordination enabled. The more clauses that match, the higher the degree of overlap between your search request and the documents that are returned.

However, in some advanced use cases, it might make sense to disable coordination. Imagine that you are looking for the synonyms jump, leap, and hop. You don't care how many of these synonyms are present, as they all represent the same concept. In fact, only one of the synonyms is likely to be present. This would be a good case for disabling the coordination factor:

```
GET /_search
{
  "query": {
    "bool": {
      "disable_coord": true,
      "should": [
        { "term": { "text": "jump" }},
        { "term": { "text": "hop"  }},
        { "term": { "text": "leap" }}
      ]
    }
  }
}
```

When you use synonyms (see Chapter 23), this is exactly what happens internally: the rewritten query disables coordination for the synonyms. Most use cases for disabling coordination are handled automatically; you don't need to worry about it.

Index-Time Field-Level Boosting

We will talk about *boosting* a field—making it more important than other fields—at query time in "Query-Time Boosting" on page 288. It is also possible to apply a boost to a field at index time. Actually, this boost is applied to every term in the field, rather than to the field itself.

To store this boost value in the index without using more space than necessary, this field-level index-time boost is combined with the field-length norm (see "Field-length norm" on page 279) and stored in the index as a single byte. This is the value returned by norm(t,d) in the preceding formula.

We strongly recommend against using field-level index-time boosts for a few reasons:

- Combining the boost with the field-length norm and storing it in a single byte means that the field-length norm loses precision. The result is that Elasticsearch is unable to distinguish between a field containing three words and a field containing five words.

- To change an index-time boost, you have to reindex all your documents. A query-time boost, on the other hand, can be changed with every query.

- If a field with an index-time boost has multiple values, the boost is multiplied by itself for every value, dramatically increasing the weight for that field.

Query-time boosting is a much simpler, cleaner, more flexible option.

With query normalization, coordination, and index-time boosting out of the way, we can now move on to the most useful tool for influencing the relevance calculation: query-time boosting.

Query-Time Boosting

In Prioritizing Clauses, we explained how you could use the boost parameter at search time to give one query clause more importance than another. For instance:

```
GET /_search
{
  "query": {
    "bool": {
      "should": [
        {
          "match": {
```

```
        "title": {
          "query": "quick brown fox",
          "boost": 2 ❶
        }
      }
    },
    {
      "match": { ❷
        "content": "quick brown fox"
      }
    }
  ]
}
}
}
}
```

❶ The title query clause is twice as important as the content query clause, because it has been boosted by a factor of 2.

❷ A query clause without a boost value has a neutral boost of 1.

Query-time boosting is the main tool that you can use to tune relevance. Any type of query accepts a boost parameter. Setting a boost of 2 doesn't simply double the final _score; the actual boost value that is applied goes through normalization and some internal optimization. However, it does imply that a clause with a boost of 2 is twice as important as a clause with a boost of 1.

Practically, there is no simple formula for deciding on the "correct" boost value for a particular query clause. It's a matter of try-it-and-see. Remember that boost is just one of the factors involved in the relevance score; it has to compete with the other factors. For instance, in the preceding example, the title field will probably already have a "natural" boost over the content field thanks to the field-length norm (titles are usually shorter than the related content), so don't blindly boost fields just because you think they should be boosted. Apply a boost and check the results. Change the boost and check again.

Boosting an Index

When searching across multiple indices, you can boost an entire index over the others with the indices_boost parameter. This could be used, as in the next example, to give more weight to documents from a more recent index:

```
GET /docs_2014_*/_search ❶
{
  "indices_boost": { ❷
    "docs_2014_10": 3,
    "docs_2014_09": 2
  },
```

```
  "query": {
    "match": {
      "text": "quick brown fox"
    }
  }
}
```

❶ This multi-index search covers all indices beginning with docs_2014_.

❷ Documents in the docs_2014_10 index will be boosted by 3, those in docs_2014_09 by 2, and any other matching indices will have a neutral boost of 1.

t.getBoost()

These boost values are represented in the "Lucene's Practical Scoring Function" on page 284 by the t.getBoost() element. Boosts are not applied at the level that they appear in the query DSL. Instead, any boost values are combined and passsed down to the individual terms. The t.getBoost() method returns any boost value applied to the term itself or to any of the queries higher up the chain.

 In fact, reading the explain output is a little more complex than that. You won't see the boost value or t.getBoost() mentioned in the explanation at all. Instead, the boost is rolled into the query Norm that is applied to a particular term. Although we said that the queryNorm is the same for every term, you will see that the query Norm for a boosted term is higher than the queryNorm for an unboosted term.

Manipulating Relevance with Query Structure

The Elasticsearch query DSL is immensely flexible. You can move individual query clauses up and down the query hierarchy to make a clause more or less important. For instance, imagine the following query:

```
quick OR brown OR red OR fox
```

We could write this as a bool query with all terms at the same level:

```
GET /_search
{
  "query": {
    "bool": {
      "should": [
        { "term": { "text": "quick" }},
        { "term": { "text": "brown" }},
        { "term": { "text": "red"   }},
        { "term": { "text": "fox"   }}
```

```
        ]
      }
    }
  }
```

But this query might score a document that contains quick, red, and brown the same as another document that contains quick, red, and fox. *Red* and *brown* are synonyms and we probably only need one of them to match. Perhaps we really want to express the query as follows:

```
quick OR (brown OR red) OR fox
```

According to standard Boolean logic, this is exactly the same as the original query, but as we have already seen in Combining Queries, a bool query does not concern itself only with whether a document matches, but also with how *well* it matches.

A better way to write this query is as follows:

```
GET /_search
{
  "query": {
    "bool": {
      "should": [
        { "term": { "text": "quick" }},
        { "term": { "text": "fox"   }},
        {
          "bool": {
            "should": [
              { "term": { "text": "brown" }},
              { "term": { "text": "red"   }}
            ]
          }
        }
      ]
    }
  }
}
```

Now, red and brown compete with each other at their own level, and quick, fox, and red OR brown are the top-level competitive terms.

We have already discussed how the match, multi_match, term, bool, and dis_max queries can be used to manipulate scoring. In the rest of this chapter, we present three other scoring-related queries: the boosting query, the constant_score query, and the function_score query.

Not Quite Not

A search on the Internet for "Apple" is likely to return results about the company, the fruit, and various recipes. We could try to narrow it down to just the company by excluding words like pie, tart, crumble, and tree, using a must_not clause in a bool query:

```
GET /_search
{
  "query": {
    "bool": {
      "must": {
        "match": {
          "text": "apple"
        }
      },
      "must_not": {
        "match": {
          "text": "pie tart fruit crumble tree"
        }
      }
    }
  }
}
```

But who is to say that we wouldn't miss a very relevant document about Apple the company by excluding tree or crumble? Sometimes, must_not can be too strict.

boosting Query

The boosting query (*http://bit.ly/1IO281f*) solves this problem. It allows us to still include results that appear to be about the fruit or the pastries, but to downgrade them—to rank them lower than they would otherwise be:

```
GET /_search
{
  "query": {
    "boosting": {
      "positive": {
        "match": {
          "text": "apple"
        }
      },
      "negative": {
        "match": {
          "text": "pie tart fruit crumble tree"
        }
      },
      "negative_boost": 0.5
    }
  }
}
```

It accepts a positive query and a negative query. Only documents that match the positive query will be included in the results list, but documents that also match the negative query will be downgraded by multiplying the original _score of the document with the negative_boost.

For this to work, the negative_boost must be less than 1.0. In this example, any documents that contain any of the negative terms will have their _score cut in half.

Ignoring TF/IDF

Sometimes we just don't care about TF/IDF. All we want to know is that a certain word appears in a field. Perhaps we are searching for a vacation home and we want to find houses that have as many of these features as possible:

- WiFi
- Garden
- Pool

The vacation home documents look something like this:

```
{ "description": "A delightful four-bedroomed house with ... " }
```

We could use a simple match query:

```
GET /_search
{
  "query": {
    "match": {
      "description": "wifi garden pool"
    }
  }
}
```

However, this isn't really *full-text search*. In this case, TF/IDF just gets in the way. We don't care whether wifi is a common term, or how often it appears in the document. All we care about is that it does appear. In fact, we just want to rank houses by the number of features they have—the more, the better. If a feature is present, it should score 1, and if it isn't, 0.

constant_score Query

Enter the constant_score (*http://bit.ly/1DIgSAK*) query. This query can wrap either a query or a filter, and assigns a score of 1 to any documents that match, regardless of TF/IDF:

```
GET /_search
{
  "query": {
    "bool": {
      "should": [
```

```
              { "constant_score": {
                "query": { "match": { "description": "wifi" }}
              }},
              { "constant_score": {
                "query": { "match": { "description": "garden" }}
              }},
              { "constant_score": {
                "query": { "match": { "description": "pool" }}
              }}
            ]
          }
        }
      }
```

Perhaps not all features are equally important—some have more value to the user than others. If the most important feature is the pool, we could boost that clause to make it count for more:

```
GET /_search
{
  "query": {
    "bool": {
      "should": [
        { "constant_score": {
          "query": { "match": { "description": "wifi" }}
        }},
        { "constant_score": {
          "query": { "match": { "description": "garden" }}
        }},
        { "constant_score": {
          "boost":    2 ❶
          "query": { "match": { "description": "pool" }}
        }}
      ]
    }
  }
}
```

❶ A matching pool clause would add a score of 2, while the other clauses would add a score of only 1 each.

> The final score for each result is not simply the sum of the scores of all matching clauses. The coordination factor and query normalization factor are still taken into account.

We could improve our vacation home documents by adding a not_analyzed features field to our vacation homes:

```
{ "features": [ "wifi", "pool", "garden" ] }
```

By default, a `not_analyzed` field has field-length norms disabled and has `index_options` set to `docs`, disabling term frequencies, but the problem remains: the inverse document frequency of each term is still taken into account.

We could use the same approach that we used previously, with the `constant_score` query:

```
GET /_search
{
  "query": {
    "bool": {
      "should": [
        { "constant_score": {
          "query": { "match": { "features": "wifi" }}
        }},
        { "constant_score": {
          "query": { "match": { "features": "garden" }}
        }},
        { "constant_score": {
          "boost":   2
          "query": { "match": { "features": "pool" }}
        }}
      ]
    }
  }
}
```

Really, though, each of these features should be treated like a filter. A vacation home either has the feature or it doesn't—a filter seems like it would be a natural fit. On top of that, if we use filters, we can benefit from filter caching.

The problem is this: filters don't score. What we need is a way of bridging the gap between filters and queries. The `function_score` query does this and a whole lot more.

function_score Query

The `function_score` query (*http://bit.ly/1sCKtHW*) is the ultimate tool for taking control of the scoring process. It allows you to apply a function to each document that matches the main query in order to alter or completely replace the original query `_score`.

In fact, you can apply different functions to *subsets* of the main result set by using filters, which gives you the best of both worlds: efficient scoring with cacheable filters.

It supports several predefined functions out of the box:

`weight`

> Apply a simple boost to each document without the boost being normalized: a `weight` of 2 results in 2 * `_score`.

`field_value_factor`

> Use the value of a field in the document to alter the `_score`, such as factoring in a `popularity` count or number of `votes`.

`random_score`

> Use consistently random scoring to sort results differently for every user, while maintaining the same sort order for a single user.

Decay functions—`linear`, `exp`, `gauss`

> Incorporate sliding-scale values like `publish_date`, `geo_location`, or `price` into the `_score` to prefer recently published documents, documents near a latitude/longitude (lat/lon) point, or documents near a specified price point.

`script_score`

> Use a custom script to take complete control of the scoring logic. If your needs extend beyond those of the functions in this list, write a custom script to implement the logic that you need.

Without the `function_score` query, we would not be able to combine the score from a full-text query with a factor like recency. We would have to sort either by `_score` or by `date`; the effect of one would obliterate the effect of the other. This query allows you to blend the two together: to still sort by full-text relevance, but giving extra weight to recently published documents, or popular documents, or products that are near the user's price point. As you can imagine, a query that supports all of this can look fairly complex. We'll start with a simple use case and work our way up the complexity ladder.

Boosting by Popularity

Imagine that we have a website that hosts blog posts and enables users to vote for the blog posts that they like. We would like more-popular posts to appear higher in the results list, but still have the full-text score as the main relevance driver. We can do this easily by storing the number of votes with each blog post:

```
PUT /blogposts/post/1
{
  "title":   "About popularity",
  "content": "In this post we will talk about...",
  "votes":   6
}
```

At search time, we can use the `function_score` query with the `field_value_factor` function to combine the number of votes with the full-text relevance score:

```
GET /blogposts/post/_search
{
  "query": {
    "function_score": { ❶
      "query": { ❷
        "multi_match": {
          "query":    "popularity",
          "fields": [ "title", "content" ]
        }
      },
      "field_value_factor": { ❸
        "field": "votes" ❹
      }
    }
  }
}
```

❶ The `function_score` query wraps the main query and the function we would like to apply.

❷ The main query is executed first.

❸ The `field_value_factor` function is applied to every document matching the main `query`.

❹ Every document *must* have a number in the `votes` field for the `function_score` to work.

In the preceding example, the final `_score` for each document has been altered as follows:

```
new_score = old_score * number_of_votes
```

This will not give us great results. The full-text `_score` range usually falls somewhere between 0 and 10. As can be seen in Figure 17-3, a blog post with 10 votes will completely swamp the effect of the full-text score, and a blog post with 0 votes will reset the score to zero.

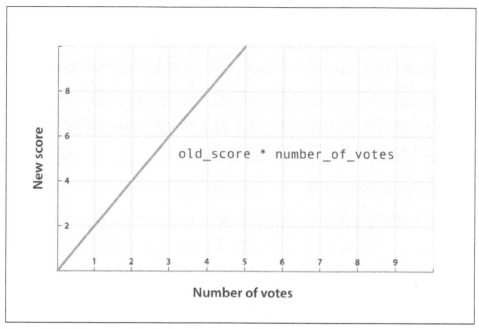

Figure 17-3. Linear popularity based on an original _score of 2.0

modifier

A better way to incorporate popularity is to smooth out the votes value with some modifier. In other words, we want the first few votes to count a lot, but for each subsequent vote to count less. The difference between 0 votes and 1 vote should be much bigger than the difference between 10 votes and 11 votes.

A typical modifier for this use case is log1p, which changes the formula to the following:

```
new_score = old_score * log(1 + number_of_votes)
```

The log function smooths out the effect of the votes field to provide a curve like the one in Figure 17-4.

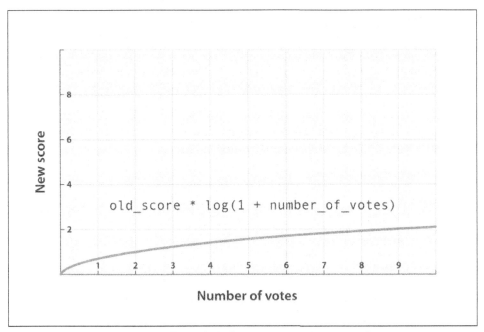

old_score * log(1 + number_of_votes)

Figure 17-4. Logarithmic popularity based on an original _score of 2.0

The request with the modifier parameter looks like the following:

```
GET /blogposts/post/_search
{
  "query": {
    "function_score": {
      "query": {
        "multi_match": {
          "query":    "popularity",
          "fields": [ "title", "content" ]
        }
      },
      "field_value_factor": {
        "field":    "votes",
        "modifier": "log1p" ❶
      }
    }
  }
}
```

❶ Set the modifier to log1p.

The available modifiers are none (the default), log, log1p, log2p, ln, ln1p, ln2p, square, sqrt, and reciprocal. You can read more about them in the field_value_factor documentation (*http://www.elasticsearch.org/guide/en/elastic search/reference/current/query-dsl-function-score-query.html#_field_value_factor*).

factor

The strength of the popularity effect can be increased or decreased by multiplying the value in the votes field by some number, called the factor:

```
GET /blogposts/post/_search
{
  "query": {
    "function_score": {
      "query": {
        "multi_match": {
          "query":    "popularity",
          "fields": [ "title", "content" ]
        }
      },
      "field_value_factor": {
        "field":    "votes",
        "modifier": "log1p",
        "factor":    2 ❶
      }
    }
  }
}
```

❶ Doubles the popularity effect

Adding in a factor changes the formula to this:

```
new_score = old_score * log(1 + factor * number_of_votes)
```

A factor greater than 1 increases the effect, and a factor less than 1 decreases the effect, as shown in Figure 17-5.

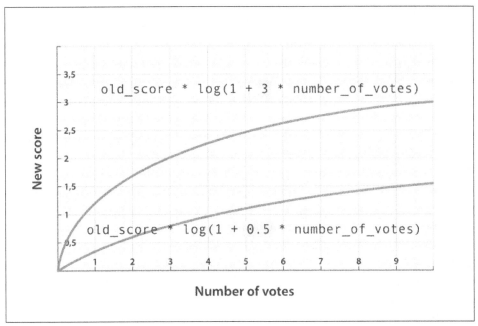

Figure 17-5. Logarithmic popularity with different factors

boost_mode

Perhaps multiplying the full-text score by the result of the `field_value_factor` function still has too large an effect. We can control how the result of a function is combined with the _score from the query by using the `boost_mode` parameter, which accepts the following values:

`multiply`
    Multiply the _score with the function result (default)

`sum`
    Add the function result to the _score

`min`
    The lower of the _score and the function result

`max`
    The higher of the _score and the function result

`replace`
    Replace the _score with the function result

If, instead of multiplying, we add the function result to the _score, we can achieve a much smaller effect, especially if we use a low `factor`:

```
GET /blogposts/post/_search
{
  "query": {
    "function_score": {
      "query": {
        "multi_match": {
          "query":     "popularity",
          "fields": [ "title", "content" ]
        }
      },
      "field_value_factor": {
        "field":     "votes",
        "modifier": "log1p",
        "factor":   0.1
      },
      "boost_mode": "sum"  ❶
    }
  }
}
```

❶ Add the function result to the _score.

The formula for the preceding request now looks like this (see Figure 17-6):

```
new_score = old_score + log(1 + 0.1 * number_of_votes)
```

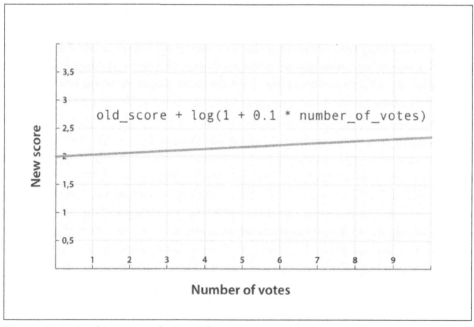

Figure 17-6. Combining popularity with sum

max_boost

Finally, we can cap the maximum effect that the function can have by using the max_boost parameter:

```
GET /blogposts/post/_search
{
  "query": {
    "function_score": {
      "query": {
        "multi_match": {
          "query":    "popularity",
          "fields": [ "title", "content" ]
        }
      },
      "field_value_factor": {
        "field":    "votes",
        "modifier": "log1p",
        "factor":   0.1
      },
      "boost_mode": "sum",
      "max_boost":  1.5 ❶
    }
  }
}
```

❶ Whatever the result of the field_value_factor function, it will never be greater than 1.5.

 The max_boost applies a limit to the result of the function only, not to the final _score.

Boosting Filtered Subsets

Let's return to the problem that we were dealing with in "Ignoring TF/IDF" on page 293, where we wanted to score vacation homes by the number of features that each home possesses. We ended that section by wishing for a way to use cached filters to affect the score, and with the function_score query we can do just that.

The examples we have shown thus far have used a single function for all documents. Now we want to divide the results into subsets by using filters (one filter per feature), and apply a different function to each subset.

The function that we will use in this example is the `weight`, which is similar to the `boost` parameter accepted by any query. The difference is that the `weight` is not normalized by Lucene into some obscure floating-point number; it is used as is.

The structure of the query has to change somewhat to incorporate multiple functions:

```
GET /_search
{
  "query": {
    "function_score": {
      "filter": { ❶
        "term": { "city": "Barcelona" }
      },
      "functions": [ ❷
        {
          "filter": { "term": { "features": "wifi" }}, ❸
          "weight": 1
        },
        {
          "filter": { "term": { "features": "garden" }}, ❸
          "weight": 1
        },
        {
          "filter": { "term": { "features": "pool" }}, ❸
          "weight": 2 ❹
        }
      ],
      "score_mode": "sum", ❺
    }
  }
}
```

❶ This `function_score` query has a `filter` instead of a `query`.

❷ The `functions` key holds a list of functions that should be applied.

❸ The function is applied only if the document matches the (optional) `filter`.

❹ The `pool` feature is more important than the others so it has a higher `weight`.

❺ The `score_mode` specifies how the values from each function should be combined.

The new features to note in this example are explained in the following sections.

filter Versus query

The first thing to note is that we have specified a `filter` instead of a `query`. In this example, we do not need full-text search. We just want to return all documents that have Barcelona in the city field, logic that is better expressed as a filter instead of a query. All documents returned by the filter will have a _score of 1. The function_score query accepts either a query or a filter. If neither is specified, it will default to using the match_all query.

functions

The functions key holds an array of functions to apply. Each entry in the array may also optionally specify a filter, in which case the function will be applied only to documents that match that filter. In this example, we apply a weight of 1 (or 2 in the case of pool) to any document that matches the filter.

score_mode

Each function returns a result, and we need a way of reducing these multiple results to a single value that can be combined with the original _score. This is the role of the score_mode parameter, which accepts the following values:

multiply
: Function results are multiplied together (default).

sum
: Function results are added up.

avg
: The average of all the function results.

max
: The highest function result is used.

min
: The lowest function result is used.

first
: Uses only the result from the first function that either doesn't have a filter or that has a filter matching the document.

In this case, we want to add the weight results from each matching filter together to produce the final score, so we have used the sum score mode.

Documents that don't match any of the filters will keep their original _score of 1.

Random Scoring

You may have been wondering what *consistently random scoring* is, or why you would ever want to use it. The previous example provides a good use case. All results from the previous example would receive a final _score of 1, 2, 3, 4, or 5. Maybe there are only a few homes that score 5, but presumably there would be a lot of homes scoring 2 or 3.

As the owner of the website, you want to give your advertisers as much exposure as possible. With the current query, results with the same _score would be returned in the same order every time. It would be good to introduce some randomness here, to ensure that all documents in a single score level get a similar amount of exposure.

We want every user to see a different random order, but we want the same user to see the same order when clicking on page 2, 3, and so forth. This is what is meant by *consistently random*.

The random_score function, which outputs a number between 0 and 1, will produce consistently random results when it is provided with the same seed value, such as a user's session ID:

```
GET /_search
{
  "query": {
    "function_score": {
      "filter": {
        "term": { "city": "Barcelona" }
      },
      "functions": [
        {
          "filter": { "term": { "features": "wifi" }},
          "weight": 1
        },
        {
          "filter": { "term": { "features": "garden" }},
          "weight": 1
        },
        {
          "filter": { "term": { "features": "pool" }},
          "weight": 2
        },
        {
          "random_score": { ❶
            "seed": "the users session id" ❷
          }
        }
      ],
      "score_mode": "sum",
    }
  }
}
```

❶ The random_score clause doesn't have any filter, so it will be applied to all documents.

---

❷ Pass the user's session ID as the seed, to make randomization consistent for that user. The same seed will result in the same randomization.

Of course, if you index new documents that match the query, the order of results will change regardless of whether you use consistent randomization or not.

The Closer, The Better

Many variables could influence the user's choice of vacation home. Maybe she would like to be close to the center of town, but perhaps would be willing to settle for a place that is a bit farther from the center if the price is low enough. Perhaps the reverse is true: she would be willing to pay more for the best location.

If we were to add a filter that excluded any vacation homes farther than 1 kilometer from the center, or any vacation homes that cost more than £100 a night, we might exclude results that the user would consider to be a good compromise.

The function_score query gives us the ability to trade off one sliding scale (like location) against another sliding scale (like price), with a group of functions known as the *decay functions*.

The three decay functions—called linear, exp, and gauss—operate on numeric fields, date fields, or lat/lon geo-points. All three take the same parameters:

origin
> The *central point*, or the best possible value for the field. Documents that fall at the origin will get a full _score of 1.0.

scale
> The rate of decay—how quickly the _score should drop the further from the ori gin that a document lies (for example, every £10 or every 100 meters).

decay
> The _score that a document at scale distance from the origin should receive. Defaults to 0.5.

offset
> Setting a nonzero offset expands the central point to cover a range of values instead of just the single point specified by the origin. All values in the range -offset <= origin <= +offset will receive the full _score of 1.0.

The only difference between these three functions is the shape of the decay curve. The difference is most easily illustrated with a graph (see Figure 17-7).

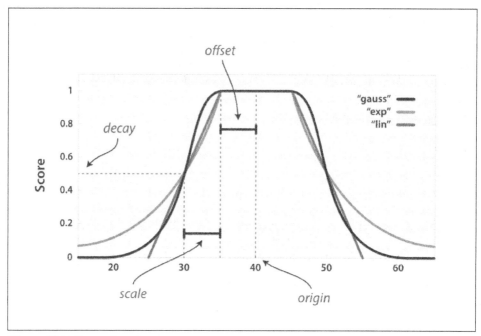

Figure 17-7. Decay function curves

The curves shown in Figure 17-7 all have their `origin`—the central point—set to 40. The `offset` is 5, meaning that all values in the range `40 - 5 <= value <= 40 + 5` are treated as though they were at the `origin`—they all get the full score of `1.0`.

Outside this range, the score starts to decay. The rate of decay is determined by the `scale` (which in this example is set to 5), and the `decay` (which is set to the default of `0.5`). The result is that all three curves return a score of `0.5` at `origin` +/- (`offset` + `scale`), or at points `30` and `50`.

The difference between `linear`, `exp`, and `gauss` is the shape of the curve at other points in the range:

- The `linear` funtion is just a straight line. Once the line hits zero, all values outside the line will return a score of `0.0`.

- The `exp` (exponential) function decays rapidly, then slows down.

- The `gauss` (Gaussian) function is bell-shaped—it decays slowly, then rapidly, then slows down again.

Which curve you choose depends entirely on how quickly you want the `_score` to decay, the further a value is from the `origin`.

To return to our example: our user would prefer to rent a vacation home close to the center of London ({ "lat": 51.50, "lon": 0.12}) and to pay no more than £100 a night, but our user considers price to be more important than distance. We could write this query as follows:

```
GET /_search
{
  "query": {
    "function_score": {
      "functions": [
        {
          "gauss": {
            "location": {  ❶
              "origin": { "lat": 51.5, "lon": 0.12 },
              "offset": "2km",
              "scale":  "3km"
            }
          }
        },
        {
          "gauss": {
            "price": {  ❷
              "origin": "50",  ❸
              "offset": "50",
              "scale":  "20"
            }
          },
          "weight": 2  ❹
        }
      ]
    }
  }
}
```

❶ The location field is mapped as a geo_point.

❷ The price field is numeric.

❸ See "Understanding the price Clause" on page 310 for the reason that origin is 50 instead of 100.

❹ The price clause has twice the weight of the location clause.

The location clause is easy to understand:

- We have specified an origin that corresponds to the center of London.
- Any location within 2km of the origin receives the full score of 1.0.

- Locations 5km (`offset` + `scale`) from the centre receive a score of `0.5`.

Understanding the price Clause

The `price` clause is a little trickier. The user's preferred price is anything up to £100, but this example sets the origin to £50. Prices can't be negative, but the lower they are, the better. Really, any price between £0 and £100 should be considered optimal.

If we were to set the `origin` to £100, then prices below £100 would receive a lower score. Instead, we set both the `origin` and the `offset` to £50. That way, the score decays only for any prices above £100 (`origin` + `offset`).

 The `weight` parameter can be used to increase or decrease the contribution of individual clauses. The `weight`, which defaults to `1.0`, is multiplied by the score from each clause before the scores are combined with the specified `score_mode`.

Scoring with Scripts

Finally, if none of the `function_score`'s built-in functions suffice, you can implement the logic that you need with a script, using the `script_score` function.

For an example, let's say that we want to factor our profit margin into the relevance calculation. In our business, the profit margin depends on three factors:

- The `price` per night of the vacation home.
- The user's membership level—some levels get a percentage `discount` above a certain price per night `threshold`.
- The negotiated `margin` as a percentage of the price-per-night, after user discounts.

The algorithm that we will use to calculate the profit for each home is as follows:

```
if (price < threshold) {
  profit = price * margin
} else {
  profit = price * (1 - discount) * margin;
}
```

We probably don't want to use the absolute profit as a score; it would overwhelm the other factors like location, popularity and features. Instead, we can express the profit as a percentage of our `target` profit. A profit margin above our target will have a positive score (greater than `1.0`), and a profit margin below our target will have a negative score (less than `1.0`):

```
if (price < threshold) {
  profit = price * margin
} else {
  profit = price * (1 - discount) * margin
}
return profit / target
```

The default scripting language in Elasticsearch is Groovy (*http://groovy.code haus.org/*), which for the most part looks a lot like JavaScript. The preceding algorithm as a Groovy script would look like this:

```
price  = doc['price'].value  ❶
margin = doc['margin'].value  ❶

if (price < threshold) {  ❷
  return price * margin / target
}
return price * (1 - discount) * margin / target  ❷
```

❶ The `price` and `margin` variables are extracted from the `price` and `margin` fields in the document.

❷ The `threshold`, `discount`, and `target` variables we will pass in as `params`.

Finally, we can add our `script_score` function to the list of other functions that we are already using:

```
GET /_search
{
  "function_score": {
    "functions": [
      { ...location clause... },  ❶
      { ...price clause... },  ❶
      {
        "script_score": {
          "params": {  ❷
            "threshold": 80,
            "discount": 0.1,
            "target": 10
          },
          "script": "price  = doc['price'].value; margin = doc['margin'].value;
          if (price < threshold) { return price * margin / target };
          return price * (1 - discount) * margin / target;"  ❸
        }
      }
    ]
  }
}
```

❶ The location and price clauses refer to the example explained in "The Closer, The Better" on page 307.

❷ By passing in these variables as params, we can change their values every time we run this query without having to recompile the script.

❸ JSON cannot include embedded newline characters. Newline characters in the script should either be escaped as \n or replaced with semicolons.

This query would return the documents that best satisfy the user's requirements for location and price, while still factoring in our need to make a profit.

The script_score function provides enormous flexibility. Within a script, you have access to the fields of the document, to the current _score, and even to the term frequencies, inverse document frequencies, and field length norms (see Text scoring in scripts (*http://bit.ly/1E3Rbbh*)).

That said, scripts can have a performance impact. If you do find that your scripts are not quite fast enough, you have three options:

- Try to precalculate as much information as possible and include it in each document.
- Groovy is fast, but not quite as fast as Java. You could reimplement your script as a native Java script. (See Native Java Scripts (*http://bit.ly/1ynBidJ*)).
- Use the rescore functionality described in "Rescoring Results" on page 251 to apply your script to only the best-scoring documents.

Pluggable Similarity Algorithms

Before we move on from relevance and scoring, we will finish this chapter with a more advanced subject: pluggable similarity algorithms. While Elasticsearch uses the "Lucene's Practical Scoring Function" on page 284 as its default similarity algorithm, it supports other algorithms out of the box, which are listed in the Similarity Modules (*http://bit.ly/14Eiw7f*) documentation.

Okapi BM25

The most interesting competitor to TF/IDF and the vector space model is called *Okapi BM25* (*http://en.wikipedia.org/wiki/Okapi_BM25*), which is considered to be a *state-of-the-art* ranking function. BM25 originates from the probabilistic relevance model (*http://en.wikipedia.org/wiki/Probabilistic_relevance_model*), rather than the vector space model, yet the algorithm has a lot in common with Lucene's practical scoring function.

Both use of term frequency, inverse document frequency, and field-length normalization, but the definition of each of these factors is a little different. Rather than explaining the BM25 formula in detail, we will focus on the practical advantages that BM25 offers.

Term-frequency saturation

Both TF/IDF and BM25 use inverse document frequency to distinguish between common (low value) words and uncommon (high value) words. Both also recognize (see "Term frequency" on page 278) that the more often a word appears in a document, the more likely is it that the document is relevant for that word.

However, common words occur commonly. The fact that a common word appears many times in one document is offset by the fact that the word appears many times in *all* documents.

However, TF/IDF was designed in an era when it was standard practice to remove the *most* common words (or *stopwords*, see Chapter 22) from the index altogether. The algorithm didn't need to worry about an upper limit for term frequency because the most frequent terms had already been removed.

In Elasticsearch, the `standard` analyzer—the default for `string` fields—doesn't remove stopwords because, even though they are words of little value, they do still have some value. The result is that, for very long documents, the sheer number of occurrences of words like `the` and `and` can artificially boost their weight.

BM25, on the other hand, does have an upper limit. Terms that appear 5 to 10 times in a document have a significantly larger impact on relevance than terms that appear just once or twice. However, as can be seen in Figure 17-8, terms that appear 20 times in a document have almost the same impact as terms that appear a thousand times or more.

This is known as *nonlinear term-frequency saturation*.

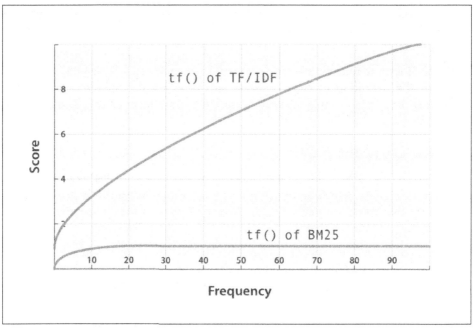

Figure 17-8. Term frequency saturation for TF/IDF and BM25

Field-length normalization

In "Field-length norm" on page 279, we said that Lucene considers shorter fields to have more weight than longer fields: the frequency of a term in a field is offset by the length of the field. However, the practical scoring function treats all fields in the same way. It will treat all `title` fields (because they are short) as more important than all body fields (because they are long).

BM25 also considers shorter fields to have more weight than longer fields, but it considers each field separately by taking the average length of the field into account. It can distinguish between a short `title` field and a `long` title field.

> In "Query-Time Boosting" on page 288, we said that the `title` field has a *natural* boost over the body field because of its length. This natural boost disappears with BM25 as differences in field length apply only within a single field.

Tuning BM25

One of the nice features of BM25 is that, unlike TF/IDF, it has two parameters that allow it to be tuned:

k1

This parameter controls how quickly an increase in term frequency results in term-frequency saturation. The default value is `1.2`. Lower values result in quicker saturation, and higher values in slower saturation.

b

This parameter controls how much effect field-length normalization should have. A value of `0.0` disables normalization completely, and a value of `1.0` normalizes fully. The default is `0.75`.

The practicalities of tuning BM25 are another matter. The default values for k1 and b should be suitable for most document collections, but the optimal values really depend on the collection. Finding good values for your collection is a matter of adjusting, checking, and adjusting again.

Changing Similarities

The similarity algorithm can be set on a per-field basis. It's just a matter of specifying the chosen algorithm in the field's mapping:

```
PUT /my_index
{
  "mappings": {
    "doc": {
      "properties": {
        "title": {
          "type":       "string",
          "similarity": "BM25" ❶
        },
        "body": {
          "type":       "string",
          "similarity": "default" ❷
        }
      }
    }
  }
}
```

❶ The `title` field uses BM25 similarity.

❷ The body field uses the default similarity (see "Lucene's Practical Scoring Function" on page 284).

Currently, it is not possible to change the `similarity` mapping for an existing field. You would need to reindex your data in order to do that.

Configuring BM25

Configuring a similarity is much like configuring an analyzer. Custom similarities can be specified when creating an index. For instance:

```
PUT /my_index
{
  "settings": {
    "similarity": {
      "my_bm25": {  ❶
        "type": "BM25",
        "b":    0  ❷
      }
    }
  },
  "mappings": {
    "doc": {
      "properties": {
        "title": {
          "type":       "string",
          "similarity": "my_bm25"  ❸
        },
        "body": {
          "type":       "string",
          "similarity": "BM25"  ❹
        }
      }
    }
  }
}
```

❶ Create a custom similarity called my_bm25, based on the built-in BM25 similarity.

❷ Disable field-length normalization. See "Tuning BM25" on page 314.

❸ Field title uses the custom similarity my_bm25.

❹ Field body uses the built-in similarity BM25.

> A custom similarity can be updated by closing the index, updating the index settings, and reopening the index. This allows you to experiment with different configurations without having to reindex your documents.

Relevance Tuning Is the Last 10%

In this chapter, we looked at a how Lucene generates scores based on TF/IDF. Understanding the score-generation process is critical so you can tune, modulate, attenuate, and manipulate the score for your particular business domain.

In practice, simple combinations of queries will get you good search results. But to get *great* search results, you'll often have to start tinkering with the previously mentioned tuning methods.

Often, applying a boost on a strategic field or rearranging a query to emphasize a particular clause will be sufficient to make your results great. Sometimes you'll need more-invasive changes. This is usually the case if your scoring requirements diverge heavily from Lucene's word-based TF/IDF model (for example, you want to score based on time or distance).

With that said, relevancy tuning is a rabbit hole that you can easily fall into and never emerge. The concept of *most relevant* is a nebulous target to hit, and different people often have different ideas about document ranking. It is easy to get into a cycle of constant fiddling without any apparent progress.

We encourage you to avoid this (very tempting) behavior and instead properly instrument your search results. Monitor how often your users click the top result, the top 10, and the first page; how often they execute a secondary query without selecting a result first; how often they click a result and immediately go back to the search results, and so forth.

These are all indicators of how relevant your search results are to the user. If your query is returning highly relevant results, users will select one of the top-five results, find what they want, and leave. Irrelevant results cause users to click around and try new search queries.

Once you have instrumentation in place, tuning your query is simple. Make a change, monitor its effect on your users, and repeat as necessary. The tools outlined in this chapter are just that: tools. You have to use them appropriately to propel your search results into the *great* category, and the only way to do that is with strong measurement of user behavior.

PART III

Dealing with Human Language

I know all those words, but that sentence makes no sense to me.
—Matt Groening

Full-text search is a battle between *precision*—returning as few irrelevant documents as possible—and *recall*—returning as many relevant documents as possible. While matching only the exact words that the user has queried would be precise, it is not enough. We would miss out on many documents that the user would consider to be relevant. Instead, we need to spread the net wider, to also search for words that are not exactly the same as the original but are related.

Wouldn't you expect a search for "quick brown fox" to match a document containing "fast brown foxes," "Johnny Walker" to match "Johnnie Walker," or "Arnolt Schwarzenneger" to match "Arnold Schwarzenegger"?

If documents exist that *do* contain exactly what the user has queried, those documents should appear at the top of the result set, but weaker matches can be included further down the list. If no documents match exactly, at least we can show the user potential matches; they may even be what the user originally intended!

There are several lines of attack:

- Remove diacritics like ´, ^, and ¨ so that a search for rôle will also match role, and vice versa. See Chapter 20.

- Remove the distinction between singular and plural—fox versus foxes—or between tenses—jumping versus jumped versus jumps—by *stemming* each word to its root form. See Chapter 21.

- Remove commonly used words or *stopwords* like `the`, `and`, and `or` to improve search performance. See Chapter 22.

- Including synonyms so that a query for `quick` could also match `fast`, or `UK` could match `United Kingdom`. See Chapter 23.

- Check for misspellings or alternate spellings, or match on *homophones*—words that sound the same, like `their` versus `there`, `meat` versus `meet` versus `mete`. See Chapter 24.

Before we can manipulate individual words, we need to divide text into words, which means that we need to know what constitutes a *word*. We will tackle this in Chapter 19.

But first, let's take a look at how to get started quickly and easily.

CHAPTER 18

Getting Started with Languages

Elasticsearch ships with a collection of language analyzers that provide good, basic, out-of-the-box support for many of the world's most common languages:

Arabic, Armenian, Basque, Brazilian, Bulgarian, Catalan, Chinese, Czech, Danish, Dutch, English, Finnish, French, Galician, German, Greek, Hindi, Hungarian, Indonesian, Irish, Italian, Japanese, Korean, Kurdish, Norwegian, Persian, Portuguese, Romanian, Russian, Spanish, Swedish, Turkish, and Thai.

These analyzers typically perform four roles:

- Tokenize text into individual words:

  `The quick brown foxes` → `[The, quick, brown, foxes]`

- Lowercase tokens:

  `The` → `the`

- Remove common *stopwords*:

  `[The, quick, brown, foxes]` → `[quick, brown, foxes]`

- Stem tokens to their root form:

  `foxes` → `fox`

Each analyzer may also apply other transformations specific to its language in order to make words from that language more searchable:

- The `english` analyzer removes the possessive `'s`:

  `John's` → `john`

- The `french` analyzer removes *elisions* like `l'` and `qu'` and *diacritics* like `¨` or `^`:

```
l'église → eglis
```

- The german analyzer normalizes terms, replacing ä and ae with a, or ß with ss, among others:

```
äußerst → ausserst
```

Using Language Analyzers

The built-in language analyzers are available globally and don't need to be configured before being used. They can be specified directly in the field mapping:

```
PUT /my_index
{
  "mappings": {
    "blog": {
      "properties": {
        "title": {
          "type":     "string",
          "analyzer": "english" ❶
        }
      }
    }
  }
}
```

❶ The title field will use the english analyzer instead of the default standard analyzer.

Of course, by passing text through the english analyzer, we lose information:

```
GET /my_index/_analyze?field=title ❶
I'm not happy about the foxes
```

❶ Emits token: i'm, happi, about, fox

We can't tell if the document mentions one fox or many foxes; the word not is a stopword and is removed, so we can't tell whether the document is happy about foxes or not. By using the english analyzer, we have increased recall as we can match more loosely, but we have reduced our ability to rank documents accurately.

To get the best of both worlds, we can use multifields to index the title field twice: once with the english analyzer and once with the standard analyzer:

```
PUT /my_index
{
  "mappings": {
    "blog": {
      "properties": {
        "title": { ❶
```

```
        "type": "string",
        "fields": {
          "english": { ❷
            "type":     "string",
            "analyzer": "english"
          }
        }
      }
    }
  }
}
```

❶ The main `title` field uses the `standard` analyzer.

❷ The `title.english` subfield uses the `english` analyzer.

With this mapping in place, we can index some test documents to demonstrate how to use both fields at query time:

```
PUT /my_index/blog/1
{ "title": "I'm happy for this fox" }

PUT /my_index/blog/2
{ "title": "I'm not happy about my fox problem" }

GET /_search
{
  "query": {
    "multi_match": {
      "type":    "most_fields", ❶
      "query":   "not happy foxes",
      "fields": [ "title", "title.english" ]
    }
  }
}
```

❶ Use the `most_fields` query type to match the same text in as many fields as possible.

Even though neither of our documents contain the word `foxes`, both documents are returned as results thanks to the word stemming on the `title.english` field. The second document is ranked as more relevant, because the word `not` matches on the `title` field.

Configuring Language Analyzers

While the language analyzers can be used out of the box without any configuration, most of them do allow you to control aspects of their behavior, specifically:

Stem-word exclusion

Imagine, for instance, that users searching for the "World Health Organization" are instead getting results for "organ health." The reason for this confusion is that both "organ" and "organization" are stemmed to the same root word: organ. Often this isn't a problem, but in this particular collection of documents, this leads to confusing results. We would like to prevent the words organization and organizations from being stemmed.

Custom stopwords

The default list of stopwords used in English are as follows:

```
a, an, and, are, as, at, be, but, by, for, if, in, into, is, it,
no, not, of, on, or, such, that, the, their, then, there, these,
they, this, to, was, will, with
```

The unusual thing about no and not is that they invert the meaning of the words that follow them. Perhaps we decide that these two words are important and that we shouldn't treat them as stopwords.

To customize the behavior of the english analyzer, we need to create a custom analyzer that uses the english analyzer as its base but adds some configuration:

```
PUT /my_index
{
  "settings": {
    "analysis": {
      "analyzer": {
        "my_english": {
          "type": "english",
          "stem_exclusion": [ "organization", "organizations" ], ❶
          "stopwords": [ ❷
            "a", "an", "and", "are", "as", "at", "be", "but", "by", "for",
            "if", "in", "into", "is", "it", "of", "on", "or", "such", "that",
            "the", "their", "then", "there", "these", "they", "this", "to",
            "was", "will", "with"
          ]
        }
      }
    }
  }
}

GET /my_index/_analyze?analyzer=my_english ❸
The World Health Organization does not sell organs.
```

❶ Prevents organization and organizations from being stemmed

❷ Specifies a custom list of stopwords

❸ Emits tokens world, health, organization, does, not, sell, organ

We discuss stemming and stopwords in much more detail in Chapter 21 and Chapter 22, respectively.

Pitfalls of Mixing Languages

If you have to deal with only a single language, count yourself lucky. Finding the right strategy for handling documents written in several languages can be challenging.

At Index Time

Multilingual documents come in three main varieties:

- One predominant language per *document*, which may contain snippets from other languages (See "One Language per Document" on page 327.)
- One predominant language per *field*, which may contain snippets from other languages (See "One Language per Field" on page 329.)
- A mixture of languages per field (See "Mixed-Language Fields" on page 331.)

The goal, although not always achievable, should be to keep languages separate. Mixing languages in the same inverted index can be problematic.

Incorrect stemming

The stemming rules for German are different from those for English, French, Swedish, and so on. Applying the same stemming rules to different languages will result in some words being stemmed correctly, some incorrectly, and some not being stemmed at all. It may even result in words from different languages with different meanings being stemmed to the same root word, conflating their meanings and producing confusing search results for the user.

Applying multiple stemmers in turn to the same text is likely to result in rubbish, as the next stemmer may try to stem an already stemmed word, compounding the problem.

Stemmer per Script

The one exception to the *only-one-stemmer* rule occurs when each language is written in a different script. For instance, in Israel it is quite possible that a single document may contain Hebrew, Arabic, Russian (Cyrillic), and English:

אזהרה - Предупреждение - تحذير - Warning

Each language uses a different script, so the stemmer for one language will not interfere with another, allowing multiple stemmers to be applied to the same text.

Incorrect inverse document frequencies

In "What Is Relevance?" on page 117, we explained that the more frequently a term appears in a collection of documents, the less weight that term has. For accurate relevance calculations, you need accurate term-frequency statistics.

A short snippet of German appearing in predominantly English text would give more weight to the German words, given that they are relatively uncommon. But mix those with documents that are predominantly German, and the short German snippets now have much less weight.

At Query Time

It is not sufficient just to think about your documents, though. You also need to think about how your users will query those documents. Often you will be able to identify the main language of the user either from the language of that user's chosen interface (for example, `mysite.de` versus `mysite.fr`) or from the `accept-language` (*http://bit.ly/1BwEl61*) HTTP header from the user's browser.

User searches also come in three main varieties:

- Users search for words in their main language.
- Users search for words in a different language, but expect results in their main language.
- Users search for words in a different language, and expect results in that language (for example, a bilingual person, or a foreign visitor in a web cafe).

Depending on the type of data that you are searching, it may be appropriate to return results in a single language (for example, a user searching for products on the Spanish version of the website) or to combine results in the identified main language of the user with results from other languages.

Usually, it makes sense to give preference to the user's language. An English-speaking user searching the Web for "deja vu" would probably prefer to see the English Wikipedia page rather than the French Wikipedia page.

Identifying Language

You may already know the language of your documents. Perhaps your documents are created within your organization and translated into a list of predefined languages. Human pre-identification is probably the most reliable method of classifying language correctly.

Perhaps, though, your documents come from an external source without any language classification, or possibly with incorrect classification. In these cases, you need

---

to use a heuristic to identify the predominant language. Fortunately, libraries are available in several languages to help with this problem.

Of particular note is the chromium-compact-language-detector (*http://bit.ly/ 1AUr3i2*) library from Mike McCandless (*http://bit.ly/1AUr85k*), which uses the open source (Apache License 2.0 (*http://bit.ly/1u9KKgI*)) Compact Language Detector (*https://code.google.com/p/cld2/*) (CLD) from Google. It is small, fast, and accurate, and can detect 160+ languages from as little as two sentences. It can even detect multiple languages within a single block of text. Bindings exist for several languages including Python, Perl, JavaScript, PHP, C#/.NET, and R.

Identifying the language of the user's search request is not quite as simple. The CLD is designed for text that is at least 200 characters in length. Shorter amounts of text, such as search keywords, produce much less accurate results. In these cases, it may be preferable to take simple heuristics into account such as the country of origin, the user's selected language, and the HTTP `accept-language` headers.

One Language per Document

A single predominant language per document requires a relatively simple setup. Documents from different languages can be stored in separate indices—`blogs-en`, `blogs-fr`, and so forth—that use the same type and the same fields for each index, just with different analyzers:

```
PUT /blogs-en
{
  "mappings": {
    "post": {
      "properties": {
        "title": {
          "type": "string",    ❶
          "fields": {
            "stemmed": {
              "type":     "string",
              "analyzer": "english"    ❷
            }
}}}}}}

PUT /blogs-fr
{
  "mappings": {
    "post": {
      "properties": {
        "title": {
          "type": "string",    ❶
          "fields": {
            "stemmed": {
              "type":     "string",
```

```
                "analyzer": "french"  ❷
            }
    }}}}}}
```

❶ Both blogs-en and blogs-fr have a type called post that contains the field
    title.

❷ The title.stemmed subfield uses a language-specific analyzer.

This approach is clean and flexible. New languages are easy to add—just create a new
index—and because each language is completely separate, we don't suffer from the
term-frequency and stemming problems described in "Pitfalls of Mixing Languages"
on page 325.

The documents of a single language can be queried independently, or queries can target multiple languages by querying multiple indices. We can even specify a preference
for particular languages with the indices_boost parameter:

```
GET /blogs-*/post/_search  ❶
{
    "query": {
        "multi_match": {
            "query":    "deja vu",
            "fields":   [ "title", "title.stemmed" ]  ❷
            "type":     "most_fields"
        }
    },
    "indices_boost": {  ❸
        "blogs-en": 3,
        "blogs-fr": 2
    }
}
```

❶ This search is performed on any index beginning with blogs-.

❷ The title.stemmed fields are queried using the analyzer specified in each index.

❸ Perhaps the user's accept-language headers showed a preference for English,
    and then French, so we boost results from each index accordingly. Any other lan-
    guages will have a neutral boost of 1.

Foreign Words

Of course, these documents may contain words or sentences in other languages, and
these words are unlikely to be stemmed correctly. With predominant-language documents, this is not usually a major problem. The user will often search for the exact
words—for instance, of a quotation from another language—rather than for inflections of a word. Recall can be improved by using techniques explained in Chapter 20.

Perhaps some words like place names should be queryable in the predominant language and in the original language, such as *Munich* and *München*. These words are effectively synonyms, which we discuss in Chapter 23.

Don't Use Types for Languages

You may be tempted to use a separate type for each language, instead of a separate index. For best results, you should avoid using types for this purpose. As explained in "Types and Mappings" on page 139, fields from different types but with the same field name are indexed into the *same inverted index*. This means that the term frequencies from each type (and thus each language) are mixed together.

To ensure that the term frequencies of one language don't pollute those of another, either use a separate index for each language, or a separate field, as explained in the next section.

One Language per Field

For documents that represent entities like products, movies, or legal notices, it is common for the same text to be translated into several languages. Although each translation could be represented in a single document in an index per language, another reasonable approach is to keep all translations in the same document:

```
{
    "title":      "Fight club",
    "title_br":   "Clube de Luta",
    "title_cz":   "Klub rvácu",
    "title_en":   "Fight club",
    "title_es":   "El club de la lucha",
    ...
}
```

Each translation is stored in a separate field, which is analyzed according to the language it contains:

```
PUT /movies
{
  "mappings": {
    "movie": {
      "properties": {
        "title": {            ❶
          "type":       "string"
        },
        "title_br": {         ❷
            "type":       "string",
            "analyzer": "brazilian"
        },
        "title_cz": {         ❷
```

```
              "type":      "string",
              "analyzer": "czech"
         },
         "title_en": { ❷
              "type":      "string",
              "analyzer": "english"
         },
         "title_es": { ❷
              "type":      "string",
              "analyzer": "spanish"
         }
       }
     }
   }
  }
}
```

❶ The title field contains the original title and uses the standard analyzer.

❷ Each of the other fields uses the appropriate analyzer for that language.

Like the *index-per-language* approach, the *field-per-language* approach maintains clean term frequencies. It is not quite as flexible as having separate indices. Although it is easy to add a new field by using the update-mapping API, those new fields may require new custom analyzers, which can only be set up at index creation time. As a workaround, you can close (*http://bit.ly/1B6s0WY*) the index, add the new analyzers with the update-settings API (*http://bit.ly/1zijFPx*), then reopen the index, but closing the index means that it will require some downtime.

The documents of a single language can be queried independently, or queries can target multiple languages by querying multiple fields. We can even specify a preference for particular languages by boosting that field:

```
GET /movies/movie/_search
{
    "query": {
        "multi_match": {
            "query":      "club de la lucha",
            "fields": [ "title*", "title_es^2" ], ❶
            "type":       "most_fields"
        }
    }
}
```

❶ This search queries any field beginning with title but boosts the title_es field by 2. All other fields have a neutral boost of 1.

Mixed-Language Fields

Usually, documents that mix multiple languages in a single field come from sources beyond your control, such as pages scraped from the Web:

```
{ "body": "Page not found / Seite nicht gefunden / Page non trouvée" }
```

They are the most difficult type of multilingual document to handle correctly. Although you can simply use the `standard` analyzer on all fields, your documents will be less searchable than if you had used an appropriate stemmer. But of course, you can't choose just one stemmer—stemmers are language specific. Or rather, stemmers are language and script specific. As discussed in "Stemmer per Script" on page 325, if every language uses a different script, then stemmers can be combined.

Assuming that your mix of languages uses the same script such as Latin, you have three choices available to you:

- Split into separate fields
- Analyze multiple times
- Use n-grams

Split into Separate Fields

The Compact Language Detector mentioned in "Identifying Language" on page 326 can tell you which parts of the document are in which language. You can split up the text based on language and use the same approach as was used in "One Language per Field" on page 329.

Analyze Multiple Times

If you primarily deal with a limited number of languages, you could use multi-fields to analyze the text once per language:

```
PUT /movies
{
  "mappings": {
    "title": {
      "properties": {
        "title": { ❶
          "type": "string",
          "fields": {
            "de": { ❷
              "type":     "string",
              "analyzer": "german"
            },
            "en": { ❷
              "type":     "string",
```

```
            "analyzer": "english"
          },
          "fr": { ❷
            "type":     "string",
            "analyzer": "french"
          },
          "es": { ❷
            "type":     "string",
            "analyzer": "spanish"
          }
        }
      }
    }
  }
}
```

❶ The main `title` field uses the `standard` analyzer.

❷ Each subfield applies a different language analyzer to the text in the `title` field.

Use n-grams

You could index all words as n-grams, using the same approach as described in "Ngrams for Compound Words" on page 273. Most inflections involve adding a suffix (or in some languages, a prefix) to a word, so by breaking each word into n-grams, you have a good chance of matching words that are similar but not exactly the same. This can be combined with the *analyze-multiple times* approach to provide a catchall field for unsupported languages:

```
PUT /movies
{
  "settings": {
    "analysis": {...} ❶
  },
  "mappings": {
    "title": {
      "properties": {
        "title": {
          "type": "string",
          "fields": {
            "de": {
              "type":     "string",
              "analyzer": "german"
            },
            "en": {
              "type":     "string",
              "analyzer": "english"
            },
            "fr": {
```

```
            "type":      "string",
            "analyzer": "french"
        },
        "es": {
            "type":      "string",
            "analyzer": "spanish"
        },
        "general": { ❷
            "type":      "string",
            "analyzer": "trigrams"
        }
    }
  }
 }
 }
 }
 }
}
```

❶ In the `analysis` section, we define the same `trigrams` analyzer as described in "Ngrams for Compound Words" on page 273.

❷ The `title.general` field uses the `trigrams` analyzer to index any language.

When querying the catchall `general` field, you can use `minimum_should_match` to reduce the number of low-quality matches. It may also be necessary to boost the other fields slightly more than the `general` field, so that matches on the the main language fields are given more weight than those on the `general` field:

```
GET /movies/movie/_search
{
    "query": {
        "multi_match": {
            "query":      "club de la lucha",
            "fields": [ "title*^1.5", "title.general" ], ❶
            "type":       "most_fields",
            "minimum_should_match": "75%" ❷
        }
    }
}
```

❶ All `title` or `title.*` fields are given a slight boost over the `title.general` field.

❷ The `minimum_should_match` parameter reduces the number of low-quality matches returned, especially important for the `title.general` field.

CHAPTER 19

Identifying Words

A word in English is relatively simple to spot: words are separated by whitespace or (some) punctuation. Even in English, though, there can be controversy: is *you're* one word or two? What about *o'clock*, *cooperate*, *half-baked*, or *eyewitness*?

Languages like German or Dutch combine individual words to create longer compound words like *Weißkopfseeadler* (white-headed sea eagle), but in order to be able to return Weißkopfseeadler as a result for the query Adler (eagle), we need to understand how to break up compound words into their constituent parts.

Asian languages are even more complex: some have no whitespace between words, sentences, or even paragraphs. Some words can be represented by a single character, but the same single character, when placed next to other characters, can form just one part of a longer word with a quite different meaning.

It should be obvious that there is no silver-bullet analyzer that will miraculously deal with all human languages. Elasticsearch ships with dedicated analyzers for many languages, and more language-specific analyzers are available as plug-ins.

However, not all languages have dedicated analyzers, and sometimes you won't even be sure which language(s) you are dealing with. For these situations, we need good standard tools that do a reasonable job regardless of language.

standard Analyzer

The standard analyzer is used by default for any full-text analyzed string field. If we were to reimplement the standard analyzer as a custom analyzer, it would be defined as follows:

```
{
    "type":       "custom",
    "tokenizer": "standard",
    "filter":  [ "lowercase", "stop" ]
}
```

In Chapter 20 and Chapter 22, we talk about the `lowercase`, and `stop` *token filters*, but for the moment, let's focus on the `standard` *tokenizer*.

standard Tokenizer

A *tokenizer* accepts a string as input, processes the string to break it into individual words, or *tokens* (perhaps discarding some characters like punctuation), and emits a *token stream* as output.

What is interesting is the algorithm that is used to *identify* words. The `whitespace` tokenizer simply breaks on whitespace—spaces, tabs, line feeds, and so forth—and assumes that contiguous nonwhitespace characters form a single token. For instance:

```
GET /_analyze?tokenizer=whitespace
You're the 1st runner home!
```

This request would return the following terms: `You're`, `the`, `1st`, `runner`, `home!`

The `letter` tokenizer, on the other hand, breaks on any character that is not a letter, and so would return the following terms: `You`, `re`, `the`, `st`, `runner`, `home`.

The `standard` tokenizer uses the Unicode Text Segmentation algorithm (as defined in Unicode Standard Annex #29 (*http://unicode.org/reports/tr29/*)) to find the boundaries *between* words, and emits everything in-between. Its knowledge of Unicode allows it to successfully tokenize text containing a mixture of languages.

Punctuation may or may not be considered part of a word, depending on where it appears:

```
GET /_analyze?tokenizer=standard
You're my 'favorite'.
```

In this example, the apostrophe in `You're` is treated as part of the word, while the single quotes in `'favorite'` are not, resulting in the following terms: `You're`, `my`, `favorite`.

> The `uax_url_email` tokenizer works in exactly the same way as the `standard` tokenizer, except that it recognizes email addresses and URLs and emits them as single tokens. The `standard` tokenizer, on the other hand, would try to break them into individual words. For instance, the email address `joe-bloggs@foo-bar.com` would result in the tokens `joe`, `bloggs`, `foo`, `bar.com`.

The `standard` tokenizer is a reasonable starting point for tokenizing most languages, especially Western languages. In fact, it forms the basis of most of the language-specific analyzers like the `english`, `french`, and `spanish` analyzers. Its support for Asian languages, however, is limited, and you should consider using the `icu_token izer` instead, which is available in the ICU plug-in.

Installing the ICU Plug-in

The ICU analysis plug-in (*https://github.com/elasticsearch/elasticsearch-analysis-icu*) for Elasticsearch uses the *International Components for Unicode* (ICU) libraries (see site.project.org (*http://site.icu-project.org*)) to provide a rich set of tools for dealing with Unicode. These include the `icu_tokenizer`, which is particularly useful for Asian languages, and a number of token filters that are essential for correct matching and sorting in all languages other than English.

 The ICU plug-in is an essential tool for dealing with languages other than English, and it is highly recommended that you install and use it. Unfortunately, because it is based on the external ICU libraries, different versions of the ICU plug-in may not be compatible with previous versions. When upgrading, you may need to reindex your data.

To install the plug-in, first shut down your Elasticsearch node and then run the following command from the Elasticsearch home directory:

```
./bin/plugin -install elasticsearch/elasticsearch-analysis-icu/$VERSION ❶
```

❶ The current `$VERSION` can be found at *https://github.com/elasticsearch/ elasticsearch-analysis-icu*.

Once installed, restart Elasticsearch, and you should see a line similar to the following in the startup logs:

```
[INFO][plugins] [Mysterio] loaded [marvel, analysis-icu], sites [marvel]
```

If you are running a cluster with multiple nodes, you will need to install the plug-in on every node in the cluster.

icu_tokenizer

The `icu_tokenizer` uses the same Unicode Text Segmentation algorithm as the `stan dard` tokenizer, but adds better support for some Asian languages by using a dictionary-based approach to identify words in Thai, Lao, Chinese, Japanese, and Korean, and using custom rules to break Myanmar and Khmer text into syllables.

For instance, compare the tokens produced by the standard and icu_tokenizers, respectively, when tokenizing "Hello. I am from Bangkok." in Thai:

```
GET /_analyze?tokenizer=standard
สวัสดี ผมมาจากกรุงเทพฯ
```

The standard tokenizer produces two tokens, one for each sentence: สวัสดี, ผมมาจาก กรุงเทพฯ. That is useful only if you want to search for the whole sentence "I am from Bangkok." but not if you want to search for just "Bangkok."

```
GET /_analyze?tokenizer=icu_tokenizer
สวัสดี ผมมาจากกรุงเทพฯ
```

The icu_tokenizer, on the other hand, is able to break up the text into the individual words (สวัสดี, ผม, มา, จาก, กรุงเทพฯ), making them easier to search.

In contrast, the standard tokenizer "over-tokenizes" Chinese and Japanese text, often breaking up whole words into single characters. Because there are no spaces between words, it can be difficult to tell whether consecutive characters are separate words or form a single word. For instance:

- 向 means *facing*, 日 means *sun*, and 葵 means *hollyhock*. When written together, 向日葵 means *sunflower*.
- 五 means *five* or *fifth*, 月 means *month*, and 雨 means *rain*. The first two characters written together as 五月 mean *the month of May*, and adding the third character, 五月雨 means *continuous rain*. When combined with a fourth character, 式, meaning *style*, the word 五月雨式 becomes an adjective for anything consecutive or unrelenting.

Although each character may be a word in its own right, tokens are more meaningful when they retain the bigger original concept instead of just the component parts:

```
GET /_analyze?tokenizer=standard
向日葵
```

```
GET /_analyze?tokenizer=icu_tokenizer
向日葵
```

The standard tokenizer in the preceding example would emit each character as a separate token: 向, 日, 葵. The icu_tokenizer would emit the single token 向日葵 (sunflower).

Another difference between the standard tokenizer and the icu_tokenizer is that the latter will break a word containing characters written in different scripts (for example, βeta) into separate tokens—β, eta—while the former will emit the word as a single token: βeta.

Tidying Up Input Text

Tokenizers produce the best results when the input text is clean, valid text, where *valid* means that it follows the punctuation rules that the Unicode algorithm expects. Quite often, though, the text we need to process is anything but clean. Cleaning it up before tokenization improves the quality of the output.

Tokenizing HTML

Passing HTML through the `standard` tokenizer or the `icu_tokenizer` produces poor results. These tokenizers just don't know what to do with the HTML tags. For example:

```
GET /_analyzer?tokenizer=standard
<p>Some d&eacute;j&agrave; vu <a href="http://somedomain.com">website</a>
```

The `standard` tokenizer confuses HTML tags and entities, and emits the following tokens: p, Some, d, eacute, j, agrave, vu, a, href, http, somedomain.com, website, a. Clearly not what was intended!

Character filters can be added to an analyzer to preprocess the text *before* it is passed to the tokenizer. In this case, we can use the `html_strip` character filter to remove HTML tags and to decode HTML entities such as é into the corresponding Unicode characters.

Character filters can be tested out via the `analyze` API by specifying them in the query string:

```
GET /_analyzer?tokenizer=standard&char_filters=html_strip
<p>Some d&eacute;j&agrave; vu <a href="http://somedomain.com">website</a>
```

To use them as part of the analyzer, they should be added to a `custom` analyzer definition:

```
PUT /my_index
{
    "settings": {
        "analysis": {
            "analyzer": {
                "my_html_analyzer": {
                    "tokenizer":    "standard",
                    "char_filter": [ "html_strip" ]
                }
            }
        }
    }
}
```

Once created, our new `my_html_analyzer` can be tested with the `analyze` API:

```
GET /my_index/_analyzer?analyzer=my_html_analyzer
<p>Some d&eacute;j&agrave; vu <a href="http://somedomain.com">website</a>
```

This emits the tokens that we expect: Some, déjà, vu, website.

Tidying Up Punctuation

The standard tokenizer and icu_tokenizer both understand that an apostrophe *within* a word should be treated as part of the word, while single quotes that *surround* a word should not. Tokenizing the text You're my 'favorite'. would correctly emit the tokens You're, my, favorite.

Unfortunately, Unicode lists a few characters that are sometimes used as apostrophes:

U+0027
>   Apostrophe (')—the original ASCII character

U+2018
>   Left single-quotation mark (')—opening quote when single-quoting

U+2019
>   Right single-quotation mark (')—closing quote when single-quoting, but also the preferred character to use as an apostrophe

Both tokenizers treat these three characters as an apostrophe (and thus as part of the word) when they appear within a word. Then there are another three apostrophe-like characters:

U+201B
>   Single high-reversed-9 quotation mark (')—same as U+2018 but differs in appearance

U+0091
>   Left single-quotation mark in ISO-8859-1—should not be used in Unicode

U+0092
>   Right single-quotation mark in ISO-8859-1—should not be used in Unicode

Both tokenizers treat these three characters as word boundaries—a place to break text into tokens. Unfortunately, some publishers use U+201B as a stylized way to write names like M'coy, and the second two characters may well be produced by your word processor, depending on its age.

Even when using the "acceptable" quotation marks, a word written with a single right quotation mark—You're—is not the same as the word written with an apostrophe—You're—which means that a query for one variant will not find the other.

Fortunately, it is possible to sort out this mess with the `mapping` character filter, which allows us to replace all instances of one character with another. In this case, we will replace all apostrophe variants with the simple U+0027 apostrophe:

```
PUT /my_index
{
  "settings": {
    "analysis": {
      "char_filter": { ❶
        "quotes": {
          "type": "mapping",
          "mappings": [ ❷
            "\\u0091=>\\u0027",
            "\\u0092=>\\u0027",
            "\\u2018=>\\u0027",
            "\\u2019=>\\u0027",
            "\\u201B=>\\u0027"
          ]
        }
      },
      "analyzer": {
        "quotes_analyzer": {
          "tokenizer":     "standard",
          "char_filter": [ "quotes" ] ❸
        }
      }
    }
  }
}
```

❶ We define a custom `char_filter` called `quotes` that maps all apostrophe variants to a simple apostrophe.

❷ For clarity, we have used the JSON Unicode escape syntax for each character, but we could just have used the characters themselves: `"'=>'"`.

❸ We use our custom `quotes` character filter to create a new analyzer called `quotes_analyzer`.

As always, we test the analyzer after creating it:

```
GET /my_index/_analyze?analyzer=quotes_analyzer
You're my 'favorite' M'Coy
```

This example returns the following tokens, with all of the in-word quotation marks replaced by apostrophes: `You're`, `my`, `favorite`, `M'Coy`.

The more effort that you put into ensuring that the tokenizer receives good-quality input, the better your search results will be.

CHAPTER 20

Normalizing Tokens

Breaking text into tokens is only half the job. To make those tokens more easily searchable, they need to go through a *normalization* process to remove insignificant differences between otherwise identical words, such as uppercase versus lowercase. Perhaps we also need to remove significant differences, to make esta, ésta, and está all searchable as the same word. Would you search for déjà vu, or just for deja vu?

This is the job of the token filters, which receive a stream of tokens from the tokenizer. You can have multiple token filters, each doing its particular job. Each receives the new token stream as output by the token filter before it.

In That Case

The most frequently used token filter is the lowercase filter, which does exactly what you would expect; it transforms each token into its lowercase form:

```
GET /_analyze?tokenizer=standard&filters=lowercase
The QUICK Brown FOX! ❶
```

❶ Emits tokens the, quick, brown, fox

It doesn't matter whether users search for fox or FOX, as long as the same analysis process is applied at query time and at search time. The lowercase filter will transform a query for FOX into a query for fox, which is the same token that we have stored in our inverted index.

To use token filters as part of the analysis process, we can create a custom analyzer:

```
PUT /my_index
{
  "settings": {
    "analysis": {
```

```
        "analyzer": {
          "my_lowercaser": {
            "tokenizer": "standard",
            "filter":  [ "lowercase" ]
          }
        }
      }
    }
  }
}
```

And we can test it out with the `analyze` API:

```
GET /my_index/_analyze?analyzer=my_lowercaser
The QUICK Brown FOX! ❶
```

❶   Emits tokens `the`, `quick`, `brown`, `fox`

You Have an Accent

English uses diacritics (like ´, ^, and ¨) only for imported words—like rôle, déjà, and däis—but usually they are optional. Other languages require diacritics in order to be correct. Of course, just because words are spelled correctly in your index doesn't mean that the user will search for the correct spelling.

It is often useful to strip diacritics from words, allowing rôle to match role, and vice versa. With Western languages, this can be done with the `asciifolding` character filter. Actually, it does more than just strip diacritics. It tries to convert many Unicode characters into a simpler ASCII representation:

- ß ⇒ ss
- æ ⇒ ae
- ł ⇒ l
- щ ⇒ m
- ?? ⇒ ??
- ❷ ⇒ 2
- ⁶ ⇒ 6

Like the `lowercase` filter, the `asciifolding` filter doesn't require any configuration but can be included directly in a `custom` analyzer:

```
PUT /my_index
{
  "settings": {
    "analysis": {
      "analyzer": {
        "folding": {
```

```
            "tokenizer": "standard",
            "filter":    [ "lowercase", "asciifolding" ]
        }
      }
    }
  }
}

GET /my_index?analyzer=folding
My œsophagus caused a débâcle ❶
```

❶ Emits my, oesophagus, caused, a, debacle

Retaining Meaning

Of course, when you strip diacritical marks from a word, you lose meaning. For instance, consider these three Spanish words:

esta

> Feminine form of the adjective *this*, as in *esta silla* (this chair) or *esta* (this one).

ésta

> An archaic form of esta.

está

> The third-person form of the verb *estar* (to be), as in *está feliz* (he is happy).

While we would like to conflate the first two forms, they differ in meaning from the third form, which we would like to keep separate. Similarly:

sé

> The first person form of the verb *saber* (to know) as in *Yo sé* (I know).

se

> The third-person reflexive pronoun used with many verbs, such as *se sabe* (it is known).

Unfortunately, there is no easy way to separate words that should have their diacritics removed from words that shouldn't. And it is quite likely that your users won't know either.

Instead, we index the text twice: once in the original form and once with diacritics removed:

```
PUT /my_index/_mapping/my_type
{
  "properties": {
    "title": {  ❶
      "type":        "string",
      "analyzer":    "standard",
```

```
        "fields": {
          "folded": {  ❷
            "type":      "string",
            "analyzer":  "folding"
          }
        }
      }
    }
  }
}
```

❶ The `title` field uses the `standard` analyzer and will contain the original word with diacritics in place.

❷ The `title.folded` field uses the `folding` analyzer, which strips the diacritical marks.

You can test the field mappings by using the `analyze` API on the sentence *Esta está loca* (This woman is crazy):

```
GET /my_index/_analyze?field=title ❶
Esta está loca
```

```
GET /my_index/_analyze?field=title.folded ❷
Esta está loca
```

❶ Emits esta, está, loca

❷ Emits esta, esta, loca

Let's index some documents to test it out:

```
PUT /my_index/my_type/1
{ "title": "Esta loca!" }
```

```
PUT /my_index/my_type/2
{ "title": "Está loca!" }
```

Now we can search across both fields, using the `multi_match` query in `most_fields` mode to combine the scores from each field:

```
GET /my_index/_search
{
  "query": {
    "multi_match": {
      "type":      "most_fields",
      "query":     "esta loca",
      "fields": [ "title", "title.folded" ]
    }
  }
}
```

Running this query through the `validate-query` API helps to explain how the query is executed:

```
GET /my_index/_validate/query?explain
{
  "query": {
    "multi_match": {
      "type":     "most_fields",
      "query":    "está loca",
      "fields": [ "title", "title.folded" ]
    }
  }
}
```

The `multi-match` query searches for the original form of the word (está) in the `title` field, and the form without diacritics `esta` in the `title.folded` field:

```
(title:está          title:loca       )
(title.folded:esta title.folded:loca)
```

It doesn't matter whether the user searches for `esta` or `está`; both documents will match because the form without diacritics exists in the the `title.folded` field. However, only the original form exists in the `title` field. This extra match will push the document containing the original form of the word to the top of the results list.

We use the `title.folded` field to *widen the net* in order to match more documents, and use the original `title` field to push the most relevant document to the top. This same technique can be used wherever an analyzer is used, to increase matches at the expense of meaning.

The `asciifolding` filter does have an option called `preserve_orig inal` that allows you to index the original token and the folded token in the same position in the same field. With this option enabled, you would end up with something like this:

```
Position 1     Position 2
---------------------------
(ésta,esta)    loca
---------------------------
```

While this appears to be a nice way to save space, it does mean that you have no way of saying, "Give me an exact match on the original word." Mixing tokens with and without diacritics can also end up interfering with term-frequency counts, resulting in less-reliable relevance calcuations.

As a rule, it is cleaner to index each field variant into a separate field, as we have done in this section.

Living in a Unicode World

When Elasticsearch compares one token with another, it does so at the byte level. In other words, for two tokens to be considered the same, they need to consist of exactly the same bytes. Unicode, however, allows you to write the same letter in different ways.

For instance, what's the difference between *é* and *é*? It depends on who you ask. According to Elasticsearch, the first one consists of the two bytes `0xC3 0xA9`, and the second one consists of three bytes, `0x65 0xCC 0x81`.

According to Unicode, the differences in how they are represented as bytes is irrelevant, and they are the same letter. The first one is the single letter é, while the second is a plain e combined with an acute accent ´.

If you get your data from more than one source, it may happen that you have the same letters encoded in different ways, which may result in one form of déjà not matching another!

Fortunately, a solution is at hand. There are four Unicode *normalization forms*, all of which convert Unicode characters into a standard format, making all characters comparable at a byte level: nfc, nfd, nfkc, nfkd.

Unicode Normalization Forms

The *composed* forms—nfc and nfkc—represent characters in the fewest bytes possible. So é is represented as the single letter é. The *decomposed* forms—nfd and nfkd—represent characters by their constituent parts, that is e + ´.

The *canonical* forms—nfc and nfd—represent ligatures like ﬃ or œ as a single character, while the *compatibility* forms—nfkc and nfkd—break down these composed characters into a simpler multiletter equivalent: f + f + i or o + e.

It doesn't really matter which normalization form you choose, as long as all your text is in the same form. That way, the same tokens consist of the same bytes. That said, the *compatibility* forms allow you to compare ligatures like ﬃ with their simpler representation, ffi.

You can use the `icu_normalizer` token filter to ensure that all of your tokens are in the same form:

```
PUT /my_index
{
  "settings": {
    "analysis": {
      "filter": {
```

```
    "nfkc_normalizer": {  ❶
      "type": "icu_normalizer",
      "name": "nfkc"
    }
  },
  "analyzer": {
    "my_normalizer": {
      "tokenizer": "icu_tokenizer",
      "filter":  [ "nfkc_normalizer" ]
    }
  }
}
}
}
```

❶ Normalize all tokens into the nfkc normalization form.

 Besides the icu_normalizer token filter mentioned previously, there is also an icu_normalizer *character* filter, which does the same job as the token filter, but does so before the text reaches the tokenizer. When using the standard tokenizer or icu_tokenizer, this doesn't really matter. These tokenizers know how to deal with all forms of Unicode correctly.

However, if you plan on using a different tokenizer, such as the ngram, edge_ngram, or pattern tokenizers, it would make sense to use the icu_normalizer character filter in preference to the token filter.

Usually, though, you will want to not only normalize the byte order of tokens, but also lowercase them. This can be done with icu_normalizer, using the custom normalization form nfkc_cf, which we discuss in the next section.

Unicode Case Folding

Humans are nothing if not inventive, and human language reflects that. Changing the case of a word seems like such a simple task, until you have to deal with multiple languages.

Take, for example, the lowercase German letter ß. Converting that to upper case gives you SS, which converted back to lowercase gives you ss. Or consider the Greek letter ς (sigma, when used at the end of a word). Converting it to uppercase results in Σ, which converted back to lowercase, gives you σ.

The whole point of lowercasing terms is to make them *more* likely to match, not less! In Unicode, this job is done by case folding rather than by lowercasing. *Case folding* is the act of converting words into a (usually lowercase) form that does not necessarily result in the correct spelling, but does allow case-insensitive comparisons.

For instance, the letter ß, which is already lowercase, is *folded* to ss. Similarly, the lowercase ς is folded to σ, to make σ, ς, and Σ comparable, no matter where the letter appears in a word.

The default normalization form that the icu_normalizer token filter uses is nfkc_cf. Like the nfkc form, this does the following:

- *Composes* characters into the shortest byte representation
- Uses *compatibility* mode to convert characters like ﬃ into the simpler ffi

But it also does this:

- *Case-folds* characters into a form suitable for case comparison

In other words, nfkc_cf is the equivalent of the lowercase token filter, but suitable for use with all languages. The *on-steroids* equivalent of the standard analyzer would be the following:

```
PUT /my_index
{
  "settings": {
    "analysis": {
      "analyzer": {
        "my_lowercaser": {
          "tokenizer": "icu_tokenizer",
          "filter":  [ "icu_normalizer" ] ❶
        }
      }
    }
  }
}
```

❶ The icu_normalizer defaults to the nfkc_cf form.

We can compare the results of running Weißkopfseeadler and WEISSKOPFSEEADLER (the uppercase equivalent) through the standard analyzer and through our Unicode-aware analyzer:

```
GET /_analyze?analyzer=standard ❶
Weißkopfseeadler WEISSKOPFSEEADLER

GET /my_index/_analyze?analyzer=my_lowercaser ❷
Weißkopfseeadler WEISSKOPFSEEADLER
```

❶ Emits tokens weißkopfseeadler, weisskopfseeadler

❷ Emits tokens weisskopfseeadler, weisskopfseeadler

The standard analyzer emits two different, incomparable tokens, while our custom analyzer produces tokens that are comparable, regardless of the original case.

Unicode Character Folding

In the same way as the lowercase token filter is a good starting point for many languages but falls short when exposed to the entire tower of Babel, so the asciifolding token filter requires a more effective Unicode *character-folding* counterpart for dealing with the many languages of the world.

The icu_folding token filter (provided by the icu plug-in) does the same job as the asciifolding filter, but extends the transformation to scripts that are not ASCII-based, such as Greek, Hebrew, Han, conversion of numbers in other scripts into their Latin equivalents, plus various other numeric, symbolic, and punctuation transformations.

The icu_folding token filter applies Unicode normalization and case folding from nfkc_cf automatically, so the icu_normalizer is not required:

```
PUT /my_index
{
  "settings": {
    "analysis": {
      "analyzer": {
        "my_folder": {
          "tokenizer": "icu_tokenizer",
          "filter": [ "icu_folding" ]
        }
      }
    }
  }
}

GET /my_index/_analyze?analyzer=my_folder
١٢٣٤٥ ❶
```

❶ The Arabic numerals ١٢٣٤٥ are folded to their Latin equivalent: 12345.

If there are particular characters that you would like to protect from folding, you can use a *UnicodeSet* (*http://icu-project.org/apiref/icu4j/com/ibm/icu/text/UnicodeSet.html*) (much like a character class in regular expressions) to specify which Unicode characters may be folded. For instance, to exclude the Swedish letters å, ä, ö, Å, Ä, and Ö from folding, you would specify a character class representing all Unicode characters, except for those letters: [^åäöÅÄÖ] (^ means *everything except*).

```
PUT /my_index
{
  "settings": {
    "analysis": {
      "filter": {
        "swedish_folding": {  ❶
          "type": "icu_folding",
          "unicodeSetFilter": "[^åäöÅÄÖ]"
        }
      },
      "analyzer": {
        "swedish_analyzer": {  ❷
          "tokenizer": "icu_tokenizer",
          "filter": [ "swedish_folding", "lowercase" ]
        }
      }
    }
  }
}
```

❶ The swedish_folding token filter customizes the icu_folding token filter to exclude Swedish letters, both uppercase and lowercase.

❷ The swedish analyzer first tokenizes words, then folds each token by using the swedish_folding filter, and then lowercases each token in case it includes some of the uppercase excluded letters: Å, Ä, or Ö.

Sorting and Collations

So far in this chapter, we have looked at how to normalize tokens for the purposes of search. The final use case to consider in this chapter is that of string sorting.

In "String Sorting and Multifields" on page 116, we explained that Elasticsearch cannot sort on an analyzed string field, and demonstrated how to use *multifields* to index the same field once as an analyzed field for search, and once as a not_analyzed field for sorting.

The problem with sorting on an analyzed field is not that it uses an analyzer, but that the analyzer tokenizes the string value into multiple tokens, like a *bag of words*, and Elasticsearch doesn't know which token to use for sorting.

Relying on a not_analyzed field for sorting is inflexible: it allows us to sort on only the exact value of the original string. However, we *can* use analyzers to achieve other sort orders, as long as our chosen analyzer always emits only a single token for each string value.

Case-Insensitive Sorting

Imagine that we have three user documents whose name fields contain Boffey, BROWN, and bailey, respectively. First we will apply the technique described in "String Sorting and Multifields" on page 116 of using a not_analyzed field for sorting:

```
PUT /my_index
{
  "mappings": {
    "user": {
      "properties": {
        "name": { ❶
          "type": "string",
          "fields": {
            "raw": { ❷
              "type":  "string",
              "index": "not_analyzed"
            }
          }
        }
      }
    }
  }
}
```

❶ The analyzed name field is used for search.

❷ The not_analyzed name.raw field is used for sorting.

We can index some documents and try sorting:

```
PUT /my_index/user/1
{ "name": "Boffey" }

PUT /my_index/user/2
{ "name": "BROWN" }

PUT /my_index/user/3
{ "name": "bailey" }

GET /my_index/user/_search?sort=name.raw
```

The preceding search request would return the documents in this order: BROWN, Bof fey, bailey. This is known as *lexicographical order* as opposed to *alphabetical order*. Essentially, the bytes used to represent capital letters have a lower value than the bytes used to represent lowercase letters, and so the names are sorted with the lowest bytes first.

That may make sense to a computer, but doesn't make much sense to human beings who would reasonably expect these names to be sorted alphabetically, regardless of case. To achieve this, we need to index each name in a way that the byte ordering corresponds to the sort order that we want.

In other words, we need an analyzer that will emit a single lowercase token:

```
PUT /my_index
{
  "settings": {
    "analysis": {
      "analyzer": {
        "case_insensitive_sort": {
          "tokenizer": "keyword",      ❶
          "filter":  [ "lowercase" ] ❷
        }
      }
    }
  }
}
```

❶ The keyword tokenizer emits the original input string as a single unchanged token.

❷ The lowercase token filter lowercases the token.

With the case_insentive_sort analyzer in place, we can now use it in our multifield:

```
PUT /my_index/_mapping/user
{
  "properties": {
    "name": {
      "type": "string",
      "fields": {
        "lower_case_sort": { ❶
          "type":      "string",
          "analyzer": "case_insensitive_sort"
        }
      }
    }
  }
}

PUT /my_index/user/1
{ "name": "Boffey" }

PUT /my_index/user/2
{ "name": "BROWN" }

PUT /my_index/user/3
{ "name": "bailey" }

GET /my_index/user/_search?sort=name.lower_case_sort
```

❶ The `name.lower_case_sort` field will provide us with case-insentive sorting.

The preceding search request returns our documents in the order that we expect: `bai ley`, `Boffey`, `BROWN`.

But is this order correct? It appears to be correct as it matches our expectations, but our expectations have probably been influenced by the fact that this book is in English and all of the letters used in our example belong to the English alphabet.

What if we were to add the German name *Böhm*?

Now our names would be returned in this order: `bailey`, `Boffey`, `BROWN`, `Böhm`. The reason that `böhm` comes after `BROWN` is that these words are still being sorted by the values of the bytes used to represent them, and an `r` is stored as the byte `0x72`, while `ö` is stored as `0xF6` and so is sorted last. The byte value of each character is an accident of history.

Clearly, the default sort order is meaningless for anything other than plain English. In fact, there is no "right" sort order. It all depends on the language you speak.

Differences Between Languages

Every language has its own sort order, and sometimes even multiple sort orders. Here are a few examples of how our four names from the previous section would be sorted in different contexts:

- English: `bailey`, `boffey`, `böhm`, `brown`
- German: `bailey`, `boffey`, `böhm`, `brown`
- German phonebook: `bailey`, `böhm`, `boffey`, `brown`
- Swedish: `bailey`, `boffey`, `brown`, `böhm`

 The reason that the German phonebook sort order places `böhm` *before* `boffey` is that ö and oe are considered synonyms when dealing with names and places, so `böhm` is sorted as if it had been written as boehm.

Unicode Collation Algorithm

Collation is the process of sorting text into a predefined order. The *Unicode Collation Algorithm*, or UCA (see *www.unicode.org/reports/tr10*) defines a method of sorting strings into the order defined in a *Collation Element Table* (usually referred to just as a *collation*).

The UCA also defines the *Default Unicode Collation Element Table*, or *DUCET*, which defines the default sort order for all Unicode characters, regardless of language. As you have already seen, there is no single correct sort order, so DUCET is designed to annoy as few people as possible as seldom as possible, but it is far from being a panacea for all sorting woes.

Instead, language-specific collations exist for pretty much every language under the sun. Most use DUCET as their starting point and add a few custom rules to deal with the peculiarities of each language.

The UCA takes a string and a collation as inputs and outputs a binary sort key. Sorting a collection of strings according to the specified collation then becomes a simple comparison of their binary sort keys.

Unicode Sorting

 The approach described in this section will probably change in a future version of Elasticsearch. Check the icu plugin documentation for the latest information.

The icu_collation token filter defaults to using the DUCET collation for sorting. This is already an improvement over the default sort. To use it, all we need to do is to create an analyzer that uses the default icu_collation filter:

```
PUT /my_index
{
  "settings": {
    "analysis": {
      "analyzer": {
        "ducet_sort": {
          "tokenizer": "keyword",
          "filter": [ "icu_collation" ]  ❶
        }
      }
    }
  }
}
```

❶ Use the default DUCET collation.

Typically, the field that we want to sort on is also a field that we want to search on, so we use the same multifield approach as we used in "Case-Insensitive Sorting" on page 353:

```
PUT /my_index/_mapping/user
{
```

```
    "properties": {
      "name": {
        "type": "string",
        "fields": {
          "sort": {
            "type": "string",
            "analyzer": "ducet_sort"
          }
        }
      }
    }
  }
}
```

With this mapping, the `name.sort` field will contain a sort key that will be used only for sorting. We haven't specified a language, so it defaults to using the DUCET collation.

Now, we can reindex our example docs and test the sorting:

```
PUT /my_index/user/_bulk
{ "index": { "_id": 1 }}
{ "name": "Boffey" }
{ "index": { "_id": 2 }}
{ "name": "BROWN" }
{ "index": { "_id": 3 }}
{ "name": "bailey" }
{ "index": { "_id": 4 }}
{ "name": "Böhm" }

GET /my_index/user/_search?sort=name.sort
```

> Note that the `sort` key returned with each document, which in ear-
> lier examples looked like brown and böhm, now looks like gobbledy-
> gook: ᵛし乏昫ꭓ侎 \u0001. The reason is that the `icu_collation`
> filter emits keys intended only for efficient sorting, not for any
> other purposes.

The preceding search returns our docs in this order: bailey, Boffey, Böhm, BROWN. This is already an improvement, as the sort order is now correct for English and German, but it is still incorrect for German phonebooks and Swedish. The next step is to customize our mapping for different languages.

Specifying a Language

The `icu_collation` filter can be configured to use the collation table for a specific language, a country-specific version of a language, or some other subset such as German phonebooks. This can be done by creating a custom version of the token filter by using the `language`, `country`, and `variant` parameters as follows:

English

```
{ "language": "en" }
```

German

```
{ "language": "de" }
```

Austrian German

```
{ "language": "de", "country": "AT" }
```

German phonebooks

```
{ "language": "en", "variant": "@collation=phonebook" }
```

 You can read more about the locales supported by ICU at: *http:// bit.ly/1u9LEdp.*

This example shows how to set up the German phonebook sort order:

```
PUT /my_index
{
  "settings": {
    "number_of_shards": 1,
    "analysis": {
      "filter": {
        "german_phonebook": {  ❶
          "type":      "icu_collation",
          "language": "de",
          "country":  "DE",
          "variant":  "@collation=phonebook"
        }
      },
      "analyzer": {
        "german_phonebook": {  ❷
          "tokenizer": "keyword",
          "filter":  [ "german_phonebook" ]
        }
      }
    }
  },
  "mappings": {
    "user": {
      "properties": {
        "name": {
          "type": "string",
          "fields": {
            "sort": {  ❸
              "type":     "string",
              "analyzer": "german_phonebook"
            }
          }
```

```
              }
            }
          }
        }
      }
    }
```

❶ First we create a version of the `icu_collation` customized for the German phonebook collation.

❷ Then we wrap that up in a custom analyzer.

❸ And we apply it to our `name.sort` field.

Reindex the data and repeat the same search as we used previously:

```
PUT /my_index/user/_bulk
{ "index": { "_id": 1 }}
{ "name": "Boffey" }
{ "index": { "_id": 2 }}
{ "name": "BROWN" }
{ "index": { "_id": 3 }}
{ "name": "bailey" }
{ "index": { "_id": 4 }}
{ "name": "Böhm" }

GET /my_index/user/_search?sort=name.sort
```

This now returns our docs in this order: `bailey`, `Böhm`, `Boffey`, `BROWN`. In the German phonebook collation, `Böhm` is the equivalent of `Boehm`, which comes before `Boffey`.

Multiple sort orders

The same field can support multiple sort orders by using a multifield for each language:

```
PUT /my_index/_mapping/_user
{
  "properties": {
    "name": {
      "type": "string",
      "fields": {
        "default": {
          "type":     "string",
          "analyzer": "ducet" ❶
        },
        "french": {
          "type":     "string",
          "analyzer": "french" ❶
        },
        "german": {
          "type":     "string",
```

```
          "analyzer": "german_phonebook" ❶
        },
        "swedish": {
          "type":     "string",
          "analyzer": "swedish" ❶
        }
      }
    }
  }
}
```

❶ We would need to create the corresponding analyzers for each of these collations.

With this mapping in place, results can be ordered correctly for French, German, and Swedish users, just by sorting on the `name.french`, `name.german`, or `name.swedish` fields. Unsupported languages can fall back to using the `name.default` field, which uses the DUCET sort order.

Customizing Collations

The `icu_collation` token filter takes many more options than just `language`, `country`, and `variant`, which can be used to tailor the sorting algorithm. Options are available that will do the following:

- Ignore diacritics
- Order uppercase first or last, or ignore case
- Take punctuation and whitespace into account or ignore it
- Sort numbers as strings or by their numeric value
- Customize existing collations or define your own custom collations

Details of these options are beyond the scope of this book, but more information can be found in the ICU plug-in documentation (*https://github.com/elasticsearch/elasticsearch-analysis-icu*) and in the ICU project collation documentation (*http://userguide.icu-project.org/collation/concepts*).

CHAPTER 21

Reducing Words to Their Root Form

Most languages of the world are *inflected*, meaning that words can change their form to express differences in the following:

- *Number*: fox, foxes
- *Tense*: pay, paid, paying
- *Gender*: waiter, waitress
- *Person*: hear, hears
- *Case*: I, me, my
- *Aspect*: ate, eaten
- *Mood*: so be it, were it so

While inflection aids expressivity, it interferes with retrievability, as a single root *word sense* (or meaning) may be represented by many different sequences of letters. English is a weakly inflected language (you could ignore inflections and still get reasonable search results), but some other languages are highly inflected and need extra work in order to achieve high-quality search results.

Stemming attempts to remove the differences between inflected forms of a word, in order to reduce each word to its root form. For instance `foxes` may be reduced to the root `fox`, to remove the difference between singular and plural in the same way that we removed the difference between lowercase and uppercase.

The root form of a word may not even be a real word. The words `jumping` and `jumpiness` may both be stemmed to `jumpi`. It doesn't matter—as long as the same terms are produced at index time and at search time, search will just work.

If stemming were easy, there would be only one implementation. Unfortunately, stemming is an inexact science that suffers from two issues: understemming and overstemming.

Understemming is the failure to reduce words with the same meaning to the same root. For example, jumped and jumps may be reduced to jump, while jumping may be reduced to jumpi. Understemming reduces retrieval relevant documents are not returned.

Overstemming is the failure to keep two words with distinct meanings separate. For instance, general and generate may both be stemmed to gener. Overstemming reduces precision: irrelevant documents are returned when they shouldn't be.

Lemmatization

A *lemma* is the canonical, or dictionary, form of a set of related words—the lemma of paying, paid, and pays is pay. Usually the lemma resembles the words it is related to but sometimes it doesn't — the lemma of is, was, am, and being is be.

Lemmatization, like stemming, tries to group related words, but it goes one step further than stemming in that it tries to group words by their *word sense*, or meaning. The same word may represent two meanings—for example,*wake* can mean *to wake up* or *a funeral*. While lemmatization would try to distinguish these two word senses, stemming would incorrectly conflate them.

Lemmatization is a much more complicated and expensive process that needs to understand the context in which words appear in order to make decisions about what they mean. In practice, stemming appears to be just as effective as lemmatization, but with a much lower cost.

First we will discuss the two classes of stemmers available in Elasticsearch—"Algorithmic Stemmers" on page 362 and "Dictionary Stemmers" on page 365—and then look at how to choose the right stemmer for your needs in "Choosing a Stemmer" on page 371. Finally, we will discuss options for tailoring stemming in "Controlling Stemming" on page 373 and "Stemming in situ" on page 375.

Algorithmic Stemmers

Most of the stemmers available in Elasticsearch are algorithmic in that they apply a series of rules to a word in order to reduce it to its root form, such as stripping the final s or es from plurals. They don't have to know anything about individual words in order to stem them.

These algorithmic stemmers have the advantage that they are available out of the box, are fast, use little memory, and work well for regular words. The downside is that they don't cope well with irregular words like be, are, and am, or mice and mouse.

One of the earliest stemming algorithms is the Porter stemmer for English, which is still the recommended English stemmer today. Martin Porter subsequently went on to create the Snowball language (*http://snowball.tartarus.org/*) for creating stemming algorithms, and a number of the stemmers available in Elasticsearch are written in Snowball.

The kstem token filter (*http://bit.ly/1IObUjZ*) is a stemmer for English which combines the algorithmic approach with a built-in dictionary. The dictionary contains a list of root words and exceptions in order to avoid conflating words incorrectly. kstem tends to stem less aggressively than the Porter stemmer.

Using an Algorithmic Stemmer

While you can use the porter_stem (*http://bit.ly/17LseXy*) or kstem (*http://bit.ly/1IObUjZ*) token filter directly, or create a language-specific Snowball stemmer with the snowball (*http://bit.ly/1Cr4tNI*) token filter, all of the algorithmic stemmers are exposed via a single unified interface: the stemmer token filter (*http://bit.ly/1AUfpDN*), which accepts the language parameter.

For instance, perhaps you find the default stemmer used by the english analyzer to be too aggressive and you want to make it less aggressive. The first step is to look up the configuration for the english analyzer in the language analyzers (*http://bit.ly/1xtdoJV*) documentation, which shows the following:

```
{
  "settings": {
    "analysis": {
      "filter": {
        "english_stop": {
          "type":       "stop",
          "stopwords":  "_english_"
        },
        "english_keywords": {
          "type":       "keyword_marker",  ❶
          "keywords":   []
        },
        "english_stemmer": {
          "type":       "stemmer",
          "language":   "english"  ❷
        },
        "english_possessive_stemmer": {
          "type":       "stemmer",
```

```
        "language":    "possessive_english" ❷
      }
    },
    "analyzer": {
      "english": {
        "tokenizer":  "standard",
        "filter": [
          "english_possessive_stemmer",
          "lowercase",
          "english_stop",
          "english_keywords",
          "english_stemmer"
        ]
      }
    }
  }
 }
}
```

❶ The keyword_marker token filter lists words that should not be stemmed. This defaults to the empty list.

❷ The english analyzer uses two stemmers: the possessive_english and the english stemmer. The possessive stemmer removes 's from any words before passing them on to the english_stop, english_keywords, and english_stem mer.

Having reviewed the current configuration, we can use it as the basis for a new analyzer, with the following changes:

- Change the english_stemmer from english (which maps to the porter_stem (*http://bit.ly/17LseXy*) token filter) to light_english (which maps to the less aggressive kstem (*http://bit.ly/1IObUjZ*) token filter).

- Add the asciifolding token filter to remove any diacritics from foreign words.

- Remove the keyword_marker token filter, as we don't need it. (We discuss this in more detail in "Controlling Stemming" on page 373.)

Our new custom analyzer would look like this:

```
PUT /my_index
{
  "settings": {
    "analysis": {
      "filter": {
        "english_stop": {
          "type":       "stop",
          "stopwords":  "_english_"
        },
```

```
        "light_english_stemmer": {
          "type":       "stemmer",
          "language":   "light_english" ❶
        },
        "english_possessive_stemmer": {
          "type":       "stemmer",
          "language":   "possessive_english"
        }
      },
      "analyzer": {
        "english": {
          "tokenizer":  "standard",
          "filter": [
            "english_possessive_stemmer",
            "lowercase",
            "english_stop",
            "light_english_stemmer", ❶
            "asciifolding" ❷
          ]
        }
      }
    }
  }
}
```

❶ Replaced the `english` stemmer with the less aggressive `light_english` stemmer

❷ Added the `asciifolding` token filter

Dictionary Stemmers

Dictionary stemmers work quite differently from algorithmic stemmers. Instead of applying a standard set of rules to each word, they simply look up the word in the dictionary. Theoretically, they could produce much better results than an algorithmic stemmer. A dictionary stemmer should be able to do the following:

- Return the correct root word for irregular forms such as `feet` and `mice`
- Recognize the distinction between words that are similar but have different word senses—for example, `organ` and `organization`

In practice, a good algorithmic stemmer usually outperforms a dictionary stemmer. There are a couple of reasons this should be so:

Dictionary quality
    A dictionary stemmer is only as good as its dictionary. The Oxford English Dictionary website estimates that the English language contains approximately

750,000 words (when inflections are included). Most English dictionaries available for computers contain about 10% of those.

The meaning of words changes with time. While stemming mobility to mobil may have made sense previously, it now conflates the idea of mobility with a mobile phone. Dictionaries need to be kept current, which is a time-consuming task. Often, by the time a dictionary has been made available, some of its entries are already out-of-date.

If a dictionary stemmer encounters a word not in its dictionary, it doesn't know how to deal with it. An algorithmic stemmer, on the other hand, will apply the same rules as before, correctly or incorrectly.

Size and performance

A dictionary stemmer needs to load all words, all prefixes, and all suffixes into memory. This can use a significant amount of RAM. Finding the right stem for a word is often considerably more complex than the equivalent process with an algorithmic stemmer.

Depending on the quality of the dictionary, the process of removing prefixes and suffixes may be more or less efficient. Less-efficient forms can slow the stemming process significantly.

Algorithmic stemmers, on the other hand, are usually simple, small, and fast.

 If a good algorithmic stemmer exists for your language, it is usually a better choice than a dictionary-based stemmer. Languages with poor (or nonexistent) algorithmic stemmers can use the Hunspell dictionary stemmer, which we discuss in the next section.

Hunspell Stemmer

Elasticsearch provides dictionary-based stemming via the hunspell token filter (*http://bit.ly/1KNFdXI*). Hunspell *hunspell.sourceforge.net* is the spell checker used by Open Office, LibreOffice, Chrome, Firefox, Thunderbird, and many other open and closed source projects.

Hunspell dictionaries can be obtained from the following:

- *extensions.openoffice.org*: Download and unzip the .oxt extension file.
- *addons.mozilla.org* (*http://mzl.la/157UORf*): Download and unzip the .xpi addon file.
- OpenOffice archive (*http://bit.ly/1ygnODR*): Download and unzip the .zip file.

A Hunspell dictionary consists of two files with the same base name—such as en_US —but with one of two extensions:

.dic

Contains all the root words, in alphabetical order, plus a code representing all possible suffixes and prefixes (which collectively are known as *affixes*)

.aff

Contains the actual prefix or suffix transformation for each code listed in the .dic file

Installing a Dictionary

The Hunspell token filter looks for dictionaries within a dedicated Hunspell directory, which defaults to ./config/hunspell/. The .dic and .aff files should be placed in a subdirectory whose name represents the language or locale of the dictionaries. For instance, we could create a Hunspell stemmer for American English with the following layout:

```
config/
  └ hunspell/ ❶
      └ en_US/ ❷
          ├ en_US.dic
          ├ en_US.aff
          └ settings.yml ❸
```

❶ The location of the Hunspell directory can be changed by setting indices.analy sis.hunspell.dictionary.location in the config/elasticsearch.yml file.

❷ en_US will be the name of the locale or language that we pass to the hunspell token filter.

❸ Per-language settings file, described in the following section.

Per-Language Settings

The settings.yml file contains settings that apply to all of the dictionaries within the language directory, such as these:

```
---
ignore_case:        true
strict_affix_parsing: true
```

The meaning of these settings is as follows:

ignore_case

Hunspell dictionaries are case sensitive by default: the surname Booker is a different word from the noun booker, and so should be stemmed differently. It may seem like a good idea to use the `hunspell` stemmer in case-sensitive mode, but that can complicate things:

- A word at the beginning of a sentence will be capitalized, and thus appear to be a proper noun.
- The input text may be all uppercase, in which case almost no words will be found.
- The user may search for names in all lowercase, in which case no capitalized words will be found.

As a general rule, it is a good idea to set `ignore_case` to `true`.

`strict_affix_parsing`
:   The quality of dictionaries varies greatly. Some dictionaries that are available online have malformed rules in the `.aff` file. By default, Lucene will throw an exception if it can't parse an affix rule. If you need to deal with a broken affix file, you can set `strict_affix_parsing` to `false` to tell Lucene to ignore the broken rules.

Custom Dictionaries

If multiple dictionaries (`.dic` files) are placed in the same directory, they will be merged together at load time. This allows you to tailor the downloaded dictionaries with your own custom word lists:

```
config/
  └ hunspell/
      └ en_US/  ❶
          ├ en_US.dic
          ├ en_US.aff  ❷
          ├ custom.dic
          └ settings.yml
```

❶   The `custom` and `en_US` dictionaries will be merged.

❷   Multiple `.aff` files are not allowed, as they could use conflicting rules.

The format of the `.dic` and `.aff` files is discussed in "Hunspell Dictionary Format" on page 370.

Creating a Hunspell Token Filter

Once your dictionaries are installed on all nodes, you can define a `hunspell` token filter that uses them:

```
PUT /my_index
{
  "settings": {
    "analysis": {
      "filter": {
        "en_US": {
          "type":     "hunspell",
          "language": "en_US"  ❶
        }
      },
      "analyzer": {
        "en_US": {
          "tokenizer":  "standard",
          "filter":     [ "lowercase", "en_US" ]
        }
      }
    }
  }
}
```

❶ The language has the same name as the directory where the dictionary lives.

You can test the new analyzer with the analyze API, and compare its output to that of the english analyzer:

```
GET /my_index/_analyze?analyzer=en_US  ❶
reorganizes

GET /_analyze?analyzer=english  ❷
reorganizes
```

❶ Returns organize

❷ Returns reorgan

An interesting property of the hunspell stemmer, as can be seen in the preceding example, is that it can remove prefixes as well as as suffixes. Most algorithmic stemmers remove suffixes only.

 Hunspell dictionaries can consume a few megabytes of RAM. Fortunately, Elasticsearch creates only a single instance of a dictionary per node. All shards that use the same Hunspell analyzer share the same instance.

Hunspell Dictionary Format

While it is not necessary to understand the format of a Hunspell dictionary in order to use the `hunspell` tokenizer, understanding the format will help you write your own custom dictionaries. It is quite simple.

For instance, in the US English dictionary, the `en_US.dic` file contains an entry for the word `analyze`, which looks like this:

```
analyze/ADSG
```

The `en_US.aff` file contains the prefix or suffix rules for the A, G, D, and S flags. Each flag consists of a number of rules, only one of which should match. Each rule has the following format:

```
[type] [flag] [letters to remove] [letters to add] [condition]
```

For instance, the following is suffix (SFX) rule D. It says that, when a word ends in a consonant (anything but `a`, `e`, `i`, `o`, or `u`) followed by a `y`, it can have the `y` removed and `ied` added (for example, `ready` → `readied`).

```
SFX   D    y   ied   [^aeiou]y
```

The rules for the A, G, D, and S flags mentioned previously are as follows:

```
SFX D Y 4
SFX D   0    d       e ❶
SFX D   y    ied     [^aeiou]y
SFX D   0    ed      [^ey]
SFX D   0    ed      [aeiou]y

SFX S Y 4
SFX S   y    ies     [^aeiou]y
SFX S   0    s       [aeiou]y
SFX S   0    es      [sxzh]
SFX S   0    s       [^sxzhy] ❷

SFX G Y 2
SFX G   e    ing     e ❸
SFX G   0    ing     [^e]

PFX A Y 1
PFX A   0    re      . ❹
```

❶   `analyze` ends in an `e`, so it can become `analyzed` by adding a `d`.

❷   `analyze` does not end in `s`, `x`, `z`, `h`, or `y`, so it can become `analyzes` by adding an `s`.

---

❸ analyze ends in an e, so it can become analyzing by removing the e and adding ing.

❹ The prefix re can be added to form reanalyze. This rule can be combined with the suffix rules to form reanalyzes, reanalyzed, reanalyzing.

More information about the Hunspell syntax can be found on the Hunspell documentation site (*http://bit.ly/1ynGhv6*).

Choosing a Stemmer

The documentation for the stemmer (*http://bit.ly/1AUfpDN*) token filter lists multiple stemmers for some languages. For English we have the following:

english
> The porter_stem (*http://bit.ly/17LseXy*) token filter.

light_english
> The kstem (*http://bit.ly/1IObUjZ*) token filter.

minimal_english
> The EnglishMinimalStemmer in Lucene, which removes plurals

lovins
> The Snowball (*http://bit.ly/1Cr4tNI*) based Lovins (*http://bit.ly/1ICyTjR*) stemmer, the first stemmer ever produced.

porter
> The Snowball (*http://bit.ly/1Cr4tNI*) based Porter (*http://bit.ly/1sCWihj*) stemmer

porter2
> The Snowball (*http://bit.ly/1Cr4tNI*) based Porter2 (*http://bit.ly/1zip3lK*) stemmer

possessive_english
> The EnglishPossessiveFilter in Lucene which removes 's

Add to that list the Hunspell stemmer with the various English dictionaries that are available.

One thing is for sure: whenever more than one solution exists for a problem, it means that none of the solutions solves the problem adequately. This certainly applies to stemming — each stemmer uses a different approach that overstems and understems words to a different degree.

The stemmer documentation page highlights the recommended stemmer for each language in bold, usually because it offers a reasonable compromise between performance and quality. That said, the recommended stemmer may not be appropriate for all use cases. There is no single right answer to the question of which is the best stemmer — it depends very much on your requirements. There are three factors to take into account when making a choice: performance, quality, and degree.

Stemmer Performance

Algorithmic stemmers are typically four or five times faster than Hunspell stemmers. "Handcrafted" algorithmic stemmers are usually, but not always, faster than their Snowball equivalents. For instance, the `porter_stem` token filter is significantly faster than the Snowball implementation of the Porter stemmer.

Hunspell stemmers have to load all words, prefixes, and suffixes into memory, which can consume a few megabytes of RAM. Algorithmic stemmers, on the other hand, consist of a small amount of code and consume very little memory.

Stemmer Quality

All languages, except Esperanto, are irregular. While more-formal words tend to follow a regular pattern, the most commonly used words often have irregular rules. Some stemming algorithms have been developed over years of research and produce reasonably high-quality results. Others have been assembled more quickly with less research and deal only with the most common cases.

While Hunspell offers the promise of dealing precisely with irregular words, it often falls short in practice. A dictionary stemmer is only as good as its dictionary. If Hunspell comes across a word that isn't in its dictionary, it can do nothing with it. Hunspell requires an extensive, high-quality, up-to-date dictionary in order to produce good results; dictionaries of this caliber are few and far between. An algorithmic stemmer, on the other hand, will happily deal with new words that didn't exist when the designer created the algorithm.

If a good algorithmic stemmer is available for your language, it makes sense to use it rather than Hunspell. It will be faster, will consume less memory, and will generally be as good or better than the Hunspell equivalent.

If accuracy and customizability is important to you, and you need (and have the resources) to maintain a custom dictionary, then Hunspell gives you greater flexibility than the algorithmic stemmers. (See "Controlling Stemming" on page 373 for customization techniques that can be used with any stemmer.)

Stemmer Degree

Different stemmers overstem and understem to a different degree. The `light_` stemmers stem less aggressively than the standard stemmers, and the `minimal_` stemmers less aggressively still. Hunspell stems aggressively.

Whether you want aggressive or light stemming depends on your use case. If your search results are being consumed by a clustering algorithm, you may prefer to match more widely (and, thus, stem more aggressively). If your search results are intended for human consumption, lighter stemming usually produces better results. Stemming nouns and adjectives is more important for search than stemming verbs, but this also depends on the language.

The other factor to take into account is the size of your document collection. With a small collection such as a catalog of 10,000 products, you probably want to stem more aggressively to ensure that you match at least some documents. If your collection is large, you likely will get good matches with lighter stemming.

Making a Choice

Start out with a recommended stemmer. If it works well enough, there is no need to change it. If it doesn't, you will need to spend some time investigating and comparing the stemmers available for language in order to find the one that best suits your purposes.

Controlling Stemming

Out-of-the-box stemming solutions are never perfect. Algorithmic stemmers, especially, will blithely apply their rules to any words they encounter, perhaps conflating words that you would prefer to keep separate. Maybe, for your use case, it is important to keep `skies` and `skiing` as distinct words rather than stemming them both down to `ski` (as would happen with the `english` analyzer).

The `keyword_marker` (*http://bit.ly/1IOeXZD*) and `stemmer_override` (*http://bit.ly/1ymcioJ*) token filters allow us to customize the stemming process.

Preventing Stemming

The `stem_exclusion` parameter for language analyzers (see "Configuring Language Analyzers" on page 323) allowed us to specify a list of words that should not be stemmed. Internally, these language analyzers use the `keyword_marker` token filter (*http://bit.ly/1IOeXZD*) to mark the listed words as *keywords*, which prevents subsequent stemming token filters from touching those words.

For instance, we can create a simple custom analyzer that uses the `porter_stem` (*http://bit.ly/17LseXy*) token filter, but prevents the word `skies` from being stemmed:

```
PUT /my_index
{
  "settings": {
    "analysis": {
      "filter": {
```

```
            "no_stem": {
              "type": "keyword_marker",
              "keywords": [ "skies" ] ❶
            }
          },
          "analyzer": {
            "my_english": {
              "tokenizer": "standard",
              "filter": [
                "lowercase",
                "no_stem",
                "porter_stem"
              ]
            }
          }
        }
      }
    }
```

❶   They keywords parameter could accept multiple words.

Testing it with the analyze API shows that just the word skies has been excluded from stemming:

```
GET /my_index/_analyze?analyzer=my_english
sky skies skiing skis ❶
```

❶   Returns: sky, skies, ski, ski

 While the language analyzers allow us only to specify an array of words in the stem_exclusion parameter, the keyword_marker token filter also accepts a keywords_path parameter that allows us to store all of our keywords in a file. The file should contain one word per line, and must be present on every node in the cluster. See "Updating Stopwords" on page 385 for tips on how to update this file.

Customizing Stemming

In the preceding example, we prevented skies from being stemmed, but perhaps we would prefer it to be stemmed to sky instead. The stemmer_override (*http://bit.ly/ 1ymcioJ*) token filter allows us to specify our own custom stemming rules. At the same time, we can handle some irregular forms like stemming mice to mouse and feet to foot:

```
PUT /my_index
{
  "settings": {
    "analysis": {
```

```
        "filter": {
          "custom_stem": {
            "type": "stemmer_override",
            "rules": [ ❶
              "skies=>sky",
              "mice=>mouse",
              "feet=>foot"
            ]
          }
        },
        "analyzer": {
          "my_english": {
            "tokenizer": "standard",
            "filter": [
              "lowercase",
              "custom_stem", ❷
              "porter_stem"
            ]
          }
        }
      }
    }
  }
}

GET /my_index/_analyze?analyzer=my_english
The mice came down from the skies and ran over my feet ❸
```

❶ Rules take the form `original=>stem`.

❷ The `stemmer_override` filter must be placed before the stemmer.

❸ Returns `the`, `mouse`, `came`, `down`, `from`, `the`, `sky`, `and`, `ran`, `over`, `my`, `foot`.

> Just as for the `keyword_marker` token filter, rules can be stored in a file whose location should be specified with the `rules_path` parameter.

Stemming in situ

For the sake of completeness, we will finish this chapter by explaining how to index stemmed words into the same field as unstemmed words. As an example, analyzing the sentence *The quick foxes jumped* would produce the following terms:

```
Pos 1: (the)
Pos 2: (quick)
Pos 3: (foxes,fox) ❶
Pos 4: (jumped,jump) ❶
```

❶ The stemmed and unstemmed forms occupy the same position.

 Read "Is Stemming in situ a Good Idea" on page 377 before using this approach.

To achieve stemming *in situ*, we will use the `keyword_repeat` (*http://bit.ly/1ynIBCe*) token filter, which, like the `keyword_marker` token filter (see "Preventing Stemming" on page 373), marks each term as a keyword to prevent the subsequent stemmer from touching it. However, it also repeats the term in the same position, and this repeated term **is** stemmed.

Using the `keyword_repeat` token filter alone would result in the following:

```
Pos 1: (the,the) ❶
Pos 2: (quick,quick) ❶
Pos 3: (foxes,fox)
Pos 4: (jumped,jump)
```

❶ The stemmed and unstemmed forms are the same, and so are repeated needlessly.

To prevent the useless repetition of terms that are the same in their stemmed and unstemmed forms, we add the `unique` (*http://bit.ly/1B6xHUY*) token filter into the mix:

```
PUT /my_index
{
  "settings": {
    "analysis": {
      "filter": {
        "unique_stem": {
          "type": "unique",
          "only_on_same_position": true ❶
        }
      },
      "analyzer": {
        "in_situ": {
          "tokenizer": "standard",
          "filter": [
            "lowercase",
            "keyword_repeat", ❷
            "porter_stem",
            "unique_stem" ❸
          ]
        }
      }
    }
  }
}
```

```
      }
    }
  }
```

❶ The `unique` token filter is set to remove duplicate tokens only when they occur in the same position.

❷ The `keyword_repeat` token filter must appear before the stemmer.

❸ The `unique_stem` filter removes duplicate terms after the stemmer has done its work.

Is Stemming in situ a Good Idea

People like the idea of stemming *in situ*: "Why use an unstemmed field *and* a stemmed field if I can just use one combined field?" But is it a good idea? The answer is almost always no. There are two problems.

The first is the inability to separate exact matches from inexact matches. In this chapter, we have seen that words with different meanings are often conflated to the same stem word: `organs` and `organization` both stem to `organ`.

In "Using Language Analyzers" on page 322, we demonstrated how to combine a query on a stemmed field (to increase recall) with a query on an unstemmed field (to improve relevance). When the stemmed and unstemmed fields are separate, the contribution of each field can be tuned by boosting one field over another (see "Prioritizing Clauses" on page 220). If, instead, the stemmed and unstemmed forms appear in the same field, there is no way to tune your search results.

The second issue has to do with how the relevance score is calculated. In "What Is Relevance?" on page 117, we explained that part of the calculation depends on the *inverse document frequency* — how often a word appears in all the documents in our index. Using in situ stemming for a document that contains the text `jump jumped jumps` would result in these terms:

```
Pos 1: (jump)
Pos 2: (jumped,jump)
Pos 3: (jumps,jump)
```

While `jumped` and `jumps` appear once each and so would have the correct IDF, `jump` appears three times, greatly reducing its value as a search term in comparison with the unstemmed forms.

For these reasons, we recommend against using stemming in situ.

CHAPTER 22

Stopwords: Performance Versus Precision

Back in the early days of information retrieval, disk space and memory were limited to a tiny fraction of what we are accustomed to today. It was essential to make your index as small as possible. Every kilobyte saved meant a significant improvement in performance. Stemming (see Chapter 21) was important, not just for making searches broader and increasing retrieval in the same way that we use it today, but also as a tool for compressing index size.

Another way to reduce index size is simply to *index fewer words*. For search purposes, some words are more important than others. A significant reduction in index size can be achieved by indexing only the more important terms.

So which terms can be left out? We can divide terms roughly into two groups:

Low-frequency terms
> Words that appear in relatively few documents in the collection. Because of their rarity, they have a high value, or *weight*.

High-frequency terms
> Common words that appear in many documents in the index, such as the, and, and is. These words have a low weight and contribute little to the relevance score.

 Of course, frequency is really a scale rather than just two points labeled *low* and *high*. We just draw a line at some arbitrary point and say that any terms below that line are low frequency and above the line are high frequency.

Which terms are low or high frequency depend on the documents themselves. The word and may be a low-frequency term if all the documents are in Chinese. In a collection of documents about databases, the word `database` may be a high-frequency term with little value as a search term for that particular collection.

That said, for any language there are words that occur very commonly and that seldom add value to a search. The default English stopwords used in Elasticsearch are as follows:

```
a, an, and, are, as, at, be, but, by, for, if, in, into, is, it,
no, not, of, on, or, such, that, the, their, then, there, these,
they, this, to, was, will, with
```

These *stopwords* can usually be filtered out before indexing with little negative impact on retrieval. But is it a good idea to do so?

Pros and Cons of Stopwords

We have more disk space, more RAM, and better compression algorithms than existed back in the day. Excluding the preceding 33 common words from the index will save only about 4MB per million documents. Using stopwords for the sake of reducing index size is no longer a valid reason. (However, there is one caveat to this statement, which we discuss in "Stopwords and Phrase Queries" on page 390.)

On top of that, by removing words from the index, we are reducing our ability to perform certain types of searches. Filtering out the words listed previously prevents us from doing the following:

- Distinguishing *happy* from *not happy*.
- Searching for the band The The.
- Finding Shakespeare's quotation "To be, or not to be"
- Using the country code for Norway: no

The primary advantage of removing stopwords is performance. Imagine that we search an index with one million documents for the word fox. Perhaps `fox` appears in only 20 of them, which means that Elastisearch has to calculate the relevance `_score` for 20 documents in order to return the top 10. Now, we change that to a search for the `OR` fox. The word `the` probably occurs in almost all the documents, which means that Elasticsearch has to calculate the `_score` for all one million documents. This second query simply cannot perform as well as the first.

Fortunately, there are techniques that we can use to keep common words searchable, while still maintaining good performance. First, we'll start with how to use stopwords.

Using Stopwords

The removal of stopwords is handled by the `stop` token filter (*http://bit.ly/1INX4tN*) which can be used when creating a `custom` analyzer (see "Using the stop Token Filter" on page 383). However, some out-of-the-box analyzers come with the `stop` filter pre-integrated:

Language analyzers (http://bit.ly/1xtdoJV)
> Each language analyzer defaults to using the appropriate stopwords list for that language. For instance, the `english` analyzer uses the `_english_` stopwords list.

`standard` *analyzer (http://bit.ly/14EpXv3)*
> Defaults to the empty stopwords list: `_none_`, essentially disabling stopwords.

`pattern` *analyzer (http://bit.ly/1u9OVct)*
> Defaults to `_none_`, like the `standard` analyzer.

Stopwords and the Standard Analyzer

To use custom stopwords in conjunction with the `standard` analyzer, all we need to do is to create a configured version of the analyzer and pass in the list of `stopwords` that we require:

```
PUT /my_index
{
  "settings": {
    "analysis": {
      "analyzer": {
        "my_analyzer": {        ❶
          "type": "standard",   ❷
          "stopwords": [ "and", "the" ] ❸
        }
      }
    }
  }
}
```

❶ This is a custom analyzer called `my_analyzer`.

❷ This analyzer is the `standard` analyzer with some custom configuration.

❸ The stopwords to filter out are `and` and `the`.

 This same technique can be used to configure custom stopword lists for any of the language analyzers.

Maintaining Positions

The output from the `analyze` API is quite interesting:

```
GET /my_index/_analyze?analyzer=my_analyzer
The quick and the dead

{
  "tokens": [
    {
      "token":        "quick",
      "start_offset": 4,
      "end_offset":   9,
      "type":         "<ALPHANUM>",
      "position":     2 ❶
    },
    {
      "token":        "dead",
      "start_offset": 18,
      "end_offset":   22,
      "type":         "<ALPHANUM>",
      "position":     5 ❶
    }
  ]
}
```

❶ Note the `position` of each token.

The stopwords have been filtered out, as expected, but the interesting part is that the `position` of the two remaining terms is unchanged: `quick` is the second word in the original sentence, and `dead` is the fifth. This is important for phrase queries—if the positions of each term had been adjusted, a phrase query for `quick dead` would have matched the preceding example incorrectly.

Specifying Stopwords

Stopwords can be passed inline, as we did in the previous example, by specifying an array:

```
"stopwords": [ "and", "the" ]
```

The default stopword list for a particular language can be specified using the `_lang_` notation:

```
"stopwords": "_english_"
```

> The predefined language-specific stopword lists available in Elasticsearch can be found in the `stop` token filter (*http://bit.ly/157YLFy*) documentation.

Stopwords can be disabled by specifying the special list: _none_. For instance, to use the english analyzer without stopwords, you can do the following:

```
PUT /my_index
{
  "settings": {
    "analysis": {
      "analyzer": {
        "my_english": {
          "type":      "english", ❶
          "stopwords": "_none_" ❷
        }
      }
    }
  }
}
```

❶ The my_english analyzer is based on the english analyzer.

❷ But stopwords are disabled.

Finally, stopwords can also be listed in a file with one word per line. The file must be present on all nodes in the cluster, and the path can be specified with the stop words_path parameter:

```
PUT /my_index
{
  "settings": {
    "analysis": {
      "analyzer": {
        "my_english": {
          "type":           "english",
          "stopwords_path": "stopwords/english.txt" ❶
        }
      }
    }
  }
}
```

❶ The path to the stopwords file, relative to the Elasticsearch config directory

Using the stop Token Filter

The stop token filter (*http://bit.ly/1AUzDNI*) can be combined with a tokenizer and other token filters when you need to create a custom analyzer. For instance, let's say that we wanted to create a Spanish analyzer with the following:

- A custom stopwords list
- The light_spanish stemmer

- The `asciifolding` filter to remove diacritics

We could set that up as follows:

```
PUT /my_index
{
  "settings": {
    "analysis": {
      "filter": {
        "spanish_stop": {
          "type":        "stop",
          "stopwords": [ "si", "esta", "el", "la" ]  ❶
        },
        "light_spanish": {  ❷
          "type":      "stemmer",
          "language": "light_spanish"
        }
      },
      "analyzer": {
        "my_spanish": {
          "tokenizer": "spanish",
          "filter": [  ❸
            "lowercase",
            "asciifolding",
            "spanish_stop",
            "light_spanish"
          ]
        }
      }
    }
  }
}
```

❶ The `stop` token filter takes the same `stopwords` and `stopwords_path` parameters as the `standard` analyzer.

❷ See "Algorithmic Stemmers" on page 362.

❸ The order of token filters is important, as explained next.

We have placed the `spanish_stop` filter after the `asciifolding` filter. This means that esta, ésta, and está will first have their diacritics removed to become just esta, which will then be removed as a stopword. If, instead, we wanted to remove esta and ésta, but not está, we would have to put the `spanish_stop` filter *before* the `ascii folding` filter, and specify both words in the stopwords list.

Updating Stopwords

A few techniques can be used to update the list of stopwords used by an analyzer. Analyzers are instantiated at index creation time, when a node is restarted, or when a closed index is reopened.

If you specify stopwords inline with the `stopwords` parameter, your only option is to close the index and update the analyzer configuration with the update index settings API (*http://bit.ly/1zijFPx*), then reopen the index.

Updating stopwords is easier if you specify them in a file with the `stopwords_path` parameter. You can just update the file (on every node in the cluster) and then force the analyzers to be re-created by either of these actions:

- Closing and reopening the index (see open/close index (*http://bit.ly/1B6s0WY*)), or
- Restarting each node in the cluster, one by one

Of course, updating the stopwords list will not change any documents that have already been indexed. It will apply only to searches and to new or updated documents. To apply the changes to existing documents, you will need to reindex your data. See "Reindexing Your Data" on page 152.

Stopwords and Performance

The biggest disadvantage of keeping stopwords is that of performance. When Elasticsearch performs a full-text search, it has to calculate the relevance `_score` on all matching documents in order to return the top 10 matches.

While most words typically occur in much fewer than 0.1% of all documents, a few words such as `the` may occur in almost all of them. Imagine you have an index of one million documents. A query for `quick brown fox` may match fewer than 1,000 documents. But a query for `the quick brown fox` has to score and sort almost all of the one million documents in your index, just in order to return the top 10!

The problem is that `the quick brown fox` is really a query for `the OR quick OR brown OR fox`—any document that contains nothing more than the almost meaningless term `the` is included in the result set. What we need is a way of reducing the number of documents that need to be scored.

and Operator

The easiest way to reduce the number of documents is simply to use the `and` operator with the `match` query, in order to make all words required.

A `match` query like this:

```
{
    "match": {
        "text": {
            "query":    "the quick brown fox",
            "operator": "and"
        }
    }
}
```

is rewritten as a `bool` query like this:

```
{
    "bool": {
        "must": [
            { "term": { "text": "the" }},
            { "term": { "text": "quick" }},
            { "term": { "text": "brown" }},
            { "term": { "text": "fox" }}
        ]
    }
}
```

The `bool` query is intelligent enough to execute each `term` query in the optimal order —it starts with the least frequent term. Because all terms are required, only documents that contain the least frequent term can possibly match. Using the and operator greatly speeds up multiterm queries.

minimum_should_match

In "Controlling Precision" on page 205, we discussed using the `mini mum_should_match` operator to trim the long tail of less-relevant results. It is useful for this purpose alone but, as a nice side effect, it offers a similar performance benefit to the and operator:

```
{
    "match": {
        "text": {
            "query": "the quick brown fox",
            "minimum_should_match": "75%"
        }
    }
}
```

In this example, at least three out of the four terms must match. This means that the only docs that need to be considered are those that contain either the least or second least frequent terms.

This offers a huge performance gain over a simple query with the default or operator! But we can do better yet…

Divide and Conquer

The terms in a query string can be divided into more-important (low-frequency) and less-important (high-frequency) terms. Documents that match only the less important terms are probably of very little interest. Really, we want documents that match as many of the more important terms as possible.

The `match` query accepts a `cutoff_frequency` parameter, which allows it to divide the terms in the query string into a low-frequency and high-frequency group. The low-frequency group (more-important terms) form the bulk of the query, while the high-frequency group (less-important terms) is used only for scoring, not for matching. By treating these two groups differently, we can gain a real boost of speed on previously slow queries.

Domain-Specific Stopwords

One of the benefits of `cutoff_frequency` is that you get *domain-specific* stopwords for free. For instance, a website about movies may use the words *movie, color, black,* and *white* so often that they could be considered almost meaningless. With the `stop` token filter, these domain-specific terms would have to be added to the stopwords list manually. However, because the `cutoff_frequency` looks at the actual frequency of terms in the index, these words would be classified as *high frequency* automatically.

Take this query as an example:

```
{
  "match": {
    "text": {
      "query": "Quick and the dead",
      "cutoff_frequency": 0.01 ❶
    }
  }
}
```

❶ Any term that occurs in more than 1% of documents is considered to be high frequency. The `cutoff_frequency` can be specified as a fraction (0.01) or as an absolute number (5).

This query uses the `cutoff_frequency` to first divide the query terms into a low-frequency group (quick, dead) and a high-frequency group (and, the). Then, the query is rewritten to produce the following bool query:

```
{
  "bool": {
    "must": { ❶
      "bool": {
        "should": [
```

```
                { "term": { "text": "quick" }},
                { "term": { "text": "dead"  }}
            ]
          }
        },
        "should": { ❷
          "bool": {
            "should": [
                { "term": { "text": "and" }},
                { "term": { "text": "the" }}
            ]
          }
        }
      }
    }
}
```

❶ At least one low-frequency/high-importance term *must* match.

❷ High-frequency/low-importance terms are entirely optional.

The must clause means that at least one of the low-frequency terms—quick or dead—
must be present for a document to be considered a match. All other documents are
excluded. The should clause then looks for the high-frequency terms and and the,
but only in the documents collected by the must clause. The sole job of the should
clause is to score a document like "Quick *and the* dead" higher than "_The_ quick but
dead". This approach greatly reduces the number of documents that need to be examined and scored.

 Setting the operator parameter to and would make *all* low-
frequency terms required, and score documents that contain *all*
high-frequency terms higher. However, matching documents
would not be required to contain all high-frequency terms. If you
would prefer all low- and high-frequency terms to be required, you
should use a bool query instead. As we saw in "and Operator" on
page 385, this is already an efficient query.

Controlling Precision

The minimum_should_match parameter can be combined with cutoff_frequency but
it applies to only the low-frequency terms. This query:

```
{
  "match": {
    "text": {
      "query": "Quick and the dead",
      "cutoff_frequency": 0.01,
      "minimum_should_match": "75%"
```

```
    }
  }
```

would be rewritten as follows:

```
{
  "bool": {
    "must": {
      "bool": {
        "should": [
          { "term": { "text": "quick" }},
          { "term": { "text": "dead"  }}
        ],
        "minimum_should_match": 1 ❶
      }
    },
    "should": { ❷
      "bool": {
        "should": [
          { "term": { "text": "and" }},
          { "term": { "text": "the" }}
        ]
      }
    }
  }
}
```

❶ Because there are only two terms, the original 75% is rounded down to 1, that is: *one out of two low-terms must match.*

❷ The high-frequency terms are still optional and used only for scoring.

Only High-Frequency Terms

An or query for high-frequency terms only—`"To be, or not to be"`—is the worst case for performance. It is pointless to score *all* the documents that contain only one of these terms in order to return just the top 10 matches. We are really interested only in documents in which the terms all occur together, so in the case where there are no low-frequency terms, the query is rewritten to make all high-frequency terms required:

```
{
  "bool": {
    "must": [
      { "term": { "text": "to" }},
      { "term": { "text": "be" }},
      { "term": { "text": "or" }},
      { "term": { "text": "not" }},
      { "term": { "text": "to" }},
      { "term": { "text": "be" }}
    ]
```

```
    }
  }
```

More Control with Common Terms

While the high/low frequency functionality in the match query is useful, sometimes you want more control over how the high- and low-frequency groups should be handled. The match query exposes a subset of the functionality available in the common terms query.

For instance, we could make all low-frequency terms required, and score only documents that have 75% of all high-frequency terms with a query like this:

```
{
  "common": {
    "text": {
      "query":                   "Quick and the dead",
      "cutoff_frequency":        0.01,
      "low_freq_operator":       "and",
      "minimum_should_match": {
        "high_freq":             "75%"
      }
    }
  }
}
```

See the common terms query (*http://bit.ly/1wdS2Qo*) reference page for more options.

Stopwords and Phrase Queries

About 5% of all queries are phrase queries (see "Phrase Matching" on page 244), but they often account for the majority of slow queries. Phrase queries can perform poorly, especially if the phrase includes very common words; a phrase like "To be, or not to be" could be considered pathological. The reason for this has to do with the amount of data that is necessary to support proximity matching.

In "Pros and Cons of Stopwords" on page 380, we said that removing stopwords saves only a small amount of space in the inverted index. That was only partially true. A typical index may contain, among other data, some or all of the following:

Terms dictionary
    A sorted list of all terms that appear in the documents in the index, and a count of the number of documents that contain each term.

Postings list
    A list of which documents contain each term.

Term frequency
    How often each term appears in each document.

Positions
> The position of each term within each document, for phrase and proximity queries.

Offsets
> The start and end character offsets of each term in each document, for snippet highlighting. Disabled by default.

Norms
> A factor used to normalize fields of different lengths, to give shorter fields more weight.

Removing stopwords from the index may save a small amount of space in the *terms dictionary* and the *postings list*, but *positions* and *offsets* are another matter. Positions and offsets data can easily double, triple, or quadruple index size.

Positions Data

Positions are enabled on `analyzed` string fields by default, so that phrase queries will work out of the box. The more often that a term appears, the more space is needed to store its position data. Very common words, by definition, appear very commonly, and their positions data can run to megabytes or gigabytes on large collections.

Running a phrase query on a high-frequency word like the might result in gigabytes of data being read from disk. That data will be stored in the kernel filesystem cache to speed up later access, which seems like a good thing, but it might cause other data to be evicted from the cache, which will slow subsequent queries.

This is clearly a problem that needs solving.

Index Options

The first question you should ask yourself is: *Do you need phrase or proximity queries?*

Often, the answer is no. For many use cases, such as logging, you need to know *whether* a term appears in a document — information that is provided by the postings list—but not *where* it appears. Or perhaps you need to use phrase queries on one or two fields, but you can disable positions data on all of the other analyzed `string` fields.

The `index_options` parameter allows you to control what information is stored in the index for each field. Valid values are as follows:

`docs`
> Only store which documents contain which terms. This is the default for `not_analyzed` string fields.

freqs

> Store docs information, plus how often each term appears in each document. Term frequencies are needed for complete TF/IDF relevance calculations, but they are not required if you just need to know whether a document contains a particular term.

positions

> Store docs and freqs, plus the position of each term in each document. This is the default for analyzed string fields, but can be disabled if phrase/proximity matching is not needed.

offsets

> Store docs, freqs, positions, and the start and end character offsets of each term in the original string. This information is used by the postings highlighter (*http://bit.ly/1u9PJ16*) but is disabled by default.

You can set index_options on fields added at index creation time, or when adding new fields by using the put-mapping API. This setting can't be changed on existing fields:

```
PUT /my_index
{
  "mappings": {
    "my_type": {
      "properties": {
        "title": {                    ❶
          "type":        "string"
        },
        "content": {                  ❷
          "type":        "string",
          "index_options": "freqs"
        }
      }
    }
  }
}
```

❶ The title field uses the default setting of positions, so it is suitable for phrase/proximity queries.

❷ The content field has positions disabled and so cannot be used for phrase/proximity queries.

Stopwords

Removing stopwords is one way of reducing the size of the positions data quite dramatically. An index with stopwords removed can still be used for phrase queries because the original positions of the remaining terms are maintained, as we saw in

"Maintaining Positions" on page 382. But of course, excluding terms from the index reduces searchability. We wouldn't be able to differentiate between the two phrases *Man in the moon* and *Man on the moon*.

Fortunately, there is a way to have our cake and eat it: the `common_grams` token filter.

common_grams Token Filter

The `common_grams` token filter is designed to make phrase queries with stopwords more efficient. It is similar to the `shingles` token filter (see "Finding Associated Words" on page 252), which creates *bigrams* out of every pair of adjacent words. It is most easily explained by example.

The `common_grams` token filter produces different output depending on whether `query_mode` is set to `false` (for indexing) or to `true` (for searching), so we have to create two separate analyzers:

```
PUT /my_index
{
  "settings": {
    "analysis": {
      "filter": {
        "index_filter": {  ❶
          "type":          "common_grams",
          "common_words": "_english_"  ❷
        },
        "search_filter": {  ❶
          "type":          "common_grams",
          "common_words": "_english_",  ❷
          "query_mode":    true
        }
      },
      "analyzer": {
        "index_grams": {  ❸
          "tokenizer": "standard",
          "filter":    [ "lowercase", "index_filter" ]
        },
        "search_grams": {  ❸
          "tokenizer": "standard",
          "filter":    [ "lowercase", "search_filter" ]
        }
      }
    }
  }
}
```

❶ First we create two token filters based on the `common_grams` token filter: `index_filter` for index time (with `query_mode` set to the default `false`), and `search_filter` for query time (with `query_mode` set to `true`).

❷ The `common_words` parameter accepts the same options as the `stopwords` parameter (see "Specifying Stopwords" on page 382). The filter also accepts a `common_words_path` parameter, which allows you to maintain the common words list in a file.

❸ Then we use each filter to create an analyzer for index time and another for query time.

With our custom analyzers in place, we can create a field that will use the `index_grams` analyzer at index time:

```
PUT /my_index/_mapping/my_type
{
  "properties": {
    "text": {
      "type":            "string",
      "index_analyzer":  "index_grams",  ❶
      "search_analyzer": "standard"  ❶
    }
  }
}
```

❶ The `text` field uses the `index_grams` analyzer at index time, but defaults to using the `standard` analyzer at search time, for reasons we will explain next.

At Index Time

If we were to analyze the phrase *The quick and brown fox* with shingles, it would produce these terms:

```
Pos 1: the_quick
Pos 2: quick_and
Pos 3: and_brown
Pos 4: brown_fox
```

Our new `index_grams` analyzer produces the following terms instead:

```
Pos 1: the, the_quick
Pos 2: quick, quick_and
Pos 3: and, and_brown
Pos 4: brown
Pos 5: fox
```

All terms are output as unigrams—the, quick, and so forth—but if a word is a common word or is followed by a common word, then it also outputs a bigram in the same position as the unigram—the_quick, quick_and, and_brown.

Unigram Queries

Because the index contains unigrams, the field can be queried using the same techniques that we have used for any other field, for example:

```
GET /my_index/_search
{
  "query": {
    "match": {
      "text": {
        "query": "the quick and brown fox",
        "cutoff_frequency": 0.01
      }
    }
  }
}
```

The preceding query string is analyzed by the search_analyzer configured for the text field—the standard analyzer in this example—to produce the terms the, quick, and, brown, fox.

Because the index for the text field contains the same unigrams as produced by the standard analyzer, search functions as it would for any normal field.

Bigram Phrase Queries

However, when we come to do phrase queries, we can use the specialized search_grams analyzer to make the process much more efficient:

```
GET /my_index/_search
{
  "query": {
    "match_phrase": {
      "text": {
        "query":    "The quick and brown fox",
        "analyzer": "search_grams" ❶
      }
    }
  }
}
```

❶ For phrase queries, we override the default search_analyzer and use the search_grams analyzer instead.

The search_grams analyzer would produce the following terms:

```
Pos 1: the_quick
Pos 2: quick_and
Pos 3: and_brown
Pos 4: brown
Pos 5: fox
```

The analyzer has stripped out all of the common word unigrams, leaving the common word bigrams and the low-frequency unigrams. Bigrams like `the_quick` are much less common than the single term `the`. This has two advantages:

- The positions data for `the_quick` is much smaller than for `the`, so it is faster to read from disk and has less of an impact on the filesystem cache.

- The term `the_quick` is much less common than `the`, so it drastically decreases the number of documents that have to be examined.

Two-Word Phrases

There is one further optimization. By far the majority of phrase queries consist of only two words. If one of those words happens to be a common word, such as

```
GET /my_index/_search
{
  "query": {
    "match_phrase": {
      "text": {
        "query":    "The quick",
        "analyzer": "search_grams"
      }
    }
  }
}
```

then the `search_grams` analyzer outputs a single token: `the_quick`. This transforms what originally could have been an expensive phrase query for `the` and `quick` into a very efficient single-term lookup.

Stopwords and Relevance

The last topic to cover before moving on from stopwords is that of relevance. Leaving stopwords in your index could make the relevance calculation less accurate, especially if your documents are very long.

As we have already discussed in "Term-frequency saturation" on page 313, the reason for this is that term-frequency/inverse document frequency doesn't impose an upper limit on the impact of term frequency. Very common words may have a low weight because of inverse document frequency but, in long documents, the sheer number of occurrences of stopwords in a single document may lead to their weight being artificially boosted.

You may want to consider using the Okapi BM25 similarity on long fields that include stopwords instead of the default Lucene similarity.

CHAPTER 23

Synonyms

While stemming helps to broaden the scope of search by simplifying inflected words to their root form, synonyms broaden the scope by relating concepts and ideas. Perhaps no documents match a query for "English queen," but documents that contain "British monarch" would probably be considered a good match.

A user might search for "the US" and expect to find documents that contain *United States*, *USA*, *U.S.A.*, *America*, or *the States*. However, they wouldn't expect to see results about the states of matter or state machines.

This example provides a valuable lesson. It demonstrates how simple it is for a human to distinguish between separate concepts, and how tricky it can be for mere machines. The natural tendency is to try to provide synonyms for every word in the language, to ensure that any document is findable with even the most remotely related terms.

This is a mistake. In the same way that we prefer light or minimal stemming to aggressive stemming, synonyms should be used only where necessary. Users understand why their results are limited to the words in their search query. They are less understanding when their results seems almost random.

Synonyms can be used to conflate words that have pretty much the same meaning, such as jump, leap, and hop, or pamphlet, leaflet, and brochure. Alternatively, they can be used to make a word more generic. For instance, bird could be used as a more general synonym for owl or pigeon, and adult could be used for man or woman.

Synonyms appear to be a simple concept but they are quite tricky to get right. In this chapter, we explain the mechanics of using synonyms and discuss the limitations and gotchas.

Synonyms are used to broaden the scope of what is considered a matching document. Just as with stemming or partial matching, synonym fields should not be used alone but should be combined with a query on a main field that contains the original text in unadulterated form. See "Most Fields" on page 229 for an explanation of how to maintain relevance when using synonyms.

Using Synonyms

Synonyms can replace existing tokens or be added to the token stream by using the synonym token filter (*http://bit.ly/1DInEGD*):

```
PUT /my_index
{
  "settings": {
    "analysis": {
      "filter": {
        "my_synonym_filter": {
          "type": "synonym",     ❶
          "synonyms": [          ❷
            "british,english",
            "queen,monarch"
          ]
        }
      },
      "analyzer": {
        "my_synonyms": {
          "tokenizer": "standard",
          "filter": [
            "lowercase",
            "my_synonym_filter"  ❸
          ]
        }
      }
    }
  }
}
```

❶ First, we define a token filter of type synonym.

❷ We discuss synonym formats in "Formatting Synonyms" on page 399.

❸ Then we create a custom analyzer that uses the my_synonym_filter.

Synonyms can be specified inline with the synonyms parameter, or in a synonyms file that must be present on every node in the cluster. The path to the synonyms file should be specified with the synonyms_path parameter, and should be either absolute or relative to the Elasticsearch config directory. See "Updating Stopwords" on page 385 for techniques that can be used to refresh the synonyms list.

Testing our analyzer with the analyze API shows the following:

```
GET /my_index/_analyze?analyzer=my_synonyms
Elizabeth is the English queen
```

```
Pos 1: (elizabeth)
Pos 2: (is)
Pos 3: (the)
Pos 4: (british,english) ❶
Pos 5: (queen,monarch) ❶
```

❶ All synonyms occupy the same position as the original term.

A document like this will match queries for any of the following: English queen, British queen, English monarch, or British monarch. Even a phrase query will work, because the position of each term has been preserved.

Using the same synonym token filter at both index time and search time is redundant. If, at index time, we replace English with the two terms english and british, then at search time we need to search for only one of those terms. Alternatively, if we don't use synonyms at index time, then at search time, we would need to convert a query for English into a query for english OR british.

Whether to do synonym expansion at search or index time can be a difficult choice. We will explore the options more in "Expand or contract" on page 400.

Formatting Synonyms

In their simplest form, synonyms are listed as comma-separated values:

```
"jump,leap,hop"
```

If any of these terms is encountered, it is replaced by all of the listed synonyms. For instance:

```
Original terms:    Replaced by:
─────────────────────────────────
jump             → (jump,leap,hop)
leap             → (jump,leap,hop)
hop              → (jump,leap,hop)
```

Alternatively, with the => syntax, it is possible to specify a list of terms to match (on the left side), and a list of one or more replacements (on the right side):

```
"u s a,united states,united states of america => usa"
"g b,gb,great britain => britain,england,scotland,wales"

Original terms:    Replaced by:
─────────────────────────────────
u s a            → (usa)
united states    → (usa)
great britain    → (britain,england,scotland,wales)
```

If multiple rules for the same synonyms are specified, they are merged together. The order of rules is not respected. Instead, the longest matching rule wins. Take the following rules as an example:

```
"united states          => usa",
"united states of america => usa"
```

If these rules conflicted, Elasticsearch would turn United States of America into the terms (usa),(of),(america). Instead, the longest sequence wins, and we end up with just the term (usa).

Expand or contract

In "Formatting Synonyms" on page 399, we have seen that it is possible to replace synonyms by *simple expansion*, *simple contraction*, or *generic expansion*. We will look at the trade-offs of each of these techniques in this section.

 This section deals with single-word synonyms only. Multiword synonyms add another layer of complexity and are discussed later in "Multiword Synonyms and Phrase Queries" on page 404.

Simple Expansion

With *simple expansion*, any of the listed synonyms is expanded into *all* of the listed synonyms:

```
"jump,hop,leap"
```

Expansion can be applied either at index time or at query time. Each has advantages (↑) and disadvantages (↓). When to use which comes down to performance versus flexibility.

	Index time	Query time
Index size	↓ Bigger index because all synonyms must be indexed.	↑ Normal.
Relevance	↓ All synonyms will have the same IDF (see "What Is Relevance?" on page 117), meaning that more commonly used words will have the same weight as less commonly used words.	↑ The IDF for each synonym will be correct.
Performance	↑ A query needs to find only the single term specified in the query string.	↓ A query for a single term is rewritten to look up all synonyms, which decreases performance.
Flexibility	↓ The synonym rules can't be changed for existing documents. For the new rules to have effect, existing documents have to be reindexed.	↑ Synonym rules can be updated without reindexing documents.

Simple Contraction

Simple contraction maps a group of synonyms on the left side to a single value on the right side:

```
"leap,hop => jump"
```

It must be applied both at index time and at query time, to ensure that query terms are mapped to the same single value that exists in the index.

This approach has some advantages and some disadvantages compared to the simple expansion approach:

Index size
  ↑ The index size is normal, as only a single term is indexed.

Relevance
  ↓ The IDF for all terms is the same, so you can't distinguish between more commonly used words and less commonly used words.

Performance

↑ A query needs to find only the single term that appears in the index.

Flexibility

↑ New synonyms can be added to the left side of the rule and applied at query time. For instance, imagine that we wanted to add the word bound to the rule specified previously. The following rule would work for queries that contain bound or for newly added documents that contain bound:

```
"leap,hop,bound => jump"
```

But we could expand the effect to also take into account *existing* documents that contain bound by writing the rule as follows:

```
"leap,hop,bound => jump,bound"
```

When you reindex your documents, you could revert to the previous rule to gain the performance benefit of querying only a single term.

Genre Expansion

Genre expansion is quite different from simple contraction or expansion. Instead of treating all synonyms as equal, genre expansion widens the meaning of a term to be more generic. Take these rules, for example:

```
"cat    => cat,pet",
"kitten => kitten,cat,pet",
"dog    => dog,pet"
"puppy  => puppy,dog,pet"
```

By applying genre expansion at index time:

- A query for `kitten` would find just documents about kittens.
- A query for `cat` would find documents abouts kittens and cats.
- A query for `pet` would find documents about kittens, cats, puppies, dogs, or pets.

Alternatively, by applying genre expansion at query time, a query for `kitten` would be expanded to return documents that mention kittens, cats, or pets specifically.

You could also have the best of both worlds by applying expansion at index time to ensure that the genres are present in the index. Then, at query time, you can choose to not apply synonyms (so that a query for `kitten` returns only documents about kittens) or to apply synonyms in order to match kittens, cats and pets (including the canine variety).

With the preceding example rules above, the IDF for `kitten` will be correct, while the IDF for `cat` and `pet` will be artificially deflated. However, this works in your favor—a genre-expanded query for `kitten OR cat OR pet` will rank documents with `kitten` highest, followed by documents with `cat`, and documents with `pet` would be right at the bottom.

Synonyms and The Analysis Chain

The example we showed in "Formatting Synonyms" on page 399, used `u s a` as a synonym. Why did we use that instead of `U.S.A.`? The reason is that the `synonym` token filter sees only the terms that the previous token filter or tokenizer has emitted.

Imagine that we have an analyzer that consists of the `standard` tokenizer, with the `lowercase` token filter followed by a `synonym` token filter. The analysis process for the text `U.S.A.` would look like this:

```
original string              → "U.S.A."
standard        tokenizer    → (U),(S),(A)
lowercase       token filter → (u),(s),(a)
synonym         token filter → (usa)
```

If we had specified the synonym as `U.S.A.`, it would never match anything because, by the time `my_synonym_filter` sees the terms, the periods have been removed and the letters have been lowercased.

This is an important point to consider. What if we want to combine synonyms with stemming, so that `jumps`, `jumped`, `jump`, `leaps`, `leaped`, and `leap` are all indexed as the single term `jump`? We could place the synonyms filter before the stemmer and list all inflections:

```
"jumps,jumped,leap,leaps,leaped => jump"
```

But the more concise way would be to place the synonyms filter after the stemmer, and to list just the root words that would be emitted by the stemmer:

```
"leap => jump"
```

Case-Sensitive Synonyms

Normally, synonym filters are placed after the `lowercase` token filter and so all synonyms are written in lowercase, but sometimes that can lead to odd conflations. For instance, a `CAT` scan and a `cat` are quite different, as are `PET` (positron emmision tomography) and a `pet`. For that matter, the surname `Little` is distinct from the adjective `little` (although if a sentence starts with the adjective, it will be uppercased anyway).

If you need use case to distinguish between word senses, you will need to place your synonym filter before the `lowercase` filter. Of course, that means that your synonym rules would need to list all of the case variations that you want to match (for example, `Little,LITTLE,little`).

Instead of that, you could have two synonym filters: one to catch the case-sensitive synonyms and one for all the case-insentive synonyms. For instance, the case-sensitive rules could look like this:

```
"CAT,CAT scan          => cat_scan"
"PET,PET scan          => pet_scan"
"Johnny Little,J Little => johnny_little"
"Johnny Small,J Small   => johnny_small"
```

And the case-insentive rules could look like this:

```
"cat                   => cat,pet"
"dog                   => dog,pet"
"cat scan,cat_scan scan => cat_scan"
"pet scan,pet_scan scan => pet_scan"
"little,small"
```

The case-sensitive rules would `CAT scan` but would match only the `CAT` in `CAT scan`. For this reason, we have the odd-looking rule `cat_scan scan` in the case-insensitive list to catch bad replacements.

 You can see how quickly it can get complicated. As always, the analyze API is your friend—use it to check that your analyzers are configured correctly. See "Testing Analyzers" on page 88.

Multiword Synonyms and Phrase Queries

So far, synonyms appear to be quite straightforward. Unfortunately, this is where things start to go wrong. For phrase queries to function correctly, Elasticsearch needs to know the position that each term occupies in the original text. Multiword synonyms can play havoc with term positions, especially when the injected synonyms are of differing lengths.

To demonstrate, we'll create a synonym token filter that uses this rule:

```
"usa,united states,u s a,united states of america"

PUT /my_index
{
  "settings": {
    "analysis": {
      "filter": {
        "my_synonym_filter": {
          "type": "synonym",
          "synonyms": [
            "usa,united states,u s a,united states of america"
          ]
        }
      }
    },
```

```
          "analyzer": {
            "my_synonyms": {
              "tokenizer": "standard",
              "filter": [
                "lowercase",
                "my_synonym_filter"
              ]
            }
          }
        }
      }
    }
  }
}

GET /my_index/_analyze?analyzer=my_synonyms&text=
The United States is wealthy
```

The tokens emitted by the `analyze` request look like this:

```
Pos 1:  (the)
Pos 2:  (usa,united,u,united)
Pos 3:  (states,s,states)
Pos 4:  (is,a,of)
Pos 5:  (wealthy,america)
```

If we were to index a document analyzed with synonyms as above, and then run a phrase query without synonyms, we'd have some surprising results. These phrases would not match:

- The usa is wealthy

- The united states of america is wealthy

- The U.S.A. is wealthy

However, these phrases would:

- United states is wealthy

- Usa states of wealthy

- The U.S. of wealthy

- U.S. is america

If we were to use synonyms at query time instead, we would see even more-bizarre matches. Look at the output of this `validate-query` request:

```
GET /my_index/_validate/query?explain
{
  "query": {
    "match_phrase": {
      "text": {
        "query": "usa is wealthy",
        "analyzer": "my_synonyms"
```

```
        }
      }
    }
  }
}
```

The explanation is as follows:

```
"(usa united u united) (is states s states) (wealthy a of) america"
```

This would match documents containg `u is of america` but wouldn't match any document that didn't contain the term `america`.

 Multiword synonyms affect highlighting in a similar way. A query for USA could end up returning a highlighted snippet such as: "The *United States is wealthy*".

Use Simple Contraction for Phrase Queries

The way to avoid this mess is to use simple contraction to inject a single term that represents all synonyms, and to use the same synonym token filter at query time:

```
PUT /my_index
{
  "settings": {
    "analysis": {
      "filter": {
        "my_synonym_filter": {
          "type": "synonym",
          "synonyms": [
            "united states,u s a,united states of america=>usa"
          ]
        }
      },
      "analyzer": {
        "my_synonyms": {
          "tokenizer": "standard",
          "filter": [
            "lowercase",
            "my_synonym_filter"
          ]
        }
      }
    }
  }
}

GET /my_index/_analyze?analyzer=my_synonyms
The United States is wealthy
```

The result of the preceding `analyze` request looks much more sane:

```
Pos 1: (the)
Pos 2: (usa)
Pos 3: (is)
Pos 5: (wealthy)
```

And repeating the `validate-query` request that we made previously yields a simple, sane explanation:

```
"usa is wealthy"
```

The downside of this approach is that, by reducing united states of america down to the single term usa, you can't use the same field to find just the word united or states. You would need to use a separate field with a different analysis chain for that purpose.

Synonyms and the query_string Query

We have tried to avoid discussing the query_string query because we don't recommend using it. In More-Complicated Queries, we said that, because the query_string query supports a terse mini *search-syntax*, it could frequently lead to surprising results or even syntax errors.

One of the gotchas of this query involves multiword synonyms. To support its search-syntax, it has to parse the query string to recognize special operators like AND, OR, +, -, field:, and so forth. (See the full query_string syntax (*http://bit.ly/151G5I1*) here.)

As part of this parsing process, it breaks up the query string on whitespace, and passes each word that it finds to the relevant analyzer separately. This means that your synonym analyzer will never receive a multiword synonym. Instead of seeing United States as a single string, the analyzer will receive United and States separately.

Fortunately, the trustworthy match query supports no such syntax, and multiword synonyms will be passed to the analyzer in their entirety.

Symbol Synonyms

The final part of this chapter is devoted to symbol synonyms, which are unlike the synonyms we have discussed until now. *Symbol synonyms* are string aliases used to represent symbols that would otherwise be removed during tokenization.

While most punctuation is seldom important for full-text search, character combinations like emoticons may be very signficant, even changing the meaning of the the text. Compare these:

- I am thrilled to be at work on Sunday.

- I am thrilled to be at work on Sunday :(

The `standard` tokenizer would simply strip out the emoticon in the second sentence, conflating two sentences that have quite different intent.

We can use the `mapping` character filter (*http://bit.ly/1ziua5n*) to replace emoticons with symbol synonyms like `emoticon_happy` and `emoticon_sad` before the text is passed to the tokenizer:

```
PUT /my_index
{
  "settings": {
    "analysis": {
      "char_filter": {
        "emoticons": {
          "type": "mapping",
          "mappings": [ ❶
            ":)=>emoticon_happy",
            ":(=>emoticon_sad"
          ]
        }
      },
      "analyzer": {
        "my_emoticons": {
          "char_filter": "emoticons",
          "tokenizer":   "standard",
          "filter":    [ "lowercase" ]
          ]
        }
      }
    }
  }
}

GET /my_index/_analyze?analyzer=my_emoticons
I am :) not :( ❷
```

❶ The `mappings` filter replaces the characters to the left of => with those to the right.

❷ Emits tokens i, am, emoticon_happy, not, emoticon_sad.

It is unlikely that anybody would ever search for `emoticon_happy`, but ensuring that important symbols like emoticons are included in the index can be helpful when doing sentiment analysis. Of course, we could equally have used real words, like `happy` and `sad`.

The mapping character filter is useful for simple replacements of exact character sequences. For more-flexible pattern matching, you can use regular expressions with the pattern_replace character filter (*http://bit.ly/1DK4hgy*).

CHAPTER 24

Typoes and Mispelings

We expect a query on structured data like dates and prices to return only documents that match exactly. However, good full-text search shouldn't have the same restriction. Instead, we can widen the net to include words that *may* match, but use the relevance score to push the better matches to the top of the result set.

In fact, full-text search that only matches exactly will probably frustrate your users. Wouldn't you expect a search for "quick brown fox" to match a document containing "fast brown foxes," "Johnny Walker" to match "Johnnie Walker," or "Arnold Shcwarzenneger" to match "Arnold Schwarzenegger"?

If documents exist that *do* contain exactly what the user has queried, they should appear at the top of the result set, but weaker matches can be included further down the list. If no documents match exactly, at least we can show the user potential matches; they may even be what the user originally intended!

We have already looked at diacritic-free matching in Chapter 20, word stemming in Chapter 21, and synonyms in Chapter 23, but all of those approaches presuppose that words are spelled correctly, or that there is only one way to spell each word.

Fuzzy matching allows for query-time matching of misspelled words, while phonetic token filters at index time can be used for *sounds-like* matching.

Fuzziness

Fuzzy matching treats two words that are "fuzzily" similar as if they were the same word. First, we need to define what we mean by *fuzziness*.

In 1965, Vladimir Levenshtein developed the Levenshtein distance (*http://en.wikipedia.org/wiki/Levenshtein_distance*), which measures the number of single-character edits required to transform one word into the other. He proposed three types of one-character edits:

- *Substitution* of one character for another: _f_ox → _b_ox
- *Insertion* of a new character: sic → sic_k_
- *Deletion* of a character:: b_l_ack → back

Frederick Damerau (*http://en.wikipedia.org/wiki/Frederick_J._Damerau*) later expanded these operations to include one more:

- *Transposition* of two adjacent characters: _st_ar → _ts_ar

For example, to convert the word bieber into beaver requires the following steps:

1. Substitute v for b: bie_b_er → bie_v_er
2. Substitute a for i: b_i_ever → b_a_ever
3. Transpose a and e: b_ae_ver → b_ea_ver

These three steps represent a Damerau-Levenshtein edit distance (*http://bit.ly/1ymgZPB*) of 3.

Clearly, bieber is a long way from beaver—they are too far apart to be considered a simple misspelling. Damerau observed that 80% of human misspellings have an edit distance of 1. In other words, 80% of misspellings could be corrected with a *single edit* to the original string.

Elasticsearch supports a maximum edit distance, specified with the fuzziness parameter, of 2.

Of course, the impact that a single edit has on a string depends on the length of the string. Two edits to the word hat can produce mad, so allowing two edits on a string of length 3 is overkill. The fuzziness parameter can be set to AUTO, which results in the following maximum edit distances:

- 0 for strings of one or two characters
- 1 for strings of three, four, or five characters
- 2 for strings of more than five characters

Of course, you may find that an edit distance of 2 is still overkill, and returns results that don't appear to be related. You may get better results, and better performance, with a maximum fuzziness of 1.

Fuzzy Query

The `fuzzy` query (*http://bit.ly/1ymh8Cu*) is the fuzzy equivalent of the `term` query. You will seldom use it directly yourself, but understanding how it works will help you to use fuzziness in the higher-level `match` query.

To understand how it works, we will first index some documents:

```
POST /my_index/my_type/_bulk
{ "index": { "_id": 1 }}
{ "text": "Surprise me!"}
{ "index": { "_id": 2 }}
{ "text": "That was surprising."}
{ "index": { "_id": 3 }}
{ "text": "I wasn't surprised."}
```

Now we can run a `fuzzy` query for the term `surprize`:

```
GET /my_index/my_type/_search
{
  "query": {
    "fuzzy": {
      "text": "surprize"
    }
  }
}
```

The `fuzzy` query is a term-level query, so it doesn't do any analysis. It takes a single term and finds all terms in the term dictionary that are within the specified `fuzziness`. The default `fuzziness` is AUTO.

In our example, `surprize` is within an edit distance of 2 from both `surprise` and `surprised`, so documents 1 and 3 match. We could reduce the matches to just `surprise` with the following query:

```
GET /my_index/my_type/_search
{
  "query": {
    "fuzzy": {
      "text": {
        "value": "surprize",
        "fuzziness": 1
      }
    }
  }
}
```

Improving Performance

The fuzzy query works by taking the original term and building a *Levenshtein automaton*—like a big graph representing all the strings that are within the specified edit distance of the original string.

The fuzzy query then uses the automation to step efficiently through all of the terms in the term dictionary to see if they match. Once it has collected all of the matching terms that exist in the term dictionary, it can compute the list of matching documents.

Of course, depending on the type of data stored in the index, a fuzzy query with an edit distance of 2 can match a very large number of terms and perform very badly. Two parameters can be used to limit the performance impact:

prefix_length
> The number of initial characters that will not be "fuzzified." Most spelling errors occur toward the end of the word, not toward the beginning. By using a prefix_length of 3, for example, you can signficantly reduce the number of matching terms.

max_expansions
> If a fuzzy query expands to three or four fuzzy options, the new options may be meaningful. If it produces 1,000 options, they are essentially meaningless. Use max_expansions to limit the total number of options that will be produced. The fuzzy query will collect matching terms until it runs out of terms or reaches the max_expansions limit.

Fuzzy match Query

The match query supports fuzzy matching out of the box:

```
GET /my_index/my_type/_search
{
  "query": {
    "match": {
      "text": {
        "query":     "SURPRIZE ME!",
        "fuzziness": "AUTO",
        "operator":  "and"
      }
    }
  }
}
```

The query string is first analyzed, to produce the terms [surprize, me], and then each term is fuzzified using the specified fuzziness.

Similarly, the `multi_match` query also supports `fuzziness`, but only when executing with type `best_fields` or `most_fields`:

```
GET /my_index/my_type/_search
{
  "query": {
    "multi_match": {
      "fields":  [ "text", "title" ],
      "query":      "SURPRIZE ME!",
      "fuzziness": "AUTO"
    }
  }
}
```

Both the `match` and `multi_match` queries also support the `prefix_length` and `max_expansions` parameters.

 Fuzziness works only with the basic `match` and `multi_match` queries. It doesn't work with phrase matching, common terms, or `cross_fields` matches.

Scoring Fuzziness

Users love fuzzy queries. They assume that these queries will somehow magically find the right combination of proper spellings. Unfortunately, the truth is somewhat more prosaic.

Imagine that we have 1,000 documents containing "Schwarzenegger," and just one document with the misspelling "Schwarzeneger." According to the theory of term frequency/inverse document frequency, the misspelling is much more relevant than the correct spelling, because it appears in far fewer documents!

In other words, if we were to treat fuzzy matches like any other match, we would favor misspellings over correct spellings, which would make for grumpy users.

 Fuzzy matching should not be used for scoring purposes—only to widen the net of matching terms in case there are misspellings.

By default, the `match` query gives all fuzzy matches the constant score of 1. This is sufficient to add potential matches onto the end of the result list, without interfering with the relevance scoring of nonfuzzy queries.

Fuzzy queries alone are much less useful than they initially appear. They are better used as part of a "bigger" feature, such as the *search-as-you-type* `completion` suggester (*http://bit.ly/1IChV5j*) or the *did-you-mean* `phrase` suggester (*http://bit.ly/1IOj5ZG*).

Phonetic Matching

In a last, desperate, attempt to match something, anything, we could resort to searching for words that sound similar, even if their spelling differs.

Several algorithms exist for converting words into a phonetic representation. The Soundex (*http://en.wikipedia.org/wiki/Soundex*) algorithm is the granddaddy of them all, and most other phonetic algorithms are improvements or specializations of Soundex, such as Metaphone (*http://en.wikipedia.org/wiki/Metaphone*) and Double Metaphone (*http://en.wikipedia.org/wiki/Metaphone#Double_Metaphone*) (which expands phonetic matching to languages other than English), Caverphone (*http://en.wikipedia.org/wiki/Caverphone*) for matching names in New Zealand, the Beider-Morse (*http://bit.ly/1E47qoB*) algorithm, which adopts the Soundex algorithm for better matching of German and Yiddish names, and the Kölner Phonetik (*http://de.wikipedia.org/wiki/K%C3%B6lner_Phonetik*) for better handling of German words.

The thing to take away from this list is that phonetic algorithms are fairly crude, and very specific to the languages they were designed for, usually either English or German. This limits their usefulness. Still, for certain purposes, and in combination with other techniques, phonetic matching can be a useful tool.

First, you will need to install the Phonetic Analysis plug-in from *http://bit.ly/1CreKJQ* on every node in the cluster, and restart each node.

Then, you can create a custom analyzer that uses one of the phonetic token filters and try it out:

```
PUT /my_index
{
  "settings": {
    "analysis": {
      "filter": {
        "dbl_metaphone": { ❶
          "type":    "phonetic",
          "encoder": "double_metaphone"
        }
      },
      "analyzer": {
        "dbl_metaphone": {
          "tokenizer": "standard",
          "filter":    "dbl_metaphone" ❷
        }
      }
```

```
      }
    }
  }
```

❶ First, configure a custom `phonetic` token filter that uses the `double_metaphone` encoder.

❷ Then use the custom token filter in a custom analyzer.

Now we can test it with the `analyze` API:

```
GET /my_index/_analyze?analyzer=dbl_metaphone
Smith Smythe
```

Each of `Smith` and `Smythe` produce two tokens in the same position: `SM0` and `XMT`. Running `John`, `Jon`, and `Johnnie` through the analyzer will all produce the two tokens `JN` and `AN`, while `Jonathon` results in the tokens `JN0N` and `ANTN`.

The phonetic analyzer can be used just like any other analyzer. First map a field to use it, and then index some data:

```
PUT /my_index/_mapping/my_type
{
  "properties": {
    "name": {
      "type": "string",
      "fields": {
        "phonetic": {  ❶
          "type":     "string",
          "analyzer": "dbl_metaphone"
        }
      }
    }
  }
}

PUT /my_index/my_type/1
{
  "name": "John Smith"
}

PUT /my_index/my_type/2
{
  "name": "Jonnie Smythe"
}
```

❶ The `name.phonetic` field uses the custom `dbl_metaphone` analyzer.

The `match` query can be used for searching:

```
GET /my_index/my_type/_search
{
```

```
    "query": {
      "match": {
        "name.phonetic": {
          "query": "Jahnnie Smeeth",
          "operator": "and"
        }
      }
    }
}
```

This query returns both documents, demonstrating just how coarse phonetic matching is. Scoring with a phonetic algorithm is pretty much worthless. The purpose of phonetic matching is not to increase precision, but to increase recall—to spread the net wide enough to catch any documents that might possibly match.

It usually makes more sense to use phonetic algorithms when retrieving results which will be consumed and post-processed by another computer, rather than by human users.

PART IV

Aggregations

Until this point, this book has been dedicated to search. With search, we have a query and we want to find a subset of documents that match the query. We are looking for the proverbial needle(s) in the haystack.

With aggregations, we zoom out to get an overview of our data. Instead of looking for individual documents, we want to analyze and summarize our complete set of data:

- How many needles are in the haystack?
- What is the average length of the needles?
- What is the median length of the needles, broken down by manufacturer?
- How many needles were added to the haystack each month?

Aggregations can answer more subtle questions too:

- What are your most popular needle manufacturers?
- Are there any unusual or anomalous clumps of needles?

Aggregations allow us to ask sophisticated questions of our data. And yet, while the functionality is completely different from search, it leverages the same data-structures. This means aggregations execute quickly and are *near real-time*, just like search.

This is extremely powerful for reporting and dashboards. Instead of performing *roll-ups* of your data (*that crusty Hadoop job that takes a week to run*), you can visualize your data in real time, allowing you to respond immediately. Your report changes as your data changes, rather than being pre-calculated, out of date and irrelevant.

Finally, aggregations operate alongside search requests. This means you can both search/filter documents *and* perform analytics at the same time, on the same data, in a single request. And because aggregations are calculated in the context of a user's search, you're not just displaying a count of four-star hotels—you're displaying a count of four-star hotels that *match their search criteria.*

Aggregations are so powerful that many companies have built large Elasticsearch clusters solely for analytics.

CHAPTER 25

High-Level Concepts

Like the query DSL, aggregations have a *composable* syntax: independent units of functionality can be mixed and matched to provide the custom behavior that you need. This means that there are only a few basic concepts to learn, but nearly limitless combinations of those basic components.

To master aggregations, you need to understand only two main concepts:

Buckets
> Collections of documents that meet a criterion

Metrics
> Statistics calculated on the documents in a bucket

That's it! Every aggregation is simply a combination of one or more buckets and zero or more metrics. To translate into rough SQL terms:

```
SELECT COUNT(color) ❶
FROM table
GROUP BY color ❷
```

❶ COUNT(color) is equivalent to a metric.

❷ GROUP BY color is equivalent to a bucket.

Buckets are conceptually similar to grouping in SQL, while metrics are similar to COUNT(), SUM(), MAX(), and so forth.

Let's dig into both of these concepts and see what they entail.

Buckets

A *bucket* is simply a collection of documents that meet a certain criteria:

- An employee would land in either the *male* or *female* bucket.
- The city of Albany would land in the *New York* state bucket.
- The date 2014-10-28 would land within the *October* bucket.

As aggregations are executed, the values inside each document are evaluated to determine whether they match a bucket's criteria. If they match, the document is placed inside the bucket and the aggregation continues.

Buckets can also be nested inside other buckets, giving you a hierarchy or conditional partitioning scheme. For example, Cincinnati would be placed inside the Ohio state bucket, and the *entire* Ohio bucket would be placed inside the USA country bucket.

Elasticsearch has a variety of buckets, which allow you to partition documents in many ways (by hour, by most-popular terms, by age ranges, by geographical location, and more). But fundamentally they all operate on the same principle: partitioning documents based on a criteria.

Metrics

Buckets allow us to partition documents into useful subsets, but ultimately what we want is some kind of metric calculated on those documents in each bucket. Bucketing is the means to an end: it provides a way to group documents in a way that you can calculate interesting metrics.

Most *metrics* are simple mathematical operations (for example, min, mean, max, and sum) that are calculated using the document values. In practical terms, metrics allow you to calculate quantities such as the average salary, or the maximum sale price, or the 95th percentile for query latency.

Combining the Two

An *aggregation* is a combination of buckets and metrics. An aggregation may have a single bucket, or a single metric, or one of each. It may even have multiple buckets nested inside other buckets. For example, we can partition documents by which country they belong to (a bucket), and then calculate the average salary per country (a metric).

Because buckets can be nested, we can derive a much more complex aggregation:

1. Partition documents by country (bucket).
2. Then partition each country bucket by gender (bucket).
3. Then partition each gender bucket by age ranges (bucket).
4. Finally, calculate the average salary for each age range (metric)

This will give you the average salary per <country, gender, age> combination. All in one request and with one pass over the data!

CHAPTER 26

Aggregation Test-Drive

We could spend the next few pages defining the various aggregations and their syntax, but aggregations are truly best learned by example. Once you learn how to think about aggregations, and how to nest them appropriately, the syntax is fairly trivial.

 A complete list of aggregation buckets and metrics can be found at the online reference documentation (*http://bit.ly/1KNL1R3*). We'll cover many of them in this chapter, but glance over it after finishing so you are familiar with the full range of capabilities.

So let's just dive in and start with an example. We are going to build some aggregations that might be useful to a car dealer. Our data will be about car transactions: the car model, manufacturer, sale price, when it sold, and more.

First we will bulk-index some data to work with:

```
POST /cars/transactions/_bulk
{ "index": {}}
{ "price" : 10000, "color" : "red", "make" : "honda", "sold" : "2014-10-28" }
{ "index": {}}
{ "price" : 20000, "color" : "red", "make" : "honda", "sold" : "2014-11-05" }
{ "index": {}}
{ "price" : 30000, "color" : "green", "make" : "ford", "sold" : "2014-05-18" }
{ "index": {}}
{ "price" : 15000, "color" : "blue", "make" : "toyota", "sold" : "2014-07-02" }
{ "index": {}}
{ "price" : 12000, "color" : "green", "make" : "toyota", "sold" : "2014-08-19" }
{ "index": {}}
{ "price" : 20000, "color" : "red", "make" : "honda", "sold" : "2014-11-05" }
{ "index": {}}
{ "price" : 80000, "color" : "red", "make" : "bmw", "sold" : "2014-01-01" }
```

```
{ "index": {}}
{ "price" : 25000, "color" : "blue", "make" : "ford", "sold" : "2014-02-12" }
```

Now that we have some data, let's construct our first aggregation. A car dealer may want to know which color car sells the best. This is easily accomplished using a simple aggregation. We will do this using a `terms` bucket:

```
GET /cars/transactions/_search?search_type=count
{
    "aggs" : { ❶
        "colors" : { ❷
            "terms" : {
                "field" : "color" ❸
            }
        }
    }
}
```

❶ Aggregations are placed under the top-level `aggs` parameter (the longer `aggregations` will also work if you prefer that).

❷ We then name the aggregation whatever we want: `colors`, in this example

❸ Finally, we define a single bucket of type `terms`.

Aggregations are executed in the context of search results, which means it is just another top-level parameter in a search request (for example, using the `/_search` endpoint). Aggregations can be paired with queries, but we'll tackle that later in Chapter 29.

 You'll notice that we used the count search_type. Because we don't care about search results—the aggregation totals—the count search_type will be faster because it omits the fetch phase.

Next we define a name for our aggregation. Naming is up to you; the response will be labeled with the name you provide so that your application can parse the results later.

Next we define the aggregation itself. For this example, we are defining a single `terms` bucket. The `terms` bucket will dynamically create a new bucket for every unique term it encounters. Since we are telling it to use the `color` field, the `terms` bucket will dynamically create a new bucket for each color.

Let's execute that aggregation and take a look at the results:

```
{
...
    "hits": {
```

```
      "hits": [] ❶
   },
   "aggregations": {
      "colors": { ❷
         "buckets": [
            {
               "key": "red", ❸
               "doc_count": 4 ❹
            },
            {
               "key": "blue",
               "doc_count": 2
            },
            {
               "key": "green",
               "doc_count": 2
            }
         ]
      }
   }
}
```

❶ No search hits are returned because we used the `search_type=count` parameter

❷ Our `colors` aggregation is returned as part of the `aggregations` field.

❸ The key to each bucket corresponds to a unique term found in the `color` field. It also always includes `doc_count`, which tells us the number of docs containing the term.

❹ The count of each bucket represents the number of documents with this color.

The response contains a list of buckets, each corresponding to a unique color (for example, red or green). Each bucket also includes a count of the number of documents that "fell into" that particular bucket. For example, there are four red cars.

The preceding example is operating entirely in real time: if the documents are searchable, they can be aggregated. This means you can take the aggregation results and pipe them straight into a graphing library to generate real-time dashboards. As soon as you sell a silver car, your graphs would dynamically update to include statistics about silver cars.

Voila! Your first aggregation!

Adding a Metric to the Mix

The previous example told us the number of documents in each bucket, which is useful. But often, our applications require more-sophisticated metrics about the documents. For example, what is the average price of cars in each bucket?

To get this information, we need to tell Elasticsearch which metrics to calculate, and on which fields. This requires *nesting* metrics inside the buckets. Metrics will calculate mathematical statistics based on the values of documents within a bucket.

Let's go ahead and add an `average` metric to our car example:

```
GET /cars/transactions/_search?search_type=count
{
   "aggs": {
      "colors": {
         "terms": {
            "field": "color"
         },
         "aggs": {   ❶
            "avg_price": {   ❷
               "avg": {
                  "field": "price"   ❸
               }
            }
         }
      }
   }
}
```

❶ We add a new `aggs` level to hold the metric.

❷ We then give the metric a name: `avg_price`.

❸ And finally, we define it as an `avg` metric over the `price` field.

As you can see, we took the previous example and tacked on a new `aggs` level. This new aggregation level allows us to nest the `avg` metric inside the `terms` bucket. Effectively, this means we will generate an average for each color.

Just like the `colors` example, we need to name our metric (`avg_price`) so we can retrieve the values later. Finally, we specify the metric itself (`avg`) and what field we want the average to be calculated on (`price`):

```
{
...
   "aggregations": {
      "colors": {
         "buckets": [
            {
```

```
            "key": "red",
            "doc_count": 4,
            "avg_price": {  ❶
                "value": 32500
            }
        },
        {
            "key": "blue",
            "doc_count": 2,
            "avg_price": {
                "value": 20000
            }
        },
        {
            "key": "green",
            "doc_count": 2,
            "avg_price": {
                "value": 21000
            }
        }
    ]
}
}
...
}
```

❶ New `avg_price` element in response

Although the response has changed minimally, the data we get out of it has grown substantially. Before, we knew there were four red cars. Now we know that the average price of red cars is $32,500. This is something that you can plug directly into reports or graphs.

Buckets Inside Buckets

The true power of aggregations becomes apparent once you start playing with different nesting schemes. In the previous examples, we saw how you could nest a metric inside a bucket, which is already quite powerful.

But the real exciting analytics come from nesting buckets inside *other buckets*. This time, we want to find out the distribution of car manufacturers for each color:

```
GET /cars/transactions/_search?search_type=count
{
    "aggs": {
        "colors": {
            "terms": {
                "field": "color"
            },
            "aggs": {
```

```
            "avg_price": { ❶
                "avg": {
                    "field": "price"
                }
            },
            "make": { ❷
                "terms": {
                    "field": "make" ❸
                }
            }
        }
    }
}
```

❶ Notice that we can leave the previous `avg_price` metric in place.

❷ Another aggregation named `make` is added to the `color` bucket.

❸ This aggregation is a `terms` bucket and will generate unique buckets for each car make.

A few interesting things happened here. First, you'll notice that the previous `avg_price` metric is left entirely intact. Each *level* of an aggregation can have many metrics or buckets. The `avg_price` metric tells us the average price for each car color. This is independent of other buckets and metrics that are also being built.

This is important for your application, since there are often many related, but entirely distinct, metrics that you need to collect. Aggregations allow you to collect all of them in a single pass over the data.

The other important thing to note is that the aggregation we added, `make`, is a `terms` bucket (nested inside the `colors` terms bucket). This means we will generate a (`color`, `make`) tuple for every unique combination in your dataset.

Let's take a look at the response (truncated for brevity, since it is now growing quite long):

```
{
...
    "aggregations": {
        "colors": {
            "buckets": [
                {
                    "key": "red",
                    "doc_count": 4,
                    "make": { ❶
                        "buckets": [
                            {
                                "key": "honda", ❷
```

```
                    "doc_count": 3
                },
                {
                    "key": "bmw",
                    "doc_count": 1
                }
            ]
        },
        "avg_price": {
            "value": 32500 ❸
        }
    },

    ...
}
```

❶   Our new aggregation is nested under each color bucket, as expected.

❷   We now see a breakdown of car makes for each color.

❸   Finally, you can see that our previous avg_price metric is still intact.

The response tells us the following:

- There are four red cars.
- The average price of a red car is $32,500.
- Three of the red cars are made by Honda, and one is a BMW.

One Final Modification

Just to drive the point home, let's make one final modification to our example before moving on to new topics. Let's add two metrics to calculate the min and max price for each make:

```
GET /cars/transactions/_search?search_type=count
{
    "aggs": {
        "colors": {
            "terms": {
                "field": "color"
            },
            "aggs": {
                "avg_price": { "avg": { "field": "price" }
                },
                "make" : {
                    "terms" : {
                        "field" : "make"
                    },
```

```
            "aggs" : {  ❶
                "min_price" : { "min": { "field": "price"} },  ❷
                "max_price" : { "max": { "field": "price"} }  ❸
            }
        }
    }
  }
 }
}
```

❶ We need to add another `aggs` level for nesting.

❷ Then we include a `min` metric.

❸ And a `max` metric.

Which gives us the following output (again, truncated):

```
{
...
    "aggregations": {
        "colors": {
            "buckets": [
                {
                    "key": "red",
                    "doc_count": 4,
                    "make": {
                        "buckets": [
                            {
                                "key": "honda",
                                "doc_count": 3,
                                "min_price": {
                                    "value": 10000  ❶
                                },
                                "max_price": {
                                    "value": 20000  ❶
                                }
                            },
                            {
                                "key": "bmw",
                                "doc_count": 1,
                                "min_price": {
                                    "value": 80000
                                },
                                "max_price": {
                                    "value": 80000
                                }
                            }
                        ]
                    },
                    "avg_price": {
                        "value": 32500
```

```
            }
        },
    ...
```

❶ The `min` and `max` metrics that we added now appear under each `make`

With those two buckets, we've expanded the information derived from this query to include the following:

- There are four red cars.
- The average price of a red car is $32,500.
- Three of the red cars are made by Honda, and one is a BMW.
- The cheapest red Honda is $10,000.
- The most expensive red Honda is $20,000.

CHAPTER 27

Building Bar Charts

One of the exciting aspects of aggregations are how easily they are converted into charts and graphs. In this chapter, we are focusing on various analytics that we can wring out of our example dataset. We will also demonstrate the types of charts aggregations can power.

The histogram bucket is particularly useful. Histograms are essentially bar charts, and if you've ever built a report or analytics dashboard, you undoubtedly had a few bar charts in it. The histogram works by specifying an interval. If we were histogramming sale prices, you might specify an interval of 20,000. This would create a new bucket every $20,000. Documents are then sorted into buckets.

For our dashboard, we want to know how many cars sold in each price range. We would also like to know the total revenue generated by that price bracket. This is calculated by summing the price of each car sold in that interval.

To do this, we use a histogram and a nested sum metric:

```
GET /cars/transactions/_search?search_type=count
{
   "aggs":{
      "price":{
         "histogram":{ ❶
            "field": "price",
            "interval": 20000
         },
         "aggs":{
            "revenue": {
               "sum": { ❷
                  "field" : "price"
               }
            }
         }
      }
```

```
          }
        }
      }
```

❶ The `histogram` bucket requires two parameters: a numeric field, and an interval that defines the bucket size.

❷ A `sum` metric is nested inside each price range, which will show us the total revenue for that bracket

As you can see, our query is built around the `price` aggregation, which contains a `histogram` bucket. This bucket requires a numeric field to calculate buckets on, and an interval size. The interval defines how "wide" each bucket is. An interval of 20000 means we will have the ranges [`0-19999, 20000-39999, ...`].

Next, we define a nested metric inside the histogram. This is a `sum` metric, which will sum up the `price` field from each document landing in that price range. This gives us the revenue for each price range, so we can see if our business makes more money from commodity or luxury cars.

And here is the response:

```
{
...
   "aggregations": {
      "price": {
         "buckets": [
            {
               "key": 0,
               "doc_count": 3,
               "revenue": {
                  "value": 37000
               }
            },
            {
               "key": 20000,
               "doc_count": 4,
               "revenue": {
                  "value": 95000
               }
            },
            {
               "key": 80000,
               "doc_count": 1,
               "revenue": {
                  "value": 80000
               }
            }
         ]
      }
```

```
      }
   }
```

The response is fairly self-explanatory, but it should be noted that the histogram keys correspond to the lower boundary of the interval. The key `0` means `0-19,999`, the key `20000` means `20,000-39,999`, and so forth.

> You'll notice that empty intervals, such as $40,000-60,000, is missing in the response. The `histogram` bucket omits these by default, since it could lead to the unintended generation of potentially enormous output.
>
> We'll discuss how to include empty buckets in the next section, "Returning Empty Buckets" on page 441.

Graphically, you could represent the preceding data in the histogram shown in Figure 27-1.

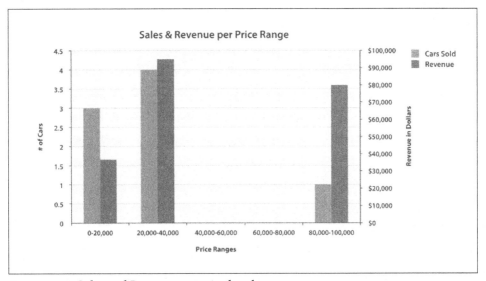

Figure 27-1. Sales and Revenue per price bracket

Of course, you can build bar charts with any aggregation that emits categories and statistics, not just the `histogram` bucket. Let's build a bar chart of popular makes, and their average price, and then calculate the standard error to add error bars on our chart. This will use the `terms` bucket and an `extended_stats` metric:

```
GET /cars/transactions/_search?search_type=count
{
   "aggs": {
      "makes": {
         "terms": {
```

```
        "field": "make",
        "size": 10
      },
      "aggs": {
        "stats": {
          "extended_stats": {
            "field": "price"
          }
        }
      }
    }
  }
}
```

This will return a list of makes (sorted by popularity) and a variety of statistics about each. In particular, we are interested in `stats.avg`, `stats.count`, and `stats.std_deviation`. Using this information, we can calculate the standard error:

```
std_err = std_deviation / count
```

This will allow us to build a chart like Figure 27-2.

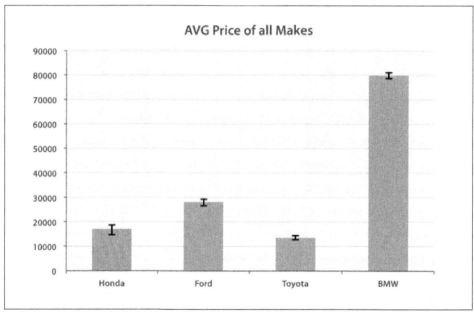

Figure 27-2. Average price of all makes, with error bars

CHAPTER 28

Looking at Time

If search is the most popular activity in Elasticsearch, building date histograms must be the second most popular. Why would you want to use a date histogram?

Imagine your data has a timestamp. It doesn't matter what the data is—Apache log events, stock buy/sell transaction dates, baseball game times—anything with a time-stamp can benefit from the date histogram. When you have a timestamp, you often want to build metrics that are expressed *over time*:

- How many cars sold each month this year?
- What was the price of this stock for the last 12 hours?
- What was the average latency of our website every hour in the last week?

While regular histograms are often represented as bar charts, date histograms tend to be converted into line graphs representing time series. Many companies use Elastic-search *solely* for analytics over time series data. The `date_histogram` bucket is their bread and butter.

The `date_histogram` bucket works similarly to the regular `histogram`. Rather than building buckets based on a numeric field representing numeric ranges, it builds buckets based on time ranges. Each bucket is therefore defined as a certain calendar size (for example, `1 month` or `2.5 days`).

Can a Regular Histogram Work with Dates?

Technically, yes. A regular `histogram` bucket will work with dates. However, it is not calendar-aware. With the `date_histogram`, you can specify intervals such as `1 month`, which knows that February is shorter than December. The `date_histogram` also has the advantage of being able to work with time zones, which allows you to customize graphs to the time zone of the user, not the server.

The regular histogram will interpret dates as numbers, which means you must specify intervals in terms of milliseconds. And the aggregation doesn't know about calendar intervals, which makes it largely useless for dates.

Our first example will build a simple line chart to answer this question: how many cars were sold each month?

```
GET /cars/transactions/_search?search_type=count
{
   "aggs": {
      "sales": {
         "date_histogram": {
            "field": "sold",
            "interval": "month",   ❶
            "format": "yyyy-MM-dd"   ❷
         }
      }
   }
}
```

❶ The interval is requested in calendar terminology (for example, one month per bucket).

❷ We provide a date format so that bucket keys are pretty.

Our query has a single aggregation, which builds a bucket per month. This will give us the number of cars sold in each month. An additional `format` parameter is provided so the buckets have "pretty" keys. Internally, dates are simply represented as a numeric value. This tends to make UI designers grumpy, however, so a prettier format can be specified using common date formatting.

The response is both expected and a little surprising (see if you can spot the surprise):

```
{
   ...
   "aggregations": {
      "sales": {
         "buckets": [
            {
```

```
            "key_as_string": "2014-01-01",
            "key": 1388534400000,
            "doc_count": 1
         },
         {
            "key_as_string": "2014-02-01",
            "key": 1391212800000,
            "doc_count": 1
         },
         {
            "key_as_string": "2014-05-01",
            "key": 1398902400000,
            "doc_count": 1
         },
         {
            "key_as_string": "2014-07-01",
            "key": 1404172800000,
            "doc_count": 1
         },
         {
            "key_as_string": "2014-08-01",
            "key": 1406851200000,
            "doc_count": 1
         },
         {
            "key_as_string": "2014-10-01",
            "key": 1412121600000,
            "doc_count": 1
         },
         {
            "key_as_string": "2014-11-01",
            "key": 1414800000000,
            "doc_count": 2
         }
      ]
   ...
}
```

The aggregation is represented in full. As you can see, we have buckets that represent months, a count of docs in each month, and our pretty key_as_string.

Returning Empty Buckets

Notice something odd about that last response?

Yep, that's right. We are missing a few months! By default, the date_histogram (and histogram too) returns only buckets that have a nonzero document count.

This means your histogram will be a minimal response. Often, this is not the behavior you want. For many applications, you would like to dump the response directly into a graphing library without doing any post-processing.

Essentially, we want buckets even if they have a count of zero. We can set two additional parameters that will provide this behavior:

```
GET /cars/transactions/_search?search_type=count
{
   "aggs": {
      "sales": {
         "date_histogram": {
            "field": "sold",
            "interval": "month",
            "format": "yyyy-MM-dd",
            "min_doc_count" : 0, ❶
            "extended_bounds" : { ❷
                "min" : "2014-01-01",
                "max" : "2014-12-31"
            }
         }
      }
   }
}
```

❶ This parameter forces empty buckets to be returned.

❷ This parameter forces the entire year to be returned.

The two additional parameters will force the response to return all months in the year, regardless of their doc count. The min_doc_count is very understandable: it forces buckets to be returned even if they are empty.

The extended_bounds parameter requires a little explanation. The min_doc_count parameter forces empty buckets to be returned, but by default Elasticsearch will return only buckets that are between the minimum and maximum value in your data.

So if your data falls between April and July, you'll have buckets representing only those months (empty or otherwise). To get the full year, we need to tell Elasticsearch that we want buckets even if they fall *before* the minimum value or *after* the maximum value.

The extended_bounds parameter does just that. Once you add those two settings, you'll get a response that is easy to plug straight into your graphing libraries and give you a graph like Figure 28-1.

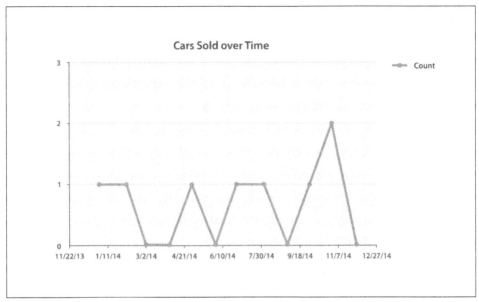

Figure 28-1. Cars sold over time

Extended Example

Just as we've seen a dozen times already, buckets can be nested in buckets for more-sophisticated behavior. For illustration, we'll build an aggregation that shows the total sum of prices for all makes, listed by quarter. Let's also calculate the sum of prices per individual make per quarter, so we can see which car type is bringing in the most money to our business:

```
GET /cars/transactions/_search?search_type=count
{
   "aggs": {
      "sales": {
         "date_histogram": {
            "field": "sold",
            "interval": "quarter", ❶
            "format": "yyyy-MM-dd",
            "min_doc_count" : 0,
            "extended_bounds" : {
                "min" : "2014-01-01",
                "max" : "2014-12-31"
            }
         },
         "aggs": {
            "per_make_sum": {
               "terms": {
                  "field": "make"
               },
```

```
              "aggs": {
                 "sum_price": {
                    "sum": { "field": "price" } ❷
                 }
              }
           },
           "total_sum": {
              "sum": { "field": "price" } ❸
           }
        }
     }
  }
}
```

❶   Note that we changed the interval from `month` to `quarter`.

❷   Calculate the sum per make.

❸   And the total sum of all makes combined together.

This returns a (heavily truncated) response:

```
{
....
"aggregations": {
   "sales": {
      "buckets": [
         {
            "key_as_string": "2014-01-01",
            "key": 1388534400000,
            "doc_count": 2,
            "total_sum": {
               "value": 105000
            },
            "per_make_sum": {
               "buckets": [
                  {
                     "key": "bmw",
                     "doc_count": 1,
                     "sum_price": {
                        "value": 80000
                     }
                  },
                  {
                     "key": "ford",
                     "doc_count": 1,
                     "sum_price": {
                        "value": 25000
                     }
                  }
               ]
            }
```

```
        },
    ...
    }
```

We can take this response and put it into a graph, showing a line chart for total sale price, and a bar chart for each individual make (per quarter), as shown in Figure 28-2.

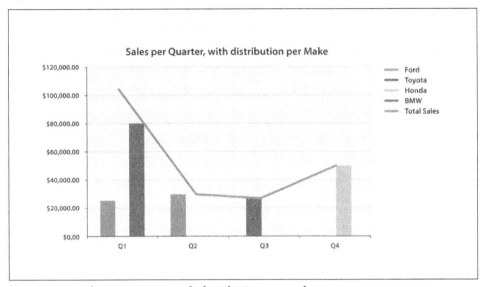

Figure 28-2. Sales per quarter, with distribution per make

The Sky's the Limit

These were obviously simple examples, but the sky really is the limit when it comes to charting aggregations. For example, Figure 28-3 shows a dashboard in Kibana built with a variety of aggregations.

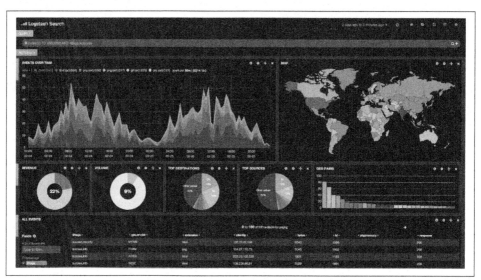

Figure 28-3. Kibana—a real time analytics dashboard built with aggregations

Because of the real-time nature of aggregations, dashboards like this are easy to query, manipulate, and interact with. This makes them ideal for nontechnical employees and analysts who need to analyze the data but cannot build a Hadoop job.

To build powerful dashboards like Kibana, however, you'll likely need some of the more advanced concepts such as scoping, filtering, and sorting aggregations.

CHAPTER 29

Scoping Aggregations

With all of the aggregation examples given so far, you may have noticed that we omitted a query from the search request. The entire request was simply an aggregation.

Aggregations can be run at the same time as search requests, but you need to understand a new concept: *scope*. By default, aggregations operate in the same scope as the query. Put another way, aggregations are calculated on the set of documents that match your query.

Let's look at one of our first aggregation examples:

```
GET /cars/transactions/_search?search_type=count
{
    "aggs" : {
        "colors" : {
            "terms" : {
                "field" : "color"
            }
        }
    }
}
```

You can see that the aggregation is in isolation. In reality, Elasticsearch assumes "no query specified" is equivalent to "query all documents." The preceding query is internally translated as follows:

```
GET /cars/transactions/_search?search_type=count
{
    "query" : {
        "match_all" : {}
    },
    "aggs" : {
        "colors" : {
            "terms" : {
```

```
                    "field" : "color"
                }
            }
        }
    }
}
```

The aggregation always operates in the scope of the query, so an isolated aggregation really operates in the scope of a `match_all` query—that is to say, all documents.

Once armed with the knowledge of scoping, we can start to customize aggregations even further. All of our previous examples calculated statistics about *all* of the data: top-selling cars, average price of all cars, most sales per month, and so forth.

With scope, we can ask questions such as "How many colors are Ford cars are available in?" We do this by simply adding a query to the request (in this case a `match` query):

```
GET /cars/transactions/_search   ❶
{
    "query" : {
        "match" : {
            "make" : "ford"
        }
    },
    "aggs" : {
        "colors" : {
            "terms" : {
                "field" : "color"
            }
        }
    }
}
```

❶   We are omitting `search_type=count` so that search hits are returned too.

By omitting the `search_type=count` this time, we can see both the search results and the aggregation results:

```
{
...
    "hits": {
        "total": 2,
        "max_score": 1.6931472,
        "hits": [
            {
                "_source": {
                    "price": 25000,
                    "color": "blue",
                    "make": "ford",
                    "sold": "2014-02-12"
                }
            },
```

```
    {
        "_source": {
            "price": 30000,
            "color": "green",
            "make": "ford",
            "sold": "2014-05-18"
        }
    }
  ]
},
"aggregations": {
    "colors": {
        "buckets": [
            {
                "key": "blue",
                "doc_count": 1
            },
            {
                "key": "green",
                "doc_count": 1
            }
        ]
    }
}
}
```

This may seem trivial, but it is the key to advanced and powerful dashboards. You can transform any static dashboard into a real-time data exploration device by adding a search bar. This allows the user to search for terms and see all of the graphs (which are powered by aggregations, and thus scoped to the query) update in real time. Try that with Hadoop!

Global Bucket

You'll often want your aggregation to be scoped to your query. But sometimes you'll want to search for a subset of data, but aggregate across *all* of your data.

For example, say you want to know the average price of Ford cars compared to the average price of *all* cars. We can use a regular aggregation (scoped to the query) to get the first piece of information. The second piece of information can be obtained by using a global bucket.

The global bucket will contain *all* of your documents, regardless of the query scope; it bypasses the scope completely. Because it is a bucket, you can nest aggregations inside it as usual:

```
GET /cars/transactions/_search?search_type=count
{
    "query" : {
        "match" : {
            "make" : "ford"
```

```
            }
        },
        "aggs" : {
            "single_avg_price": {
                "avg" : { "field" : "price" } ❶
            },
            "all": {
                "global" : {}, ❷
                "aggs" : {
                    "avg_price": {
                        "avg" : { "field" : "price" } ❸
                    }

                }
            }
        }
    }
}
```

❶   This aggregation operates in the query scope (for example, all docs matching
    `ford`)

❷   The `global` bucket has no parameters.

❸   This aggregation operates on the all documents, regardless of the make.

The `single_avg_price` metric calculation is based on all documents that fall under
the query scope—all `ford` cars. The `avg_price` metric is nested under a `global`
bucket, which means it ignores scoping entirely and calculates on all the documents.
The average returned for that aggregation represents the average price of all cars.

If you've made it this far in the book, you'll recognize the mantra: use a filter wherever you can. The same applies to aggregations, and in the next chapter we show you
how to filter an aggregation instead of just limiting the query scope.

CHAPTER 30

Filtering Queries and Aggregations

A natural extension to aggregation scoping is filtering. Because the aggregation operates in the context of the query scope, any filter applied to the query will also apply to the aggregation.

Filtered Query

If we want to find all cars over $10,000 and also calculate the average price for those cars, we can simply use a `filtered` query:

```
GET /cars/transactions/_search?search_type=count
{
    "query" : {
        "filtered": {
            "filter": {
                "range": {
                    "price": {
                        "gte": 10000
                    }
                }
            }
        }
    },
    "aggs" : {
        "single_avg_price": {
            "avg" : { "field" : "price" }
        }
    }
}
```

Fundamentally, using a `filtered` query is no different from using a `match` query, as we discussed in the previous chapter. The query (which happens to include a filter)

451

returns a certain subset of documents, and the aggregation operates on those documents.

Filter Bucket

But what if you would like to filter just the aggregation results? Imagine we are building the search page for our car dealership. We want to display search results according to what the user searches for. But we also want to enrich the page by including the average price of cars (matching the search) that were sold in the last month.

We can't use simple scoping here, since there are two different criteria. The search results must match ford, but the aggregation results must match ford AND sold > now - 1M.

To solve this problem, we can use a special bucket called filter. You specify a filter, and when documents match the filter's criteria, they are added to the bucket.

Here is the resulting query:

```
GET /cars/transactions/_search?search_type=count
{
    "query":{
        "match": {
            "make": "ford"
        }
    },
    "aggs":{
        "recent_sales": {
            "filter": {  ❶
                "range": {
                    "sold": {
                        "from": "now-1M"
                    }
                }
            },
            "aggs": {
                "average_price":{
                    "avg": {
                        "field": "price"  ❷
                    }
                }
            }
        }
    }
}
```

❶ Using the filter bucket to apply a filter in addition to the query scope.

❷ This `avg` metric will therefore average only docs that are both `ford` and sold in the last month.

Since the `filter` bucket operates like any other bucket, you are free to nest other buckets and metrics inside. All nested components will "inherit" the filter. This allows you to filter selective portions of the aggregation as required.

Post Filter

So far, we have a way to filter both the search results and aggregations (a `filtered` query), as well as filtering individual portions of the aggregation (`filter` bucket).

You may be thinking to yourself, "hmm…is there a way to filter *just* the search results but not the aggregation?" The answer is to use a `post_filter`.

This is a top-level search-request element that accepts a filter. The filter is applied *after* the query has executed (hence the `post` moniker: it runs *post query* execution). Because it operates after the query has executed, it does not affect the query scope—and thus does not affect the aggregations either.

We can use this behavior to apply additional filters to our search criteria that don't affect things like categorical facets in your UI. Let's design another search page for our car dealer. This page will allow the user to search for a car and filter by color. Color choices are populated via an aggregation:

```
GET /cars/transactions/_search?search_type=count
{
    "query": {
        "match": {
            "make": "ford"
        }
    },
    "post_filter": {        ❶
        "term" : {
            "color" : "green"
        }
    },
    "aggs" : {
        "all_colors": {
            "terms" : { "field" : "color" }
        }
    }
}
```

❶ The `post_filter` element is a `top-level` element and filters just the search hits.

The `query` portion is finding all `ford` cars. We are then building a list of colors with a `terms` aggregation. Because aggregations operate in the query scope, the list of colors will correspond with the colors that Ford cars are painted.

Finally, the `post_filter` will filter the search results to show only green `ford` cars. This happens *after* the query is executed, so the aggregations are unaffected.

This is often important for coherent UIs. Imagine that a user clicks a category in your UI (for example, green). The expectation is that the search results are filtered, but *not* the UI options. If you applied a `filtered` query, the UI would instantly transform to show *only* green as an option—not what the user wants!

Performance consideration

Use a `post_filter` *only* if you need to differentially filter search results and aggregations. Sometimes people will use `post_filter` for regular searches.

Don't do this! The nature of the `post_filter` means it runs *after* the query, so any performance benefit of filtering (such as caches) is lost completely.

The `post_filter` should be used only in combination with aggregations, and only when you need differential filtering.

Recap

Choosing the appropriate type of filtering—search hits, aggregations, or both—often boils down to how you want your user interface to behave. Choose the appropriate filter (or combinations) depending on how you want to display results to your user.

- A `filtered` query affects both search results and aggregations.
- A `filter` bucket affects just aggregations.
- A `post_filter` affects just search results.

CHAPTER 31

Sorting Multivalue Buckets

Multivalue buckets—the `terms`, `histogram`, and `date_histogram`—dynamically produce many buckets. How does Elasticsearch decide the order that these buckets are presented to the user?

By default, buckets are ordered by `doc_count` in descending order. This is a good default because often we want to find the documents that maximize some criteria: price, population, frequency. But sometimes you'll want to modify this sort order, and there are a few ways to do it, depending on the bucket.

Intrinsic Sorts

These sort modes are *intrinsic* to the bucket: they operate on data that bucket generates, such as `doc_count`. They share the same syntax but differ slightly depending on the bucket being used.

Let's perform a `terms` aggregation but sort by `doc_count`, in ascending order:

```
GET /cars/transactions/_search?search_type=count
{
    "aggs" : {
        "colors" : {
            "terms" : {
              "field" : "color",
              "order": {
                "_count" : "asc" ❶
              }
            }
        }
    }
}
```

❶ Using the _count keyword, we can sort by doc_count, in ascending order.

We introduce an order object into the aggregation, which allows us to sort on one of several values:

_count

Sort by document count. Works with terms, histogram, date_histogram.

_term

Sort by the string value of a term alphabetically. Works only with terms.

_key

Sort by the numeric value of each bucket's key (conceptually similar to _term). Works only with histogram and date_histogram.

Sorting by a Metric

Often, you'll find yourself wanting to sort based on a metric's calculated value. For our car sales analytics dashboard, we may want to build a bar chart of sales by car color, but order the bars by the average price, ascending.

We can do this by adding a metric to our bucket, and then referencing that metric from the order parameter:

```
GET /cars/transactions/_search?search_type=count
{
    "aggs" : {
        "colors" : {
            "terms" : {
              "field" : "color",
              "order": {
                "avg_price" : "asc" ❷
              }
            },
            "aggs": {
                "avg_price": {
                    "avg": {"field": "price"} ❶
                }
            }
        }
    }
}
```

❶ The average price is calculated for each bucket.

❷ Then the buckets are ordered by the calculated average in ascending order.

This lets you override the sort order with any metric, simply by referencing the name of the metric. Some metrics, however, emit multiple values. The extended_stats metric is a good example: it provides half a dozen individual metrics.

If you want to sort on a multivalue metric, you just need to use the dot-path to the metric of interest:

```
GET /cars/transactions/_search?search_type=count
{
    "aggs" : {
        "colors" : {
            "terms" : {
              "field" : "color",
              "order": {
                "stats.variance" : "asc" ❶
              }
            },
            "aggs": {
                "stats": {
                    "extended_stats": {"field": "price"}
                }
            }
        }
    }
}
```

❶ Using dot notation, we can sort on the metric we are interested in.

In this example we are sorting on the variance of each bucket, so that colors with the least variance in price will appear before those that have more variance.

Sorting Based on "Deep" Metrics

In the prior examples, the metric was a direct child of the bucket. An average price was calculated for each term. It is possible to sort on *deeper* metrics, which are grandchildren or great-grandchildren of the bucket—with some limitations.

You can define a path to a deeper, nested metric by using angle brackets (>), like so: my_bucket>another_bucket>metric.

The caveat is that each nested bucket in the path must be a *single-value* bucket. A filter bucket produces a single bucket: all documents that match the filtering criteria. Multivalue buckets (such as terms) generate many dynamic buckets, which makes it impossible to specify a deterministic path.

Currently, there are only three single-value buckets: filter, global, and reverse_nested. As a quick example, let's build a histogram of car prices, but order the buckets by the variance in price of red and green (but not blue) cars in each price range:

```
GET /cars/transactions/_search?search_type=count
{
    "aggs" : {
        "colors" : {
            "histogram" : {
              "field" : "price",
              "interval": 20000,
              "order": {
                "red_green_cars>stats.variance" : "asc"  ❶
              }
            },
            "aggs": {
                "red_green_cars": {
                    "filter": { "terms": {"color": ["red", "green"]}},  ❷
                    "aggs": {
                        "stats": {"extended_stats": {"field" : "price"}}  ❸
                    }
                }
            }
        }
    }
}
```

❶ Sort the buckets generated by the histogram according to the variance of a nested metric.

❷ Because we are using a single-value `filter`, we can use nested sorting.

❸ Sort on the stats generated by this metric.

In this example, you can see that we are accessing a nested metric. The `stats` metric is a child of `red_green_cars`, which is in turn a child of `colors`. To sort on that metric, we define the path as `red_green_cars>stats.variance`. This is allowed because the `filter` bucket is a single-value bucket.

CHAPTER 32

Approximate Aggregations

Life is easy if all your data fits on a single machine. Classic algorithms taught in CS201 will be sufficient for all your needs. But if all your data fits on a single machine, there would be no need for distributed software like Elasticsearch at all. But once you start distributing data, algorithm selection needs to be made carefully.

Some algorithms are amenable to distributed execution. All of the aggregations discussed thus far execute in a single pass and give exact results. These types of algorithms are often referred to as *embarrassingly parallel*, because they parallelize to multiple machines with little effort. When performing a max metric, for example, the underlying algorithm is very simple:

1. Broadcast the request to all shards.

2. Look at the price field for each document. If price > current_max, replace current_max with price.

3. Return the maximum price from all shards to the coordinating node.

4. Find the maximum price returned from all shards. This is the true maximum.

The algorithm scales linearly with machines because the algorithm requires no coordination (the machines don't need to discuss intermediate results), and the memory footprint is very small (a single integer representing the maximum).

Not all algorithms are as simple as taking the maximum value, unfortunately. More complex operations require algorithms that make conscious trade-offs in performance and memory utilization. There is a triangle of factors at play: big data, exactness, and real-time latency.

You get to choose two from this triangle:

Exact + real time
> Your data fits in the RAM of a single machine. The world is your oyster; use any algorithm you want. Results will be 100% accurate and relatively fast.

Big data + exact
> A classic Hadoop installation. Can handle petabytes of data and give you exact answers—but it may take a week to give you that answer.

Big data + real time
> Approximate algorithms that give you accurate, but not exact, results.

Elasticsearch currently supports two approximate algorithms (`cardinality` and `per` `centiles`). These will give you accurate results, but not 100% exact. In exchange for a little bit of estimation error, these algorithms give you fast execution and a small memory footprint.

For *most* domains, highly accurate results that return *in real time* across *all your data* is more important than 100% exactness. At first blush, this may be an alien concept to you. *"We need exact answers!"* you may yell. But consider the implications of a 0.5% error:

- The true 99th percentile of latency for your website is 132ms.
- An approximation with 0.5% error will be within +/- 0.66ms of 132ms.
- The approximation returns in milliseconds, while the "true" answer may take seconds, or be impossible.

For simply checking on your website's latency, do you care if the approximate answer is 132.66ms instead of 132ms? Certainly, not all domains can tolerate approximations —but the vast majority will have no problem. Accepting an approximate answer is more often a *cultural* hurdle rather than a business or technical imperative.

Finding Distinct Counts

The first approximate aggregation provided by Elasticsearch is the `cardinality` metric. This provides the cardinality of a field, also called a *distinct* or *unique* count. You may be familiar with the SQL version:

```
SELECT DISTINCT(color)
FROM cars
```

Distinct counts are a common operation, and answer many fundamental business questions:

- How many unique visitors have come to my website?
- How many unique cars have we sold?

- How many distinct users purchased a product each month?

We can use the `cardinality` metric to determine the number of car colors being sold at our dealership:

```
GET /cars/transactions/_search?search_type=count
{
    "aggs" : {
        "distinct_colors" : {
            "cardinality" : {
              "field" : "color"
            }
        }
    }
}
```

This returns a minimal response showing that we have sold three different-colored cars:

```
...
"aggregations": {
  "distinct_colors": {
    "value": 3
  }
}
...
```

We can make our example more useful: how many colors were sold each month? For that metric, we just nest the `cardinality` metric under a `date_histogram`:

```
GET /cars/transactions/_search?search_type=count
{
  "aggs" : {
      "months" : {
        "date_histogram": {
          "field": "sold",
          "interval": "month"
        },
        "aggs": {
          "distinct_colors" : {
              "cardinality" : {
                "field" : "color"
              }
          }
        }
      }
  }
}
```

Understanding the Trade-offs

As mentioned at the top of this chapter, the `cardinality` metric is an approximate algorithm. It is based on the HyperLogLog++ (*http://bit.ly/1u6UWwd*) (HLL) algorithm. HLL works by hashing your input and using the bits from the hash to make probabilistic estimations on the cardinality.

You don't need to understand the technical details (although if you're interested, the paper is a great read!), but you should be aware of the *properties* of the algorithm:

- Configurable precision, which controls memory usage (more precise == more memory).
- Excellent accuracy on low-cardinality sets.
- Fixed memory usage. Whether there are thousands or billions of unique values, memory usage depends on only the configured precision.

To configure the precision, you must specify the `precision_threshold` parameter. This threshold defines the point under which cardinalities are expected to be very close to accurate. Consider this example:

```
GET /cars/transactions/_search?search_type=count
{
    "aggs" : {
        "distinct_colors" : {
            "cardinality" : {
              "field" : "color",
              "precision_threshold" : 100 ❶
            }
        }
    }
}
```

❶ `precision_threshold` accepts a number from 0–40,000. Larger values are treated as equivalent to 40,000.

This example will ensure that fields with 100 or fewer distinct values will be extremely accurate. Although not guaranteed by the algorithm, if a cardinality is under the threshold, it is almost always 100% accurate. Cardinalities above this will begin to trade accuracy for memory savings, and a little error will creep into the metric.

For a given threshold, the HLL data-structure will use about `precision_threshold` * 8 bytes of memory. So you must balance how much memory you are willing to sacrifice for additional accuracy.

Practically speaking, a threshold of `100` maintains an error under 5% even when counting millions of unique values.

Optimizing for Speed

If you want a distinct count, you *usually* want to query your entire dataset (or nearly all of it). Any operation on all your data needs to execute quickly, for obvious reasons. HyperLogLog is very fast already—it simply hashes your data and does some bit-twiddling.

But if speed is important to you, we can optimize it a little bit further. Since HLL simply needs the hash of the field, we can precompute that hash at index time. When the query executes, we can skip the hash computation and load the value directly out of fielddata.

Precomputing hashes is useful only on very large and/or high-cardinality fields. Calculating the hash on these fields is non-negligible at query time.

However, numeric fields hash very quickly, and storing the original numeric often requires the same (or less) memory. This is also true on low-cardinality string fields; there are internal optimizations that guarantee that hashes are calculated only once per unique value.

Basically, precomputing hashes is not guaranteed to make all fields faster — only those that have high cardinality and/or large strings. And remember, precomputing simply shifts the cost to index time. You still pay the price; you just choose *when* to pay it.

To do this, we need to add a new multifield to our data. We'll delete our index, add a new mapping that includes the hashed field, and then reindex:

```
DELETE /cars/

PUT /cars/
{
  "mappings": {
    "color": {
      "type": "string",
      "fields": {
        "hash": {
          "type": "murmur3" ❶
        }
      }
    }
  }
}

POST /cars/transactions/_bulk
{ "index": {}}
{ "price" : 10000, "color" : "red", "make" : "honda", "sold" : "2014-10-28" }
```

```
{ "index": {}}
{ "price" : 20000, "color" : "red", "make" : "honda", "sold" : "2014-11-05" }
{ "index": {}}
{ "price" : 30000, "color" : "green", "make" : "ford", "sold" : "2014-05-18" }
{ "index": {}}
{ "price" : 15000, "color" : "blue", "make" : "toyota", "sold" : "2014-07-02" }
{ "index": {}}
{ "price" : 12000, "color" : "green", "make" : "toyota", "sold" : "2014-08-19" }
{ "index": {}}
{ "price" : 20000, "color" : "red", "make" : "honda", "sold" : "2014-11-05" }
{ "index": {}}
{ "price" : 80000, "color" : "red", "make" : "bmw", "sold" : "2014-01-01" }
{ "index": {}}
{ "price" : 25000, "color" : "blue", "make" : "ford", "sold" : "2014-02-12" }
```

❶ This multifield is of type murmur3, which is a hashing function.

Now when we run an aggregation, we use the color.hash field instead of the color field:

```
GET /cars/transactions/_search?search_type=count
{
    "aggs" : {
        "distinct_colors" : {
            "cardinality" : {
                "field" : "color.hash" ❶
            }
        }
    }
}
```

❶ Notice that we specify the hashed multifield, rather than the original.

Now the cardinality metric will load the values (the precomputed hashes) from "color.hash" and use those in place of dynamically hashing the original value.

The savings per document is small, but if hashing each field adds 10 nanoseconds and your aggregation touches 100 million documents, that adds 1 second per query. If you find yourself using cardinality across many documents, perform some profiling to see if precomputing hashes makes sense for your deployment.

Calculating Percentiles

The other approximate metric offered by Elasticsearch is the percentiles metric. Percentiles show the point at which a certain percentage of observed values occur. For example, the 95th percentile is the value that is greater than 95% of the data.

Percentiles are often used to find outliers. In (statistically) normal distributions, the 0.13th and 99.87th percentiles represent three standard deviations from the mean.

Any data that falls outside three standard deviations is often considered an anomaly because it is so different from the average value.

To be more concrete, imagine that you are running a large website and it is your job to guarantee fast response times to visitors. You must therefore monitor your website latency to determine whether you are meeting your goal.

A common metric to use in this scenario is the average latency. But this is a poor choice (despite being common), because averages can easily hide outliers. A median metric also suffers the same problem. You could try a maximum, but this metric is easily skewed by just a single outlier.

This graph in Figure 32-1 visualizes the problem. If you rely on simple metrics like mean or median, you might see a graph that looks like Figure 32-1.

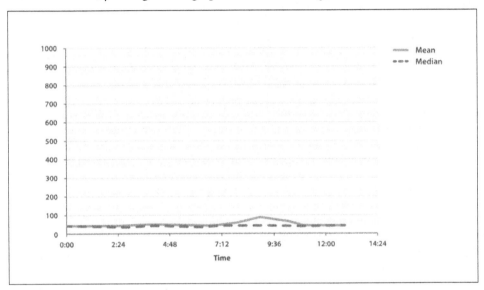

Figure 32-1. Average request latency over time

Everything looks fine. There is a slight bump, but nothing to be concerned about. But if we load up the 99th percentile (the value that accounts for the slowest 1% of latencies), we see an entirely different story, as shown in Figure 32-2.

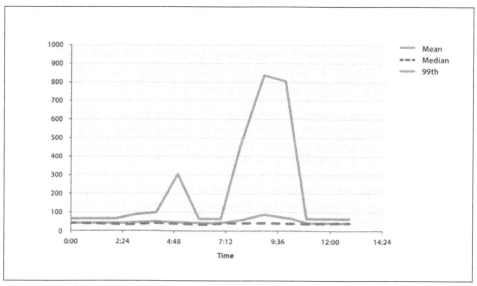

Figure 32-2. Average request latency with 99th percentile over time

Whoa! At 9:30 a.m., the mean is only 75ms. As a system administrator, you wouldn't look at this value twice. Everything normal! But the 99th percentile is telling you that 1% of your customers are seeing latency in excess of 850ms—a very different story. There is also a smaller spike at 4:48 a.m. that wasn't even noticeable in the mean/median.

This is just one use-case for a percentile. Percentiles can also be used to quickly eyeball the distribution of data, check for skew or bimodalities, and more.

Percentile Metric

Let's load a new dataset (the car data isn't going to work well for percentiles). We are going to index a bunch of website latencies and run a few percentiles over it:

```
POST /website/logs/_bulk
{ "index": {}}
{ "latency" : 100, "zone" : "US", "timestamp" : "2014-10-28" }
{ "index": {}}
{ "latency" : 80, "zone" : "US", "timestamp" : "2014-10-29" }
{ "index": {}}
{ "latency" : 99, "zone" : "US", "timestamp" : "2014-10-29" }
{ "index": {}}
{ "latency" : 102, "zone" : "US", "timestamp" : "2014-10-28" }
{ "index": {}}
{ "latency" : 75, "zone" : "US", "timestamp" : "2014-10-28" }
{ "index": {}}
{ "latency" : 82, "zone" : "US", "timestamp" : "2014-10-29" }
{ "index": {}}
```

```
{ "latency" : 100, "zone" : "EU", "timestamp" : "2014-10-28" }
{ "index": {}}
{ "latency" : 280, "zone" : "EU", "timestamp" : "2014-10-29" }
{ "index": {}}
{ "latency" : 155, "zone" : "EU", "timestamp" : "2014-10-29" }
{ "index": {}}
{ "latency" : 623, "zone" : "EU", "timestamp" : "2014-10-28" }
{ "index": {}}
{ "latency" : 380, "zone" : "EU", "timestamp" : "2014-10-28" }
{ "index": {}}
{ "latency" : 319, "zone" : "EU", "timestamp" : "2014-10-29" }
```

This data contains three values: a latency, a data center zone, and a date timestamp. Let's run `percentiles` over the whole dataset to get a feel for the distribution:

```
GET /website/logs/_search?search_type=count
{
    "aggs" : {
        "load_times" : {
            "percentiles" : {
                "field" : "latency" ❶
            }
        },
        "avg_load_time" : {
            "avg" : {
                "field" : "latency" ❷
            }
        }
    }
}
```

❶ The `percentiles` metric is applied to the `latency` field.

❷ For comparison, we also execute an `avg` metric on the same field.

By default, the `percentiles` metric will return an array of predefined percentiles: [1, 5, 25, 50, 75, 95, 99]. These represent common percentiles that people are interested in—the extreme percentiles at either end of the spectrum, and a few in the middle. In the response, we see that the fastest latency is around 75ms, while the slowest is almost 600ms. In contrast, the average is sitting near 200ms, which is much less informative:

```
...
"aggregations": {
  "load_times": {
    "values": {
        "1.0": 75.55,
        "5.0": 77.75,
        "25.0": 94.75,
        "50.0": 101,
        "75.0": 289.75,
```

```
        "95.0": 489.34999999999985,
        "99.0": 596.2700000000002
      }
    },
    "avg_load_time": {
      "value": 199.58333333333334
    }
  }
}
```

So there is clearly a wide distribution in latencies. Let's see whether it is correlated to the geographic zone of the data center:

```
GET /website/logs/_search?search_type=count
{
    "aggs" : {
        "zones" : {
            "terms" : {
                "field" : "zone" ❶
            },
            "aggs" : {
                "load_times" : {
                    "percentiles" : { ❷
                      "field" : "latency",
                      "percents" : [50, 95.0, 99.0] ❸
                    }
                },
                "load_avg" : {
                    "avg" : {
                        "field" : "latency"
                    }
                }
            }
        }
    }
}
```

❶ First we separate our latencies into buckets, depending on their zone.

❷ Then we calculate the percentiles per zone.

❸ The percents parameter accepts an array of percentiles that we want returned, since we are interested in only slow latencies.

From the response, we can see the EU zone is much slower than the US zone. On the US side, the 50th percentile is very close to the 99th percentile—and both are close to the average.

In contrast, the EU zone has a large difference between the 50th and 99th percentile. It is now obvious that the EU zone is dragging down the latency statistics, and we know that 50% of the EU zone is seeing 300ms+ latencies.

```
...
"aggregations": {
  "zones": {
    "buckets": [
      {
        "key": "eu",
        "doc_count": 6,
        "load_times": {
          "values": {
            "50.0": 299.5,
            "95.0": 562.25,
            "99.0": 610.85
          }
        },
        "load_avg": {
          "value": 309.5
        }
      },
      {
        "key": "us",
        "doc_count": 6,
        "load_times": {
          "values": {
            "50.0": 90.5,
            "95.0": 101.5,
            "99.0": 101.9
          }
        },
        "load_avg": {
          "value": 89.66666666666667
        }
      }
    ]
  }
}
...
```

Percentile Ranks

There is another, closely related metric called `percentile_ranks`. The `percentiles` metric tells you the lowest value below which a given percentage of documents fall. For instance, if the 50th percentile is 119ms, then 50% of documents have values of no more than 119ms. The `percentile_ranks` tells you which percentile a specific value belongs to. The `percentile_ranks` of 119ms is the 50th percentile. It is basically a two-way relationship. For example:

- The 50th percentile is 119ms.
- The 119ms percentile rank is the 50th percentile.

So imagine that our website must maintain an SLA of 210ms response times or less. And, just for fun, your boss has threatened to fire you if response times creep over 800ms. Understandably, you would like to know what percentage of requests are actually meeting that SLA (and hopefully at least under 800ms!).

For this, you can apply the percentile_ranks metric instead of percentiles:

```
GET /website/logs/_search?search_type=count
{
    "aggs" : {
        "zones" : {
            "terms" : {
                "field" : "zone"
            },
            "aggs" : {
                "load_times" : {
                    "percentile_ranks" : {
                      "field" : "latency",
                      "values" : [210, 800] ❶
                    }
                }
            }
        }
    }
}
```

❶ The percentile_ranks metric accepts an array of values that you want ranks for.

After running this aggregation, we get two values back:

```
"aggregations": {
  "zones": {
    "buckets": [
        {
           "key": "eu",
           "doc_count": 6,
           "load_times": {
              "values": {
                  "210.0": 31.944444444444443,
                  "800.0": 100
              }
           }
        },
        {
           "key": "us",
           "doc_count": 6,
           "load_times": {
              "values": {
                  "210.0": 100,
                  "800.0": 100
              }
           }
        }
```

```
            }
        ]
    }
}
```

This tells us three important things:

- In the EU zone, the percentile rank for 210ms is 31.94%.
- In the US zone, the percentile rank for 210ms is 100%.
- In both EU and US, the percentile rank for 800ms is 100%.

In plain english, this means that the EU zone is meeting the SLA only 32% of the time, while the US zone is always meeting the SLA. But luckily for you, both zones are under 800ms, so you won't be fired (yet!).

The `percentile_ranks` metric provides the same information as `percentiles`, but presented in a different format that may be more convenient if you are interested in specific value(s).

Understanding the Trade-offs

Like cardinality, calculating percentiles requires an approximate algorithm. The naive implementation would maintain a sorted list of all values—but this clearly is not possible when you have billions of values distributed across dozens of nodes.

Instead, `percentiles` uses an algorithm called TDigest (introduced by Ted Dunning in Computing Extremely Accurate Quantiles Using T-Digests (*http://bit.ly/1DIpOWK*)). As with HyperLogLog, it isn't necessary to understand the full technical details, but it is good to know the properties of the algorithm:

- Percentile accuracy is proportional to how *extreme* the percentile is. This means that percentiles such as the 1st or 99th are more accurate than the 50th. This is just a property of how the data structure works, but it happens to be a nice property, because most people care about extreme percentiles.
- For small sets of values, percentiles are highly accurate. If the dataset is small enough, the percentiles may be 100% exact.
- As the quantity of values in a bucket grows, the algorithm begins to approximate the percentiles. It is effectively trading accuracy for memory savings. The exact level of inaccuracy is difficult to generalize, since it depends on your data distribution and volume of data being aggregated.

Similar to `cardinality`, you can control the memory-to-accuracy ratio by changing a parameter: `compression`.

The TDigest algorithm uses nodes to approximate percentiles: the more nodes available, the higher the accuracy (and the larger the memory footprint) proportional to the volume of data. The compression parameter limits the maximum number of nodes to 20 * compression.

Therefore, by increasing the compression value, you can increase the accuracy of your percentiles at the cost of more memory. Larger compression values also make the algorithm slower since the underlying tree data structure grows in size, resulting in more expensive operations. The default compression value is 100.

A node uses roughly 32 bytes of memory, so in a worst-case scenario (for example, a large amount of data that arrives sorted and in order), the default settings will produce a TDigest roughly 64KB in size. In practice, data tends to be more random, and the TDigest will use less memory.

CHAPTER 33

Significant Terms

The `significant_terms` (SigTerms) aggregation is rather different from the rest of the aggregations. All the aggregations we have seen so far are essentially simple math operations. By combining the various building blocks, you can build sophisticated aggregations and reports about your data.

`significant_terms` has a different agenda. To some, it may even look a bit like machine learning. The `significant_terms` aggregation finds *uncommonly common* terms in your data-set.

What do we mean by *uncommonly common*? These are terms that are statistically unusual — data that appears more frequently than the background rate would suggest. These statistical anomalies are usually indicative of something interesting in your data.

For example, imagine you are in charge of detecting and tracking down credit card fraud. Customers call and complain about unusual transactions appearing on their credit card — their account has been compromised. These transactions are just symptoms of a larger problem. Somewhere in the recent past, a merchant has either knowingly stolen the customers' credit card information, or has unknowingly been compromised themselves.

Your job is to find the *common point of compromise*. If you have 100 customers complaining of unusual transactions, those customers likely share a single merchant—and it is this merchant that is likely the source of blame.

Of course, it is a little more nuanced than just finding a merchant that all customers share. For example, many of the customers will have large merchants like Amazon in their recent transaction history. We can rule out Amazon, however, since many uncompromised credit cards also have Amazon as a recent merchant.

This is an example of a *commonly common* merchant. Everyone, whether compromised or not, shares the merchant. This makes it of little interest to us.

On the opposite end of the spectrum, you have tiny merchants such as the corner drug store. These are *commonly uncommon*—only one or two customers have transactions from the merchant. We can rule these out as well. Since all of the compromised cards did not interact with the merchant, we can be sure it was not to blame for the security breach.

What we want are *uncommonly common* merchants. These are merchants that every compromised card shares, but that are not well represented in the background noise of uncompromised cards. These merchants are statistical anomalies; they appear more frequently than they should. It is highly likely that these uncommonly common merchants are to blame.

significant_terms aggregation does just this. It analyzes your data and finds terms that appear with a frequency that is statistically anomalous compared to the background data.

What you *do* with this statistical anomaly depends on the data. With the credit card data, you might be looking for fraud. With ecommerce, you might be looking for an unidentified demographic so you can market to them more efficiently. If you are analyzing logs, you might find one server that throws a certain type of error more often than it should. The applications of significant_terms is nearly endless.

significant_terms Demo

Because the significant_terms aggregation works by analyzing statistics, you need to have a certain threshold of data for it to become effective. That means we won't be able to index a small amount of example data for the demo.

Instead, we have a pre-prepared dataset of around 80,000 documents. This is saved as a snapshot (for more information about snapshots and restore, see "Backing Up Your Cluster" on page 659) in our public demo repository. You can "restore" this dataset into your cluster by using these commands:

```
PUT /_snapshot/sigterms ❶
{
    "type": "url",
    "settings": {
        "url": "http://download.elasticsearch.org/definitiveguide/sigterms_demo/"
    }
}

GET /_snapshot/sigterms/_all ❷

POST /_snapshot/sigterms/snapshot/_restore ❸
```

```
GET /mlmovies,mlratings/_recovery ❹
```

❶ Register a new read-only URL repository pointing at the demo snapshot

❷ (Optional) Inspect the repository to learn details about available snapshots

❸ Begin the Restore process. This will download two indices into your cluster: mlmo
vies and mlratings

❹ (Optional) Monitor the Restore process using the Recovery API

> The dataset is around 50 MB and may take some time to download.

In this demo, we are going to look at movie ratings by users of MovieLens. At Movie-Lens, users make movie recommendations so other users can find new movies to watch. For this demo, we are going to recommend movies by using signifi
cant_terms based on an input movie.

Let's take a look at some sample data, to get a feel for what we are working with. There are two indices in this dataset, mlmovies and mlratings. Let's look at mlmovies first:

```
GET mlmovies/_search ❶

{
   "took": 4,
   "timed_out": false,
   "_shards": {...},
   "hits": {
      "total": 10681,
      "max_score": 1,
      "hits": [
         {
            "_index": "mlmovies",
            "_type": "mlmovie",
            "_id": "2",
            "_score": 1,
            "_source": {
               "offset": 2,
               "bytes": 34,
               "title": "Jumanji (1995)"
            }
         },
         ....
```

❶ Execute a search without a query, so that we can see a random sampling of docs.

Each document in mlmovies represents a single movie. The two important pieces of data are the _id of the movie and the title of the movie. You can ignore offset and bytes; they are artifacts of the process used to extract this data from the original CSV files. There are 10,681 movies in this dataset.

Now let's look at mlratings:

```
GET mlratings/_search

{
   "took": 3,
   "timed_out": false,
   "_shards": {...},
   "hits": {
      "total": 69796,
      "max_score": 1,
      "hits": [
         {
            "_index": "mlratings",
            "_type": "mlrating",
            "_id": "00IC-2jDQFiQkpD6vhbFYA",
            "_score": 1,
            "_source": {
               "offset": 1,
               "bytes": 108,
               "movie": [122,185,231,292,
                  316,329,355,356,362,364,370,377,420,
                  466,480,520,539,586,588,589,594,616
               ],
               "user": 1
            }
         },
         ...
```

Here we can see the recommendations of individual users. Each document represents a single user, denoted by the user ID field. The movie field holds a list of movies that this user watched and recommended.

Recommending Based on Popularity

The first strategy we could take is trying to recommend movies based on popularity. Given a particular movie, we find all users who recommended that movie. Then we aggregate all their recommendations and take the top five most popular.

We can express that easily with a terms aggregation and some filtering. Let's look at *Talladega Nights*, a comedy about NASCAR racing starring Will Ferrell. Ideally, our recommender should find other comedies in a similar style (and more than likely also starring Will Ferrell).

First we need to find the *Talladega Nights* ID:

```
GET mlmovies/_search
{
  "query": {
    "match": {
      "title": "Talladega Nights"
    }
  }
}
```

```
    ...
    "hits": [
      {
        "_index": "mlmovies",
        "_type": "mlmovie",
        "_id": "46970",          ❶
        "_score": 3.658795,
        "_source": {
          "offset": 9575,
          "bytes": 74,
          "title": "Talladega Nights: The Ballad of Ricky Bobby (2006)"
        }
      },
      ...
```

❶ *Talladega Nights* is ID 46970.

Armed with the ID, we can now filter the ratings and apply our `terms` aggregation to find the most popular movies from people who also like *Talladega Nights*:

```
GET mlratings/_search?search_type=count  ❶
{
  "query": {
    "filtered": {
      "filter": {
        "term": {
          "movie": 46970       ❷
        }
      }
    }
  },
  "aggs": {
    "most_popular": {
      "terms": {
        "field": "movie",      ❸
        "size": 6
      }
    }
  }
}
```

❶ We execute our query on mlratings this time, and specify search_type=count since we are interested only in the aggregation results.

❷ Apply a filter on the ID corresponding to *Talladega Nights*.

❸ Finally, find the most popular movies by using a terms bucket.

We perform the search on the mlratings index, and apply a filter for the ID of *Talladega Nights*. Since aggregations operate on query scope, this will effectively filter the aggregation results to only the users who recommended *Talladega Nights*. Finally, we execute a terms aggregation to bucket the most popular movies. We are requesting the top six results, since it is likely that *Talladega Nights* itself will be returned as a hit (and we don't want to recommend the same movie).

The results come back like so:

```
{
...
  "aggregations": {
    "most_popular": {
      "buckets": [
        {
          "key": 46970,
          "key_as_string": "46970",
          "doc_count": 271
        },
        {
          "key": 2571,
          "key_as_string": "2571",
          "doc_count": 197
        },
        {
          "key": 318,
          "key_as_string": "318",
          "doc_count": 196
        },
        {
          "key": 296,
          "key_as_string": "296",
          "doc_count": 183
        },
        {
          "key": 2959,
          "key_as_string": "2959",
          "doc_count": 183
        },
        {
          "key": 260,
          "key_as_string": "260",
          "doc_count": 90
```

```
        }
      ]
    }
  }
...
```

We need to correlate these back to their original titles, which can be done with a simple filtered query:

```
GET mlmovies/_search
{
  "query": {
    "filtered": {
      "filter": {
        "ids": {
          "values": [2571,318,296,2959,260]
        }
      }
    }
  }
}
```

And finally, we end up with the following list:

1. Matrix, The

2. Shawshank Redemption

3. Pulp Fiction

4. Fight Club

5. Star Wars Episode IV: A New Hope

OK—well that is certainly a good list! I like all of those movies. But that's the problem: most *everyone* likes that list. Those movies are universally well-liked, which means they are popular on everyone's recommendations. The list is basically a recommendation of popular movies, not recommendations related to *Talladega Nights*.

This is easily verified by running the aggregation again, but without the filter on *Talladega Nights*. This will give a top-five most popular movie list:

```
GET mlratings/_search?search_type=count
{
  "aggs": {
    "most_popular": {
      "terms": {
        "field": "movie",
        "size": 5
      }
    }
  }
}
```

This returns a list that is very similar:

1. Shawshank Redemption
2. Silence of the Lambs, The
3. Pulp Fiction
4. Forrest Gump
5. Star Wars Episode IV: A New Hope

Clearly, just checking the most popular movies is not sufficient to build a good, discriminating recommender.

Recommending Based on Statistics

Now that the scene is set, let's try using `significant_terms`. `significant_terms` will analyze the group of people who enjoy *Talladega Nights* (the *foreground* group) and determine what movies are most popular. It will then construct a list of popular films for everyone (the *background* group) and compare the two.

The statistical anomalies will be the movies that are *over-represented* in the foreground compared to the background. Theoretically, this should be a list of comedies, since people who enjoy Will Ferrell comedies will recommend them at a higher rate than the background population of people.

Let's give it a shot:

```
GET mlratings/_search?search_type=count
{
  "query": {
    "filtered": {
      "filter": {
        "term": {
          "movie": 46970
        }
      }
    }
  },
  "aggs": {
    "most_sig": {
      "significant_terms": { ❶
        "field": "movie",
        "size": 6
      }
    }
  }
}
```

❶ The setup is nearly identical — we just use `significant_terms` instead of `terms`.

As you can see, the query is nearly the same. We filter for users who liked *Talladega Nights*; this forms the foreground group. By default, significant_terms will use the entire index as the background, so we don't need to do anything special.

The results come back as a list of buckets similar to terms, but with some extra metadata:

```
    ...
    "aggregations": {
        "most_sig": {
            "doc_count": 271, ❶
            "buckets": [
                {
                    "key": 46970,
                    "key_as_string": "46970",
                    "doc_count": 271,
                    "score": 256.549815498155,
                    "bg_count": 271
                },
                {
                    "key": 52245, ❷
                    "key_as_string": "52245",
                    "doc_count": 59, ❸
                    "score": 17.66462367106966,
                    "bg_count": 185 ❹
                },
                {
                    "key": 8641,
                    "key_as_string": "8641",
                    "doc_count": 107,
                    "score": 13.884387742677438,
                    "bg_count": 762
                },
                {
                    "key": 58156,
                    "key_as_string": "58156",
                    "doc_count": 17,
                    "score": 9.746428133759462,
                    "bg_count": 28
                },
                {
                    "key": 52973,
                    "key_as_string": "52973",
                    "doc_count": 95,
                    "score": 9.65770100311672,
                    "bg_count": 857
                },
                {
                    "key": 35836,
                    "key_as_string": "35836",
                    "doc_count": 128,
                    "score": 9.199001116457955,
```

```
        "bg_count": 1610
      }
    ]
  ...
```

❶ The top-level doc_count shows the number of docs in the foreground group.

❷ Each bucket lists the key (for example, movie ID) being aggregated.

❸ A doc_count for that bucket.

❹ And a background count, which shows the rate at which this value appears in the entire background.

You can see that the first bucket we get back is *Talladega Nights*. It is found in all 271 documents, which is not surprising. Let's look at the next bucket: key 52245.

This ID corresponds to *Blades of Glory*, a comedy about male figure skating that also stars Will Ferrell. We can see that it was recommended 59 times by the people who also liked *Talladega Nights*. This means that 21% of the foreground group recommended *Blades of Glory* (59 / 271 = 0.2177).

In contrast, *Blades of Glory* was recommended only 185 times in the entire dataset, which equates to a mere 0.26% (185 / 69796 = 0.00265). *Blades of Glory* is therefore a statistical anomaly: it is uncommonly common in the group of people who like *Talladega Nights*. We just found a good recommendation!

If we look at the entire list, they are all comedies that would fit as good recommendations (many of which also star Will Ferrell):

1. Blades of Glory
2. Anchorman: The Legend of Ron Burgundy
3. Semi-Pro
4. Knocked Up
5. 40-Year-Old Virgin, The

This is just one example of the power of significant_terms. Once you start using significant_terms, you find many situations where you don't want the most popular—you want the most uncommonly common. This simple aggregation can uncover some surprisingly sophisticated trends in your data.

CHAPTER 34

Controlling Memory Use and Latency

Fielddata

Aggregations work via a data structure known as *fielddata* (briefly introduced in "Fielddata" on page 121). Fielddata is often the largest consumer of memory in an Elasticsearch cluster, so it is important to understand how it works.

 Fielddata can be loaded on the fly into memory, or built at index time and stored on disk. Later, we will talk about on-disk fielddata in "Doc Values" on page 495. For now we will focus on in-memory fielddata, as it is currently the default mode of operation in Elasticsearch. This may well change in a future version.

Fielddata exists because inverted indices are efficient only for certain operations. The inverted index excels at finding documents that contain a term. It does not perform well in the opposite direction: determining which terms exist in a single document. Aggregations need this secondary access pattern.

Consider the following inverted index:

```
Term       Doc_1   Doc_2   Doc_3
-----------------------------------
brown   |   X   |   X   |
dog     |   X   |       |   X
dogs    |       |   X   |   X
fox     |   X   |       |   X
foxes   |       |   X   |
in      |       |   X   |
jumped  |   X   |       |   X
lazy    |   X   |   X   |
leap    |       |   X   |
over    |   X   |   X   |   X
```

```
quick   |   X   |   X   |   X
summer  |       |   X   |
the     |   X   |       |   X
--------------------------------------
```

If we want to compile a complete list of terms in any document that mentions brown, we might build a query like so:

```
GET /my_index/_search
{
  "query" : {
    "match" : {
      "body" : "brown"
    }
  },
  "aggs" : {
    "popular_terms": {
      "terms" : {
        "field" : "body"
      }
    }
  }
}
```

The query portion is easy and efficient. The inverted index is sorted by terms, so first we find brown in the terms list, and then scan across all the columns to see which documents contain brown. We can very quickly see that Doc_1 and Doc_2 contain the token brown.

Then, for the aggregation portion, we need to find all the unique terms in Doc_1 and Doc_2. Trying to do this with the inverted index would be a very expensive process: we would have to iterate over every term in the index and collect tokens from Doc_1 and Doc_2 columns. This would be slow and scale poorly: as the number of terms and documents grows, so would the execution time.

Fielddata addresses this problem by inverting the relationship. While the inverted index maps terms to the documents containing the term, fielddata maps documents to the terms contained by the document:

```
Doc     Terms
------------------------------------------------------------------
Doc_1 | brown, dog, fox, jumped, lazy, over, quick, the
Doc_2 | brown, dogs, foxes, in, lazy, leap, over, quick, summer
Doc_3 | dog, dogs, fox, jumped, over, quick, the
------------------------------------------------------------------
```

Once the data has been uninverted, it is trivial to collect the unique tokens from Doc_1 and Doc_2. Go to the rows for each document, collect all the terms, and take the union of the two sets.

The fielddata cache is per segment. In other words, when a new segment becomes visible to search, the fielddata cached from old segments remains valid. Only the data for the new segment needs to be loaded into memory.

Thus, search and aggregations are closely intertwined. Search finds documents by using the inverted index. Aggregations collect and aggregate values from fielddata, which is itself generated from the inverted index.

The rest of this chapter covers various functionality that either decreases fielddata's memory footprint or increases execution speed.

Fielddata is not just used for aggregations. It is required for any operation that needs to look up the value contained in a specific document. Besides aggregations, this includes sorting, scripts that access field values, parent-child relationships (see Chapter 42), and certain types of queries or filters, such as the geo_distance filter.

Aggregations and Analysis

Some aggregations, such as the terms bucket, operate on string fields. And string fields may be either analyzed or not_analyzed, which begs the question: how does analysis affect aggregations?

The answer is "a lot," but it is best shown through an example. First, index some documents representing various states in the US:

```
POST /agg_analysis/data/_bulk
{ "index": {}}
{ "state" : "New York" }
{ "index": {}}
{ "state" : "New Jersey" }
{ "index": {}}
{ "state" : "New Mexico" }
{ "index": {}}
{ "state" : "New York" }
{ "index": {}}
{ "state" : "New York" }
```

We want to build a list of unique states in our dataset, complete with counts. Simple— let's use a terms bucket:

```
GET /agg_analysis/data/_search?search_type=count
{
    "aggs" : {
        "states" : {
            "terms" : {
                "field" : "state"
```

```
                        }
                    }
                }
            }
```

This gives us these results:

```
{
...
    "aggregations": {
        "states": {
            "buckets": [
                {
                    "key": "new",
                    "doc_count": 5
                },
                {
                    "key": "york",
                    "doc_count": 3
                },
                {
                    "key": "jersey",
                    "doc_count": 1
                },
                {
                    "key": "mexico",
                    "doc_count": 1
                }
            ]
        }
    }
}
```

Oh dear, that's not at all what we want! Instead of counting states, the aggregation is counting individual words. The underlying reason is simple: aggregations are built from the inverted index, and the inverted index is *post-analysis.*

When we added those documents to Elasticsearch, the string "New York" was ana-lyzed/tokenized into ["new", "york"]. These individual tokens were then used to populate fielddata, and ultimately we see counts for new instead of New York.

This is obviously not the behavior that we wanted, but luckily it is easily corrected.

We need to define a multifield for state and set it to not_analyzed. This will prevent New York from being analyzed, which means it will stay a single token in the aggrega-tion. Let's try the whole process over, but this time specify a *raw* multifield:

```
DELETE /agg_analysis/
PUT /agg_analysis
{
    "mappings": {
        "data": {
```

```
      "properties": {
        "state" : {
          "type": "string",
          "fields": {
            "raw" : {
              "type": "string",
              "index": "not_analyzed"❶
            }
          }
        }
      }
    }
  }
}

POST /agg_analysis/data/_bulk
{ "index": {}}
{ "state" : "New York" }
{ "index": {}}
{ "state" : "New Jersey" }
{ "index": {}}
{ "state" : "New Mexico" }
{ "index": {}}
{ "state" : "New York" }
{ "index": {}}
{ "state" : "New York" }

GET /agg_analysis/data/_search?search_type=count
{
  "aggs" : {
    "states" : {
        "terms" : {
            "field" : "state.raw" ❷
        }
    }
  }
}
```

❶ This time we explicitly map the state field and include a not_analyzed sub-field.

❷ The aggregation is run on state.raw instead of state.

Now when we run our aggregation, we get results that make sense:

```
{
...
   "aggregations": {
      "states": {
         "buckets": [
            {
                "key": "New York",
```

```
          "doc_count": 3
        },
        {
          "key": "New Jersey",
          "doc_count": 1
        },
        {
          "key": "New Mexico",
          "doc_count": 1
        }
      ]
    }
  }
}
```

In practice, this kind of problem is easy to spot. Your aggregations will simply return strange buckets, and you'll remember the analysis issue. It is a generalization, but there are not many instances where you want to use an analyzed field in an aggregation. When in doubt, add a multifield so you have the option for both.

High-Cardinality Memory Implications

There is another reason to avoid aggregating analyzed fields: high-cardinality fields consume a large amount of memory when loaded into fielddata. The analysis process often (although not always) generates a large number of tokens, many of which are unique. This increases the overall cardinality of the field and contributes to more memory pressure.

Some types of analysis are *extremely* unfriendly with regards to memory. Consider an n-gram analysis process. The term New York might be n-grammed into the following tokens:

- ne
- ew
- w
- y
- yo
- or
- rk

You can imagine how the n-gramming process creates a huge number of unique tokens, especially when analyzing paragraphs of text. When these are loaded into memory, you can easily exhaust your heap space.

So, before aggregating across fields, take a second to verify that the fields are not_ana
lyzed. And if you want to aggregate analyzed fields, ensure that the analysis process
is not creating an obscene number of tokens.

 At the end of the day, it doesn't matter whether a field is analyzed
or not_analyzed. The more unique values in a field—the higher
the cardinality of the field—the more memory that is required.
This is especially true for string fields, where every unique string
must be held in memory—longer strings use more memory.

Limiting Memory Usage

In order for aggregations (or any operation that requires access to field values) to be
fast, access to fielddata must be fast, which is why it is loaded into memory. But loading too much data into memory will cause slow garbage collections as the JVM tries
to find extra space in the heap, or possibly even an OutOfMemory exception.

It may surprise you to find that Elasticsearch does not load into fielddata just the values for the documents that match your query. It loads the values for *all documents in
your index*, even documents with a different _type!

The logic is: if you need access to documents X, Y, and Z for this query, you will probably need access to other documents in the next query. It is cheaper to load all values
once, and to *keep them in memory*, than to have to scan the inverted index on every
request.

The JVM heap is a limited resource that should be used wisely. A number of mechanisms exist to limit the impact of fielddata on heap usage. These limits are important
because abuse of the heap will cause node instability (thanks to slow garbage collections) or even node death (with an OutOfMemory exception).

Choosing a Heap Size

There are two rules to apply when setting the Elasticsearch heap size, with the
$ES_HEAP_SIZE environment variable:

No more than 50% of available RAM
  Lucene makes good use of the filesystem caches, which are managed by the kernel. Without enough filesystem cache space, performance will suffer.

No more than 32 GB: If the heap is less than 32 GB, the JVM can use compressed
pointers, which saves a lot of memory: 4 bytes per pointer instead of 8 bytes.

+ Increasing the heap from 32 GB to 34 GB would mean that you have much *less* memory available, because all pointers are taking double the space. Also, with bigger heaps, garbage collection becomes more costly and can result in node instability.

This limit has a direct impact on the amount of memory that can be devoted to field-data.

Fielddata Size

The `indices.fielddata.cache.size` controls how much heap space is allocated to fielddata. When you run a query that requires access to new field values, it will load the values into memory and then try to add them to fielddata. If the resulting field-data size would exceed the specified `size`, other values would be evicted in order to make space.

By default, this setting is *unbounded*—Elasticsearch will never evict data from field-data.

This default was chosen deliberately: fielddata is not a transient cache. It is an in-memory data structure that must be accessible for fast execution, and it is expensive to build. If you have to reload data for every request, performance is going to be awful.

A bounded size forces the data structure to evict data. We will look at when to set this value, but first a warning:

This setting is a safeguard, not a solution for insufficient memory.

If you don't have enough memory to keep your fielddata resident in memory, Elasticsearch will constantly have to reload data from disk, and evict other data to make space. Evictions cause heavy disk I/O and generate a large amount of garbage in memory, which must be garbage collected later on.

Imagine that you are indexing logs, using a new index every day. Normally you are interested in data from only the last day or two. Although you keep older indices around, you seldom need to query them. However, with the default settings, the field-data from the old indices is never evicted! fielddata will just keep on growing until you trip the fielddata circuit breaker (see "Circuit Breaker" on page 492), which will prevent you from loading any more fielddata.

At that point, you're stuck. While you can still run queries that access fielddata from the old indices, you can't load any new values. Instead, we should evict old values to make space for the new values.

To prevent this scenario, place an upper limit on the fielddata by adding this setting to the `config/elasticsearch.yml` file:

```
indices.fielddata.cache.size:  40% ❶
```

❶ Can be set to a percentage of the heap size, or a concrete value like 5gb

With this setting in place, the least recently used fielddata will be evicted to make space for newly loaded data.

 There is another setting that you may see online: `indices.field data.cache.expire`.

We beg that you *never* use this setting! It will likely be deprecated in the future.

This setting tells Elasticsearch to evict values from fielddata if they are older than `expire`, whether the values are being used or not.

This is *terrible* for performance. Evictions are costly, and this effectively *schedules* evictions on purpose, for no real gain.

There isn't a good reason to use this setting; we literally cannot theory-craft a hypothetically useful situation. It exists only for backward compatibility at the moment. We mention the setting in this book only since, sadly, it has been recommended in various articles on the Internet as a good performance tip.

It is not. Never use it!

Monitoring fielddata

It is important to keep a close watch on how much memory is being used by fielddata, and whether any data is being evicted. High eviction counts can indicate a serious resource issue and a reason for poor performance.

Fielddata usage can be monitored:

- per-index using the `indices-stats` API (*http://bit.ly/1BwZ61b*):

    ```
    GET /_stats/fielddata?fields=*
    ```

- per-node using the `nodes-stats` API (*http://bit.ly/1586yDn*):

    ```
    GET /_nodes/stats/indices/fielddata?fields=*
    ```

- Or even per-index per-node:

    ```
    GET /_nodes/stats/indices/fielddata?level=indices&fields=*
    ```

By setting `?fields=*`, the memory usage is broken down for each field.

Circuit Breaker

An astute reader might have noticed a problem with the fielddata size settings. fielddata size is checked *after* the data is loaded. What happens if a query arrives that tries to load more into fielddata than available memory? The answer is ugly: you would get an OutOfMemoryException.

Elasticsearch includes a *fielddata circuit breaker* that is designed to deal with this situation. The circuit breaker estimates the memory requirements of a query by introspecting the fields involved (their type, cardinality, size, and so forth). It then checks to see whether loading the required fielddata would push the total fielddata size over the configured percentage of the heap.

If the estimated query size is larger than the limit, the circuit breaker is *tripped* and the query will be aborted and return an exception. This happens *before* data is loaded, which means that you won't hit an OutOfMemoryException.

Available Circuit Breakers

Elasticsearch has a family of circuit breakers, all of which work to ensure that memory limits are not exceeded:

`indices.breaker.fielddata.limit`
> The `fielddata` circuit breaker limits the size of fielddata to 60% of the heap, by default.

`indices.breaker.request.limit`
> The `request` circuit breaker estimates the size of structures required to complete other parts of a request, such as creating aggregation buckets, and limits them to 40% of the heap, by default.

`indices.breaker.total.limit`
> The `total` circuit breaker wraps the `request` and `fielddata` circuit breakers to ensure that the combination of the two doesn't use more than 70% of the heap by default.

The circuit breaker limits can be specified in the `config/elasticsearch.yml` file, or can be updated dynamically on a live cluster:

```
PUT /_cluster/settings
{
  "persistent" : {
    "indices.breaker.fielddata.limit" : "40%" ❶
  }
}
```

❶ The limit is a percentage of the heap.

It is best to configure the circuit breaker with a relatively conservative value. Remember that fielddata needs to share the heap with the `request` circuit breaker, the indexing memory buffer, the filter cache, Lucene data structures for open indices, and various other transient data structures. For this reason, it defaults to a fairly conservative 60%. Overly optimistic settings can cause potential OOM exceptions, which will take down an entire node.

On the other hand, an overly conservative value will simply return a query exception that can be handled by your application. An exception is better than a crash. These exceptions should also encourage you to reassess your query: why *does* a single query need more than 60% of the heap?

In "Fielddata Size" on page 490, we spoke about adding a limit to the size of fielddata, to ensure that old unused fielddata can be evicted. The relationship between `indices.fielddata.cache.size` and `indices.breaker.fielddata.limit` is an important one. If the circuit-breaker limit is lower than the cache size, no data will ever be evicted. In order for it to work properly, the circuit breaker limit *must* be higher than the cache size.

It is important to note that the circuit breaker compares estimated query size against the total heap size, *not* against the actual amount of heap memory used. This is done for a variety of technical reasons (for example, the heap may look full but is actually just garbage waiting to be collected, which is hard to estimate properly). But as the end user, this means the setting needs to be conservative, since it is comparing against total heap, not *free* heap.

Fielddata Filtering

Imagine that you are running a website that allows users to listen to their favorite songs. To make it easier for them to manage their music library, users can tag songs with whatever tags make sense to them. You will end up with a lot of tracks tagged with `rock`, `hiphop`, and `electronica`, but also with some tracks tagged with `my_16th_birthday_favorite_anthem`.

Now imagine that you want to show users the most popular three tags for each song. It is highly likely that tags like `rock` will show up in the top three, but `my_16th_birthday_favorite_anthem` is very unlikely to make the grade. However, in order to calculate the most popular tags, you have been forced to load all of these one-off terms into memory.

Thanks to fielddata filtering, we can take control of this situation. We *know* that we're interested in only the most popular terms, so we can simply avoid loading any terms that fall into the less interesting long tail:

```
PUT /music/_mapping/song
{
  "properties": {
    "tag": {
      "type": "string",
      "fielddata": { ❶
        "filter": {
          "frequency": { ❷
            "min":                0.01, ❸
            "min_segment_size": 500    ❹
          }
        }
      }
    }
  }
}
```

❶ The `fielddata` key allows us to configure how fielddata is handled for this field.

❷ The `frequency` filter allows us to filter fielddata loading based on term frequencies.

❸ Load only terms that occur in at least 1% of documents in this segment.

❹ Ignore any segments that have fewer than 500 documents.

With this mapping in place, only terms that appear in at least 1% of the documents *in that segment* will be loaded into memory. You can also specify a `max` term frequency, which could be used to exclude terms that are *too* common, such as stopwords.

Term frequencies, in this case, are calculated per segment. This is a limitation of the implementation: fielddata is loaded per segment, and at that point the only term frequencies that are visible are the frequencies for that segment. However, this limitation has interesting properties: it allows newly popular terms to rise to the top quickly.

Let's say that a new genre of song becomes popular one day. You would like to include the tag for this new genre in the most popular list, but if you were relying on term frequencies calculated across the whole index, you would have to wait for the new tag to become as popular as `rock` and `electronica`. Because of the way frequency filtering is implemented, the newly added tag will quickly show up as a high-frequency tag within new segments, so will quickly float to the top.

The `min_segment_size` parameter tells Elasticsearch to ignore segments below a certain size. If a segment holds only a few documents, the term frequencies are too coarse to have any meaning. Small segments will soon be merged into bigger segments, which will then be big enough to take into account.

 Filtering terms by frequency is not the only option. You can also decide to load only those terms that match a regular expression. For instance, you could use a `regex` filter on tweets to load only hashtags into memory — terms the start with a #. This assumes that you are using an analyzer that preserves punctuation, like the `whitespace` analyzer.

Fielddata filtering can have a *massive* impact on memory usage. The trade-off is fairly obvious: you are essentially ignoring data. But for many applications, the trade-off is reasonable since the data is not being used anyway. The memory savings is often more important than including a large and relatively useless long tail of terms.

Doc Values

In-memory fielddata is limited by the size of your heap. While this is a problem that can be solved by scaling horizontally—you can always add more nodes—you will find that heavy use of aggregations and sorting can exhaust your heap space while other resources on the node are underutilized.

While fielddata defaults to loading values into memory on the fly, this is not the only option. It can also be written to disk at index time in a way that provides all the functionality of in-memory fielddata, but without the heap memory usage. This alternative format is called *doc values*.

Doc values were added to Elasticsearch in version 1.0.0 but, until recently, they were much slower than in-memory fielddata. By benchmarking and profiling performance, various bottlenecks have been identified—in both Elasticsearch and Lucene—and removed.

Doc values are now only about 10–25% slower than in-memory fielddata, and come with two major advantages:

- They live on disk instead of in heap memory. This allows you to work with quantities of fielddata that would normally be too large to fit into memory. In fact, your heap space (`$ES_HEAP_SIZE`) can now be set to a smaller size, which improves the speed of garbage collection and, consequently, node stability.

- Doc values are built at index time, not at search time. While in-memory fielddata has to be built on the fly at search time by uninverting the inverted index, doc values are prebuilt and much faster to initialize.

The trade-off is a larger index size and slightly slower fielddata access. Doc values are remarkably efficient, so for many queries you might not even notice the slightly slower speed. Combine that with faster garbage collections and improved initialization times and you may notice a net gain.

The more filesystem cache space that you have available, the better doc values will perform. If the files holding the doc values are resident in the filesystem cache, then accessing the files is almost equivalent to reading from RAM. And the filesystem cache is managed by the kernel instead of the JVM.

Enabling Doc Values

Doc values can be enabled for numeric, date, Boolean, binary, and geo-point fields, and for `not_analyzed` string fields. They do not currently work with `analyzed` string fields. Doc values are enabled per field in the field mapping, which means that you can combine in-memory fielddata with doc values:

```
PUT /music/_mapping/song
{
  "properties" : {
    "tag": {
      "type":      "string",
      "index" :    "not_analyzed",
      "doc_values": true ❶
    }
  }
}
```

❶ Setting `doc_values` to `true` at field creation time is all that is required to use disk-based fielddata instead of in-memory fielddata.

That's it! Queries, aggregations, sorting, and scripts will function as normal; they'll just be using doc values now. There is no other configuration necessary.

> Use doc values freely. The more you use them, the less stress you place on the heap. It is possible that doc values will become the default format in the near future.

Preloading Fielddata

The default behavior of Elasticsearch is to load in-memory fielddata *lazily*. The first time Elasticsearch encounters a query that needs fielddata for a particular field, it will load that entire field into memory for each segment in the index.

For small segments, this requires a negligible amount of time. But if you have a few 5 GB segments and need to load 10 GB of fielddata into memory, this process could take tens of seconds. Users accustomed to subsecond response times would all of a sudden be hit by an apparently unresponsive website.

There are three methods to combat this latency spike:

- Eagerly load fielddata
- Eagerly load global ordinals
- Prepopulate caches with warmers

All are variations on the same concept: preload the fielddata so that there is no latency spike when the user needs to execute a search.

Eagerly Loading Fielddata

The first tool is called *eager loading* (as opposed to the default lazy loading). As new segments are created (by refreshing, flushing, or merging), fields with eager loading enabled will have their per-segment fielddata preloaded *before* the segment becomes visible to search.

This means that the first query to hit the segment will not need to trigger fielddata loading, as the in-memory cache has already been populated. This prevents your users from experiencing the *cold cache* latency spike.

Eager loading is enabled on a per-field basis, so you can control which fields are preloaded:

```
PUT /music/_mapping/_song
{
  "price_usd": {
    "type": "integer",
    "fielddata": {
      "loading" : "eager" ❶
    }
  }
}
```

❶ By setting `fielddata.loading: eager`, we tell Elasticsearch to preload this field's contents into memory.

Fielddata loading can be set to `lazy` or `eager` on existing fields, using the `update-mapping` API.

Eager loading simply shifts the cost of loading fielddata. Instead of paying at query time, you pay at refresh time.

Large segments will take longer to refresh than small segments. Usually, large segments are created by merging smaller segments that are already visible to search, so the slower refresh time is not important.

Global Ordinals

One of the techniques used to reduce the memory usage of string fielddata is called *ordinals.*

Imagine that we have a billion documents, each of which has a `status` field. There are only three statuses: `status_pending`, `status_published`, `status_deleted`. If we were to hold the full string status in memory for every document, we would use 14 to 16 bytes per document, or about 15 GB.

Instead, we can identify the three unique strings, sort them, and number them: 0, 1, 2.

```
Ordinal | Term
------------------
0       | status_deleted
1       | status_pending
2       | status_published
```

The original strings are stored only once in the ordinals list, and each document just uses the numbered ordinal to point to the value that it contains.

```
Doc     | Ordinal
------------------------
0       | 1  # pending
1       | 1  # pending
2       | 2  # published
3       | 0  # deleted
```

This reduces memory usage from 15 GB to less than 1 GB!

But there is a problem. Remember that fielddata caches are *per segment*. If one segment contains only two statuses—`status_deleted` and `status_published`—then the resulting ordinals (0 and 1) will not be the same as the ordinals for a segment that contains all three statuses.

If we try to run a `terms` aggregation on the `status` field, we need to aggregate on the actual string values, which means that we need to identify the same values across all segments. A naive way of doing this would be to run the aggregation on each segment, return the string values from each segment, and then reduce them into an overall result. While this would work, it would be slow and CPU intensive.

Instead, we use a structure called *global ordinals*. Global ordinals are a small in-memory data structure built on top of fielddata. Unique values are identified *across all segments* and stored in an ordinals list like the one we have already described.

Now, our `terms` aggregation can just aggregate on the global ordinals, and the conversion from ordinal to actual string value happens only once at the end of the aggregation. This increases performance of aggregations (and sorting) by a factor of three or four.

Building global ordinals

Of course, nothing in life is free. Global ordinals cross all segments in an index, so if a new segment is added or an old segment is deleted, the global ordinals need to be rebuilt. Rebuilding requires reading every unique term in every segment. The higher the cardinality—the more unique terms that exist—the longer this process takes.

Global ordinals are built on top of in-memory fielddata and doc values. In fact, they are one of the major reasons that doc values perform as well as they do.

Like fielddata loading, global ordinals are built lazily, by default. The first request that requires fielddata to hit an index will trigger the building of global ordinals. Depending on the cardinality of the field, this can result in a significant latency spike for your users. Once global ordinals have been rebuilt, they will be reused until the segments in the index change: after a refresh, a flush, or a merge.

Eager global ordinals

Individual string fields can be configured to prebuild global ordinals eagerly:

```
PUT /music/_mapping/_song
{
  "song_title": {
    "type": "string",
    "fielddata": {
      "loading" : "eager_global_ordinals" ❶
    }
  }
}
```

❶ Setting `eager_global_ordinals` also implies loading fielddata eagerly.

Just like the eager preloading of fielddata, eager global ordinals are built before a new segment becomes visible to search.

Ordinals are only built and used for strings. Numerical data (integers, geopoints, dates, etc) doesn't need an ordinal mapping, since the value itself acts as an intrinsic ordinal mapping.

Therefore, you can only enable eager global ordinals for string fields.

Doc values can also have their global ordinals built eagerly:

```
PUT /music/_mapping/_song
{
  "song_title": {
    "type":         "string",
    "doc_values": true,
    "fielddata": {
      "loading" : "eager_global_ordinals" ❶
    }
  }
}
```

❶ In this case, fielddata is not loaded into memory, but doc values are loaded into the filesystem cache.

Unlike fielddata preloading, eager building of global ordinals can have an impact on the *real-time* aspect of your data. For very high cardinality fields, building global ordinals can delay a refresh by several seconds. The choice is between paying the cost on each refresh, or on the first query after a refresh. If you index often and query seldom, it is probably better to pay the price at query time instead of on every refresh.

Make your global ordinals pay for themselves. If you have very high cardinality fields that take seconds to rebuild, increase the `refresh_interval` so that global ordinals remain valid for longer. This will also reduce CPU usage, as you will need to rebuild global ordinals less often.

Index Warmers

Finally, we come to *index warmers*. Warmers predate eager fielddata loading and eager global ordinals, but they still serve a purpose. An index warmer allows you to specify a query and aggregations that should be run before a new segment is made visible to search. The idea is to prepopulate, or *warm*, caches so your users never see a spike in latency.

Originally, the most important use for warmers was to make sure that fielddata was pre-loaded, as this is usually the most costly step. This is now better controlled with the techniques we discussed previously. However, warmers can be used to prebuild filter caches, and can still be used to preload fielddata should you so choose.

Let's register a warmer and then talk about what's happening:

```
PUT /music/_warmer/warmer_1 ❶
{
  "query" : {
    "filtered" : {
      "filter" : {
        "bool": {
          "should": [ ❷
            { "term": { "tag": "rock"      }},
            { "term": { "tag": "hiphop"    }},
            { "term": { "tag": "electronics" }}
          ]
        }
      }
    }
  },
  "aggs" : {
    "price" : {
      "histogram" : {
        "field" : "price", ❸
        "interval" : 10
      }
    }
  }
}
```

❶ Warmers are associated with an index (music) and are registered using the
   _warmer endpoint and a unique ID (warmer_1).

❷ The three most popular music genres have their filter caches prebuilt.

❸ The fielddata and global ordinals for the price field will be preloaded.

Warmers are registered against a specific index. Each warmer is given a unique ID,
because you can have multiple warmers per index.

Then you just specify a query, any query. It can include queries, filters, aggregations,
sort values, scripts—literally any valid query DSL. The point is to register queries that
are representative of the traffic that your users will generate, so that appropriate
caches can be prepopulated.

When a new segment is created, Elasticsearch will *literally* execute the queries registered in your warmers. The act of executing these queries will force caches to be
loaded. Only after all warmers have been executed will the segment be made visible to
search.

Similar to eager loading, warmers shift the cost of cold caches to refresh time. When registering warmers, it is important to be judicious. You *could* add thousands of warmers to make sure every cache is populated—but that will drastically increase the time it takes for new segments to be made searchable.

In practice, select a handful of queries that represent the majority of your user's queries and register those.

Some administrative details (such as getting existing warmers and deleting warmers) that have been omitted from this explanation. Refer to the warmers documentation (*http://bit.ly/1AUGwys*) for the rest of the details.

Preventing Combinatorial Explosions

The `terms` bucket dynamically builds buckets based on your data; it doesn't know up front how many buckets will be generated. While this is fine with a single aggregation, think about what can happen when one aggregation contains another aggregation, which contains another aggregation, and so forth. The combination of unique values in each of these aggregations can lead to an explosion in the number of buckets generated.

Imagine we have a modest dataset that represents movies. Each document lists the actors in that movie:

```
{
  "actors" : [
    "Fred Jones",
    "Mary Jane",
    "Elizabeth Worthing"
  ]
}
```

If we want to determine the top 10 actors and their top costars, that's trivial with an aggregation:

```
{
  "aggs" : {
    "actors" : {
      "terms" : {
        "field" : "actors",
        "size" :  10
      },
      "aggs" : {
        "costars" : {
          "terms" : {
            "field" : "actors",
            "size" :  5
          }
```

```
            }
          }
        }
      }
    }
  }
```

This will return a list of the top 10 actors, and for each actor, a list of their top five costars. This seems like a very modest aggregation; only 50 values will be returned!

However, this seemingly innocuous query can easily consume a vast amount of memory. You can visualize a `terms` aggregation as building a tree in memory. The `actors` aggregation will build the first level of the tree, with a bucket for every actor. Then, nested under each node in the first level, the `costars` aggregation will build a second level, with a bucket for every costar, as seen in Figure 34-1. That means that a single movie will generate n^2 buckets!

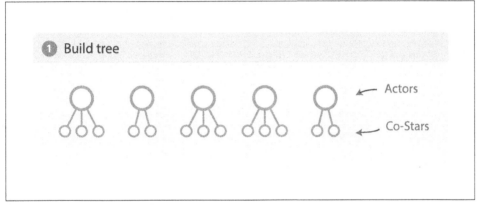

Figure 34-1. Build full depth tree

To use some real numbers, imagine each movie has 10 actors on average. Each movie will then generate 10^2 == 100 buckets. If you have 20,000 movies, that's roughly 2,000,000 generated buckets.

Now, remember, our aggregation is simply asking for the top 10 actors and their costars, totaling 50 values. To get the final results, we have to generate that tree of 2,000,000 buckets, sort it, and finally prune it such that only the top 10 actors are left. This is illustrated in Figure 34-2 and Figure 34-3.

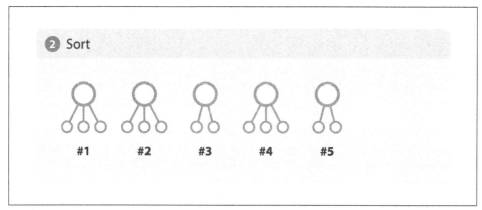

Figure 34-2. Sort tree

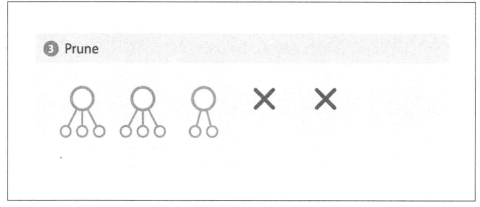

Figure 34-3. Prune tree

At this point you should be quite distraught. Twenty thousand documents is paltry, and the aggregation is pretty tame. What if you had 200 million documents, wanted the top 100 actors and their top 20 costars, as well as the costars' costars?

You can appreciate how quickly combinatorial expansion can grow, making this strategy untenable. There is not enough memory in the world to support uncontrolled combinatorial explosions.

Depth-First Versus Breadth-First

Elasticsearch allows you to change the *collection mode* of an aggregation, for exactly this situation. The strategy we outlined previously—building the tree fully and then pruning—is called *depth-first* and it is the default. Depth-first works well for the majority of aggregations, but can fall apart in situations like our actors and costars example.

For these special cases, you should use an alternative collection strategy called *breadth-first*. This strategy works a little differently. It executes the first layer of aggregations, and *then* performs a pruning phase before continuing, as illustrated in Figure 34-4 through Figure 34-6.

In our example, the `actors` aggregation would be executed first. At this point, we have a single layer in the tree, but we already know who the top 10 actors are! There is no need to keep the other actors since they won't be in the top 10 anyway.

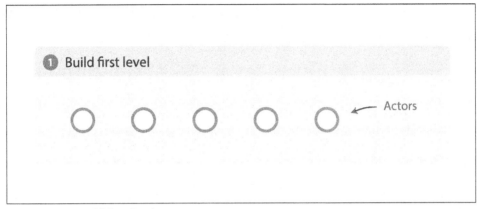

Figure 34-4. Build first level

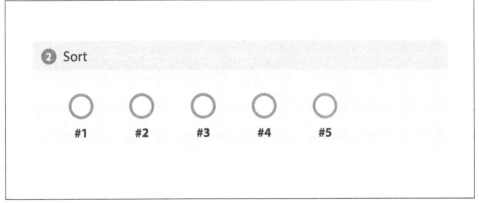

Figure 34-5. Sort first level

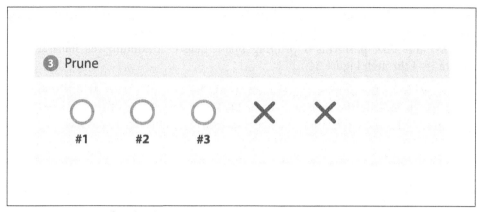

Figure 34-6. Prune first level

Since we already know the top ten actors, we can safely prune away the rest of the long tail. After pruning, the next layer is populated based on *its* execution mode, and the process repeats until the aggregation is done, as illustrated in Figure 34-7. This prevents the combinatorial explosion of buckets and drastically reduces memory requirements for classes of queries that are amenable to breadth-first.

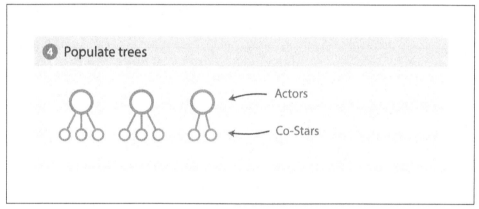

Figure 34-7. Populate full depth for remaining nodes

To use breadth-first, simply enable it via the `collect` parameter:

```
{
  "aggs" : {
    "actors" : {
      "terms" : {
        "field" :        "actors",
        "size" :         10,
        "collect_mode" : "breadth_first" ❶
      },
      "aggs" : {
```

```
      "costars" : {
        "terms" : {
          "field" : "actors",
          "size" :  5
        }
      }
    }
  }
 }
}
```

❶ Enable breadth_first on a per-aggregation basis.

Breadth-first should be used only when you expect more buckets to be generated than documents landing in the buckets. Breadth-first works by caching document data at the bucket level, and then replaying those documents to child aggregations after the pruning phase.

The memory requirement of a breadth-first aggregation is linear to the number of documents in each bucket prior to pruning. For many aggregations, the number of documents in each bucket is very large. Think of a histogram with monthly intervals: you might have thousands or hundreds of thousands of documents per bucket. This makes breadth-first a bad choice, and is why depth-first is the default.

But for the actor example—which generates a large number of buckets, but each bucket has relatively few documents—breadth-first is much more memory efficient, and allows you to build aggregations that would otherwise fail.

CHAPTER 35

Closing Thoughts

This section covered a lot of ground, and a lot of deeply technical issues. Aggregations bring a power and flexibility to Elasticsearch that is hard to overstate. The ability to nest buckets and metrics, to quickly approximate cardinality and percentiles, to find statistical anomalies in your data, all while operating on near-real-time data and in parallel to full-text search—these are game-changers to many organizations.

It is a feature that, once you start using it, you'll find dozens of other candidate uses. Real-time reporting and analytics is central to many organizations (be it over business intelligence or server logs).

But with great power comes great responsibility, and for Elasticsearch that often means proper memory stewardship. Memory is often the limiting factor in Elasticsearch deployments, particularly those that heavily utilize aggregations. Because aggregation data is loaded to fielddata—and this is an in-memory data structure—managing efficient memory usage is important.

The management of this memory can take several forms, depending on your particular use-case:

- At a data level, by making sure you analyze (or `not_analyze`) your data appropriately so that it is memory-friendly
- During indexing, by configuring heavy fields to use disk-based doc values instead of in-memory fielddata
- At search time, by utilizing approximate aggregations and data filtering
- At a node level, by setting hard memory and dynamic circuit-breaker limits
- At an operations level, by monitoring memory usage and controlling slow garbage-collection cycles, potentially by adding more nodes to the cluster

Most deployments will use one or more of the preceding methods. The exact combination is highly dependent on your particular environment. Some organizations need blisteringly fast responses and opt to simply add more nodes. Other organizations are limited by budget and choose doc values and approximate aggregations.

Whatever the path you take, it is important to assess the available options and create both a short- and long-term plan. Decide how your memory situation exists today and what (if anything) needs to be done. Then decide what will happen in six months or one year as your data grows. What methods will you use to continue scaling?

It is better to plan out these life cycles of your cluster ahead of time, rather than panicking at 3 a.m. because your cluster is at 90% heap utilization.

PART V

Geolocation

Gone are the days when we wander around a city with paper maps. Thanks to smartphones, we now know exactly where we are all the time, and we expect websites to use that information. I'm not interested in restaurants in Greater London—I want to know about restaurants within a 5-minute walk of my current location.

But geolocation is only one part of the puzzle. The beauty of Elasticsearch is that it allows you to combine geolocation with full-text search, structured search, and analytics.

For instance: show me restaurants that mention *vitello tonnato*, are within a 5-minute walk, and are open at 11 p.m., and then rank them by a combination of user rating, distance, and price. Another example: show me a map of vacation rental properties available in August throughout the city, and calculate the average price per zone.

Elasticsearch offers two ways of representing geolocations: latitude-longitude points using the `geo_point` field type, and complex shapes defined in GeoJSON (*http://en.wikipedia.org/wiki/GeoJSON*), using the `geo_shape` field type.

Geo-points allow you to find points within a certain distance of another point, to calculate distances between two points for sorting or relevance scoring, or to aggregate into a grid to display on a map. *Geo-shapes*, on the other hand, are used purely for filtering. They can be used to decide whether two shapes overlap, or whether one shape completely contains other shapes.

CHAPTER 36

Geo-Points

A *geo-point* is a single latitude/longitude point on the Earth's surface. Geo-points can be used to calculate distance from a point, to determine whether a point falls within a bounding box, or in aggregations.

Geo-points cannot be automatically detected with dynamic mapping. Instead, geo_point fields should be mapped explicitly:

```
PUT /attractions
{
  "mappings": {
    "restaurant": {
      "properties": {
        "name": {
          "type": "string"
        },
        "location": {
          "type": "geo_point"
        }
      }
    }
  }
}
```

Lat/Lon Formats

With the location field defined as a geo_point, we can proceed to index documents containing latitude/longitude pairs, which can be formatted as strings, arrays, or objects:

```
PUT /attractions/restaurant/1
{
  "name":      "Chipotle Mexican Grill",
  "location": "40.715, -74.011" ❶
}

PUT /attractions/restaurant/2
{
  "name":      "Pala Pizza",
  "location": { ❷
    "lat":      40.722,
    "lon":     -73.989
  }
}

PUT /attractions/restaurant/3
{
  "name":      "Mini Munchies Pizza",
  "location": [ -73.983, 40.719 ] ❸
}
```

❶ A string representation, with "lat,lon".

❷ An object representation with lat and lon explicitly named.

❸ An array representation with [lon,lat].

Everybody gets caught at least once: string geo-points are "lati
tude,longitude", while array geo-points are [longitude,lati
tude]—the opposite order!

Originally, both strings and arrays in Elasticsearch used latitude
followed by longitude. However, it was decided early on to switch
the order for arrays in order to conform with GeoJSON.

The result is a bear trap that captures all unsuspecting users on
their journey to full geolocation nirvana.

Filtering by Geo-Point

Four geo-point filters can be used to include or exclude documents by geolocation:

geo_bounding_box
    Find geo-points that fall within the specified rectangle.

geo_distance
    Find geo-points within the specified distance of a central point.

`geo_distance_range`

Find geo-points within a specified minimum and maximum distance from a central point.

`geo_polygon`

Find geo-points that fall within the specified polygon. *This filter is very expensive.* If you find yourself wanting to use it, you should be looking at geo-shapes instead.

All of these filters work in a similar way: the `lat`/`lon` values are loaded into memory for *all documents in the index*, not just the documents that match the query (see "Fielddata" on page 121). Each filter performs a slightly different calculation to check whether a point falls into the containing area.

 Geo-filters are expensive — they should be used on as few documents as possible. First remove as many documents as you can with cheaper filters, like `term` or `range` filters, and apply the geo-filters last.

The `bool` filter will do this for you automatically. First it applies any bitset-based filters (see "All About Caching" on page 194) to exclude as many documents as it can as cheaply as possible. Then it applies the more expensive geo or script filters to each remaining document in turn.

geo_bounding_box Filter

This is by far the most efficient geo-filter because its calculation is very simple. You provide it with the `top`, `bottom`, `left`, and `right` coordinates of a rectangle, and all it does is compare the latitude with the left and right coordinates, and the longitude with the top and bottom coordinates:

```
GET /attractions/restaurant/_search
{
  "query": {
    "filtered": {
      "filter": {
        "geo_bounding_box": {
          "location": { ❶
            "top_left": {
              "lat":  40.8,
              "lon": -74.0
            },
            "bottom_right": {
              "lat":  40.7,
              "lon": -73.0
            }
          }
        }
```

```
          }
        }
      }
    }
  }
}
```

❶ These coordinates can also be specified as bottom_left and top_right.

Optimizing Bounding Boxes

The geo_bounding_box is the one geo-filter that doesn't require all geo-points to be loaded into memory. Because all it has to do is check whether the lat and lon values fall within the specified ranges, it can use the inverted index to do a glorified range filter.

To use this optimization, the geo_point field must be mapped to index the lat and lon values separately:

```
PUT /attractions
{
  "mappings": {
    "restaurant": {
      "properties": {
        "name": {
          "type": "string"
        },
        "location": {
          "type":    "geo_point",
          "lat_lon": true ❶
        }
      }
    }
  }
}
```

❶ The location.lat and location.lon fields will be indexed separately. These fields can be used for searching, but their values cannot be retrieved.

Now, when we run our query, we have to tell Elasticsearch to use the indexed lat and lon values:

```
GET /attractions/restaurant/_search
{
  "query": {
    "filtered": {
      "filter": {
        "geo_bounding_box": {
          "type":    "indexed", ❶
          "location": {
            "top_left": {
```

```
            "lat":  40.8,
            "lon": -74.0
        },
        "bottom_right": {
            "lat":  40.7,
            "lon":  -73.0
        }
    }
}
```

❶ Setting the type parameter to indexed (instead of the default memory) tells Elas-
    ticsearch to use the inverted index for this filter.

 While a geo_point field can contain multiple geo-points, the
lat_lon optimization can be used only on fields that contain a
single geo-point.

geo_distance Filter

The geo_distance filter draws a circle around the specified location and finds all
documents that have a geo-point within that circle:

```
GET /attractions/restaurant/_search
{
  "query": {
    "filtered": {
      "filter": {
        "geo_distance": {
          "distance": "1km", ❶
          "location": { ❷
            "lat":  40.715,
            "lon": -73.988
          }
        }
      }
    }
  }
}
```

❶ Find all location fields within 1km of the specified point. See Distance Units
    (http://bit.ly/1ynS64j) for a list of the accepted units.

❷ The central point can be specified as a string, an array, or (as in this example) an object. See "Lat/Lon Formats" on page 513.

A geo-distance calculation is expensive. To optimize performance, Elasticsearch draws a box around the circle and first uses the less expensive bounding-box calculation to exclude as many documents as it can. It runs the geo-distance calculation on only those points that fall within the bounding box.

 Do your users really require an accurate circular filter to be applied to their results? Using a rectangular bounding box is much more efficient than geo-distance and will usually serve their purposes just as well.

Faster Geo-Distance Calculations

The distance between two points can be calculated using algorithms, which trade performance for accuracy:

arc

> The slowest but most accurate is the arc calculation, which treats the world as a sphere. Accuracy is still limited because the world isn't really a sphere.

plane

> The plane calculation, which treats the world as if it were flat, is faster but less accurate. It is most accurate at the equator and becomes less accurate toward the poles.

sloppy_arc

> So called because it uses the SloppyMath Lucene class to trade accuracy for speed, the sloppy_arc calculation uses the Haversine formula (*http://en.wikipedia.org/wiki/Haversine_formula*) to calculate distance. It is four to five times as fast as arc, and distances are 99.9% accurate. This is the default calculation.

You can specify a different calculation as follows:

```
GET /attractions/restaurant/_search
{
  "query": {
    "filtered": {
      "filter": {
        "geo_distance": {
          "distance":      "1km",
          "distance_type": "plane", ❶
          "location": {
            "lat":  40.715,
            "lon": -73.988
          }
```

```
              }
            }
          }
        }
      }
    }
```

❶ Use the faster but less accurate `plane` calculation.

 Will your users really care if a restaurant is a few meters outside their specified radius? While some geo applications require great accuracy, less-accurate but faster calculations will suit the majority of use cases just fine.

geo_distance_range Filter

The only difference between the `geo_distance` and `geo_distance_range` filters is that the latter has a doughnut shape and excludes documents within the central hole.

Instead of specifying a single `distance` from the center, you specify a minimum distance (with `gt` or `gte`) and maximum distance (with `lt` or `lte`), just like a `range` filter:

```
GET /attractions/restaurant/_search
{
  "query": {
    "filtered": {
      "filter": {
        "geo_distance_range": {
          "gte":    "1km", ❶
          "lt":     "2km", ❶
          "location": {
            "lat":  40.715,
            "lon": -73.988
          }
        }
      }
    }
  }
}
```

❶ Matches locations that are at least 1km from the center, and less than 2km from the center.

Caching geo-filters

The results of geo-filters are not cached by default, for two reasons:

- Geo-filters are usually used to find entities that are near to a user's current location. The problem is that users move, and no two users are in exactly the same location. A cached filter would have little chance of being reused.

- Filters are cached as bitsets that represent all documents in a segment. Imagine that our query excludes all documents but one in a particular segment. An uncached geo-filter just needs to check the one remaining document, but a cached geo-filter would need to check all of the documents in the segment.

That said, caching can be used to good effect with geo-filters. Imagine that your index contains restaurants from all over the United States. A user in New York is not interested in restaurants in San Francisco. We can treat New York as a *hot spot* and draw a big bounding box around the city and neighboring areas.

This `geo_bounding_box` filter can be cached and reused whenever we have a user within the city limits of New York. It will exclude all restaurants from the rest of the country. We can then use an uncached, more specific `geo_bounding_box` or `geo_dis tance` filter to narrow the remaining results to those that are close to the user:

```
GET /attractions/restaurant/_search
{
  "query": {
    "filtered": {
      "filter": {
        "bool": {
          "must": [
            {
              "geo_bounding_box": {
                "type": "indexed",
                "_cache": true, ❶
                "location": {
                  "top_left": {
                    "lat":  40,8,
                    "lon": -74.1
                  },
                  "bottom_right": {
                    "lat":  40.4,
                    "lon": -73.7
                  }
                }
              }
            },
            {
              "geo_distance": { ❷
                "distance": "1km",
                "location": {
                  "lat":  40.715,
                  "lon": -73.988
                }
              }
            }
```

```
            }
          ]
        }
       }
      }
     }
    }
   }
```

❶ The cached bounding box filter reduces all results down to those in the greater New York area.

❷ The more costly `geo_distance` filter narrows the results to those within 1km of the user.

Reducing Memory Usage

Each `lat/lon` pair requires 16 bytes of memory, memory that is in short supply. It needs this much memory in order to provide very accurate results. But as we have commented before, such exacting precision is seldom required.

You can reduce the amount of memory that is used by switching to a `compressed` fielddata format and by specifying how precise you need your geo-points to be. Even reducing precision to 1mm reduces memory usage by a third. A more realistic setting of 3m reduces usage by 62%, and 1km saves a massive 75%!

This setting can be changed on a live index with the `update-mapping` API:

```
POST /attractions/_mapping/restaurant
{
  "location": {
    "type": "geo_point",
    "fielddata": {
      "format":    "compressed",
      "precision": "1km" ❶
    }
  }
}
```

❶ Each `lat/lon` pair will require only 4 bytes, instead of 16.

Alternatively, you can avoid using memory for geo-points altogether, either by using the technique described in "Optimizing Bounding Boxes" on page 516, or by storing geo-points as doc values:

```
PUT /attractions
{
  "mappings": {
    "restaurant": {
      "properties": {
```

```
      "name": {
        "type": "string"
      },
      "location": {
        "type":        "geo_point",
        "doc_values": true ❶
      }
    }
  }
 }
}
```

❶ Geo-points will not be loaded into memory, but instead stored on disk.

Mapping a geo-point to use doc values can be done only when the field is first created. There is a small performance cost in using doc values instead of fielddata, but
with memory in such short supply, it is often worth doing.

Sorting by Distance

Search results can be sorted by distance from a point:

 While you *can* sort by distance, "Scoring by Distance" on page 524
is usually a better solution.

```
GET /attractions/restaurant/_search
{
  "query": {
    "filtered": {
      "filter": {
        "geo_bounding_box": {
          "type":        "indexed",
          "location": {
            "top_left": {
              "lat":  40,8,
              "lon": -74.0
            },
            "bottom_right": {
              "lat":  40.4,
              "lon": -73.0
            }
          }
        }
      }
    }
  },
  "sort": [
```

```
{
  "_geo_distance": {
    "location": {           ❶
      "lat":  40.715,
      "lon": -73.998
    },
    "order":        "asc",
    "unit":         "km",   ❷
    "distance_type": "plane" ❸
  }
}
]
}
```

❶ Calculate the distance between the specified lat/lon point and the geo-point in the location field of each document.

❷ Return the distance in km in the sort keys for each result.

❸ Use the faster but less accurate plane calculation.

You may ask yourself: why do we specify the distance unit? For sorting, it doesn't matter whether we compare distances in miles, kilometers, or light years. The reason is that the actual value used for sorting is returned with each result, in the sort element:

```
...
"hits": [
  {
    "_index": "attractions",
    "_type": "restaurant",
    "_id": "2",
    "_score": null,
    "_source": {
      "name": "New Malaysia",
      "location": {
        "lat": 40.715,
        "lon": -73.997
      }
    },
    "sort": [
      0.08425653647614346 ❶
    ]
  },
...
```

❶ This restaurant is 0.084km from the location we specified.

You can set the unit to return these values in whatever form makes sense for your application.

Geo-distance sorting can also handle multiple geo-points, both in the document and in the sort parameters. Use the sort_mode to specify whether it should use the min, max, or avg distance between each combination of locations. This can be used to return "friends nearest to my work and home locations."

Scoring by Distance

It may be that distance is the only important factor in deciding the order in which results are returned, but more frequently we need to combine distance with other factors, such as full-text relevance, popularity, and price.

In these situations, we should reach for the function_score query that allows us to blend all of these factors into an overall score. See "The Closer, The Better" on page 307 for an example that uses geo-distance to influence scoring.

The other drawback of sorting by distance is performance: the distance has to be calculated for all matching documents. The function_score query, on the other hand, can be executed during the rescore phase, limiting the number of calculations to just the top *n* results.

CHAPTER 37

Geohashes

Geohashes (*http://en.wikipedia.org/wiki/Geohash*) are a way of encoding lat/lon points as strings. The original intention was to have a URL-friendly way of specifying geolocations, but geohashes have turned out to be a useful way of indexing geo-points and geo-shapes in databases.

Geohashes divide the world into a grid of 32 cells—4 rows and 8 columns—each represented by a letter or number. The g cell covers half of Greenland, all of Iceland, and most of Great Britian. Each cell can be further divided into another 32 cells, which can be divided into another 32 cells, and so on. The gc cell covers Ireland and England, gcp covers most of London and part of Southern England, and gcpuuz94k is the entrance to Buckingham Palace, accurate to about 5 meters.

In other words, the longer the geohash string, the more accurate it is. If two geohashes share a prefix— and gcpuuz—then it implies that they are near each other. The longer the shared prefix, the closer they are.

That said, two locations that are right next to each other may have completely different geohashes. For instance, the Millenium Dome (*http://en.wikipedia.org/wiki/Millennium_Dome*) in London has geohash u10hbp, because it falls into the u cell, the next top-level cell to the east of the g cell.

Geo-points can index their associated geohashes automatically, but more important, they can also index all geohash *prefixes*. Indexing the location of the entrance to Buckingham Palace—latitude 51.501568 and longitude -0.141257—would index all of the geohashes listed in the following table, along with the approximate dimensions of each geohash cell:

Geohash	Level	Dimensions
g	1	~ 5,004km x 5,004km
gc	2	~ 1,251km x 625km
gcp	3	~ 156km x 156km
gcpu	4	~ 39km x 19.5km
gcpuu	5	~ 4.9km x 4.9km
gcpuuz	6	~ 1.2km x 0.61km
gcpuuz9	7	~ 152.8m x 152.8m
gcpuuz94	8	~ 38.2m x 19.1m
gcpuuz94k	9	~ 4.78m x 4.78m
gcpuuz94kk	10	~ 1.19m x 0.60m
gcpuuz94kkp	11	~ 14.9cm x 14.9cm
gcpuuz94kkp5	12	~ 3.7cm x 1.8cm

The geohash_cell filter (*http://bit.ly/1DIqyex*) can use these geohash prefixes to find locations near a specified lat/lon point.

Mapping Geohashes

The first step is to decide just how much precision you need. Although you could index all geo-points with the default full 12 levels of precision, do you really need to be accurate to within a few centimeters? You can save yourself a lot of space in the index by reducing your precision requirements to something more realistic, such as 1km:

```
PUT /attractions
{
  "mappings": {
    "restaurant": {
      "properties": {
        "name": {
          "type": "string"
        },
        "location": {
          "type":                    "geo_point",
```

```
            "geohash_prefix":    true, ❶
            "geohash_precision": "1km" ❷
          }
        }
      }
    }
  }
```

❶ Setting `geohash_prefix` to `true` tells Elasticsearch to index all geohash prefixes, up to the specified precision.

❷ The precision can be specified as an absolute number, representing the length of the geohash, or as a distance. A precision of `1km` corresponds to a geohash of length 7.

With this mapping in place, geohash prefixes of lengths 1 to 7 will be indexed, providing geohashes accurate to about 150 meters.

geohash_cell Filter

The `geohash_cell` filter simply translates a `lat/lon` location into a geohash with the specified precision and finds all locations that contain that geohash—a very efficient filter indeed.

```
GET /attractions/restaurant/_search
{
  "query": {
    "filtered": {
      "filter": {
        "geohash_cell": {
          "location": {
            "lat":  40.718,
            "lon": -73.983
          },
          "precision": "2km" ❶
        }
      }
    }
  }
}
```

❶ The `precision` cannot be more precise than that specified in the `geohash_preci sion` mapping.

This filter translates the `lat/lon` point into a geohash of the appropriate length—in this example `dr5rsk`—and looks for all locations that contain that exact term.

However, the filter as written in the preceding example may not return all restaurants within 5km of the specified point. Remember that a geohash is just a rectangle, and the point may fall anywhere within that rectangle. If the point happens to fall near the edge of a geohash cell, the filter may well exclude any restaurants in the adjacent cell.

To fix that, we can tell the filter to include the neigboring cells, by setting `neighbors` to `true`:

```
GET /attractions/restaurant/_search
{
  "query": {
    "filtered": {
      "filter": {
        "geohash_cell": {
          "location": {
            "lat":  40.718,
            "lon": -73.983
          },
          "neighbors": true, ❶
          "precision": "2km"
        }
      }
    }
  }
}
```

❶ This filter will look for the resolved geohash and all surrounding geohashes.

Clearly, looking for a geohash with precision 2km plus all the neighboring cells results in quite a large search area. This filter is not built for accuracy, but it is very efficient and can be used as a prefiltering step before applying a more accurate geo-filter.

 Specifying the `precision` as a distance can be misleading. A `precision` of 2km is converted to a geohash of length 6, which actually has dimensions of about 1.2km x 0.6km. You may find it more understandable to specify an actual length such as 5 or 6.

The other advantage that this filter has over a `geo_bounding_box` filter is that it supports multiple locations per field. The `lat_lon` option that we discussed in "Optimizing Bounding Boxes" on page 516 is efficient, but only when there is a single `lat`/`lon` point per field.

CHAPTER 38

Geo-aggregations

Although filtering or scoring results by geolocation is useful, it is often more useful to be able to present information to the user on a map. A search may return way too many results to be able to display each geo-point individually, but geo-aggregations can be used to cluster geo-points into more manageable buckets.

Three aggregations work with fields of type `geo_point`:

`geo_distance`
    Groups documents into concentric circles around a central point.

`geohash_grid`
    Groups documents by geohash cell, for display on a map.

`geo_bounds`
    Returns the `lat`/`lon` coordinates of a bounding box that would encompass all of the geo-points. This is useful for choosing the correct zoom level when displaying a map.

geo_distance Aggregation

The `geo_distance` agg is useful for searches such as to "find all pizza restaurants within 1km of me." The search results should, indeed, be limited to the 1km radius specified by the user, but we can add "another result found within 2km":

```
GET /attractions/restaurant/_search
{
  "query": {
    "filtered": {
      "query": {
        "match": {  ❶
          "name": "pizza"
```

```
        }
      },
      "filter": {
        "geo_bounding_box": {
          "location": { ❷
            "top_left": {
              "lat":  40,8,
              "lon": -74.1
            },
            "bottom_right": {
              "lat":  40.4,
              "lon": -73.7
            }
          }
        }
      }
    }
  },
  "aggs": {
    "per_ring": {
      "geo_distance": { ❸
        "field":    "location",
        "unit":     "km",
        "origin": {
          "lat":    40.712,
          "lon":    -73.988
        },
        "ranges": [
          { "from": 0, "to": 1 },
          { "from": 1, "to": 2 }
        ]
      }
    }
  },
  "post_filter": { ❹
    "geo_distance": {
      "distance":  "1km",
      "location": {
        "lat":    40.712,
        "lon":    -73.988
      }
    }
  }
}
```

❶ The main query looks for restaurants with `pizza` in the name.

❷ The bounding box filters these results down to just those in the greater New York area.

❸ The `geo_distance` agg counts the number of results within 1km of the user, and between 1km and 2km from the user.

❹ Finally, the `post_filter` reduces the search results to just those restaurants within 1km of the user.

The response from the preceding request is as follows:

```
"hits": {
  "total":      1,
  "max_score": 0.15342641,
  "hits": [ ❶
     {
        "_index": "attractions",
        "_type":  "restaurant",
        "_id":    "3",
        "_score": 0.15342641,
        "_source": {
           "name": "Mini Munchies Pizza",
           "location": [
              -73.983,
               40.719
           ]
        }
     }
  ]
},
"aggregations": {
  "per_ring": { ❷
     "buckets": [
        {
           "key":       "*-1.0",
           "from":       0,
           "to":         1,
           "doc_count": 1
        },
        {
           "key":       "1.0-2.0",
           "from":       1,
           "to":         2,
           "doc_count": 1
        }
     ]
  }
}
}
```

❶ The `post_filter` has reduced the search hits to just the single pizza restaurant within 1km of the user.

❷ The aggregation includes the search result plus the other pizza restaurant within 2km of the user.

In this example, we have counted the number of restaurants that fall into each concentric ring. Of course, we could nest subaggregations under the per_rings aggregation to calculate the average price per ring, the maximum popularity, and more.

geohash_grid Aggregation

The number of results returned by a query may be far too many to display each geopoint individually on a map. The geohash_grid aggregation buckets nearby geopoints together by calculating the geohash for each point, at the level of precision that you define.

The result is a grid of cells—one cell per geohash—that can be displayed on a map. By changing the precision of the geohash, you can summarize information across the whole world, by country, or by city block.

The aggregation is *sparse*—it returns only cells that contain documents. If your geohashes are too precise and too many buckets are generated, it will return, by default, the 10,000 most populous cells—those containing the most documents. However, it still needs to generate *all* the buckets in order to figure out which are the most populous 10,000. You need to control the number of buckets generated by doing the following:

1. Limit the result with a geo_bounding_box filter.

2. Choose an appropriate precision for the size of your bounding box.

```
GET /attractions/restaurant/_search?search_type=count
{
  "query": {
    "filtered": {
      "filter": {
        "geo_bounding_box": {
          "location": { ❶
            "top_left": {
              "lat":  40,8,
              "lon": -74.1
            },
            "bottom_right": {
              "lat":  40.4,
              "lon": -73.7
            }
          }
        }
      }
    }
  }
}
```

```
    },
  "aggs": {
    "new_york": {
      "geohash_grid": {  ❷
        "field":      "location",
        "precision": 5
      }
    }
  }
}
```

❶ The bounding box limits the scope of the search to the greater New York area.

❷ Geohashes of precision 5 are approximately 5km x 5km.

Geohashes with precision 5 measure about 25km^2 each, so 10,000 cells at this precision would cover 250,000km^2. The bounding box that we specified measures approximately 44km x 33km, or about 1,452km^2, so we are well within safe limits; we definitely won't create too many buckets in memory.

The response from the preceding request looks like this:

```
...
"aggregations": {
  "new_york": {
    "buckets": [  ❶
      {
        "key": "dr5rs",
        "doc_count": 2
      },
      {
        "key": "dr5re",
        "doc_count": 1
      }
    ]
  }
}
...
```

❶ Each bucket contains the geohash as the key.

Again, we didn't specify any subaggregations, so all we got back was the document count. We could have asked for popular restaurant types, average price, or other details.

To plot these buckets on a map, you need a library that understands how to convert a geohash into the equivalent bounding box or central point. Libraries exist in JavaScript and other languages that will perform this conversion for you, but you can also use information from "geo_bounds Aggregation" on page 534 to perform a similar job.

geo_bounds Aggregation

In our previous example, we filtered our results by using a bounding box that covered the greater New York area. However, our results were all located in downtown Manhattan. When displaying a map for our user, it makes sense to zoom into the area of the map that contains the data; there is no point in showing lots of empty space.

The geo_bounds aggregation does exactly this: it calculates the smallest bounding box that is needed to encapsulate all of the geo-points:

```
GET /attractions/restaurant/_search?search_type=count
{
  "query": {
    "filtered": {
      "filter": {
        "geo_bounding_box": {
          "location": {
            "top_left": {
              "lat":  40,8,
              "lon": -74.1
            },
            "bottom_right": {
              "lat":  40.4,
              "lon": -73.9
            }
          }
        }
      }
    }
  },
  "aggs": {
    "new_york": {
      "geohash_grid": {
        "field":     "location",
        "precision": 5
      }
    },
    "map_zoom": {  ❶
      "geo_bounds": {
        "field":     "location"
      }
    }
  }
```

```
    }
  }
```

❶ The geo_bounds aggregation will calculate the smallest bounding box required to encapsulate all of the documents matching our query.

The response now includes a bounding box that we can use to zoom our map:

```
...
"aggregations": {
  "map_zoom": {
    "bounds": {
      "top_left": {
        "lat":  40.722,
        "lon": -74.011
      },
      "bottom_right": {
        "lat":  40.715,
        "lon": -73.983
      }
    }
  }
},
...
```

In fact, we could even use the geo_bounds aggregation inside each geohash cell, in case the geo-points inside a cell are clustered in just a part of the cell:

```
GET /attractions/restaurant/_search?search_type=count
{
  "query": {
    "filtered": {
      "filter": {
        "geo_bounding_box": {
          "location": {
            "top_left": {
              "lat":  40,8,
              "lon": -74.1
            },
            "bottom_right": {
              "lat":  40.4,
              "lon": -73.9
            }
          }
        }
      }
    }
  },
  "aggs": {
    "new_york": {
      "geohash_grid": {
        "field":     "location",
        "precision": 5
      },
```

```
      "aggs": {
        "cell": {  ❶
          "geo_bounds": {
            "field": "location"
          }
        }
      }
    }
  }
}
```

❶ The cell_bounds subaggregation is calculated for every geohash cell.

Now the points in each cell have a bounding box:

```
...
"aggregations": {
  "new_york": {
    "buckets": [
      {
        "key": "dr5rs",
        "doc_count": 2,
        "cell": {
          "bounds": {
            "top_left": {
              "lat":  40.722,
              "lon": -73.989
            },
            "bottom_right": {
              "lat":  40.719,
              "lon": -73.983
            }
          }
        }
      },
...
```

CHAPTER 39

Geo-shapes

Geo-shapes use a completely different approach than geo-points. A circle on a computer screen does not consist of a perfect continuous line. Instead it is drawn by coloring adjacent pixels as an approximation of a circle. Geo-shapes work in much the same way.

Complex shapes—such as points, lines, polygons, multipolygons, and polygons with holes,--are "painted" onto a grid of geohash cells, and the shape is converted into a list of the geohashes of all the cells that it touches.

 Actually, two types of grids can be used with geo-shapes: geohashes, which we have already discussed and which are the default encoding, and *quad trees*. Quad trees are similar to geohashes except that there are only four cells at each level, instead of 32. The difference comes down to a choice of encoding.

All of the geohashes that compose a shape are indexed as if they were terms. With this information in the index, it is easy to determine whether one shape intersects with another, as they will share the same geohash terms.

That is the extent of what you can do with geo-shapes: determine the relationship between a query shape and a shape in the index. The `relation` can be one of the following:

`intersects`
  The query shape overlaps with the indexed shape (default).

`disjoint`
  The query shape does *not* overlap at all with the indexed shape.

within
> The indexed shape is entirely within the query shape.

Geo-shapes cannot be used to caculate distance, cannot be used for sorting or scoring, and cannot be used in aggregations.

Mapping geo-shapes

Like fields of type `geo_point`, geo-shapes have to be mapped explicitly before they can be used:

```
PUT /attractions
{
  "mappings": {
    "landmark": {
      "properties": {
        "name": {
          "type": "string"
        },
        "location": {
          "type": "geo_shape"
        }
      }
    }
  }
}
```

There are two important settings that you should consider changing `precision` and `distance_error_pct`.

precision

The `precision` parameter controls the maximum length of the geohashes that are generated. It defaults to a precision of 9, which equates to a geohash with dimensions of about 5m x 5m. That is probably far more precise than you need.

The lower the precision, the fewer terms that will be indexed and the faster the search will be. But of course, the lower the precision, the less accurate are your geo-shapes. Consider just how accurate you need your shapes to be—even one or two levels of precision can represent a significant savings.

You can specify precisions by using distances—for example, `50m` or `2km`—but ultimately these distances are converted to the same levels as described in Chapter 37.

distance_error_pct

When indexing a polygon, the big central continuous part can be represented cheaply by a short geohash. It is the edges that matter. Edges require much smaller geohashes to represent them with any accuracy.

If you're indexing a small landmark, you want the edges to be quite accurate. It wouldn't be good to have one monument overlapping with the next. When indexing an entire country, you don't need quite as much precision. Fifty meters here or there isn't likely to start any wars.

The distance_error_pct specifies the maximum allowable error based on the size of the shape. It defaults to 0.025, or 2.5%. In other words, big shapes (like countries) are allowed to have fuzzier edges than small shapes (like monuments).

The default of 0.025 is a good starting point, but the more error that is allowed, the fewer terms that are required to index a shape.

Indexing geo-shapes

Shapes are represented using GeoJSON (*http://geojson.org/*), a simple open standard for encoding two-dimensional shapes in JSON. Each shape definition contains the type of shape—point, line, polygon, envelope,—and one or more arrays of longitude/latitude points.

In GeoJSON, coordinates are always written as *longitude* followed by *latitude.*

For instance, we can index a polygon representing Dam Square in Amsterdam as follows:

```
PUT /attractions/landmark/dam_square
{
    "name" : "Dam Square, Amsterdam",
    "location" : {
        "type" : "polygon",        ❶
        "coordinates" : [[          ❷
          [ 4.89218, 52.37356 ],
          [ 4.89205, 52.37276 ],
          [ 4.89301, 52.37274 ],
          [ 4.89392, 52.37250 ],
          [ 4.89431, 52.37287 ],
          [ 4.89331, 52.37346 ],
          [ 4.89305, 52.37326 ],
          [ 4.89218, 52.37356 ]
```

```
      ]]
    }
  }
```

❶ The type parameter indicates the type of shape that the coordinates represent.

❷ The list of lon/lat points that describe the polygon.

The excess of square brackets in the example may look confusing, but the GeoJSON syntax is quite simple:

1. Each lon/lat point is represented as an array:

   ```
   [lon,lat]
   ```

2. A list of points is wrapped in an array to represent a polygon:

   ```
   [[lon,lat],[lon,lat], ... ]
   ```

3. A shape of type polygon can optionally contain several polygons; the first represents the polygon proper, while any subsequent polygons represent holes in the first:

   ```
   [
     [[lon,lat],[lon,lat], ... ],  # main polygon
     [[lon,lat],[lon,lat], ... ],  # hole in main polygon
     ...
   ]
   ```

See the Geo-shape mapping documentation (*http://bit.ly/1G2nMCT*) for more details about the supported shapes.

Querying geo-shapes

The unusual thing about the geo_shape query (*http://bit.ly/1AjFrxE*) and geo_shape filter (*http://bit.ly/1G2ocsZ*) is that they allow us to query using shapes, rather than just points.

For instance, if our user steps out of the central train station in Amsterdam, we could find all landmarks within a 1km radius with a query like this:

```
GET /attractions/landmark/_search
{
  "query": {
    "geo_shape": {
      "location": {  ❶
        "shape": {  ❷
          "type":    "circle",  ❸
          "radius": "1km"
          "coordinates": [  ❹
            4.89994,
```

```
                52.37815
            ]
          }
        }
      }
    }
  }
}
```

❶ The query looks at geo-shapes in the `location` field.

❷ The `shape` key indicates that the shape is specified inline in the query.

❸ The shape is a circle, with a radius of 1km.

❹ This point is situated at the entrance of the central train station in Amsterdam.

By default, the query (or filter—do the same job) looks for indexed shapes that intersect with the query shape. The `relation` parameter can be set to `disjoint` to find indexed shapes that don't intersect with the query shape, or `within` to find indexed shapes that are completely contained by the query shape.

For instance, we could find all landmarks in the center of Amsterdam with this query:

```
GET /attractions/landmark/_search
{
  "query": {
    "geo_shape": {
      "location": {
        "relation": "within", ❶
        "shape": {
          "type": "polygon",
          "coordinates": [[ ❷
              [4.88330,52.38617],
              [4.87463,52.37254],
              [4.87875,52.36369],
              [4.88939,52.35850],
              [4.89840,52.35755],
              [4.91909,52.36217],
              [4.92656,52.36594],
              [4.93368,52.36615],
              [4.93342,52.37275],
              [4.92690,52.37632],
              [4.88330,52.38617]
          ]]
        }
      }
    }
  }
}
```

❶ Match only indexed shapes that are completely within the query shape.

❷ This polygon represents the center of Amsterdam.

Querying with Indexed Shapes

With shapes that are often used in queries, it can be more convenient to store them in the index and to refer to them by name in the query. Take our example of central Amsterdam in the previous example. We could store it as a document of type `neighborhood`.

First, we set up the mapping in the same way as we did for `landmark`:

```
PUT /attractions/_mapping/neighborhood
{
  "properties": {
    "name": {
      "type": "string"
    },
    "location": {
      "type": "geo_shape"
    }
  }
}
```

Then we can index a shape for central Amsterdam:

```
PUT /attractions/neighborhood/central_amsterdam
{
  "name" : "Central Amsterdam",
  "location" : {
      "type" : "polygon",
      "coordinates" : [[
        [4.88330,52.38617],
        [4.87463,52.37254],
        [4.87875,52.36369],
        [4.88939,52.35850],
        [4.89840,52.35755],
        [4.91909,52.36217],
        [4.92656,52.36594],
        [4.93368,52.36615],
        [4.93342,52.37275],
        [4.92690,52.37632],
        [4.88330,52.38617]
      ]]
  }
}
```

After the shape is indexed, we can refer to it by `index`, `type`, and `id` in the query itself:

```
GET /attractions/landmark/_search
{
  "query": {
    "geo_shape": {
      "location": {
        "relation": "within",
        "indexed_shape": {  ❶
          "index": "attractions",
          "type":  "neighborhood",
          "id":    "central_amsterdam",
          "path":  "location"
        }
      }
    }
  }
}
```

❶ By specifying indexed_shape instead of shape, Elasticsearch knows that it needs
   to retrieve the query shape from the specified document and path.

There is nothing special about the shape for central Amsterdam. We could equally
use our existing shape for Dam Square in queries. This query finds neighborhoods
that intersect with Dam Square:

```
GET /attractions/neighborhood/_search
{
  "query": {
    "geo_shape": {
      "location": {
        "indexed_shape": {
          "index": "attractions",
          "type":  "landmark",
          "id":    "dam_square",
          "path":  "location"
        }
      }
    }
  }
}
```

Geo-shape Filters and Caching

The geo_shape query and filter perform the same function. The query simply acts as
a filter: any matching documents receive a relevance _score of 1. Query results cannot be cached, but filter results can be.

The results are not cached by default. Just as with geo-points, any change in the coordinates in a shape are likely to produce a different set of geohashes, so there is little
point in caching filter results. That said, if you filter using the same shapes repeatedly,
it can be worth caching the results, by setting _cache to true:

```
GET /attractions/neighborhood/_search
{
  "query": {
    "filtered": {
      "filter": {
        "geo_shape": {
          "_cache": true, ❶
          "location": {
            "indexed_shape": {
              "index": "attractions",
              "type":  "landmark",
              "id":    "dam_square",
              "path":  "location"
            }
          }
        }
      }
    }
  }
}
```

❶ The results of this geo_shape filter will be cached.

PART VI

Modeling Your Data

Elasticsearch is a different kind of beast, especially if you come from the world of SQL. It comes with many benefits: performance, scale, near real-time search, and analytics across massive amounts of data. And it is easy to get going! Just download and start using it.

But it is not magic. To get the most out of Elasticsearch, you need to understand how it works and how to make it work for your needs.

Handling relationships between entities is not as obvious as it is with a dedicated relational store. The golden rule of a relational database—normalize your data—does not apply to Elasticsearch. In Chapter 40, Chapter 41, and Chapter 42 we discuss the pros and cons of the available approaches.

Then in Chapter 43 we talk about the features that Elasticsearch offers that enable you to scale out quickly and flexibly. Scale is not one-size-fits-all. You need to think about how data flows through your system, and design your model accordingly. Time-based data like log events or social network streams require a very different approach than more static collections of documents.

And finally, we talk about the one thing in Elasticsearch that doesn't scale.

CHAPTER 40

Handling Relationships

In the real world, relationships matter: blog posts have comments, bank accounts have transactions, customers have bank accounts, orders have order lines, and directories have files and subdirectories.

Relational databases are specifically designed—and this will not come as a surprise to you—to manage relationships:

- Each entity (or *row*, in the relational world) can be uniquely identified by a *primary key*.

- Entities are *normalized*. The data for a unique entity is stored only once, and related entities store just its primary key. Changing the data of an entity has to happen in only one place.

- Entities can be joined at query time, allowing for cross-entity search.

- Changes to a single entity are *atomic, consistent, isolated,* and *durable.* (See *ACID Transactions* (*http://en.wikipedia.org/wiki/ACID_transactions*) for more on this subject.)

- Most relational databases support ACID transactions across multiple entities.

But relational databases do have their limitations, besides their poor support for full-text search. Joining entities at query time is expensive—more joins that are required, the more expensive the query. Performing joins between entities that live on different hardware is so expensive that it is just not practical. This places a limit on the amount of data that can be stored on a single server.

Elasticsearch, like most NoSQL databases, treats the world as though it were flat. An index is a flat collection of independent documents. A single document should contain all of the information that is required to decide whether it matches a search request.

While changing the data of a single document in Elasticsearch is ACIDic (*http:// en.wikipedia.org/wiki/ACID_transactions*), transactions involving multiple documents are not. There is no way to roll back the index to its previous state if part of a transaction fails.

This FlatWorld has its advantages:

- Indexing is fast and lock-free.
- Searching is fast and lock-free.
- Massive amounts of data can be spread across multiple nodes, because each document is independent of the others.

But relationships matter. Somehow, we need to bridge the gap between FlatWorld and the real world. Four common techniques are used to manage relational data in Elasticsearch:

- Application-side joins
- Data denormalization
- Nested objects
- Parent/child relationships

Often the final solution will require a mixture of a few of these techniques.

Application-side Joins

We can (partly) emulate a relational database by implementing joins in our application. For instance, let's say we are indexing users and their blog posts. In the relational world, we would do something like this:

```
PUT /my_index/user/1 ❶
{
  "name":     "John Smith",
  "email":    "john@smith.com",
  "dob":      "1970/10/24"
}

PUT /my_index/blogpost/2 ❶
{
  "title":    "Relationships",
  "body":     "It's complicated...",
  "user":     1 ❷
}
```

❶ The index, type, and id of each document together function as a primary key.

❷ The blogpost links to the user by storing the user's id. The index and type aren't required as they are hardcoded in our application.

Finding blog posts by user with ID 1 is easy:

```
GET /my_index/blogpost/_search
{
  "query": {
    "filtered": {
      "filter": {
        "term": { "user": 1 }
      }
    }
  }
}
```

To find blogposts by a user called John, we would need to run two queries: the first would look up all users called John in order to find their IDs, and the second would pass those IDs in a query similar to the preceding one:

```
GET /my_index/user/_search
{
  "query": {
    "match": {
      "name": "John"
    }
  }
}

GET /my_index/blogpost/_search
{
  "query": {
    "filtered": {
      "filter": {
        "terms": { "user": [1] }  ❶
      }
    }
  }
}
```

❶ The values in the terms filter would be populated with the results from the first query.

The main advantage of application-side joins is that the data is normalized. Changing the user's name has to happen in only one place: the user document. The disadvantage is that you have to run extra queries in order to join documents at search time.

In this example, there was only one user who matched our first query, but in the real world we could easily have millions of users named John. Including all of their IDs in the second query would make for a very large query, and one that has to do millions of term lookups.

This approach is suitable when the first entity (the user in this example) has a small number of documents and, preferably, they seldom change. This would allow the application to cache the results and avoid running the first query often.

Denormalizing Your Data

The way to get the best search performance out of Elasticsearch is to use it as it is intended, by denormalizing (*http://en.wikipedia.org/wiki/Denormalization*) your data at index time. Having redundant copies of data in each document that requires access to it removes the need for joins.

If we want to be able to find a blog post by the name of the user who wrote it, include the user's name in the blog-post document itself:

```
PUT /my_index/user/1
{
  "name":     "John Smith",
  "email":    "john@smith.com",
  "dob":      "1970/10/24"
}

PUT /my_index/blogpost/2
{
  "title":    "Relationships",
  "body":     "It's complicated...",
  "user":     {
    "id":       1,
    "name":     "John Smith" ❶
  }
}
```

❶ Part of the user's data has been denormalized into the blogpost document.

Now, we can find blog posts about relationships by users called John with a single query:

```
GET /my_index/blogpost/_search
{
  "query": {
    "bool": {
      "must": [
        { "match": { "title":     "relationships" }},
        { "match": { "user.name": "John"           }}
      ]
    }
  }
}
```

The advantage of data denormalization is speed. Because each document contains all of the information that is required to determine whether it matches the query, there is no need for expensive joins.

Field Collapsing

A common requirement is the need to present search results grouped by a particular field. We might want to return the most relevant blog posts *grouped* by the user's name. Grouping by name implies the need for a `terms` aggregation. To be able to group on the user's *whole* name, the name field should be available in its original `not_analyzed` form, as explained in "Aggregations and Analysis" on page 485:

```
PUT /my_index/_mapping/blogpost
{
  "properties": {
    "user": {
      "properties": {
        "name": {  ❶
          "type": "string",
          "fields": {
            "raw": {  ❷
              "type":  "string",
              "index": "not_analyzed"
            }
          }
        }
      }
    }
  }
}
```

❶ The user.name field will be used for full-text search.

❷ The user.name.raw field will be used for grouping with the terms aggregation.

Then add some data:

```
PUT /my_index/user/1
{
  "name": "John Smith",
  "email": "john@smith.com",
  "dob": "1970/10/24"
}

PUT /my_index/blogpost/2
{
  "title": "Relationships",
  "body": "It's complicated...",
  "user": {
    "id": 1,
```

```
      "name": "John Smith"
    }
  }

PUT /my_index/user/3
{
  "name": "Alice John",
  "email": "alice@john.com",
  "dob": "1979/01/04"
}

PUT /my_index/blogpost/4
{
  "title": "Relationships are cool",
  "body": "It's not complicated at all...",
  "user": {
    "id": 3,
    "name": "Alice John"
  }
}
```

Now we can run a query looking for blog posts about `relationships`, by users called John, and group the results by user, thanks to the `top_hits` aggregation (*http://bit.ly/1CrlWFQ*):

```
GET /my_index/blogpost/_search?search_type=count ❶
{
  "query": { ❷
    "bool": {
      "must": [
        { "match": { "title":      "relationships" }},
        { "match": { "user.name": "John"            }}
      ]
    }
  },
  "aggs": {
    "users": {
      "terms": {
        "field":    "user.name.raw",          ❸
        "order": { "top_score": "desc" } ❹
      },
      "aggs": {
        "top_score": { "max":      { "script":  "_score"        }}, ❹
        "blogposts": { "top_hits": { "_source": "title", "size": 5 }} ❺
      }
    }
  }
}
```

❶ The blog posts that we are interested in are returned under the blogposts aggregation, so we can disable the usual search hits by setting the search_type=count.

❷ The query returns blog posts about relationships by users named John.

❸ The terms aggregation creates a bucket for each user.name.raw value.

❹ The top_score aggregation orders the terms in the users aggregation by the top-scoring document in each bucket.

❺ The top_hits aggregation returns just the title field of the five most relevant blog posts for each user.

The abbreviated response is shown here:

```
...
"hits": {
   "total":      2,
   "max_score": 0,
   "hits":       []  ❶
},
"aggregations": {
   "users": {
      "buckets": [
         {
            "key":         "John Smith",  ❷
            "doc_count": 1,
            "blogposts": {
               "hits": {  ❸
                  "total":      1,
                  "max_score": 0.35258877,
                  "hits": [
                     {
                        "_index": "my_index",
                        "_type":   "blogpost",
                        "_id":     "2",
                        "_score": 0.35258877,
                        "_source": {
                           "title": "Relationships"
                        }
                     }
                  ]
               }
            },
            "top_score": {  ❹
               "value": 0.3525887727737427
            }
         },
         ...
```

❶ The hits array is empty because we set `search_type=count`.

❷ There is a bucket for each user who appeared in the top results.

❸ Under each user bucket there is a `blogposts.hits` array containing the top results for that user.

❹ The user buckets are sorted by the user's most relevant blog post.

Using the `top_hits` aggregation is the equivalent of running a query to return the names of the users with the most relevant blog posts, and then running the same query for each user, to get their best blog posts. But it is much more efficient.

The top hits returned in each bucket are the result of running a light *mini-query* based on the original main query. The mini-query supports the usual features that you would expect from search such as highlighting and pagination.

Denormalization and Concurrency

Of course, data denormalization has downsides too. The first disadvantage is that the index will be bigger because the `_source` document for every blog post is bigger, and there are more indexed fields. This usually isn't a huge problem. The data written to disk is highly compressed, and disk space is cheap. Elasticsearch can happily cope with the extra data.

The more important issue is that, if the user were to change his name, all of his blog posts would need to be updated too. Fortunately, users don't often change names. Even if they did, it is unlikely that a user would have written more than a few thousand blog posts, so updating blog posts with the `scroll` and `bulk` APIs would take less than a second.

However, let's consider a more complex scenario in which changes are common, far reaching, and, most important, concurrent.

In this example, we are going to emulate a filesystem with directory trees in Elasticsearch, much like a filesystem on Linux: the root of the directory is /, and each directory can contain files and subdirectories.

We want to be able to search for files that live in a particular directory, the equivalent of this:

```
grep "some text" /clinton/projects/elasticsearch/*
```

This requires us to index the path of the directory where the file lives:

```
PUT /fs/file/1
{
  "name":      "README.txt", ❶
```

```
    "path":     "/clinton/projects/elasticsearch",  ❷
    "contents": "Starting a new Elasticsearch project is easy..."
}
```

❶ The filename

❷ The full path to the directory holding the file

 Really, we should also index directory documents so we can list all
files and subdirectories within a directory, but for brevity's sake, we
will ignore that requirement.

We also want to be able to search for files that live anywhere in the directory tree
below a particular directory, the equivalent of this:

```
grep -r "some text" /clinton
```

To support this, we need to index the path hierarchy:

- /clinton
- /clinton/projects
- /clinton/projects/elasticsearch

This hierarchy can be generated automatically from the path field using the
path_hierarchy tokenizer (*http://bit.ly/1AjGltZ*):

```
PUT /fs
{
  "settings": {
    "analysis": {
      "analyzer": {
        "paths": {  ❶
          "tokenizer": "path_hierarchy"
        }
      }
    }
  }
}
```

❶ The custom paths analyzer uses the path_hierarchy tokenizer with its default
settings. See path_hierarchy tokenizer (*http://bit.ly/1AjGltZ*).

The mapping for the file type would look like this:

```
PUT /fs/_mapping/file
{
  "properties": {
```

```
    "name": { ❶
      "type":  "string",
      "index": "not_analyzed"
    },
    "path": { ❷
      "type":  "string",
      "index": "not_analyzed",
      "fields": {
        "tree": { ❷
          "type":     "string",
          "analyzer": "paths"
        }
      }
    }
  }
}
}
```

❶ The name field will contain the exact name.

❷ The path field will contain the exact directory name, while the path.tree field
will contain the path hierarchy.

Once the index is set up and the files have been indexed, we can perform a search for
files containing elasticsearch in just the /clinton/projects/elasticsearch
directory like this:

```
GET /fs/file/_search
{
  "query": {
    "filtered": {
      "query": {
        "match": {
          "contents": "elasticsearch"
        }
      },
      "filter": {
        "term": { ❶
          "path": "/clinton/projects/elasticsearch"
        }
      }
    }
  }
}
```

❶ Find files in this directory only.

Every file that lives in any subdirectory under /clinton will include the term /clin
ton in the path.tree field. So we can search for all files in any subdirectory of /clin
ton as follows:

```
GET /fs/file/_search
{
  "query": {
    "filtered": {
      "query": {
        "match": {
          "contents": "elasticsearch"
        }
      },
      "filter": {
        "term": { ❶
          "path.tree": "/clinton"
        }
      }
    }
  }
}
```

❶ Find files in this directory or in any of its subdirectories.

Renaming Files and Directories

So far, so good. Renaming a file is easy—a simple `update` or `index` request is all that is
required. You can even use optimistic concurrency control to ensure that your change
doesn't conflict with the changes from another user:

```
PUT /fs/file/1?version=2 ❶
{
  "name":     "README.asciidoc",
  "path":     "/clinton/projects/elasticsearch",
  "contents": "Starting a new Elasticsearch project is easy..."
}
```

❶ The `version` number ensures that the change is applied only if the document in
the index has this same version number.

We can even rename a directory, but this means updating all of the files that exist
anywhere in the path hierarchy beneath that directory. This may be quick or slow,
depending on how many files need to be updated. All we would need to do is to use
scan-and-scroll to retrieve all the files, and the `bulk` API to update them. The process
isn't atomic, but all files will quickly move to their new home.

Solving Concurrency Issues

The problem comes when we want to allow more than one person to rename files or
directories *at the same time*. Imagine that you rename the `/clinton` directory, which
contains hundreds of thousands of files. Meanwhile, another user renames the single

file `/clinton/projects/elasticsearch/README.txt`. That user's change, although it started after yours, will probably finish more quickly.

One of two things will happen:

- You have decided to use `version` numbers, in which case your mass rename will fail with a version conflict when it hits the renamed `README.asciidoc` file.
- You didn't use versioning, and your changes will overwrite the changes from the other user.

The problem is that Elasticsearch does not support ACID transactions (*http://en.wiki pedia.org/wiki/ACID_transactions*). Changes to individual documents are ACIDic, but not changes involving multiple documents.

If your main data store is a relational database, and Elasticsearch is simply being used as a search engine or as a way to improve performance, make your changes in the database first and replicate those changes to Elasticsearch after they have succeeded. This way, you benefit from the ACID transactions available in the database, and all changes to Elasticsearch happen in the right order. Concurrency is dealt with in the relational database.

If you are not using a relational store, these concurrency issues need to be dealt with at the Elasticsearch level. The following are three practical solutions using Elastic-search, all of which involve some form of locking:

- Global Locking
- Document Locking
- Tree Locking

 The solutions described in this section could also be implemented by applying the same principles while using an external system instead of Elasticsearch.

Global Locking

We can avoid concurrency issues completely by allowing only one process to make changes at any time. Most changes will involve only a few files and will complete very quickly. A rename of a top-level directory may block all other changes for longer, but these are likely to be much less frequent.

Because document-level changes in Elasticsearch are ACIDic, we can use the existence or absence of a document as a global lock. To request a lock, we try to `create` the global-lock document:

```
PUT /fs/lock/global/_create
{}
```

If this `create` request fails with a conflict exception, another process has already been granted the global lock and we will have to try again later. If it succeeds, we are now the proud owners of the global lock and we can continue with our changes. Once we are finished, we must release the lock by deleting the global lock document:

```
DELETE /fs/lock/global
```

Depending on how frequent changes are, and how long they take, a global lock could restrict the performance of a system significantly. We can increase parallelism by making our locking more fine-grained.

Document Locking

Instead of locking the whole filesystem, we could lock individual documents by using the same technique as previously described. A process could use a scan-and-scroll request to retrieve the IDs of all documents that would be affected by the change, and would need to create a lock file for each of them:

```
PUT /fs/lock/_bulk
{ "create": { "_id": 1}}   ❶
{ "process_id": 123     }  ❷
{ "create": { "_id": 2}}
{ "process_id": 123     }
...
```

❶ The ID of the `lock` document would be the same as the ID of the file that should be locked.

❷ The `process_id` is a unique ID that represents the process that wants to perform the changes.

If some files are already locked, parts of the `bulk` request will fail and we will have to try again.

Of course, if we try to lock *all* of the files again, the `create` statements that we used previously will fail for any file that is already locked by us! Instead of a simple `create` statement, we need an `update` request with an `upsert` parameter and this `script`:

```
if ( ctx._source.process_id != process_id ) {   ❶
  assert false;   ❷
}
ctx.op = 'noop';   ❸
```

❶ `process_id` is a parameter that we pass into the script.

❷ `assert false` will throw an exception, causing the update to fail.

❸ Changing the op from `update` to `noop` prevents the update request from making any changes, but still returns success.

The full `update` request looks like this:

```
POST /fs/lock/1/_update
{
  "upsert": { "process_id": 123 },
  "script": "if ( ctx._source.process_id != process_id )
  { assert false }; ctx.op = 'noop';"
  "params": {
    "process_id": 123
  }
}
```

If the document doesn't already exist, the `upsert` document will be inserted—much the same as the `create` request we used previously. However, if the document *does* exist, the script will look at the `process_id` stored in the document. If it is the same as ours, it aborts the update (`noop`) and returns success. If it is different, the `assert false` throws an exception and we know that the lock has failed.

Once all locks have been successfully created, the rename operation can begin. Afterward, we must release all of the locks, which we can do with a `delete-by-query` request:

```
POST /fs/_refresh ❶

DELETE /fs/lock/_query
{
  "query": {
    "term": {
      "process_id": 123
    }
  }
}
```

❶ The `refresh` call ensures that all `lock` documents are visible to the `delete-by-query` request.

Document-level locking enables fine-grained access control, but creating lock files for millions of documents can be expensive. In certain scenarios, such as this example with directory trees, it is possible to achieve fine-grained locking with much less work.

Tree Locking

Rather than locking every involved document, as in the previous option, we could lock just part of the directory tree. We will need exclusive access to the file or directory that we want to rename, which can be achieved with an *exclusive lock* document:

```
{ "lock_type": "exclusive" }
```

And we need shared locks on any parent directories, with a *shared lock* document:

```
{
  "lock_type":  "shared",
  "lock_count": 1 ❶
}
```

❶ The lock_count records the number of processes that hold a shared lock.

A process that wants to rename /clinton/projects/elasticsearch/README.txt needs an *exclusive* lock on that file, and a *shared* lock on /clinton, /clinton/projects, and /clinton/projects/elasticsearch.

A simple create request will suffice for the exclusive lock, but the shared lock needs a scripted update to implement some extra logic:

```
if (ctx._source.lock_type == 'exclusive') {
  assert false; ❶
}
ctx._source.lock_count++ ❷
```

❶ If the lock_type is exclusive, the assert statement will throw an exception, causing the update request to fail.

❷ Otherwise, we increment the lock_count.

This script handles the case where the lock document already exists, but we will also need an upsert document to handle the case where it doesn't exist yet. The full update request is as follows:

```
POST /fs/lock/%2Fclinton/_update ❶
{
  "upsert": { ❷
    "lock_type":  "shared",
    "lock_count": 1
  },
  "script": "if (ctx._source.lock_type == 'exclusive')
  { assert false }; ctx._source.lock_count++"
}
```

❶ The ID of the document is /clinton, which is URL-encoded to %2fclinton.

❷ The upsert document will be inserted if the document does not already exist.

Once we succeed in gaining a shared lock on all of the parent directories, we try to create an exclusive lock on the file itself:

```
PUT /fs/lock/%2Fclinton%2fprojects%2felasticsearch%2fREADME.txt/_create
{ "lock_type": "exclusive" }
```

Now, if somebody else wants to rename the /clinton directory, they would have to gain an exclusive lock on that path:

```
PUT /fs/lock/%2Fclinton/_create
{ "lock_type": "exclusive" }
```

This request would fail because a lock document with the same ID already exists. The other user would have to wait until our operation is done and we have released our locks. The exclusive lock can just be deleted:

```
DELETE /fs/lock/%2Fclinton%2fprojects%2felasticsearch%2fREADME.txt
```

The shared locks need another script that decrements the lock_count and, if the count drops to zero, deletes the lock document:

```
if (--ctx._source.lock_count == 0) {
  ctx.op = 'delete' ❶
}
```

❶ Once the lock_count reaches 0, the ctx.op is changed from update to delete.

This update request would need to be run for each parent directory in reverse order, from longest to shortest:

```
POST /fs/lock/%2Fclinton%2fprojects%2felasticsearch/_update
{
  "script": "if (--ctx._source.lock_count == 0) { ctx.op = 'delete' } "
}
```

Tree locking gives us fine-grained concurrency control with the minimum of effort. Of course, it is not applicable to every situation—the data model must have some sort of access path like the directory tree for it to work.

None of the three options—global, document, or tree locking—deals with the thorniest problem associated with locking: what happens if the process holding the lock dies?

The unexpected death of a process leaves us with two problems:

- How do we know that we can release the locks held by the dead process?

- How do we clean up the change that the dead process did not manage to complete?

These topics are beyond the scope of this book, but you will need to give them some thought if you decide to use locking.

While denormalization is a good choice for many projects, the need for locking schemes can make for complicated implementations. Instead, Elasticsearch provides two models that help us deal with related entities: *nested objects* and *parent-child relationships*.

CHAPTER 41

Nested Objects

Given the fact that creating, deleting, and updating a single document in Elasticsearch is atomic, it makes sense to store closely related entities within the same document. For instance, we could store an order and all of its order lines in one document, or we could store a blog post and all of its comments together, by passing an array of `com ments`:

```
PUT /my_index/blogpost/1
{
  "title": "Nest eggs",
  "body":  "Making your money work...",
  "tags":  [ "cash", "shares" ],
  "comments": [ ❶
    {
      "name":    "John Smith",
      "comment": "Great article",
      "age":     28,
      "stars":   4,
      "date":    "2014-09-01"
    },
    {
      "name":    "Alice White",
      "comment": "More like this please",
      "age":     31,
      "stars":   5,
      "date":    "2014-10-22"
    }
  ]
}
```

❶ If we rely on dynamic mapping, the `comments` field will be autocreated as an `object` field.

Because all of the content is in the same document, there is no need to join blog posts and comments at query time, so searches perform well.

The problem is that the preceding document would match a query like this:

```
GET /_search
{
  "query": {
    "bool": {
      "must": [
        { "match": { "name": "Alice" }},
        { "match": { "age":  28       }} ❶
      ]
    }
  }
}
```

❶ Alice is 31, not 28!

The reason for this cross-object matching, as discussed in "Arrays of Inner Objects" on page 97, is that our beautifully structured JSON document is flattened into a simple key-value format in the index that looks like this:

```
{
  "title":           [ eggs, nest ],
  "body":            [ making, money, work, your ],
  "tags":            [ cash, shares ],
  "comments.name":   [ alice, john, smith, white ],
  "comments.comment": [ article, great, like, more, please, this ],
  "comments.age":    [ 28, 31 ],
  "comments.stars":  [ 4, 5 ],
  "comments.date":   [ 2014-09-01, 2014-10-22 ]
}
```

The correlation between Alice and 31, or between John and 2014-09-01, has been irretrievably lost. While fields of type object (see "Multilevel Objects" on page 96) are useful for storing a *single* object, they are useless, from a search point of view, for storing an array of objects.

This is the problem that *nested objects* are designed to solve. By mapping the comments field as type nested instead of type object, each nested object is indexed as a *hidden separate document*, something like this:

```
{ ❶
  "comments.name":    [ john, smith ],
  "comments.comment": [ article, great ],
  "comments.age":     [ 28 ],
  "comments.stars":   [ 4 ],
  "comments.date":    [ 2014-09-01 ]
}
{ ❷
  "comments.name":    [ alice, white ],
```

```
  "comments.comment": [ like, more, please, this ],
  "comments.age":     [ 31 ],
  "comments.stars":   [ 5 ],
  "comments.date":    [ 2014-10-22 ]
}
{ ❸
  "title":            [ eggs, nest ],
  "body":             [ making, money, work, your ],
  "tags":             [ cash, shares ]
}
```

❶ First nested object

❷ Second nested object

❸ The *root* or parent document

By indexing each nested object separately, the fields within the object maintain their relationships. We can run queries that will match only if the match occurs within the same nested object.

Not only that, because of the way that nested objects are indexed, joining the nested documents to the root document at query time is fast—almost as fast as if they were a single document.

These extra nested documents are hidden; we can't access them directly. To update, add, or remove a nested object, we have to reindex the whole document. It's important to note that, the result returned by a search request is not the nested object alone; it is the whole document.

Nested Object Mapping

Setting up a nested field is simple—where you would normally specify type object, make it type nested instead:

```
PUT /my_index
{
  "mappings": {
    "blogpost": {
      "properties": {
        "comments": {
          "type": "nested", ❶
          "properties": {
            "name":    { "type": "string" },
            "comment": { "type": "string" },
            "age":     { "type": "short"  },
            "stars":   { "type": "short"  },
            "date":    { "type": "date"   }
          }
```

```
          }
        }
      }
    }
  }
```

❶ A nested field accepts the same parameters as a field of type object.

That's all that is required. Any comments objects would now be indexed as separate nested documents. See the nested type reference docs (*http://bit.ly/1KNQEP9*) for more.

Querying a Nested Object

Because nested objects are indexed as separate hidden documents, we can't query them directly. Instead, we have to use the nested query (*http://bit.ly/1ziFQoR*) or nes ted filter (*http://bit.ly/1IOp94r*) to access them:

```
GET /my_index/blogpost/_search
{
  "query": {
    "bool": {
      "must": [
        { "match": { "title": "eggs" }},  ❶
        {
          "nested": {
            "path": "comments",  ❷
            "query": {
              "bool": {
                "must": [  ❸
                  { "match": { "comments.name": "john" }},
                  { "match": { "comments.age":  28      }}
                ]
        }}}}
      ]
}}}
```

❶ The title clause operates on the root document.

❷ The nested clause "steps down" into the nested comments field. It no longer has access to fields in the root document, nor fields in any other nested document.

❸ The comments.name and comments.age clauses operate on the same nested document.

A `nested` field can contain other `nested` fields. Similarly, a `nested` query can contain other `nested` queries. The nesting hierarchy is applied as you would expect.

Of course, a `nested` query could match several nested documents. Each matching nested document would have its own relevance score, but these multiple scores need to be reduced to a single score that can be applied to the root document.

By default, it averages the scores of the matching nested documents. This can be controlled by setting the `score_mode` parameter to `avg`, `max`, `sum`, or even `none` (in which case the root document gets a constant score of `1.0`).

```
GET /my_index/blogpost/_search
{
  "query": {
    "bool": {
      "must": [
        { "match": { "title": "eggs" }},
        {
          "nested": {
            "path":        "comments",
            "score_mode": "max", ❶
            "query": {
              "bool": {
                "must": [
                  { "match": { "comments.name": "john" }},
                  { "match": { "comments.age":  28      }}
                ]
        }}}}
      ]
}}}
```

❶ Give the root document the `_score` from the best-matching nested document.

 A `nested` filter behaves much like a `nested` query, except that it doesn't accept the `score_mode` parameter. It can be used only in *filter context*—such as inside a `filtered` query—and it behaves like any other filter: it includes or excludes, but it doesn't score.

While the results of the `nested` filter itself are not cached, the usual caching rules apply to the filter *inside* the `nested` filter.

Sorting by Nested Fields

It is possible to sort by the value of a nested field, even though the value exists in a separate nested document. To make the result more interesting, we will add another record:

```
PUT /my_index/blogpost/2
{
  "title": "Investment secrets",
  "body":  "What they don't tell you ...",
  "tags":  [ "shares", "equities" ],
  "comments": [
    {
      "name":    "Mary Brown",
      "comment": "Lies, lies, lies",
      "age":     42,
      "stars":   1,
      "date":    "2014-10-18"
    },
    {
      "name":    "John Smith",
      "comment": "You're making it up!",
      "age":     28,
      "stars":   2,
      "date":    "2014-10-16"
    }
  ]
}
```

Imagine that we want to retrieve blog posts that received comments in October, ordered by the lowest number of stars that each blog post received. The search request would look like this:

```
GET /_search
{
  "query": {
    "nested": {  ❶
      "path": "comments",
      "filter": {
        "range": {
          "comments.date": {
            "gte": "2014-10-01",
            "lt":  "2014-11-01"
          }
        }
      }
    }
  },
  "sort": {
    "comments.stars": {  ❷
      "order": "asc",     ❷
      "mode":  "min",     ❷
```

```
      "nested_filter": {  ❸
        "range": {
          "comments.date": {
            "gte": "2014-10-01",
            "lt":  "2014-11-01"
          }
        }
      }
    }
  }
}
```

❶ The `nested` query limits the results to blog posts that received a comment in October.

❷ Results are sorted in ascending (`asc`) order by the lowest value (`min`) in the `com ment.stars` field in any matching comments.

❸ The `nested_filter` in the sort clause is the same as the `nested` query in the main query clause. The reason is explained next.

Why do we need to repeat the query conditions in the `nested_filter`? The reason is that sorting happens after the query has been executed. The query matches blog posts that received comments in October, but it returns blog post documents as the result. If we didn't include the `nested_filter` clause, we would end up sorting based on any comments that the blog post has ever received, not just those received in October.

Nested Aggregations

In the same way as we need to use the special `nested` query to gain access to nested objects at search time, the dedicated `nested` aggregation allows us to aggregate fields in nested objects:

```
GET /my_index/blogpost/_search?search_type=count
{
  "aggs": {
    "comments": {  ❶
      "nested": {
        "path": "comments"
      },
      "aggs": {
        "by_month": {
          "date_histogram": {  ❷
            "field":    "comments.date",
            "interval": "month",
            "format":   "yyyy-MM"
          },
          "aggs": {
```

```
          "avg_stars": {
            "avg": {  ❸
              "field": "comments.stars"
            }
          }
        }
      }
    }
  }
}
```

❶ The nested aggregation "steps down" into the nested comments object.

❷ Comments are bucketed into months based on the comments.date field.

❸ The average number of stars is calculated for each bucket.

The results show that aggregation has happened at the nested document level:

```
...
"aggregations": {
  "comments": {
    "doc_count": 4,  ❶
    "by_month": {
      "buckets": [
        {
          "key_as_string": "2014-09",
          "key": 1409529600000,
          "doc_count": 1,  ❶
          "avg_stars": {
            "value": 4
          }
        },
        {
          "key_as_string": "2014-10",
          "key": 1412121600000,
          "doc_count": 3,  ❶
          "avg_stars": {
            "value": 2.6666666666666665
          }
        }
      ]
    }
  }
}
...
```

❶ There are a total of four comments: one in September and three in October.

reverse_nested Aggregation

A `nested` aggregation can access only the fields within the nested document. It can't see fields in the root document or in a different nested document. However, we can *step out* of the nested scope back into the parent with a `reverse_nested` aggregation.

For instance, we can find out which `tags` our commenters are interested in, based on the age of the commenter. The `comment.age` is a nested field, while the `tags` are in the root document:

```
GET /my_index/blogpost/_search?search_type=count
{
  "aggs": {
    "comments": {
      "nested": {  ❶
        "path": "comments"
      },
      "aggs": {
        "age_group": {
          "histogram": {  ❷
            "field":    "comments.age",
            "interval": 10
          },
          "aggs": {
            "blogposts": {
              "reverse_nested": {},  ❸
              "aggs": {
                "tags": {
                  "terms": {  ❹
                    "field": "tags"
                  }
                }
              }
            }
          }
        }
      }
    }
  }
}
```

❶ The `nested` agg steps down into the `comments` object.

❷ The `histogram` agg groups on the `comments.age` field, in buckets of 10 years.

❸ The `reverse_nested` agg steps back up to the root document.

❹ The `terms` agg counts popular terms per age group of the commenter.

The abbreviated results show us the following:

```
  ..
  "aggregations": {
    "comments": {
      "doc_count": 4, ❶
      "age_group": {
        "buckets": [
          {
            "key": 20, ❷
            "doc_count": 2, ❷
            "blogposts": {
              "doc_count": 2, ❸
              "tags": {
                "doc_count_error_upper_bound": 0,
                "buckets": [ ❹
                  { "key": "shares",   "doc_count": 2 },
                  { "key": "cash",     "doc_count": 1 },
                  { "key": "equities", "doc_count": 1 }
                ]
              }
            }
          }
        ]
      },
    },
  ...
```

❶ There are four comments.

❷ There are two comments by commenters between the ages of 20 and 30.

❸ Two blog posts are associated with those comments.

❹ The popular tags in those blog posts are shares, cash, and equities.

When to Use Nested Objects

Nested objects are useful when there is one main entity, like our blogpost, with a limited number of closely related but less important entities, such as comments. It is useful to be able to find blog posts based on the content of the comments, and the nested query and filter provide for fast query-time joins.

The disadvantages of the nested model are as follows:

- To add, change, or delete a nested document, the whole document must be reindexed. This becomes more costly the more nested documents there are.
- Search requests return the whole document, not just the matching nested documents. Although there are plans afoot to support returning the best -matching nested documents with the root document, this is not yet supported.

Sometimes you need a complete separation between the main document and its associated entities. This separation is provided by the *parent-child relationship*.

CHAPTER 42

Parent-Child Relationship

The *parent-child* relationship is similar in nature to the nested model: both allow you to associate one entity with another. The difference is that, with nested objects, all entities live within the same document while, with parent-child, the parent and children are completely separate documents.

The parent-child functionality allows you to associate one document type with another, in a *one-to-many* relationship—one parent to many children. The advantages that parent-child has over `nested` objects are as follows:

- The parent document can be updated without reindexing the children.
- Child documents can be added, changed, or deleted without affecting either the parent or other children. This is especially useful when child documents are large in number and need to be added or changed frequently.
- Child documents can be returned as the results of a search request.

Elasticsearch maintains a map of which parents are associated with which children. It is thanks to this map that query-time joins are fast, but it does place a limitation on the parent-child relationship: *the parent document and all of its children must live on the same shard*.

 At the time of going to press, the parent-child ID map is held in memory as part of fielddata. There are plans afoot to change the default setting to use doc values by default instead.

Parent-Child Mapping

All that is needed in order to establish the parent-child relationship is to specify which document type should be the parent of a child type. This must be done at index creation time, or with the update-mapping API before the child type has been created.

As an example, let's say that we have a company that has branches in many cities. We would like to associate employees with the branch where they work. We need to be able to search for branches, individual employees, and employees who work for particular branches, so the nested model will not help. We could, of course, use application-side-joins or data denormalization here instead, but for demonstration purposes we will use parent-child.

All that we have to do is to tell Elasticsearch that the employee type has the branch document type as its _parent, which we can do when we create the index:

```
PUT /company
{
  "mappings": {
    "branch": {},
    "employee": {
      "_parent": {
        "type": "branch" ❶
      }
    }
  }
}
```

❶ Documents of type employee are children of type branch.

Indexing Parents and Children

Indexing parent documents is no different from any other document. Parents don't need to know anything about their children:

```
POST /company/branch/_bulk
{ "index": { "_id": "london" }}
{ "name": "London Westminster", "city": "London", "country": "UK" }
{ "index": { "_id": "liverpool" }}
{ "name": "Liverpool Central", "city": "Liverpool", "country": "UK" }
{ "index": { "_id": "paris" }}
{ "name": "Champs Élysées", "city": "Paris", "country": "France" }
```

When indexing child documents, you must specify the ID of the associated parent document:

```
PUT /company/employee/1?parent=london ❶
{
```

```
    "name":   "Alice Smith",
    "dob":    "1970-10-24",
    "hobby":  "hiking"
}
```

❶ This employee document is a child of the london branch.

This parent ID serves two purposes: it creates the link between the parent and the child, and it ensures that the child document is stored on the same shard as the parent.

In "Routing a Document to a Shard" on page 63, we explained how Elasticsearch uses a routing value, which defaults to the _id of the document, to decide which shard a document should belong to. The routing value is plugged into this simple formula:

```
shard = hash(routing) % number_of_primary_shards
```

However, if a parent ID is specified, it is used as the routing value instead of the _id. In other words, both the parent and the child use the same routing value—the _id of the parent—and so they are both stored on the same shard.

The parent ID needs to be specified on all single-document requests: when retrieving a child document with a GET request, or when indexing, updating, or deleting a child document. Unlike a search request, which is forwarded to all shards in an index, these single-document requests are forwarded only to the shard that holds the document— if the parent ID is not specified, the request will probably be forwarded to the wrong shard.

The parent ID should also be specified when using the bulk API:

```
POST /company/employee/_bulk
{ "index": { "_id": 2, "parent": "london" }}
{ "name": "Mark Thomas", "dob": "1982-05-16", "hobby": "diving" }
{ "index": { "_id": 3, "parent": "liverpool" }}
{ "name": "Barry Smith", "dob": "1979-04-01", "hobby": "hiking" }
{ "index": { "_id": 4, "parent": "paris" }}
{ "name": "Adrien Grand", "dob": "1987-05-11", "hobby": "horses" }
```

If you want to change the parent value of a child document, it is not sufficient to just reindex or update the child document—the new parent document may be on a different shard. Instead, you must first delete the old child, and then index the new child.

Finding Parents by Their Children

The has_child query and filter can be used to find parent documents based on the contents of their children. For instance, we could find all branches that have employees born after 1980 with a query like this:

```
GET /company/branch/_search
{
  "query": {
    "has_child": {
      "type": "employee",
      "query": {
        "range": {
          "dob": {
            "gte": "1980-01-01"
          }
        }
      }
    }
  }
}
```

Like the nested query, the has_child query could match several child documents,
each with a different relevance score. How these scores are reduced to a single score
for the parent document depends on the score_mode parameter. The default setting is
none, which ignores the child scores and assigns a score of 1.0 to the parents, but it
also accepts avg, min, max, and sum.

The following query will return both london and liverpool, but london will get a
better score because Alice Smith is a better match than Barry Smith:

```
GET /company/branch/_search
{
  "query": {
    "has_child": {
      "type":       "employee",
      "score_mode": "max"
      "query": {
        "match": {
          "name": "Alice Smith"
        }
      }
    }
  }
}
```

 The default score_mode of none is significantly faster than the
other modes because Elasticsearch doesn't need to calculate the
score for each child document. Set it to avg, min, max, or sum only
if you care about the score.

min_children and max_children

The `has_child` query and filter both accept the `min_children` and `max_children` parameters, which will return the parent document only if the number of matching children is within the specified range.

This query will match only branches that have at least two employees:

```
GET /company/branch/_search
{
  "query": {
    "has_child": {
      "type":         "employee",
      "min_children": 2, ❶
      "query": {
        "match_all": {}
      }
    }
  }
}
```

❶ A branch must have at least two employees in order to match.

The performance of a `has_child` query or filter with the `min_children` or `max_children` parameters is much the same as a `has_child` query with scoring enabled.

---

has_child Filter

The `has_child` filter works in the same way as the `has_child` query, except that it doesn't support the `score_mode` parameter. It can be used only in *filter context*—such as inside a `filtered` query—and behaves like any other filter: it includes or excludes, but doesn't score.

While the results of a `has_child` filter are not cached, the usual caching rules apply to the filter *inside* the `has_child` filter.

Finding Children by Their Parents

While a `nested` query can always return only the root document as a result, parent and child documents are independent and each can be queried independently. The `has_child` query allows us to return parents based on data in their children, and the `has_parent` query returns children based on data in their parents.

It looks very similar to the `has_child` query. This example returns employees who work in the UK:

```
GET /company/employee/_search
{
  "query": {
    "has_parent": {
      "type": "branch",  ❶
      "query": {
        "match": {
          "country": "UK"
        }
      }
    }
  }
}
```

❶ Returns children who have parents of type branch

The has_parent query also supports the score_mode, but it accepts only two settings: none (the default) and score. Each child can have only one parent, so there is no need to reduce multiple scores into a single score for the child. The choice is simply between using the score (score) or not (none).

---

has_parent Filter

The has_parent filter works in the same way as the has_parent query, except that it doesn't support the score_mode parameter. It can be used only in *filter context*—such as inside a filtered query—and behaves like any other filter: it includes or excludes, but doesn't score.

While the results of a has_parent filter are not cached, the usual caching rules apply to the filter *inside* the has_parent filter.

Children Aggregation

Parent-child supports a children aggregation (*http://bit.ly/1xtpjaz*) as a direct analog to the nested aggregation discussed in "Nested Aggregations" on page 571. A parent aggregation (the equivalent of reverse_nested) is not supported.

This example demonstrates how we could determine the favorite hobbies of our employees by country:

```
GET /company/branch/_search?search_type=count
{
  "aggs": {
    "country": {
      "terms": {  ❶
        "field": "country"
      },
```

```
      "aggs": {
        "employees": {
          "children": { ❷
            "type": "employee"
          },
          "aggs": {
            "hobby": {
              "terms": { ❸
                "field": "employee.hobby"
              }
            }
          }
        }
      }
    }
  }
}
```

❶ The country field in the branch documents.

❷ The children aggregation joins the parent documents with their associated chil-
    dren of type employee.

❸ The hobby field from the employee child documents.

Grandparents and Grandchildren

The parent-child relationship can extend across more than one generation—grandchildren can have grandparents—but it requires an extra step to ensure that documents from all generations are indexed on the same shard.

Let's change our previous example to make the country type a parent of the branch
type:

```
PUT /company
{
  "mappings": {
    "country": {},
    "branch": {
      "_parent": {
        "type": "country" ❶
      }
    },
    "employee": {
      "_parent": {
        "type": "branch" ❷
      }
    }
  }
}
```

❶ branch is a child of country.

❷ employee is a child of branch.

Countries and branches have a simple parent-child relationship, so we use the same process as we used in "Indexing Parents and Children" on page 576:

```
POST /company/country/_bulk
{ "index": { "_id": "uk" }}
{ "name": "UK" }
{ "index": { "_id": "france" }}
{ "name": "France" }

POST /company/branch/_bulk
{ "index": { "_id": "london", "parent": "uk" }}
{ "name": "London Westmintster" }
{ "index": { "_id": "liverpool", "parent": "uk" }}
{ "name": "Liverpool Central" }
{ "index": { "_id": "paris", "parent": "france" }}
{ "name": "Champs Élysées" }
```

The parent ID has ensured that each branch document is routed to the same shard as its parent country document. However, look what would happen if we were to use the same technique with the employee grandchildren:

```
PUT /company/employee/1?parent=london
{
  "name":  "Alice Smith",
  "dob":   "1970-10-24",
  "hobby": "hiking"
}
```

The shard routing of the employee document would be decided by the parent ID—london—but the london document was routed to a shard by *its own* parent ID—uk. It is very likely that the grandchild would end up on a different shard from its parent and grandparent, which would prevent the same-shard parent-child mapping from functioning.

Instead, we need to add an extra routing parameter, set to the ID of the grandparent, to ensure that all three generations are indexed on the same shard. The indexing request should look like this:

```
PUT /company/employee/1?parent=london&routing=uk ❶
{
  "name":  "Alice Smith",
  "dob":   "1970-10-24",
  "hobby": "hiking"
}
```

❶ The routing value overrides the parent value.

The `parent` parameter is still used to link the employee document with its parent, but the `routing` parameter ensures that it is stored on the same shard as its parent and grandparent. The `routing` value needs to be provided for all single-document requests.

Querying and aggregating across generations works, as long as you step through each generation. For instance, to find countries where employees enjoy hiking, we need to join countries with branches, and branches with employees:

```
GET /company/country/_search
{
  "query": {
    "has_child": {
      "type": "branch",
      "query": {
        "has_child": {
          "type": "employee",
          "query": {
            "match": {
              "hobby": "hiking"
            }
          }
        }
      }
    }
  }
}
```

Practical Considerations

Parent-child joins can be a useful technique for managing relationships when index-time performance is more important than search-time performance, but it comes at a significant cost. Parent-child queries can be 5 to 10 times slower than the equivalent nested query!

Memory Use

At the time of going to press, the parent-child ID map is still held in memory. There are plans to change the map to use doc values instead, which will be a big memory saving. Until that happens, you need to be aware of the following: the string `_id` field of every parent document has to be held in memory, and every child document requires 8 bytes (a long value) of memory. Actually, it's a bit less thanks to compression, but this gives you a rough idea.

You can check how much memory is being used by the parent-child cache by consulting the `indices-stats` API (for a summary at the index level) or the `node-stats` API (for a summary at the node level):

```
GET /_nodes/stats/indices/id_cache?human ❶
```

❶ Returns memory use of the ID cache summarized by node in a human-friendly format.

Global Ordinals and Latency

Parent-child uses global ordinals to speed up joins. Regardless of whether the parent-child map uses an in-memory cache or on-disk doc values, global ordinals still need to be rebuilt after any change to the index.

The more parents in a shard, the longer global ordinals will take to build. Parent-child is best suited to situations where there are many children for each parent, rather than many parents and few children.

Global ordinals, by default, are built lazily: the first parent-child query or aggregation after a refresh will trigger building of global ordinals. This can introduce a significant latency spike for your users. You can use `eager_global_ordinals` to shift the cost of building global ordinals from query time to refresh time, by mapping the `_parent` field as follows:

```
PUT /company
{
  "mappings": {
    "branch": {},
    "employee": {
      "_parent": {
        "type": "branch",
        "fielddata": {
          "loading": "eager_global_ordinals" ❶
        }
      }
    }
  }
}
```

❶ Global ordinals for the `_parent` field will be built before a new segment becomes visible to search.

With many parents, global ordinals can take several seconds to build. In this case, it makes sense to increase the `refresh_interval` so that refreshes happen less often and global ordinals remain valid for longer. This will greatly reduce the CPU cost of rebuilding global ordinals every second.

Multigenerations and Concluding Thoughts

The ability to join multiple generations (see "Grandparents and Grandchildren" on page 581) sounds attractive until you think of the costs involved:

- The more joins you have, the worse performance will be.
- Each generation of parents needs to have their string _id fields stored in memory, which can consume a lot of RAM.

As you consider your relationship schemes and whether parent-child is right for you, consider this advice about parent-child relationships:

- Use parent-child relationships sparingly, and only when there are many more children than parents.
- Avoid using multiple parent-child joins in a single query.
- Avoid scoring by using the has_child filter, or the has_child query with score_mode set to none.
- Keep the parent IDs short, so that they require less memory.

Above all: think about the other relationship techniques that we have discussed before reaching for parent-child.

CHAPTER 43

Designing for Scale

Elasticsearch is used by some companies to index and search petabytes of data every day, but most of us start out with something a little more humble in size. Even if we aspire to be the next Facebook, it is unlikely that our bank balance matches our aspirations. We need to build for what we have today, but in a way that will allow us to scale out flexibly and rapidly.

Elasticsearch is built to scale. It will run very happily on your laptop or in a cluster containing hundreds of nodes, and the experience is almost identical. Growing from a small cluster to a large cluster is almost entirely automatic and painless. Growing from a large cluster to a very large cluster requires a bit more planning and design, but it is still relatively painless.

Of course, it is not magic. Elasticsearch has its limitations too. If you are aware of those limitations and work with them, the growing process will be pleasant. If you treat Elasticsearch badly, you could be in for a world of pain.

The default settings in Elasticsearch will take you a long way, but to get the most bang for your buck, you need to think about how data flows through your system. We will talk about two common data flows: time-based data (such as log events or social network streams, where relevance is driven by recency), and user-based data (where a large document collection can be subdivided by user or customer).

This chapter will help you make the right decisions up front, to avoid nasty surprises later.

The Unit of Scale

In "Dynamically Updatable Indices" on page 157, we explained that a shard is a *Lucene index* and that an Elasticsearch index is a collection of shards. Your application talks to an index, and Elasticsearch routes your requests to the appropriate shards.

A shard is the *unit of scale*. The smallest index you can have is one with a single shard. This may be more than sufficient for your needs—a single shard can hold a lot of data —but it limits your ability to scale.

Imagine that our cluster consists of one node, and in our cluster we have one index, which has only one shard:

```
PUT /my_index
{
  "settings": {
    "number_of_shards":   1, ❶
    "number_of_replicas": 0
  }
}
```

❶ Create an index with one primary shard and zero replica shards.

This setup may be small, but it serves our current needs and is cheap to run.

 At the moment we are talking about only *primary* shards. We discuss *replica* shards in "Replica Shards" on page 592.

One glorious day, the Internet discovers us, and a single node just can't keep up with the traffic. We decide to add a second node, as per Figure 43-1. What happens?

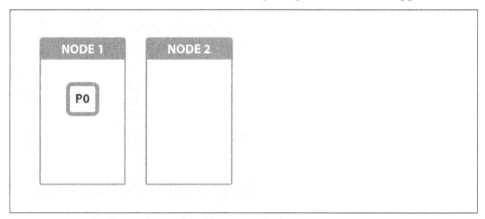

Figure 43-1. An index with one shard has no scale factor

The answer is: nothing. Because we have only one shard, there is nothing to put on the second node. We can't increase the number of shards in the index, because the number of shards is an important element in the algorithm used to route documents to shards:

```
shard = hash(routing) % number_of_primary_shards
```

Our only option now is to reindex our data into a new, bigger index that has more shards, but that will take time that we can ill afford. By planning ahead, we could have avoided this problem completely by *overallocating*.

Shard Overallocation

A shard lives on a single node, but a node can hold multiple shards. Imagine that we created our index with two primary shards instead of one:

```
PUT /my_index
{
  "settings": {
    "number_of_shards":   2, ❶
    "number_of_replicas": 0
  }
}
```

❶ Create an index with two primary shards and zero replica shards.

With a single node, both shards would be assigned to the same node. From the point of view of our application, everything functions as it did before. The application communicates with the index, not the shards, and there is still only one index.

This time, when we add a second node, Elasticsearch will automatically move one shard from the first node to the second node, as depicted in Figure 43-2. Once the relocation has finished, each shard will have access to twice the computing power that it had before.

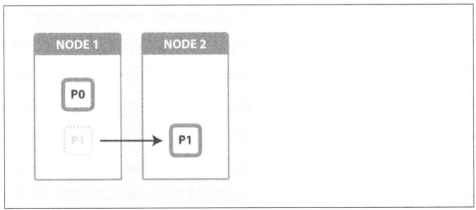

Figure 43-2. An index with two shards can take advantage of a second node

We have been able to double our capacity by simply copying a shard across the network to the new node. The best part is, we achieved this with zero downtime. All indexing and search requests continued to function normally while the shard was being moved.

A new index in Elasticsearch is allotted five primary shards by default. That means that we can spread that index out over a maximum of five nodes, with one shard on each node. That's a lot of capacity, and it happens without you having to think about it at all!

Shard Splitting

Users often ask why Elasticsearch doesn't support *shard-splitting*—the ability to split each shard into two or more pieces. The reason is that shard-splitting is a bad idea:

- Splitting a shard is almost equivalent to reindexing your data. It's a much heavier process than just copying a shard from one node to another.

- Splitting is exponential. You start with one shard, then split into two, and then four, eight, sixteen, and so on. Splitting doesn't allow you to increase capacity by just 50%.

- Shard splitting requires you to have enough capacity to hold a second copy of your index. Usually, by the time you realize that you need to scale out, you don't have enough free space left to perform the split.

In a way, Elasticsearch does support shard splitting. You can always reindex your data to a new index with the appropriate number of shards (see "Reindexing Your Data" on page 152). It is still a more intensive process than moving shards around, and still requires enough free space to complete, but at least you can control the number of shards in the new index.

Kagillion Shards

The first thing that new users do when they learn about shard overallocation is to say to themselves:

> I don't know how big this is going to be, and I can't change the index size later on, so to be on the safe side, I'll just give this index 1,000 shards…
>
> —A new user

One thousand shards—really? And you don't think that, perhaps, between now and the time you need to buy *one thousand nodes*, that you may need to rethink your data model once or twice and have to reindex?

A shard is not free. Remember:

- A shard is a Lucene index under the covers, which uses file handles, memory, and CPU cycles.

- Every search request needs to hit a copy of every shard in the index. That's fine if every shard is sitting on a different node, but not if many shards have to compete for the same resources.

- Term statistics, used to calculate relevance, are per shard. Having a small amount of data in many shards leads to poor relevance.

 A little overallocation is good. A kagillion shards is bad. It is difficult to define what constitutes too many shards, as it depends on their size and how they are being used. A hundred shards that are seldom used may be fine, while two shards experiencing very heavy usage could be too many. Monitor your nodes to ensure that they have enough spare capacity to deal with exceptional conditions.

Scaling out should be done in phases. Build in enough capacity to get to the next phase. Once you get to the next phase, you have time to think about the changes you need to make to reach the phase after that.

Capacity Planning

If 1 shard is too few and 1,000 shards are too many, how do I know how many shards I need? This is a question that is impossible to answer in the general case. There are just too many variables: the hardware that you use, the size and complexity of your documents, how you index and analyze those documents, the types of queries that you run, the aggregations that you perform, how you model your data, and more.

Fortunately, it is an easy question to answer in the specific case—yours:

1. Create a cluster consisting of a single server, with the hardware that you are considering using in production.

2. Create an index with the same settings and analyzers that you plan to use in production, but with only one primary shard and no replicas.

3. Fill it with real documents (or as close to real as you can get).

4. Run real queries and aggregations (or as close to real as you can get).

Essentially, you want to replicate real-world usage and to push this single shard until it "breaks." Even the definition of *breaks* depends on you: some users require that all responses return within 50ms; others are quite happy to wait for 5 seconds.

Once you define the capacity of a single shard, it is easy to extrapolate that number to your whole index. Take the total amount of data that you need to index, plus some extra for future growth, and divide by the capacity of a single shard. The result is the number of primary shards that you will need.

 Capacity planning should not be your first step.

First look for ways to optimize how you are using Elasticsearch. Perhaps you have inefficient queries, not enough RAM, or you have left swap enabled?

We have seen new users who, frustrated by initial performance, immediately start trying to tune the garbage collector or adjust the number of threads, instead of tackling the simple problems like removing wildcard queries.

Replica Shards

Up until now we have spoken only about primary shards, but we have another tool in our belt: replica shards. The main purpose of replicas is for failover, as discussed in Chapter 2: if the node holding a primary shard dies, a replica is promoted to the role of primary.

At index time, a replica shard does the same amount of work as the primary shard. New documents are first indexed on the primary and then on any replicas. Increasing the number of replicas does not change the capacity of the index.

However, replica shards can serve read requests. If, as is often the case, your index is search heavy, you can increase search performance by increasing the number of replicas, but only if you also *add extra hardware*.

Let's return to our example of an index with two primary shards. We increased capacity of the index by adding a second node. Adding more nodes would not help us to add indexing capacity, but we could take advantage of the extra hardware at search time by increasing the number of replicas:

```
POST /my_index/_settings
{
  "number_of_replicas": 1
}
```

Having two primary shards, plus a replica of each primary, would give us a total of four shards: one for each node, as shown in Figure 43-3.

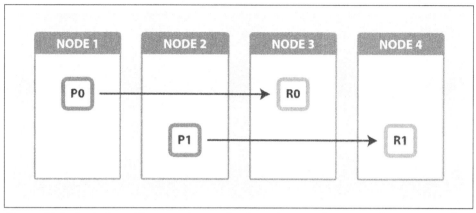

Figure 43-3. An index with two primary shards and one replica can scale out across four nodes

Balancing Load with Replicas

Search performance depends on the response times of the slowest node, so it is a good idea to try to balance out the load across all nodes. If we added just one extra node instead of two, we would end up with two nodes having one shard each, and one node doing double the work with two shards.

We can even things out by adjusting the number of replicas. By allocating two replicas instead of one, we end up with a total of six shards, which can be evenly divided between three nodes, as shown in Figure 43-4:

```
POST /my_index/_settings
{
  "number_of_replicas": 2
}
```

As a bonus, we have also increased our availability. We can now afford to lose two nodes and still have a copy of all our data.

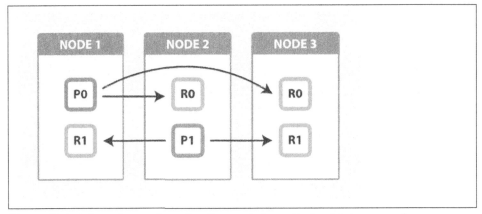

Figure 43-4. Adjust the number of replicas to balance the load between nodes

 The fact that node 3 holds two replicas and no primaries is not important. Replicas and primaries do the same amount of work; they just play slightly different roles. There is no need to ensure that primaries are distributed evenly across all nodes.

Multiple Indices

Finally, remember that there is no rule that limits your application to using only a single index. When we issue a search request, it is forwarded to a copy (a primary or a replica) of all the shards in an index. If we issue the same search request on multiple indices, the exact same thing happens—there are just more shards involved.

 Searching 1 index of 50 shards is exactly equivalent to searching 50 indices with 1 shard each: both search requests hit 50 shards.

This can be a useful fact to remember when you need to add capacity on the fly. Instead of having to reindex your data into a bigger index, you can just do the following:

- Create a new index to hold new data.
- Search across both indices to retrieve new and old data.

In fact, with a little forethought, adding a new index can be done in a completely transparent way, without your application ever knowing that anything has changed.

In "Index Aliases and Zero Downtime" on page 153, we spoke about using an index alias to point to the current version of your index. For instance, instead of naming your index `tweets`, name it `tweets_v1`. Your application would still talk to `tweets`, but in reality that would be an alias that points to `tweets_v1`. This allows you to switch the alias to point to a newer version of the index on the fly.

A similar technique can be used to expand capacity by adding a new index. It requires a bit of planning because you will need two aliases: one for searching and one for indexing:

```
PUT /tweets_1/_alias/tweets_search ❶
PUT /tweets_1/_alias/tweets_index ❶
```

❶   Both the `tweets_search` and the `tweets_index` alias point to index `tweets_1`.

New documents should be indexed into `tweets_index`, and searches should be performed against `tweets_search`. For the moment, these two aliases point to the same index.

When we need extra capacity, we can create a new index called `tweets_2` and update the aliases as follows:

```
POST /_aliases
{
  "actions": [
    { "add":    { "index": "tweets_2", "alias": "tweets_search" }}, ❶
    { "remove": { "index": "tweets_1", "alias": "tweets_index"  }}, ❷
    { "add":    { "index": "tweets_2", "alias": "tweets_index"  }} ❷
  ]
}
```

❶   Add index `tweets_2` to the `tweets_search` alias.

❷   Switch `tweets_index` from `tweets_1` to `tweets_2`.

A search request can target multiple indices, so having the search alias point to `tweets_1` and `tweets_2` is perfectly valid. However, indexing requests can target only a single index. For this reason, we have to switch the index alias to point to only the new index.

A document GET request, like an indexing request, can target only one index. This makes retrieving a document by ID a bit more complicated in this scenario. Instead, run a search request with the `ids` query (*http://bit.ly/1C4Q0cf*), or do a `multi-get` (*http://bit.ly/1sDd2EX*) request on `tweets_1` and `tweets_2`.

Using multiple indices to expand index capacity on the fly is of particular benefit when dealing with time-based data such as logs or social-event streams, which we discuss in the next section.

Time-Based Data

One of the most common use cases for Elasticsearch is for logging, so common in fact that Elasticsearch provides an integrated logging platform called the *ELK stack*—Elasticsearch, Logstash, and Kibana—to make the process easy.

Logstash (*http://www.elasticsearch.org/overview/logstash*) collects, parses, and enriches logs before indexing them into Elasticsearch. Elasticsearch acts as a centralized logging server, and Kibana (*http://www.elasticsearch.org/overview/kibana*) is a graphic frontend that makes it easy to query and visualize what is happening across your network in near real-time.

Most traditional use cases for search engines involve a relatively static collection of documents that grows slowly. Searches look for the most relevant documents, regardless of when they were created.

Logging—and other time-based data streams such as social-network activity—are very different in nature. The number of documents in the index grows rapidly, often accelerating with time. Documents are almost never updated, and searches mostly target the most recent documents. As documents age, they lose value.

We need to adapt our index design to function with the flow of time-based data.

Index per Time Frame

If we were to have one big index for documents of this type, we would soon run out of space. Logging events just keep on coming, without pause or interruption. We could delete the old events, with a `delete-by-query`:

```
DELETE /logs/event/_query
{
  "query": {
    "range": {
      "@timestamp": {  ❶
        "lt": "now-90d"
      }
    }
  }
}
```

❶ Deletes all documents where Logstash's `@timestamp` field is older than 90 days.

But this approach is *very inefficient*. Remember that when you delete a document, it is only *marked* as deleted (see "Deletes and Updates" on page 160). It won't be physically deleted until the segment containing it is merged away.

Instead, use an *index per time frame*. You could start out with an index per year (logs_2014) or per month (logs_2014-10). Perhaps, when your website gets really busy, you need to switch to an index per day (logs_2014-10-24). Purging old data is easy: just delete old indices.

This approach has the advantage of allowing you to scale as and when you need to. You don't have to make any difficult decisions up front. Every day is a new opportunity to change your indexing time frames to suit the current demand. Apply the same logic to how big you make each index. Perhaps all you need is one primary shard per week initially. Later, maybe you need five primary shards per day. It doesn't matter—you can adjust to new circumstances at any time.

Aliases can help make switching indices more transparent. For indexing, you can point logs_current to the index currently accepting new log events, and for searching, update last_3_months to point to all indices for the previous three months:

```
POST /_aliases
{
  "actions": [
    { "add":    { "alias": "logs_current",  "index": "logs_2014-10" }}, ❶
    { "remove": { "alias": "logs_current",  "index": "logs_2014-09" }}, ❶
    { "add":    { "alias": "last_3_months", "index": "logs_2014-10" }}, ❷
    { "remove": { "alias": "last_3_months", "index": "logs_2014-07" }}  ❷
  ]
}
```

❶   Switch logs_current from September to October.

❷   Add October to last_3_months and remove July.

Index Templates

Elasticsearch doesn't require you to create an index before using it. With logging, it is often more convenient to rely on index autocreation than to have to create indices manually.

Logstash uses the timestamp from an event to derive the index name. By default, it indexes into a different index every day, so an event with a @timestamp of 2014-10-01 00:00:01 will be sent to the index logstash-2014.10.01. If that index doesn't already exist, it will be created for us.

Usually we want some control over the settings and mappings of the new index. Perhaps we want to limit the number of shards to 1, and we want to disable the _all field. Index templates can be used to control which settings should be applied to newly created indices:

```
PUT /_template/my_logs ❶
{
  "template": "logstash-*", ❷
  "order":    1, ❸
  "settings": {
    "number_of_shards": 1 ❹
  },
  "mappings": {
    "_default_": { ❺
      "_all": {
        "enabled": false
      }
    }
  },
  "aliases": {
    "last_3_months": {} ❻
  }
}
```

❶ Create a template called my_logs.

❷ Apply this template to all indices beginning with logstash-.

❸ This template should override the default logstash template that has a lower order.

❹ Limit the number of primary shards to 1.

❺ Disable the _all field for all types.

❻ Add this index to the last_3_months alias.

This template specifies the default settings that will be applied to any index whose name begins with logstash-, whether it is created manually or automatically. If we think the index for tomorrow will need more capacity than today, we can update the index to use a higher number of shards.

The template even adds the newly created index into the last_3_months alias, although removing the old indices from that alias will have to be done manually.

Retiring Data

As time-based data ages, it becomes less relevant. It's possible that we will want to see what happened last week, last month, or even last year, but for the most part, we're interested in only the here and now.

The nice thing about an index per time frame is that it enables us to easily delete old data: just delete the indices that are no longer relevant:

```
DELETE /logs_2013*
```

Deleting a whole index is much more efficient than deleting individual documents: Elasticsearch just removes whole directories.

But deleting an index is very *final*. There are a number of things we can do to help data age gracefully, before we decide to delete it completely.

Migrate Old Indices

With logging data, there is likely to be one *hot* index—the index for today. All new documents will be added to that index, and almost all queries will target that index. It should use your best hardware.

How does Elasticsearch know which servers are your best servers? You tell it, by assigning arbitrary tags to each server. For instance, you could start a node as follows:

```
./bin/elasticsearch --node.box_type strong
```

The box_type parameter is completely arbitrary—you could have named it whatever you like—but you can use these arbitrary values to tell Elasticsearch where to allocate an index.

We can ensure that today's index is on our strongest boxes by creating it with the following settings:

```
PUT /logs_2014-10-01
{
  "settings": {
    "index.routing.allocation.include.box_type" : "strong"
  }
}
```

Yesterday's index no longer needs to be on our strongest boxes, so we can move it to the nodes tagged as medium by updating its index settings:

```
POST /logs_2014-09-30/_settings
{
  "index.routing.allocation.include.box_type" : "medium"
}
```

Optimize Indices

Yesterday's index is unlikely to change. Log events are static: what happened in the past stays in the past. If we merge each shard down to just a single segment, it'll use fewer resources and will be quicker to query. We can do this with the "optimize API" on page 170.

It would be a bad idea to optimize the index while it was still allocated to the `strong` boxes, as the optimization process could swamp the I/O on those nodes and impact the indexing of today's logs. But the `medium` boxes aren't doing very much at all, so we are safe to optimize.

Yesterday's index may have replica shards. If we issue an optimize request, it will optimize the primary shard and the replica shards, which is a waste. Instead, we can remove the replicas temporarily, optimize, and then restore the replicas:

```
POST /logs_2014-09-30/_settings
{ "number_of_replicas": 0 }

POST /logs_2014-09-30/_optimize?max_num_segments=1

POST /logs_2014-09-30/_settings
{ "number_of_replicas": 1 }
```

Of course, without replicas, we run the risk of losing data if a disk suffers catastrophic failure. You may want to back up the data first, with the `snapshot-restore` API (*http://bit.ly/14ED13A*).

Closing Old Indices

As indices get even older, they reach a point where they are almost never accessed. We could delete them at this stage, but perhaps you want to keep them around just in case somebody asks for them in six months.

These indices can be closed. They will still exist in the cluster, but they won't consume resources other than disk space. Reopening an index is much quicker than restoring it from backup.

Before closing, it is worth flushing the index to make sure that there are no transactions left in the transaction log. An empty transaction log will make index recovery faster when it is reopened:

```
POST /logs_2014-01-*/_flush ❶
POST /logs_2014-01-*/_close ❷
POST /logs_2014-01-*/_open ❸
```

❶ Flush all indices from January to empty the transaction logs.

❷ Close all indices from January.

❸ When you need access to them again, reopen them with the open API.

Archiving Old Indices

Finally, very old indices can be archived off to some long-term storage like a shared disk or Amazon's S3 using the `snapshot-restore` API (*http://bit.ly/14ED13A*), just in case you may need to access them in the future. Once a backup exists, the index can be deleted from the cluster.

User-Based Data

Often, users start using Elasticsearch because they need to add full-text search or analytics to an existing application. They create a single index that holds all of their documents. Gradually, others in the company realize how much benefit Elasticsearch brings, and they want to add their data to Elasticsearch as well.

Fortunately, Elasticsearch supports multitenancy (*http://en.wikipedia.org/wiki/Multitenancy*) so each new user can have her own index in the same cluster. Occasionally, somebody will want to search across the documents for all users, which they can do by searching across all indices, but most of the time, users are interested in only their own documents.

Some users have more documents than others, and some users will have heavier search loads than others, so the ability to specify the number of primary shards and replica shards that each index should have fits well with the index-per-user model. Similarly, busier indices can be allocated to stronger boxes with shard allocation filtering. (See "Migrate Old Indices" on page 599.)

 Don't just use the default number of primary shards for every index. Think about how much data that index needs to hold. It may be that all you need is one shard—any more is a waste of resources.

Most users of Elasticsearch can stop here. A simple index-per-user approach is sufficient for the majority of cases.

In exceptional cases, you may find that you need to support a large number of users, all with similar needs. An example might be hosting a search engine for thousands of email forums. Some forums may have a huge amount of traffic, but the majority of forums are quite small. Dedicating an index with a single shard to a small forum is overkill—a single shard could hold the data for many forums.

What we need is a way to share resources across users, to give the impression that each user has his own index without wasting resources on small users.

Shared Index

We can use a large shared index for the many smaller forums by indexing the forum identifier in a field and using it as a filter:

```
PUT /forums
{
  "settings": {
    "number_of_shards": 10 ❶
  },
  "mappings": {
    "post": {
      "properties": {
        "forum_id": { ❷
          "type":  "string",
          "index": "not_analyzed"
        }
      }
    }
  }
}

PUT /forums/post/1
{
  "forum_id": "baking", ❷
  "title":    "Easy recipe for ginger nuts",
  ...
}
```

❶ Create an index large enough to hold thousands of smaller forums.

❷ Each post must include a `forum_id` to identify which forum it belongs to.

We can use the `forum_id` as a filter to search within a single forum. The filter will exclude most of the documents in the index (those from other forums), and filter caching will ensure that responses are fast:

```
GET /forums/post/_search
{
  "query": {
    "filtered": {
      "query": {
        "match": {
          "title": "ginger nuts"
        }
      },
      "filter": {
        "term": { ❶
          "forum_id": {
            "baking"
          }
```

```
          }
        }
      }
    }
  }
```

❶ The term filter is cached by default.

This approach works, but we can do better. The posts from a single forum would fit easily onto one shard, but currently they are scattered across all ten shards in the index. This means that every search request has to be forwarded to a primary or replica of all ten shards. What would be ideal is to ensure that all the posts from a single forum are stored on the same shard.

In "Routing a Document to a Shard" on page 63, we explained that a document is allocated to a particular shard by using this formula:

```
shard = hash(routing) % number_of_primary_shards
```

The routing value defaults to the document's _id, but we can override that and provide our own custom routing value, such as forum_id. All documents with the same routing value will be stored on the same shard:

```
PUT /forums/post/1?routing=baking ❶
{
  "forum_id": "baking", ❶
  "title":    "Easy recipe for ginger nuts",
  ...
}
```

❶ Using forum_id as the routing value ensures that all posts from the same forum are stored on the same shard.

When we search for posts in a particular forum, we can pass the same routing value to ensure that the search request is run on only the single shard that holds our documents:

```
GET /forums/post/_search?routing=baking ❶
{
  "query": {
    "filtered": {
      "query": {
        "match": {
          "title": "ginger nuts"
        }
      },
      "filter": {
        "term": { ❷
          "forum_id": {
            "baking"
          }
```

```
          }
        }
      }
    }
  }
```

❶ The query is run on only the shard that corresponds to this `routing` value.

❷ We still need the filter, as a single shard can hold posts from many forums.

Multiple forums can be queried by passing a comma-separated list of `routing` values, and including each `forum_id` in a `terms` filter:

```
GET /forums/post/_search?routing=baking,cooking,recipes
{
  "query": {
    "filtered": {
      "query": {
        "match": {
          "title": "ginger nuts"
        }
      },
      "filter": {
        "terms": {
          "forum_id": {
            [ "baking", "cooking", "recipes" ]
          }
        }
      }
    }
  }
}
```

While this approach is technically efficient, it looks a bit clumsy because of the need to specify `routing` values and `terms` filters on every query or indexing request. Index aliases to the rescue!

Faking Index per User with Aliases

To keep our design simple and clean, we would like our application to believe that we have a dedicated index per user—or per forum in our example—even if the reality is that we are using one big shared index. To do that, we need some way to hide the `routing` value and the filter on `forum_id`.

Index aliases allow us to do just that. When you associate an alias with an index, you can also specify a filter and routing values:

```
PUT /forums/_alias/baking
{
  "routing": "baking",
```

```
    "filter": {
      "term": {
        "forum_id": "baking"
      }
    }
  }
}
```

Now, we can treat the `baking` alias as if it were its own index. Documents indexed into the `baking` alias automatically get the custom routing value applied:

```
PUT /baking/post/1 ❶
{
  "forum_id": "baking", ❶
  "title":    "Easy recipe for ginger nuts",
  ...
}
```

❶ We still need the `forum_id` field for the filter to work, but the custom routing value is now implicit.

Queries run against the `baking` alias are run just on the shard associated with the custom routing value, and the results are automatically filtered by the filter we specified:

```
GET /baking/post/_search
{
  "query": {
    "match": {
      "title": "ginger nuts"
    }
  }
}
```

Multiple aliases can be specified when searching across multiple forums:

```
GET /baking,recipes/post/_search ❶
{
  "query": {
    "match": {
      "title": "ginger nuts"
    }
  }
}
```

❶ Both `routing` values are applied, and results can match either filter.

One Big User

Big, popular forums start out as small forums. One day we will find that one shard in our shared index is doing a lot more work than the other shards, because it holds the documents for a forum that has become very popular. That forum now needs its own index.

The index aliases that we're using to fake an index per user give us a clean migration path for the big forum.

The first step is to create a new index dedicated to the forum, and with the appropriate number of shards to allow for expected growth:

```
PUT /baking_v1
{
  "settings": {
    "number_of_shards": 3
  }
}
```

The next step is to migrate the data from the shared index into the dedicated index, which can be done using scan-and-scroll and the bulk API. As soon as the migration is finished, the index alias can be updated to point to the new index:

```
POST /_aliases
{
  "actions": [
    { "remove": { "alias": "baking", "index": "forums"    }},
    { "add":    { "alias": "baking", "index": "baking_v1" }}
  ]
}
```

Updating the alias is atomic; it's like throwing a switch. Your application continues talking to the baking API and is completely unaware that it now points to a new dedicated index.

The dedicated index no longer needs the filter or the routing values. We can just rely on the default sharding that Elasticsearch does using each document's _id field.

The last step is to remove the old documents from the shared index, which can be done with a delete-by-query request, using the original routing value and forum ID:

```
DELETE /forums/post/_query?routing=baking
{
  "query": {
    "term": {
      "forum_id": "baking"
    }
  }
}
```

The beauty of this index-per-user model is that it allows you to reduce resources, keeping costs low, while still giving you the flexibility to scale out when necessary, and with zero downtime.

Scale Is Not Infinite

Throughout this chapter we have spoken about many of the ways that Elasticsearch can scale. Most scaling problems can be solved by adding more nodes. But one resource is finite and should be treated with respect: the cluster state.

The *cluster state* is a data structure that holds the following cluster-level information:

- Cluster-level settings
- Nodes that are part of the cluster
- Indices, plus their settings, mappings, analyzers, warmers, and aliases
- The shards associated with each index, plus the node on which they are allocated

You can view the current cluster state with this request:

```
GET /_cluster/state
```

The cluster state exists on every node in the cluster, including client nodes. This is how any node can forward a request directly to the node that holds the requested data—every node knows where every document lives.

Only the master node is allowed to update the cluster state. Imagine that an indexing request introduces a previously unknown field. The node holding the primary shard for the document must forward the new mapping to the master node. The master node incorporates the changes in the cluster state, and publishes a new version to all of the nodes in the cluster.

Search requests *use* the cluster state, but they don't change it. The same applies to document-level CRUD requests unless, of course, they introduce a new field that requires a mapping update. By and large, the cluster state is static and is not a bottleneck.

However, remember that this same data structure has to exist in memory on every node, and must be published to every node whenever it is updated. The bigger it is, the longer that process will take.

The most common problem that we see with the cluster state is the introduction of too many fields. A user might decide to use a separate field for every IP address, or every referer URL. The following example keeps track of the number of times a page has been visited by using a different field name for every unique referer:

```
POST /counters/pageview/home_page/_update
{
  "script": "ctx._source[referer]++",
  "params": {
    "referer": "http://www.foo.com/links?bar=baz"
  }
}
```

This approach is catastrophically bad! It will result in millions of fields, all of which have to be stored in the cluster state. Every time a new referer is seen, a new field is added to the already bloated cluster state, which then has to be published to every node in the cluster.

A much better approach is to use nested objects, with one field for the parameter name—referer&#x2014and another field for its associated value—count:

```
"counters": [
  { "referer": "http://www.foo.com/links?bar=baz",  "count": 2 },
  { "referer": "http://www.linkbait.com/article_3", "count": 10 },
  ...
]
```

The nested approach may increase the number of documents, but Elasticsearch is built to handle that. The important thing is that it keeps the cluster state small and agile.

Eventually, despite your best intentions, you may find that the number of nodes and indices and mappings that you have is just too much for one cluster. At this stage, it is probably worth dividing the problem into multiple clusters. Thanks to tribe nodes (*http://www.elasticsearch.org/guide/en/elasticsearch/reference/current/modules-tribe.html*), you can even run searches across multiple clusters, as if they were one big cluster.

PART VII

Administration, Monitoring, and Deployment

The majority of this book is aimed at building applications by using Elasticsearch as the backend. This section is a little different. Here, you will learn how to manage Elasticsearch itself. Elasticsearch is a complex piece of software, with many moving parts. Many APIs are designed to help you manage your Elasticsearch deployment.

In this chapter, we cover three main topics:

- Monitoring your cluster's vital statistics, understanding which behaviors are normal and which should be cause for alarm, and interpreting various stats provided by Elasticsearch

- Deploying your cluster to production, including best practices and important configuration that should (or should not!) be changed

- Performing post-deployment logistics, such as a rolling restart or backup of your cluster

Monitoring

Elasticsearch is often deployed as a cluster of nodes. A variety of APIs let you manage and monitor the cluster itself, rather than interact with the data stored within the cluster.

As with most functionality in Elasticsearch, there is an overarching design goal that tasks should be performed through an API rather than by modifying static configuration files. This becomes especially important as your cluster scales. Even with a provisioning system (such as Puppet, Chef, and Ansible), a single HTTP API call is often simpler than pushing new configurations to hundreds of physical machines.

To that end, this chapter presents the various APIs that allow you to dynamically tweak, tune, and configure your cluster. It also covers a host of APIs that provide statistics about the cluster itself so you can monitor for health and performance.

Marvel for Monitoring

At the very beginning of the book ("Installing Marvel" on page 5), we encouraged you to install Marvel, a management monitoring tool for Elasticsearch, because it would enable interactive code samples throughout the book.

If you didn't install Marvel then, we encourage you to install it now. This chapter introduces a large number of APIs that emit an even larger number of statistics. These stats track everything from heap memory usage and garbage collection counts to open file descriptors. These statistics are invaluable for debugging a misbehaving cluster.

The problem is that these APIs provide a single data point: the statistic *right now*. Often you'll want to see historical data too, so you can plot a trend. Knowing memory usage at this instant is helpful, but knowing memory usage *over time* is much more useful.

Furthermore, the output of these APIs can get truly hairy as your cluster grows. Once you have a dozen nodes, let alone a hundred, reading through stacks of JSON becomes very tedious.

Marvel periodically polls these APIs and stores the data back in Elasticsearch. This allows Marvel to query and aggregate the metrics, and then provide interactive graphs in your browser. There are no proprietary statistics that Marvel exposes; it uses the same stats APIs that are accessible to you. But it does greatly simplify the collection and graphing of those statistics.

Marvel is free to use in development, so you should definitely try it out!

Cluster Health

An Elasticsearch cluster may consist of a single node with a single index. Or it may have a hundred data nodes, three dedicated masters, a few dozen client nodes—all operating on a thousand indices (and tens of thousands of shards).

No matter the scale of the cluster, you'll want a quick way to assess the status of your cluster. The `Cluster Health` API fills that role. You can think of it as a 10,000-foot view of your cluster. It can reassure you that everything is all right, or alert you to a problem somewhere in your cluster.

Let's execute a `cluster-health` API and see what the response looks like:

```
GET _cluster/health
```

Like other APIs in Elasticsearch, `cluster-health` will return a JSON response. This makes it convenient to parse for automation and alerting. The response contains some critical information about your cluster:

```
{
   "cluster_name": "elasticsearch_zach",
   "status": "green",
   "timed_out": false,
   "number_of_nodes": 1,
   "number_of_data_nodes": 1,
   "active_primary_shards": 10,
   "active_shards": 10,
   "relocating_shards": 0,
   "initializing_shards": 0,
   "unassigned_shards": 0
}
```

The most important piece of information in the response is the `status` field. The status may be one of three values:

green
> All primary and replica shards are allocated. Your cluster is 100% operational.

yellow
> All primary shards are allocated, but at least one replica is missing. No data is missing, so search results will still be complete. However, your high availability is compromised to some degree. If *more* shards disappear, you might lose data. Think of yellow as a warning that should prompt investigation.

red
> At least one primary shard (and all of its replicas) are missing. This means that you are missing data: searches will return partial results, and indexing into that shard will return an exception.

The green/yellow/red status is a great way to glance at your cluster and understand what's going on. The rest of the metrics give you a general summary of your cluster:

- number_of_nodes and number_of_data_nodes are fairly self-descriptive.

- active_primary_shards indicates the number of primary shards in your cluster. This is an aggregate total across all indices.

- active_shards is an aggregate total of *all* shards across all indices, which includes replica shards.

- relocating_shards shows the number of shards that are currently moving from one node to another node. This number is often zero, but can increase when Elasticsearch decides a cluster is not properly balanced, a new node is added, or a node is taken down, for example.

- initializing_shards is a count of shards that are being freshly created. For example, when you first create an index, the shards will all briefly reside in initializing state. This is typically a transient event, and shards shouldn't linger in initializing too long. You may also see initializing shards when a node is first restarted: as shards are loaded from disk, they start as initializing.

- unassigned_shards are shards that exist in the cluster state, but cannot be found in the cluster itself. A common source of unassigned shards are unassigned replicas. For example, an index with five shards and one replica will have five unassigned replicas in a single-node cluster. Unassigned shards will also be present if your cluster is red (since primaries are missing).

Drilling Deeper: Finding Problematic Indices

Imagine something goes wrong one day, and you notice that your cluster health looks like this:

```
{
    "cluster_name": "elasticsearch_zach",
    "status": "red",
    "timed_out": false,
    "number_of_nodes": 8,
    "number_of_data_nodes": 8,
    "active_primary_shards": 90,
    "active_shards": 180,
    "relocating_shards": 0,
    "initializing_shards": 0,
    "unassigned_shards": 20
}
```

OK, so what can we deduce from this health status? Well, our cluster is red, which means we are missing data (primary + replicas). We know our cluster has 10 nodes, but see only 8 data nodes listed in the health. Two of our nodes have gone missing. We see that there are 20 unassigned shards.

That's about all the information we can glean. The nature of those missing shards are still a mystery. Are we missing 20 indices with 1 primary shard each? Or 1 index with 20 primary shards? Or 10 indices with 1 primary + 1 replica? Which index?

To answer these questions, we need to ask cluster-health for a little more information by using the level parameter:

```
GET _cluster/health?level=indices
```

This parameter will make the cluster-health API add a list of indices in our cluster and details about each of those indices (status, number of shards, unassigned shards, and so forth):

```
{
    "cluster_name": "elasticsearch_zach",
    "status": "red",
    "timed_out": false,
    "number_of_nodes": 8,
    "number_of_data_nodes": 8,
    "active_primary_shards": 90,
    "active_shards": 180,
    "relocating_shards": 0,
    "initializing_shards": 0,
    "unassigned_shards": 20
    "indices": {
        "v1": {
            "status": "green",
            "number_of_shards": 10,
            "number_of_replicas": 1,
            "active_primary_shards": 10,
            "active_shards": 20,
            "relocating_shards": 0,
            "initializing_shards": 0,
            "unassigned_shards": 0
```

```
    },
    "v2": {
      "status": "red",  ❶
      "number_of_shards": 10,
      "number_of_replicas": 1,
      "active_primary_shards": 0,
      "active_shards": 0,
      "relocating_shards": 0,
      "initializing_shards": 0,
      "unassigned_shards": 20 ❷
    },
    "v3": {
      "status": "green",
      "number_of_shards": 10,
      "number_of_replicas": 1,
      "active_primary_shards": 10,
      "active_shards": 20,
      "relocating_shards": 0,
      "initializing_shards": 0,
      "unassigned_shards": 0
    },
    ....
  }
}
```

❶ We can now see that the v2 index is the index that has made the cluster red.

❷ And it becomes clear that all 20 missing shards are from this index.

Once we ask for the indices output, it becomes immediately clear which index is having problems: the v2 index. We also see that the index has 10 primary shards and one replica, and that all 20 shards are missing. Presumably these 20 shards were on the two nodes that are missing from our cluster.

The level parameter accepts one more option:

```
GET _cluster/health?level=shards
```

The shards option will provide a very verbose output, which lists the status and location of every shard inside every index. This output is sometimes useful, but because of the verbosity can be difficult to work with. Once you know the index that is having problems, other APIs that we discuss in this chapter will tend to be more helpful.

Blocking for Status Changes

The cluster-health API has another neat trick that is useful when building unit and integration tests, or automated scripts that work with Elasticsearch. You can specify a wait_for_status parameter, which will only return after the status is satisfied. For example:

```
GET _cluster/health?wait_for_status=green
```

This call will *block* (not return control to your program) until the `cluster-health` has turned `green`, meaning all primary and replica shards have been allocated. This is important for automated scripts and tests.

If you create an index, Elasticsearch must broadcast the change in cluster state to all nodes. Those nodes must initialize those new shards, and then respond to the master that the shards are `Started`. This process is fast, but because network latency may take 10–20ms.

If you have an automated script that (a) creates an index and then (b) immediately attempts to index a document, this operation may fail, because the index has not been fully initialized yet. The time between (a) and (b) will likely be less than 1ms—not nearly enough time to account for network latency.

Rather than sleeping, just have your script/test call `cluster-health` with a `wait_for_status` parameter. As soon as the index is fully created, the `cluster-health` will change to `green`, the call will return control to your script, and you may begin indexing.

Valid options are `green`, `yellow`, and `red`. The call will return when the requested status (or one "higher") is reached. For example, if you request `yellow`, a status change to `yellow` or `green` will unblock the call.

Monitoring Individual Nodes

`Cluster-health` is at one end of the spectrum—a very high-level overview of everything in your cluster. The `node-stats` API is at the other end. It provides a bewildering array of statistics about each node in your cluster.

`Node-stats` provides so many stats that, until you are accustomed to the output, you may be unsure which metrics are most important to keep an eye on. We'll highlight the most important metrics to monitor (but we encourage you to log all the metrics provided—or use Marvel—because you'll never know when you need one stat or another).

The `node-stats` API can be executed with the following:

```
GET _nodes/stats
```

Starting at the top of the output, we see the cluster name and our first node:

```
{
   "cluster_name": "elasticsearch_zach",
   "nodes": {
      "UNr6ZMf5Qk-YCPA_L18BOQ": {
         "timestamp": 1408474151742,
```

```
    "name": "Zach",
    "transport_address": "inet[zacharys-air/192.168.1.131:9300]",
    "host": "zacharys-air",
    "ip": [
       "inet[zacharys-air/192.168.1.131:9300]",
       "NONE"
    ],
...
```

The nodes are listed in a hash, with the key being the UUID of the node. Some information about the node's network properties are displayed (such as transport address, and host). These values are useful for debugging discovery problems, where nodes won't join the cluster. Often you'll see that the port being used is wrong, or the node is binding to the wrong IP address/interface.

indices Section

The `indices` section lists aggregate statistics for all the indices that reside on this particular node:

```
"indices": {
    "docs": {
       "count": 6163666,
       "deleted": 0
    },
    "store": {
       "size_in_bytes": 2301398179,
       "throttle_time_in_millis": 122850
    },
```

The returned statistics are grouped into the following sections:

- docs shows how many documents reside on this node, as well as the number of deleted docs that haven't been purged from segments yet.

- The `store` portion indicates how much physical storage is consumed by the node. This metric includes both primary and replica shards. If the throttle time is large, it may be an indicator that your disk throttling is set too low (discussed in "Segments and Merging" on page 656).

```
"indexing": {
    "index_total": 803441,
    "index_time_in_millis": 367654,
    "index_current": 99,
    "delete_total": 0,
    "delete_time_in_millis": 0,
    "delete_current": 0
},
"get": {
    "total": 6,
    "time_in_millis": 2,
```

```
      "exists_total": 5,
      "exists_time_in_millis": 2,
      "missing_total": 1,
      "missing_time_in_millis": 0,
      "current": 0
   },
   "search": {
      "open_contexts": 0,
      "query_total": 123,
      "query_time_in_millis": 531,
      "query_current": 0,
      "fetch_total": 3,
      "fetch_time_in_millis": 55,
      "fetch_current": 0
   },
   "merges": {
      "current": 0,
      "current_docs": 0,
      "current_size_in_bytes": 0,
      "total": 1128,
      "total_time_in_millis": 21338523,
      "total_docs": 7241313,
      "total_size_in_bytes": 5724869463
   },
```

- indexing shows the number of docs that have been indexed. This value is a monotonically increasing counter; it doesn't decrease when docs are deleted. Also note that it is incremented anytime an *index* operation happens internally, which includes things like updates.

  Also listed are times for indexing, the number of docs currently being indexed, and similar statistics for deletes.

- get shows statistics about get-by-ID statistics. This includes GET and HEAD requests for a single document.

- search describes the number of active searches (open_contexts), number of queries total, and the amount of time spent on queries since the node was started. The ratio between query_time_in_millis / query_total can be used as a rough indicator for how efficient your queries are. The larger the ratio, the more time each query is taking, and you should consider tuning or optimization.

  The fetch statistics detail the second half of the query process (the *fetch* in query-then-fetch). If more time is spent in fetch than query, this can be an indicator of slow disks or very large documents being fetched, or potentially search requests with paginations that are too large (for example, size: 10000).

- merges contains information about Lucene segment merges. It will tell you the number of merges that are currently active, the number of docs involved, the cumulative size of segments being merged, and the amount of time spent on merges in total.

Merge statistics can be important if your cluster is write heavy. Merging consumes a large amount of disk I/O and CPU resources. If your index is write heavy and you see large merge numbers, be sure to read "Indexing Performance Tips" on page 653.

Note: updates and deletes will contribute to large merge numbers too, since they cause segment *fragmentation* that needs to be merged out eventually.

```
"filter_cache": {
   "memory_size_in_bytes": 48,
   "evictions": 0
},
"id_cache": {
   "memory_size_in_bytes": 0
},
"fielddata": {
   "memory_size_in_bytes": 0,
   "evictions": 0
},
"segments": {
   "count": 319,
   "memory_in_bytes": 65812120
},
...
```

- `filter_cache` indicates the amount of memory used by the cached filter bitsets, and the number of times a filter has been evicted. A large number of evictions *could* indicate that you need to increase the filter cache size, or that your filters are not caching well (for example, they are churning heavily because of high cardinality, such as caching now date expressions).

  However, evictions are a difficult metric to evaluate. Filters are cached on a per-segment basis, and evicting a filter from a small segment is much less expensive than evicting a filter from a large segment. It's possible that you have many evictions, but they all occur on small segments, which means they have little impact on query performance.

  Use the eviction metric as a rough guideline. If you see a large number, investigate your filters to make sure they are caching well. Filters that constantly evict, even on small segments, will be much less effective than properly cached filters.

- `id_cache` shows the memory usage by parent/child mappings. When you use parent/children, the `id_cache` maintains an in-memory join table that maintains the relationship. This statistic will show you how much memory is being used. There is little you can do to affect this memory usage, since it has a fairly linear relationship with the number of parent/child docs. It is heap-resident, however, so it's a good idea to keep an eye on it.

- `field_data` displays the memory used by fielddata, which is used for aggregations, sorting, and more. There is also an eviction count. Unlike `filter_cache`, the eviction count here is useful: it should be zero or very close. Since field data is not a cache, any eviction is costly and should be avoided. If you see evictions here, you need to reevaluate your memory situation, fielddata limits, queries, or all three.

- `segments` will tell you the number of Lucene segments this node currently serves. This can be an important number. Most indices should have around 50–150 segments, even if they are terabytes in size with billions of documents. Large numbers of segments can indicate a problem with merging (for example, merging is not keeping up with segment creation). Note that this statistic is the aggregate total of all indices on the node, so keep that in mind.

The `memory` statistic gives you an idea of the amount of memory being used by the Lucene segments themselves. This includes low-level data structures such as posting lists, dictionaries, and bloom filters. A very large number of segments will increase the amount of overhead lost to these data structures, and the memory usage can be a handy metric to gauge that overhead.

OS and Process Sections

The `OS` and `Process` sections are fairly self-explanatory and won't be covered in great detail. They list basic resource statistics such as CPU and load. The `OS` section describes it for the entire `OS`, while the `Process` section shows just what the Elasticsearch JVM process is using.

These are obviously useful metrics, but are often being measured elsewhere in your monitoring stack. Some stats include the following:

- CPU
- Load
- Memory usage
- Swap usage
- Open file descriptors

JVM Section

The `jvm` section contains some critical information about the JVM process that is running Elasticsearch. Most important, it contains garbage collection details, which have a large impact on the stability of your Elasticsearch cluster.

Garbage Collection Primer

Before we describe the stats, it is useful to give a crash course in garbage collection and its impact on Elasticsearch. If you are familar with garbage collection in the JVM, feel free to skip down.

Java is a *garbage-collected* language, which means that the programmer does not manually manage memory allocation and deallocation. The programmer simply writes code, and the Java Virtual Machine (JVM) manages the process of allocating memory as needed, and then later cleaning up that memory when no longer needed.

When memory is allocated to a JVM process, it is allocated in a big chunk called the *heap*. The JVM then breaks the heap into two groups, referred to as *generations*:

Young (or Eden)
>   The space where newly instantiated objects are allocated. The young generation space is often quite small, usually 100 MB–500 MB. The young-gen also contains two *survivor* spaces.

Old
>   The space where older objects are stored. These objects are expected to be long-lived and persist for a long time. The old-gen is often much larger than then young-gen, and Elasticsearch nodes can see old-gens as large as 30 GB.

When an object is instantiated, it is placed into young-gen. When the young generation space is full, a young-gen garbage collection (GC) is started. Objects that are still "alive" are moved into one of the survivor spaces, and "dead" objects are removed. If an object has survived several young-gen GCs, it will be "tenured" into the old generation.

A similar process happens in the old generation: when the space becomes full, a garbage collection is started and dead objects are removed.

Nothing comes for free, however. Both the young- and old-generation garbage collectors have phases that "stop the world." During this time, the JVM literally halts execution of the program so it can trace the object graph and collect dead objects. During this stop-the-world phase, nothing happens. Requests are not serviced, pings are not responded to, shards are not relocated. The world quite literally stops.

This isn't a big deal for the young generation; its small size means GCs execute quickly. But the old-gen is quite a bit larger, and a slow GC here could mean 1s or even 15s of pausing—which is unacceptable for server software.

The garbage collectors in the JVM are *very* sophisticated algorithms and do a great job minimizing pauses. And Elasticsearch tries very hard to be *garbage-collection friendly*, by intelligently reusing objects internally, reusing network buffers, and offering features like "Doc Values" on page 495. But ultimately, GC frequency and duration is a metric that needs to be watched by you, since it is the number one culprit for cluster instability.

A cluster that is frequently experiencing long GC will be a cluster that is under heavy load with not enough memory. These long GCs will make nodes drop off the cluster for brief periods. This instability causes shards to relocate frequently as Elasticsearch tries to keep the cluster balanced and enough replicas available. This in turn increases network traffic and disk I/O, all while your cluster is attempting to service the normal indexing and query load.

In short, long GCs are bad and need to be minimized as much as possible.

Because garbage collection is so critical to Elasticsearch, you should become intimately familiar with this section of the node-stats API:

```
"jvm": {
    "timestamp": 1408556438203,
    "uptime_in_millis": 14457,
    "mem": {
        "heap_used_in_bytes": 457252160,
        "heap_used_percent": 44,
        "heap_committed_in_bytes": 1038876672,
        "heap_max_in_bytes": 1038876672,
        "non_heap_used_in_bytes": 38680680,
        "non_heap_committed_in_bytes": 38993920,
```

- The jvm section first lists some general stats about heap memory usage. You can see how much of the heap is being used, how much is committed (actually allocated to the process), and the max size the heap is allowed to grow to. Ideally, heap_committed_in_bytes should be identical to heap_max_in_bytes. If the committed size is smaller, the JVM will have to resize the heap eventually—and this is a very expensive process. If your numbers are not identical, see "Heap: Sizing and Swapping" on page 645 for how to configure it correctly.

The heap_used_percent metric is a useful number to keep an eye on. Elasticsearch is configured to initiate GCs when the heap reaches 75% full. If your node is consistently >= 75%, your node is experiencing *memory pressure*. This is a warning sign that slow GCs may be in your near future.

If the heap usage is consistently >=85%, you are in trouble. Heaps over 90–95% are in risk of horrible performance with long 10–30s GCs at best, and out-of-memory (OOM) exceptions at worst.

```
    "pools": {
      "young": {
        "used_in_bytes": 138467752,
        "max_in_bytes": 279183360,
        "peak_used_in_bytes": 279183360,
        "peak_max_in_bytes": 279183360
      },
      "survivor": {
        "used_in_bytes": 34865152,
        "max_in_bytes": 34865152,
        "peak_used_in_bytes": 34865152,
        "peak_max_in_bytes": 34865152
      },
      "old": {
        "used_in_bytes": 283919256,
        "max_in_bytes": 724828160,
        "peak_used_in_bytes": 283919256,
        "peak_max_in_bytes": 724828160
      }
    }
  }
},
```

- The young, survivor, and old sections will give you a breakdown of memory usage of each generation in the GC. These stats are handy for keeping an eye on relative sizes, but are often not overly important when debugging problems.

```
"gc": {
  "collectors": {
    "young": {
      "collection_count": 13,
      "collection_time_in_millis": 923
    },
    "old": {
      "collection_count": 0,
      "collection_time_in_millis": 0
    }
  }
}
```

- gc section shows the garbage collection counts and cumulative time for both young and old generations. You can safely ignore the young generation counts for the most part: this number will usually be large. That is perfectly normal.

In contrast, the old generation collection count should remain small, and have a small collection_time_in_millis. These are cumulative counts, so it is hard to give an exact number when you should start worrying (for example, a node with a one-year uptime will have a large count even if it is healthy). This is one of the reasons that tools such as Marvel are so helpful. GC counts *over time* are the important consideration.

Time spent GC'ing is also important. For example, a certain amount of garbage is generated while indexing documents. This is normal and causes a GC every now and then. These GCs are almost always fast and have little effect on the node: young generation takes a millisecond or two, and old generation takes a few hundred milliseconds. This is much different from 10-second GCs.

Our best advice is to collect collection counts and duration periodically (or use Marvel) and keep an eye out for frequent GCs. You can also enable slow-GC logging, discussed in "Logging" on page 652.

Threadpool Section

Elasticsearch maintains threadpools internally. These threadpools cooperate to get work done, passing work between each other as necessary. In general, you don't need to configure or tune the threadpools, but it is sometimes useful to see their stats so you can gain insight into how your cluster is behaving.

There are about a dozen threadpools, but they all share the same format:

```
"index": {
    "threads": 1,
    "queue": 0,
    "active": 0,
    "rejected": 0,
    "largest": 1,
    "completed": 1
}
```

Each threadpool lists the number of threads that are configured (`threads`), how many of those threads are actively processing some work (`active`), and how many work units are sitting in a queue (`queue`).

If the queue fills up to its limit, new work units will begin to be rejected, and you will see that reflected in the `rejected` statistic. This is often a sign that your cluster is starting to bottleneck on some resources, since a full queue means your node/cluster is processing at maximum speed but unable to keep up with the influx of work.

Bulk Rejections

If you are going to encounter queue rejections, it will most likely be caused by bulk indexing requests. It is easy to send many bulk requests to Elasticsearch by using concurrent import processes. More is better, right?

In reality, each cluster has a certain limit at which it can not keep up with ingestion. Once this threshold is crossed, the queue will quickly fill up, and new bulks will be rejected.

This is a *good thing*. Queue rejections are a useful form of back pressure. They let you know that your cluster is at maximum capacity, which is much better than sticking data into an in-memory queue. Increasing the queue size doesn't increase performance; it just hides the problem. If your cluster can process only 10,000 docs per second, it doesn't matter whether the queue is 100 or 10,000,000—your cluster can still process only 10,000 docs per second.

The queue simply hides the performance problem and carries a real risk of data-loss. Anything sitting in a queue is by definition not processed yet. If the node goes down, all those requests are lost forever. Furthermore, the queue eats up a lot of memory, which is not ideal.

It is much better to handle queuing in your application by gracefully handling the back pressure from a full queue. When you receive bulk rejections, you should take these steps:

1. Pause the import thread for 3–5 seconds.
2. Extract the rejected actions from the bulk response, since it is probable that many of the actions were successful. The bulk response will tell you which succeeded and which were rejected.
3. Send a new bulk request with just the rejected actions.
4. Repeat from step 1 if rejections are encountered again.

Using this procedure, your code naturally adapts to the load of your cluster and naturally backs off.

Rejections are not errors: they just mean you should try again later.

There are a dozen threadpools. Most you can safely ignore, but a few are good to keep an eye on:

indexing
: Threadpool for normal indexing requests

bulk
: Bulk requests, which are distinct from the nonbulk indexing requests

get
: Get-by-ID operations

search
: All search and query requests

merging
: Threadpool dedicated to managing Lucene merges

FS and Network Sections

Continuing down the `node-stats` API, you'll see a bunch of statistics about your file-system: free space, data directory paths, disk I/O stats, and more. If you are not monitoring free disk space, you can get those stats here. The disk I/O stats are also handy, but often more specialized command-line tools (`iostat`, for example) are more useful.

Obviously, Elasticsearch has a difficult time functioning if you run out of disk space —so make sure you don't.

There are also two sections on network statistics:

```
"transport": {
    "server_open": 13,
    "rx_count": 11696,
    "rx_size_in_bytes": 1525774,
    "tx_count": 10282,
    "tx_size_in_bytes": 1440101928
},
"http": {
    "current_open": 4,
    "total_opened": 23
},
```

- `transport` shows some basic stats about the *transport address*. This relates to inter-node communication (often on port 9300) and any transport client or node client connections. Don't worry if you see many connections here; Elasticsearch maintains a large number of connections between nodes.

- `http` represents stats about the HTTP port (often 9200). If you see a very large `total_opened` number that is constantly increasing, that is a sure sign that one of your HTTP clients is not using keep-alive connections. Persistent, keep-alive connections are important for performance, since building up and tearing down sockets is expensive (and wastes file descriptors). Make sure your clients are configured appropriately.

Circuit Breaker

Finally, we come to the last section: stats about the fielddata circuit breaker (introduced in "Circuit Breaker" on page 492):

```
"fielddata_breaker": {
    "maximum_size_in_bytes": 623326003,
    "maximum_size": "594.4mb",
    "estimated_size_in_bytes": 0,
    "estimated_size": "0b",
    "overhead": 1.03,
    "tripped": 0
}
```

Here, you can determine the maximum circuit-breaker size (for example, at what size the circuit breaker will trip if a query attempts to use more memory). This section will also let you know the number of times the circuit breaker has been tripped, and the currently configured overhead. The overhead is used to pad estimates, because some queries are more difficult to estimate than others.

The main thing to watch is the `tripped` metric. If this number is large or consistently increasing, it's a sign that your queries may need to be optimized or that you may need to obtain more memory (either per box or by adding more nodes).

Cluster Stats

The `cluster-stats` API provides similar output to the `node-stats`. There is one crucial difference: Node Stats shows you statistics per node, while `cluster-stats` shows you the sum total of all nodes in a single metric.

This provides some useful stats to glance at. You can see for example, that your entire cluster is using 50% of the available heap or that filter cache is not evicting heavily. Its main use is to provide a quick summary that is more extensive than the `cluster-health`, but less detailed than `node-stats`. It is also useful for clusters that are very large, which makes `node-stats` output difficult to read.

The API may be invoked as follows:

```
GET _cluster/stats
```

Index Stats

So far, we have been looking at *node-centric* statistics: How much memory does this node have? How much CPU is being used? How many searches is this node servicing?

Sometimes it is useful to look at statistics from an *index-centric* perspective: How many search requests is *this index* receiving? How much time is spent fetching docs in *that index*?

To do this, select the index (or indices) that you are interested in and execute an Index stats API:

```
GET my_index/_stats ❶

GET my_index,another_index/_stats ❷

GET _all/_stats ❸
```

❶ Stats for my_index.

❷ Stats for multiple indices can be requested by separating their names with a comma.

❸ Stats indices can be requested using the special _all index name.

The stats returned will be familar to the node-stats output: search fetch get index bulk segment counts and so forth

Index-centric stats can be useful for identifying or verifying *hot* indices inside your cluster, or trying to determine why some indices are faster/slower than others.

In practice, however, node-centric statistics tend to be more useful. Entire nodes tend to bottleneck, not individual indices. And because indices are usually spread across multiple nodes, index-centric statistics are usually not very helpful because they aggregate data from different physical machines operating in different environments.

Index-centric stats are a useful tool to keep in your repertoire, but are not usually the first tool to reach for.

Pending Tasks

There are certain tasks that only the master can perform, such as creating a new index or moving shards around the cluster. Since a cluster can have only one master, only one node can ever process cluster-level metadata changes. For 99.9999% of the time, this is never a problem. The queue of metadata changes remains essentially zero.

In some *rare* clusters, the number of metadata changes occurs faster than the master can process them. This leads to a buildup of pending actions that are queued.

The pending-tasks API will show you what (if any) cluster-level metadata changes are pending in the queue:

```
GET _cluster/pending_tasks
```

Usually, the response will look like this:

```
{
   "tasks": []
}
```

This means there are no pending tasks. If you have one of the rare clusters that bottle-necks on the master node, your pending task list may look like this:

```
{
   "tasks": [
      {
         "insert_order": 101,
         "priority": "URGENT",
         "source": "create-index [foo_9], cause [api]",
         "time_in_queue_millis": 86,
         "time_in_queue": "86ms"
      },
      {
         "insert_order": 46,
         "priority": "HIGH",
         "source": "shard-started ([foo_2][1], node[tMTocMvQQgGCkj7QDHl30A], [P],
         s[INITIALIZING]), reason [after recovery from gateway]",
         "time_in_queue_millis": 842,
         "time_in_queue": "842ms"
      },
      {
         "insert_order": 45,
         "priority": "HIGH",
         "source": "shard-started ([foo_2][0], node[tMTocMvQQgGCkj7QDHl30A], [P],
         s[INITIALIZING]), reason [after recovery from gateway]",
         "time_in_queue_millis": 858,
         "time_in_queue": "858ms"
      }
   ]
}
```

You can see that tasks are assigned a priority (URGENT is processed before HIGH, for example), the order it was inserted, how long the action has been queued and what the action is trying to perform. In the preceding list, there is a create-index action and two shard-started actions pending.

When Should I Worry About Pending Tasks?

As mentioned, the master node is rarely the bottleneck for clusters. The only time it could bottleneck is if the cluster state is both very large *and* updated frequently.

For example, if you allow customers to create as many dynamic fields as they wish, and have a unique index for each customer every day, your cluster state will grow very large. The cluster state includes (among other things) a list of all indices, their types, and the fields for each index.

So if you have 100,000 customers, and each customer averages 1,000 fields and 90 days of retention—that's nine billion fields to keep in the cluster state. Whenever this changes, the nodes must be notified.

The master must process these changes, which requires nontrivial CPU overhead, plus the network overhead of pushing the updated cluster state to all nodes.

It is these clusters that may begin to see cluster-state actions queuing up. There is no easy solution to this problem, however. You have three options:

- Obtain a beefier master node. Vertical scaling just delays the inevitable, unfortunately.
- Restrict the dynamic nature of the documents in some way, so as to limit the cluster-state size.
- Spin up another cluster after a certain threshold has been crossed.

cat API

If you work from the command line often, the `cat` APIs will be helpful to you. Named after the linux `cat` command, these APIs are designed to work like *nix command-line tools.

They provide statistics that are identical to all the previously discussed APIs (Health, `node-stats`, and so forth), but present the output in tabular form instead of JSON. This is *very* convenient for a system administrator, and you just want to glance over your cluster or find nodes with high memory usage.

Executing a plain `GET` against the `cat` endpoint will show you all available APIs:

```
GET /_cat

=^.^=
/_cat/allocation
/_cat/shards
/_cat/shards/{index}
/_cat/master
/_cat/nodes
/_cat/indices
/_cat/indices/{index}
/_cat/segments
/_cat/segments/{index}
/_cat/count
/_cat/count/{index}
/_cat/recovery
/_cat/recovery/{index}
/_cat/health
/_cat/pending_tasks
/_cat/aliases
/_cat/aliases/{alias}
/_cat/thread_pool
/_cat/plugins
```

```
/_cat/fielddata
/_cat/fielddata/{fields}
```

Many of these APIs should look familiar to you (and yes, that's a cat at the top :)).
Let's take a look at the Cat Health API:

```
GET /_cat/health
```

```
1408723713 12:08:33 elasticsearch_zach yellow 1 1 114 114 0 0 114
```

The first thing you'll notice is that the response is plain text in tabular form, not
JSON. The second thing you'll notice is that there are no column headers enabled by
default. This is designed to emulate *nix tools, since it is assumed that once you
become familiar with the output, you no longer want to see the headers.

To enable headers, add the ?v parameter:

```
GET /_cat/health?v
```

```
epoch    time    cluster status node.total node.data shards pri relo init
1408[..] 12[..] el[..]  1        1          114 114   0   0      114
unassign
```

Ah, much better. We now see the timestamp, cluster name, status, the number of
nodes in the cluster, and more—all the same information as the cluster-health API.

Let's look at node-stats in the cat API:

```
GET /_cat/nodes?v
```

```
host          ip            heap.percent ram.percent load node.role master name
zacharys-air 192.168.1.131           45          72 1.85 d          *      Zach
```

We see some stats about the nodes in our cluster, but the output is basic compared to
the full node-stats output. You can include many additional metrics, but rather than
consulting the documentation, let's just ask the cat API what is available.

You can do this by adding ?help to any API:

```
GET /_cat/nodes?help
```

```
id            | id,nodeId         | unique node id
pid           | p                 | process id
host          | h                 | host name
ip            | i                 | ip address
port          | po                | bound transport port
version       | v                 | es version
build         | b                 | es build hash
jdk           | j                 | jdk version
disk.avail    | d,disk,diskAvail  | available disk space
heap.percent  | hp,heapPercent    | used heap ratio
heap.max      | hm,heapMax        | max configured heap
ram.percent   | rp,ramPercent     | used machine memory ratio
```

```
ram.max          | rm,ramMax           | total machine memory
load             | l                   | most recent load avg
uptime           | u                   | node uptime
node.role        | r,role,dc,nodeRole  | d:data node, c:client node
master           | m                   | m:master-eligible, *:current master
...
...
```

(Note that the output has been truncated for brevity).

The first column shows the full name, the second column shows the short name, and the third column offers a brief description about the parameter. Now that we know some column names, we can ask for those explicitly by using the ?h parameter:

```
GET /_cat/nodes?v&h=ip,port,heapPercent,heapMax

ip            port heapPercent heapMax
192.168.1.131 9300          53 990.7mb
```

Because the cat API tries to behave like *nix utilities, you can pipe the output to other tools such as sort grep or awk. For example, we can find the largest index in our cluster by using the following:

```
% curl 'localhost:9200/_cat/indices?bytes=b' | sort -rnk8

yellow test_names             5 1 3476004 0 376324705 376324705
yellow .marvel-2014.08.19     1 1  263878 0 160777194 160777194
yellow .marvel-2014.08.15     1 1  234482 0 143020770 143020770
yellow .marvel-2014.08.09     1 1  222532 0 138177271 138177271
yellow .marvel-2014.08.18     1 1  225921 0 138116185 138116185
yellow .marvel-2014.07.26     1 1  173423 0 132031505 132031505
yellow .marvel-2014.08.21     1 1  219857 0 128414798 128414798
yellow .marvel-2014.07.27     1 1   75202 0  56320862  56320862
yellow wavelet               5 1    5979 0  54815185  54815185
yellow .marvel-2014.07.28     1 1   57483 0  43006141  43006141
yellow .marvel-2014.07.21     1 1   31134 0  27558507  27558507
yellow .marvel-2014.08.01     1 1   41100 0  27000476  27000476
yellow kibana-int            5 1       2 0     17791     17791
yellow t                     5 1       7 0     15280     15280
yellow website               5 1      12 0     12631     12631
yellow agg_analysis          5 1       5 0      5804      5804
yellow v2                    5 1       2 0      5410      5410
yellow v1                    5 1       2 0      5367      5367
yellow bank                  1 1      16 0      4303      4303
yellow v                     5 1       1 0      2954      2954
yellow p                     5 1       2 0      2939      2939
yellow b0001_072320141238    5 1       1 0      2923      2923
yellow ipaddr                5 1       1 0      2917      2917
yellow v2a                   5 1       1 0      2895      2895
yellow movies                5 1       1 0      2738      2738
yellow cars                  5 1       0 0      1249      1249
yellow wavelet2              5 1       0 0       615       615
```

By adding `?bytes=b`, we disable the human-readable formatting on numbers and force them to be listed as bytes. This output is then piped into `sort` so that our indices are ranked according to size (the eighth column).

Unfortunately, you'll notice that the Marvel indices are clogging up the results, and we don't really care about those indices right now. Let's pipe the output through `grep` and remove anything mentioning Marvel:

```
% curl 'localhost:9200/_cat/indices?bytes=b' | sort -rnk8 | grep -v marvel
```

```
yellow test_names            5 1 3476004 0 376324705 376324705
yellow wavelet               5 1    5979 0  54815185  54815185
yellow kibana-int            5 1       2 0     17791     17791
yellow t                     5 1       7 0     15280     15280
yellow website               5 1      12 0     12631     12631
yellow agg_analysis          5 1       5 0      5804      5804
yellow v2                    5 1       2 0      5410      5410
yellow v1                    5 1       2 0      5367      5367
yellow bank                  1 1      16 0      4303      4303
yellow v                     5 1       1 0      2954      2954
yellow p                     5 1       2 0      2939      2939
yellow b0001_072320141238    5 1       1 0      2923      2923
yellow ipaddr                5 1       1 0      2917      2917
yellow v2a                   5 1       1 0      2895      2895
yellow movies                5 1       1 0      2738      2738
yellow cars                  5 1       0 0      1249      1249
yellow wavelet2              5 1       0 0       615       615
```

Voila! After piping through `grep` (with `-v` to invert the matches), we get a sorted list of indices without Marvel cluttering it up.

This is just a simple example of the flexibility of `cat` at the command line. Once you get used to using `cat`, you'll see it like any other *nix tool and start going crazy with piping, sorting, and grepping. If you are a system admin and spend any time SSH'd into boxes, definitely spend some time getting familiar with the `cat` API.

CHAPTER 45

Production Deployment

If you have made it this far in the book, hopefully you've learned a thing or two about Elasticsearch and are ready to deploy your cluster to production. This chapter is not meant to be an exhaustive guide to running your cluster in production, but it covers the key things to consider before putting your cluster live.

Three main areas are covered:

- Logistical considerations, such as hardware recommendations and deployment strategies
- Configuration changes that are more suited to a production environment
- Post-deployment considerations, such as security, maximizing indexing performance, and backups

Hardware

If you've been following the normal development path, you've probably been playing with Elasticsearch on your laptop or on a small cluster of machines laying around. But when it comes time to deploy Elasticsearch to production, there are a few recommendations that you should consider. Nothing is a hard-and-fast rule; Elasticsearch is used for a wide range of tasks and on a bewildering array of machines. But these recommendations provide good starting points based on our experience with production clusters.

Memory

If there is one resource that you will run out of first, it will likely be memory. Sorting and aggregations can both be memory hungry, so enough heap space to accommodate these is important. Even when the heap is comparatively small, extra memory can be given to the OS filesystem cache. Because many data structures used by Lucene are disk-based formats, Elasticsearch leverages the OS cache to great effect.

A machine with 64 GB of RAM is the ideal sweet spot, but 32 GB and 16 GB machines are also common. Less than 8 GB tends to be counterproductive (you end up needing many, many small machines), and greater than 64 GB has problems that we will discuss in "Heap: Sizing and Swapping" on page 645.

CPUs

Most Elasticsearch deployments tend to be rather light on CPU requirements. As such, the exact processor setup matters less than the other resources. You should choose a modern processor with multiple cores. Common clusters utilize two to eight core machines.

If you need to choose between faster CPUs or more cores, choose more cores. The extra concurrency that multiple cores offers will far outweigh a slightly faster clock speed.

Disks

Disks are important for all clusters, and doubly so for indexing-heavy clusters (such as those that ingest log data). Disks are the slowest subsystem in a server, which means that write-heavy clusters can easily saturate their disks, which in turn become the bottleneck of the cluster.

If you can afford SSDs, they are by far superior to any spinning media. SSD-backed nodes see boosts in both query and indexing performance. If you can afford it, SSDs are the way to go.

Check Your I/O Scheduler

If you are using SSDs, make sure your OS I/O scheduler is configured correctly. When you write data to disk, the I/O scheduler decides when that data is *actually* sent to the disk. The default under most *nix distributions is a scheduler called cfq (Completely Fair Queuing).

This scheduler allocates *time slices* to each process, and then optimizes the delivery of these various queues to the disk. It is optimized for spinning media: the nature of rotating platters means it is more efficient to write data to disk based on physical layout.

This is inefficient for SSD, however, since there are no spinning platters involved. Instead, deadline or noop should be used instead. The deadline scheduler optimizes based on how long writes have been pending, while noop is just a simple FIFO queue.

> This simple change can have dramatic impacts. We've seen a 500-fold improvement to write throughput just by using the correct scheduler.

If you use spinning media, try to obtain the fastest disks possible (high-performance server disks, 15k RPM drives).

Using RAID 0 is an effective way to increase disk speed, for both spinning disks and SSD. There is no need to use mirroring or parity variants of RAID, since high availability is built into Elasticsearch via replicas.

Finally, avoid network-attached storage (NAS). People routinely claim their NAS solution is faster and more reliable than local drives. Despite these claims, we have never seen NAS live up to its hype. NAS is often slower, displays larger latencies with a wider deviation in average latency, and is a single point of failure.

Network

A fast and reliable network is obviously important to performance in a distributed system. Low latency helps ensure that nodes can communicate easily, while high bandwidth helps shard movement and recovery. Modern data-center networking (1 GbE, 10 GbE) is sufficient for the vast majority of clusters.

Avoid clusters that span multiple data centers, even if the data centers are colocated in close proximity. Definitely avoid clusters that span large geographic distances.

Elasticsearch clusters assume that all nodes are equal—not that half the nodes are actually 150ms distant in another data center. Larger latencies tend to exacerbate problems in distributed systems and make debugging and resolution more difficult.

Similar to the NAS argument, everyone claims that their pipe between data centers is robust and low latency. This is true—until it isn't (a network failure will happen eventually; you can count on it). From our experience, the hassle of managing cross–data center clusters is simply not worth the cost.

General Considerations

It is possible nowadays to obtain truly enormous machines: hundreds of gigabytes of RAM with dozens of CPU cores. Conversely, it is also possible to spin up thousands of small virtual machines in cloud platforms such as EC2. Which approach is best?

In general, it is better to prefer medium-to-large boxes. Avoid small machines, because you don't want to manage a cluster with a thousand nodes, and the overhead of simply running Elasticsearch is more apparent on such small boxes.

At the same time, avoid the truly enormous machines. They often lead to imbalanced resource usage (for example, all the memory is being used, but none of the CPU) and can add logistical complexity if you have to run multiple nodes per machine.

Java Virtual Machine

You should always run the most recent version of the Java Virtual Machine (JVM), unless otherwise stated on the Elasticsearch website. Elasticsearch, and in particular Lucene, is a demanding piece of software. The unit and integration tests from Lucene often expose bugs in the JVM itself. These bugs range from mild annoyances to serious segfaults, so it is best to use the latest version of the JVM where possible.

Java 7 is strongly preferred over Java 6. Either Oracle or OpenJDK are acceptable. They are comparable in performance and stability.

If your application is written in Java and you are using the transport client or node client, make sure the JVM running your application is identical to the server JVM. In few locations in Elasticsearch, Java's native serialization is used (IP addresses, exceptions, and so forth). Unfortunately, Oracle has been known to change the serialization format between minor releases, leading to strange errors. This happens rarely, but it is best practice to keep the JVM versions identical between client and server.

Please Do Not Tweak JVM Settings

The JVM exposes dozens (hundreds even!) of settings, parameters, and configurations. They allow you to tweak and tune almost every aspect of the JVM.

When a knob is encountered, it is human nature to want to turn it. We implore you to squash this desire and *not* use custom JVM settings. Elasticsearch is a complex piece of software, and the current JVM settings have been tuned over years of real-world usage.

It is easy to start turning knobs, producing opaque effects that are hard to measure, and eventually detune your cluster into a slow, unstable mess. When debugging clusters, the first step is often to remove all custom configurations. About half the time, this alone restores stability and performance.

Transport Client Versus Node Client

If you are using Java, you may wonder when to use the transport client versus the node client. As discussed at the beginning of the book, the transport client acts as a communication layer between the cluster and your application. It knows the API and can automatically round-robin between nodes, sniff the cluster for you, and more. But it is *external* to the cluster, similar to the REST clients.

The node client, on the other hand, is actually a node within the cluster (but does not hold data, and cannot become master). Because it is a node, it knows the entire cluster state (where all the nodes reside, which shards live in which nodes, and so forth). This means it can execute APIs with one less network hop.

There are uses-cases for both clients:

- The transport client is ideal if you want to decouple your application from the cluster. For example, if your application quickly creates and destroys connections to the cluster, a transport client is much "lighter" than a node client, since it is not part of a cluster.

  Similarly, if you need to create thousands of connections, you don't want to have thousands of node clients join the cluster. The TC will be a better choice.

- On the flipside, if you need only a few long-lived, persistent connection objects to the cluster, a node client can be a bit more efficient since it knows the cluster layout. But it ties your application into the cluster, so it may pose problems from a firewall perspective.

Configuration Management

If you use configuration management already (Puppet, Chef, Ansible), you can skip this tip.

If you don't use configuration management tools yet, you should! Managing a handful of servers by `parallel-ssh` may work now, but it will become a nightmare as you grow your cluster. It is almost impossible to edit 30 configuration files by hand without making a mistake.

Configuration management tools help make your cluster consistent by automating the process of config changes. It may take a little time to set up and learn, but it will pay itself off handsomely over time.

Important Configuration Changes

Elasticsearch ships with *very good* defaults, especially when it comes to performance-related settings and options. When in doubt, just leave the settings alone. We have witnessed countless dozens of clusters ruined by errant settings because the administrator thought he could turn a knob and gain 100-fold improvement.

Please read this entire section! All configurations presented are equally important, and are not listed in any particular order. Please read through all configuration options and apply them to your cluster.

Other databases may require tuning, but by and large, Elasticsearch does not. If you are hitting performance problems, the solution is usually better data layout or more nodes. There are very few "magic knobs" in Elasticsearch. If there were, we'd have turned them already!

With that said, there are some *logistical* configurations that should be changed for production. These changes are necessary either to make your life easier, or because there is no way to set a good default (because it depends on your cluster layout).

Assign Names

Elasticseach by default starts a cluster named `elasticsearch`. It is wise to rename your production cluster to something else, simply to prevent accidents whereby someone's laptop joins the cluster. A simple change to `elasticsearch_production` can save a lot of heartache.

This can be changed in your `elasticsearch.yml` file:

```
cluster.name: elasticsearch_production
```

Similarly, it is wise to change the names of your nodes. As you've probably noticed by now, Elasticsearch assigns a random Marvel superhero name to your nodes at startup. This is cute in development—but less cute when it is 3a.m. and you are trying to remember which physical machine was Tagak the Leopard Lord.

More important, since these names are generated on startup, each time you restart your node, it will get a new name. This can make logs confusing, since the names of all the nodes are constantly changing.

Boring as it might be, we recommend you give each node a name that makes sense to you—a plain, descriptive name. This is also configured in your `elasticsearch.yml`:

```
node.name: elasticsearch_005_data
```

Paths

By default, Elasticsearch will place the plug-ins, logs, and—most important—your data in the installation directory. This can lead to unfortunate accidents, whereby the installation directory is accidentally overwritten by a new installation of Elasticsearch. If you aren't careful, you can erase all your data.

Don't laugh—we've seen it happen more than a few times.

The best thing to do is relocate your data directory outside the installation location. You can optionally move your plug-in and log directories as well.

This can be changed as follows:

```
path.data: /path/to/data1,/path/to/data2 ❶

# Path to log files:
path.logs: /path/to/logs

# Path to where plugins are installed:
path.plugins: /path/to/plugins
```

❶ Notice that you can specify more than one directory for data by using comma-separated lists.

Data can be saved to multiple directories, and if each directory is mounted on a different hard drive, this is a simple and effective way to set up a software RAID 0. Elasticsearch will automatically stripe data between the different directories, boosting performance

Minimum Master Nodes

The `minimum_master_nodes` setting is *extremely* important to the stability of your cluster. This setting helps prevent *split brains*, the existence of two masters in a single cluster.

When you have a split brain, your cluster is at danger of losing data. Because the master is considered the supreme ruler of the cluster, it decides when new indices can be created, how shards are moved, and so forth. If you have *two* masters, data integrity becomes perilous, since you have two nodes that think they are in charge.

This setting tells Elasticsearch to not elect a master unless there are enough master-eligible nodes available. Only then will an election take place.

This setting should always be configured to a quorum (majority) of your master-eligible nodes. A quorum is (`number of master-eligible nodes / 2) + 1`. Here are some examples:

- If you have ten regular nodes (can hold data, can become master), a quorum is 6.
- If you have three dedicated master nodes and a hundred data nodes, the quorum is 2, since you need to count only nodes that are master eligible.
- If you have two regular nodes, you are in a conundrum. A quorum would be 2, but this means a loss of one node will make your cluster inoperable. A setting of 1 will allow your cluster to function, but doesn't protect against split brain. It is best to have a minimum of three nodes in situations like this.

This setting can be configured in your `elasticsearch.yml` file:

```
discovery.zen.minimum_master_nodes: 2
```

But because Elasticsearch clusters are dynamic, you could easily add or remove nodes that will change the quorum. It would be extremely irritating if you had to push new configurations to each node and restart your whole cluster just to change the setting.

For this reason, `minimum_master_nodes` (and other settings) can be configured via a dynamic API call. You can change the setting while your cluster is online:

```
PUT /_cluster/settings
{
    "persistent" : {
        "discovery.zen.minimum_master_nodes" : 2
    }
}
```

This will become a persistent setting that takes precedence over whatever is in the static configuration. You should modify this setting whenever you add or remove master-eligible nodes.

Recovery Settings

Several settings affect the behavior of shard recovery when your cluster restarts. First, we need to understand what happens if nothing is configured.

Imagine you have ten nodes, and each node holds a single shard—either a primary or a replica—in a 5 primary / 1 replica index. You take your entire cluster offline for maintenance (installing new drives, for example). When you restart your cluster, it just so happens that five nodes come online before the other five.

Maybe the switch to the other five is being flaky, and they didn't receive the restart command right away. Whatever the reason, you have five nodes online. These five nodes will gossip with each other, elect a master, and form a cluster. They notice that data is no longer evenly distributed, since five nodes are missing from the cluster, and immediately start replicating new shards between each other.

Finally, your other five nodes turn on and join the cluster. These nodes see that *their* data is being replicated to other nodes, so they delete their local data (since it is now redundant, and may be outdated). Then the cluster starts to rebalance even more, since the cluster size just went from five to ten.

During this whole process, your nodes are thrashing the disk and network, moving data around—for no good reason. For large clusters with terabytes of data, this useless shuffling of data can take a *really long time*. If all the nodes had simply waited for the cluster to come online, all the data would have been local and nothing would need to move.

Now that we know the problem, we can configure a few settings to alleviate it. First, we need to give Elasticsearch a hard limit:

```
gateway.recover_after_nodes: 8
```

This will prevent Elasticsearch from starting a recovery until at least eight nodes are present. The value for this setting is a matter of personal preference: how many nodes do you want present before you consider your cluster functional? In this case, we are setting it to 8, which means the cluster is inoperable unless there are eight nodes.

Then we tell Elasticsearch how many nodes *should* be in the cluster, and how long we want to wait for all those nodes:

```
gateway.expected_nodes: 10
gateway.recover_after_time: 5m
```

What this means is that Elasticsearch will do the following:

- Wait for eight nodes to be present
- Begin recovering after 5 minutes *or* after ten nodes have joined the cluster, whichever comes first.

These three settings allow you to avoid the excessive shard swapping that can occur on cluster restarts. It can literally make recovery take seconds instead of hours.

Prefer Unicast over Multicast

Elasticsearch is configured to use multicast discovery out of the box. Multicast works by sending UDP pings across your local network to discover nodes. Other Elasticsearch nodes will receive these pings and respond. A cluster is formed shortly after.

Multicast is excellent for development, since you don't need to do anything. Turn a few nodes on, and they automatically find each other and form a cluster.

This ease of use is the exact reason you should disable it in production. The last thing you want is for nodes to accidentally join your production network, simply because they received an errant multicast ping. There is nothing wrong with multicast *per se*. Multicast simply leads to silly problems, and can be a bit more fragile (for example, a network engineer fiddles with the network without telling you—and all of a sudden nodes can't find each other anymore).

In production, it is recommended to use unicast instead of multicast. This works by providing Elasticsearch a list of nodes that it should try to contact. Once the node contacts a member of the unicast list, it will receive a full cluster state that lists all nodes in the cluster. It will then proceed to contact the master and join.

This means your unicast list does not need to hold all the nodes in your cluster. It just needs enough nodes that a new node can find someone to talk to. If you use dedicated masters, just list your three dedicated masters and call it a day. This setting is configured in your `elasticsearch.yml`:

```
discovery.zen.ping.multicast.enabled: false ❶
discovery.zen.ping.unicast.hosts: ["host1", "host2:port"]
```

❶   Make sure you disable multicast, since it can operate in parallel with unicast.

Don't Touch These Settings!

There are a few hotspots in Elasticsearch that people just can't seem to avoid tweaking. We understand: knobs just beg to be turned. But of all the knobs to turn, these you should *really* leave alone. They are often abused and will contribute to terrible stability or terrible performance. Or both.

Garbage Collector

As briefly introduced in "Garbage Collection Primer" on page 621, the JVM uses a garbage collector to free unused memory. This tip is really an extension of the last tip, but deserves its own section for emphasis:

Do not change the default garbage collector!

The default GC for Elasticsearch is Concurrent-Mark and Sweep (CMS). This GC runs concurrently with the execution of the application so that it can minimize pauses. It does, however, have two stop-the-world phases. It also has trouble collecting large heaps.

Despite these downsides, it is currently the best GC for low-latency server software like Elasticsearch. The official recommendation is to use CMS.

There is a newer GC called the Garbage First GC (G1GC). This newer GC is designed to minimize pausing even more than CMS, and operate on large heaps. It works by dividing the heap into regions and predicting which regions contain the most reclaimable space. By collecting those regions first (*garbage first*), it can minimize pauses and operate on very large heaps.

Sounds great! Unfortunately, G1GC is still new, and fresh bugs are found routinely. These bugs are usually of the segfault variety, and will cause hard crashes. The Lucene test suite is brutal on GC algorithms, and it seems that G1GC hasn't had the kinks worked out yet.

We would like to recommend G1GC someday, but for now, it is simply not stable enough to meet the demands of Elasticsearch and Lucene.

Threadpools

Everyone *loves* to tweak threadpools. For whatever reason, it seems people cannot resist increasing thread counts. Indexing a lot? More threads! Searching a lot? More threads! Node idling 95% of the time? More threads!

The default threadpool settings in Elasticsearch are very sensible. For all threadpools (except search) the threadcount is set to the number of CPU cores. If you have eight cores, you can be running only eight threads simultaneously. It makes sense to assign only eight threads to any particular threadpool.

Search gets a larger threadpool, and is configured to # cores * 3.

You might argue that some threads can block (such as on a disk I/O operation), which is why you need more threads. This is not a problem in Elasticsearch: much of the disk I/O is handled by threads managed by Lucene, not Elasticsearch.

Furthermore, threadpools cooperate by passing work between each other. You don't need to worry about a networking thread blocking because it is waiting on a disk write. The networking thread will have long since handed off that work unit to another threadpool and gotten back to networking.

Finally, the compute capacity of your process is finite. Having more threads just forces the processor to switch thread contexts. A processor can run only one thread at a time, so when it needs to switch to a different thread, it stores the current state (registers, and so forth) and loads another thread. If you are lucky, the switch will happen on the same core. If you are unlucky, the switch may migrate to a different core and require transport on an inter-core communication bus.

This context switching eats up cycles simply by doing administrative housekeeping; estimates can peg it as high as 30μs on modern CPUs. So unless the thread will be blocked for longer than 30μs, it is highly likely that that time would have been better spent just processing and finishing early.

People routinely set threadpools to silly values. On eight core machines, we have run across configs with 60, 100, or even 1000 threads. These settings will simply thrash the CPU more than getting real work done.

So. Next time you want to tweak a threadpool, please don't. And if you *absolutely cannot resist*, please keep your core count in mind and perhaps set the count to double. More than that is just a waste.

Heap: Sizing and Swapping

The default installation of Elasticsearch is configured with a 1 GB heap. For just about every deployment, this number is far too small. If you are using the default heap values, your cluster is probably configured incorrectly.

There are two ways to change the heap size in Elasticsearch. The easiest is to set an environment variable called ES_HEAP_SIZE. When the server process starts, it will read this environment variable and set the heap accordingly. As an example, you can set it via the command line as follows:

```
export ES_HEAP_SIZE=10g
```

Alternatively, you can pass in the heap size via a command-line argument when starting the process, if that is easier for your setup:

```
./bin/elasticsearch -Xmx=10g -Xms=10g ❶
```

❶ Ensure that the min (Xms) and max (Xmx) sizes are the same to prevent the heap from resizing at runtime, a very costly process.

Generally, setting the ES_HEAP_SIZE environment variable is preferred over setting explicit -Xmx and -Xms values.

Give Half Your Memory to Lucene

A common problem is configuring a heap that is *too* large. You have a 64 GB machine —and by golly, you want to give Elasticsearch all 64 GB of memory. More is better!

Heap is definitely important to Elasticsearch. It is used by many in-memory data structures to provide fast operation. But with that said, there is another major user of memory that is *off heap*: Lucene.

Lucene is designed to leverage the underlying OS for caching in-memory data structures. Lucene segments are stored in individual files. Because segments are immutable, these files never change. This makes them very cache friendly, and the underlying OS will happily keep hot segments resident in memory for faster access.

Lucene's performance relies on this interaction with the OS. But if you give all available memory to Elasticsearch's heap, there won't be any left over for Lucene. This can seriously impact the performance of full-text search.

The standard recommendation is to give 50% of the available memory to Elasticsearch heap, while leaving the other 50% free. It won't go unused; Lucene will happily gobble up whatever is left over.

Don't Cross 32 GB!

There is another reason to not allocate enormous heaps to Elasticsearch. As it turns out, the JVM uses a trick to compress object pointers when heaps are less than ~32 GB.

In Java, all objects are allocated on the heap and referenced by a pointer. Ordinary object pointers (OOP) point at these objects, and are traditionally the size of the

CPU's native *word*: either 32 bits or 64 bits, depending on the processor. The pointer references the exact byte location of the value.

For 32-bit systems, this means the maximum heap size is 4 GB. For 64-bit systems, the heap size can get much larger, but the overhead of 64-bit pointers means there is more wasted space simply because the pointer is larger. And worse than wasted space, the larger pointers eat up more bandwidth when moving values between main memory and various caches (LLC, L1, and so forth).

Java uses a trick called compressed oops (*https://wikis.oracle.com/display/HotSpotInternals/CompressedOops*) to get around this problem. Instead of pointing at exact byte locations in memory, the pointers reference *object offsets*. This means a 32-bit pointer can reference four billion *objects*, rather than four billion bytes. Ultimately, this means the heap can grow to around 32 GB of physical size while still using a 32-bit pointer.

Once you cross that magical ~30–32 GB boundary, the pointers switch back to ordinary object pointers. The size of each pointer grows, more CPU-memory bandwidth is used, and you effectively lose memory. In fact, it takes until around 40–50 GB of allocated heap before you have the same *effective* memory of a 32 GB heap using compressed oops.

The moral of the story is this: even when you have memory to spare, try to avoid crossing the 32 GB heap boundary. It wastes memory, reduces CPU performance, and makes the GC struggle with large heaps.

I Have a Machine with 1 TB RAM!

The 32 GB line is fairly important. So what do you do when your machine has a lot of memory? It is becoming increasingly common to see super-servers with 300–500 GB of RAM.

First, we would recommend avoiding such large machines (see "Hardware" on page 635).

But if you already have the machines, you have two practical options:

- Are you doing mostly full-text search? Consider giving 32 GB to Elasticsearch and letting Lucene use the rest of memory via the OS filesystem cache. All that memory will cache segments and lead to blisteringly fast full-text search.

- Are you doing a lot of sorting/aggregations? You'll likely want that memory in the heap then. Instead of one node with 32 GB+ of RAM, consider running two or more nodes on a single machine. Still adhere to the 50% rule, though. So if your machine has 128 GB of RAM, run two nodes, each with 32 GB. This means 64 GB will be used for heaps, and 64 will be left over for Lucene.

  If you choose this option, set `cluster.routing.allocation.same_shard.host: true` in your config. This will prevent a primary and a replica shard from colocating to the same physical machine (since this would remove the benefits of replica high availability).

Swapping Is the Death of Performance

It should be obvious, but it bears spelling out clearly: swapping main memory to disk will *crush* server performance. Think about it: an in-memory operation is one that needs to execute quickly.

If memory swaps to disk, a 100-microsecond operation becomes one that take 10 milliseconds. Now repeat that increase in latency for all other 10us operations. It isn't difficult to see why swapping is terrible for performance.

The best thing to do is disable swap completely on your system. This can be done temporarily:

```
sudo swapoff -a
```

To disable it permanently, you'll likely need to edit your */etc/fstab*. Consult the documentation for your OS.

If disabling swap completely is not an option, you can try to lower `swappiness`. This value controls how aggressively the OS tries to swap memory. This prevents swapping under normal circumstances, but still allows the OS to swap under emergency memory situations.

For most Linux systems, this is configured using the `sysctl` value:

```
vm.swappiness = 1 ❶
```

❶ A `swappiness` of 1 is better than 0, since on some kernel versions a `swappiness` of 0 can invoke the OOM-killer.

Finally, if neither approach is possible, you should enable `mlockall`. file. This allows the JVM to lock its memory and prevent it from being swapped by the OS. In your `elasticsearch.yml`, set this:

```
bootstrap.mlockall: true
```

File Descriptors and MMap

Lucene uses a *very* large number of files. At the same time, Elasticsearch uses a large number of sockets to communicate between nodes and HTTP clients. All of this requires available file descriptors.

Sadly, many modern Linux distributions ship with a paltry 1,024 file descriptors allowed per process. This is *far* too low for even a small Elasticsearch node, let alone one that is handling hundreds of indices.

You should increase your file descriptor count to something very large, such as 64,000. This process is irritatingly difficult and highly dependent on your particular OS and distribution. Consult the documentation for your OS to determine how best to change the allowed file descriptor count.

Once you think you've changed it, check Elasticsearch to make sure it really does have enough file descriptors:

```
GET /_nodes/process

{
   "cluster_name": "elasticsearch__zach",
   "nodes": {
      "TGn9iO2_QQKb0kavcLbnDw": {
         "name": "Zach",
         "transport_address": "inet[/192.168.1.131:9300]",
         "host": "zacharys-air",
         "ip": "192.168.1.131",
         "version": "2.0.0-SNAPSHOT",
         "build": "612f461",
         "http_address": "inet[/192.168.1.131:9200]",
         "process": {
            "refresh_interval_in_millis": 1000,
            "id": 19808,
```

```
            "max_file_descriptors": 64000, ❶
            "mlockall": true
        }
      }
    }
  }
```

❶ The `max_file_descriptors` field shows the number of available descriptors that
   the Elasticsearch process can access.

Elasticsearch also uses a mix of NioFS and MMapFS for the various files. Ensure that
you configure the maximum map count so that there is ample virtual memory available for mmapped files. This can be set temporarily:

```
sysctl -w vm.max_map_count=262144
```

Or you can set it permanently by modifying vm.max_map_count setting in your /etc/
sysctl.conf.

Revisit This List Before Production

You are likely reading this section before you go into production. The details covered
in this chapter are good to be generally aware of, but it is critical to revisit this entire
list right before deploying to production.

Some of the topics will simply stop you cold (such as too few available file descriptors). These are easy enough to debug because they are quickly apparent. Other
issues, such as split brains and memory settings, are visible only after something bad
happens. At that point, the resolution is often messy and tedious.

It is much better to proactively prevent these situations from occurring by configuring your cluster appropriately *before* disaster strikes. So if you are going to dog-ear
(or bookmark) one section from the entire book, this chapter would be a good candidate. The week before deploying to production, simply flip through the list presented
here and check off all the recommendations.

CHAPTER 46

Post-Deployment

Once you have deployed your cluster in production, there are some tools and best practices to keep your cluster running in top shape. In this short chapter, we talk about configuring settings dynamically, tweaking logging levels, improving indexing performance, and backing up your cluster.

Changing Settings Dynamically

Many settings in Elasticsearch are dynamic and can be modified through the API. Configuration changes that force a node (or cluster) restart are strenuously avoided. And while it's possible to make the changes through the static configs, we recommend that you use the API instead.

The `cluster-update` API operates in two modes:

Transient
> These changes are in effect until the cluster restarts. Once a full cluster restart takes place, these settings are erased.

Persistent
> These changes are permanently in place unless explicitly changed. They will survive full cluster restarts and override the static configuration files.

Transient versus persistent settings are supplied in the JSON body:

```
PUT /_cluster/settings
{
    "persistent" : {
        "discovery.zen.minimum_master_nodes" : 2 ❶
    },
    "transient" : {
        "indices.store.throttle.max_bytes_per_sec" : "50mb" ❷
```

```
        }
    }
```

❶ This persistent setting will survive full cluster restarts.

❷ This transient setting will be removed after the first full cluster restart.

A complete list of settings that can be updated dynamically can be found in the online reference docs (*http://www.elasticsearch.org/guide/en/elasticsearch/reference/current/ cluster-update-settings.html*).

Logging

Elasticsearch emits a number of logs, which are placed in `ES_HOME/logs`. The default logging level is `INFO`. It provides a moderate amount of information, but is designed to be rather light so that your logs are not enormous.

When debugging problems, particularly problems with node discovery (since this often depends on finicky network configurations), it can be helpful to bump up the logging level to `DEBUG`.

You *could* modify the `logging.yml` file and restart your nodes—but that is both tedious and leads to unnecessary downtime. Instead, you can update logging levels through the `cluster-settings` API that we just learned about.

To do so, take the logger you are interested in and prepend `logger.` to it. Let's turn up the discovery logging:

```
PUT /_cluster/settings
{
    "transient" : {
        "logger.discovery" : "DEBUG"
    }
}
```

While this setting is in effect, Elasticsearch will begin to emit `DEBUG`-level logs for the `discovery` module.

> Avoid `TRACE`. It is extremely verbose, to the point where the logs are no longer useful.

Slowlog

There is another log called the *slowlog*. The purpose of this log is to catch queries and indexing requests that take over a certain threshold of time. It is useful for hunting down user-generated queries that are particularly slow.

By default, the slowlog is not enabled. It can be enabled by defining the action (query, fetch, or index), the level that you want the event logged at (WARN, DEBUG, and so forth) and a time threshold.

This is an index-level setting, which means it is applied to individual indices:

```
PUT /my_index/_settings
{
    "index.search.slowlog.threshold.query.warn" : "10s",   ❶
    "index.search.slowlog.threshold.fetch.debug": "500ms",  ❷
    "index.indexing.slowlog.threshold.index.info": "5s"  ❸
}
```

❶ Emit a WARN log when queries are slower than 10s.

❷ Emit a DEBUG log when fetches are slower than 500ms.

❸ Emit an INFO log when indexing takes longer than 5s.

You can also define these thresholds in your elasticsearch.yml file. Indices that do not have a threshold set will inherit whatever is configured in the static config.

Once the thresholds are set, you can toggle the logging level like any other logger:

```
PUT /_cluster/settings
{
    "transient" : {
        "logger.index.search.slowlog" : "DEBUG",  ❶
        "logger.index.indexing.slowlog" : "WARN"  ❷
    }
}
```

❶ Set the search slowlog to DEBUG level.

❷ Set the indexing slowlog to WARN level.

Indexing Performance Tips

If you are in an indexing-heavy environment, such as indexing infrastructure logs, you may be willing to sacrifice some search performance for faster indexing rates. In these scenarios, searches tend to be relatively rare and performed by people internal to your organization. They are willing to wait several seconds for a search, as opposed to a consumer facing a search that must return in milliseconds.

Because of this unique position, certain trade-offs can be made that will increase your indexing performance.

These Tips Apply Only to Elasticsearch 1.3+

This book is written for the most recent versions of Elasticsearch, although much of the content works on older versions.

The tips presented in this section, however, are *explicitly* for version 1.3+. There have been multiple performance improvements and bugs fixed that directly impact indexing. In fact, some of these recommendations will *reduce* performance on older versions because of the presence of bugs or performance defects.

Test Performance Scientifically

Performance testing is always difficult, so try to be as scientific as possible in your approach. Randomly fiddling with knobs and turning on ingestion is not a good way to tune performance. If there are too many *causes*, it is impossible to determine which one had the best *effect*. A reasonable approach to testing is as follows:

1. Test performance on a single node, with a single shard and no replicas.

2. Record performance under 100% default settings so that you have a baseline to measure against.

3. Make sure performance tests run for a long time (30+ minutes) so you can evaluate long-term performance, not short-term spikes or latencies. Some events (such as segment merging, and GCs) won't happen right away, so the performance profile can change over time.

4. Begin making single changes to the baseline defaults. Test these rigorously, and if performance improvement is acceptable, keep the setting and move on to the next one.

Using and Sizing Bulk Requests

This should be fairly obvious, but use bulk indexing requests for optimal performance. Bulk sizing is dependent on your data, analysis, and cluster configuration, but a good starting point is 5–15 MB per bulk. Note that this is physical size. Document count is not a good metric for bulk size. For example, if you are indexing 1,000 documents per bulk, keep the following in mind:

- 1,000 documents at 1 KB each is 1 MB.
- 1,000 documents at 100 KB each is 100 MB.

Those are drastically different bulk sizes. Bulks need to be loaded into memory at the coordinating node, so it is the physical size of the bulk that is more important than the document count.

Start with a bulk size around 5–15 MB and slowly increase it until you do not see performance gains anymore. Then start increasing the concurrency of your bulk ingestion (multiple threads, and so forth).

Monitor your nodes with Marvel and/or tools such as `iostat`, `top`, and `ps` to see when resources start to bottleneck. If you start to receive `EsRejectedExecutionExcep tion`, your cluster can no longer keep up: at least one resource has reached capacity. Either reduce concurrency, provide more of the limited resource (such as switching from spinning disks to SSDs), or add more nodes.

 When ingesting data, make sure bulk requests are round-robined across all your data nodes. Do not send all requests to a single node, since that single node will need to store all the bulks in memory while processing.

Storage

Disks are usually the bottleneck of any modern server. Elasticsearch heavily uses disks, and the more throughput your disks can handle, the more stable your nodes will be. Here are some tips for optimizing disk I/O:

- Use SSDs. As mentioned elsewhere, they are superior to spinning media.
- Use RAID 0. Striped RAID will increase disk I/O, at the obvious expense of potential failure if a drive dies. Don't use mirrored or parity RAIDS since replicas provide that functionality.
- Alternatively, use multiple drives and allow Elasticsearch to stripe data across them via multiple `path.data` directories.
- Do not use remote-mounted storage, such as NFS or SMB/CIFS. The latency introduced here is antithetical to performance.
- If you are on EC2, beware of EBS. Even the SSD-backed EBS options are often slower than local instance storage.

Segments and Merging

Segment merging is computationally expensive, and can eat up a lot of disk I/O. Merges are scheduled to operate in the background because they can take a long time to finish, especially large segments. This is normally fine, because the rate of large segment merges is relatively rare.

But sometimes merging falls behind the ingestion rate. If this happens, Elasticsearch will automatically throttle indexing requests to a single thread. This prevents a *segment explosion* problem, in which hundreds of segments are generated before they can be merged. Elasticsearch will log INFO-level messages stating now throttling indexing when it detects merging falling behind indexing.

Elasticsearch defaults here are conservative: you don't want search performance to be impacted by background merging. But sometimes (especially on SSD, or logging scenarios), the throttle limit is too low.

The default is 20 MB/s, which is a good setting for spinning disks. If you have SSDs, you might consider increasing this to 100–200 MB/s. Test to see what works for your system:

```
PUT /_cluster/settings
{
    "persistent" : {
        "indices.store.throttle.max_bytes_per_sec" : "100mb"
    }
}
```

If you are doing a bulk import and don't care about search at all, you can disable merge throttling entirely. This will allow indexing to run as fast as your disks will allow:

```
PUT /_cluster/settings
{
    "transient" : {
        "indices.store.throttle.type" : "none" ❶
    }
}
```

❶ Setting the throttle type to none disables merge throttling entirely. When you are done importing, set it back to merge to reenable throttling.

If you are using spinning media instead of SSD, you need to add this to your elasticsearch.yml:

```
index.merge.scheduler.max_thread_count: 1
```

Spinning media has a harder time with concurrent I/O, so we need to decrease the number of threads that can concurrently access the disk per index. This setting will

---

allow `max_thread_count + 2` threads to operate on the disk at one time, so a setting of 1 will allow three threads.

For SSDs, you can ignore this setting. The default is `Math.min(3, Runtime.getRun time().availableProcessors() / 2)`, which works well for SSD.

Finally, you can increase `index.translog.flush_threshold_size` from the default 200 MB to something larger, such as 1 GB. This allows larger segments to accumulate in the translog before a flush occurs. By letting larger segments build, you flush less often, and the larger segments merge less often. All of this adds up to less disk I/O overhead and better indexing rates.

Other

Finally, there are some other considerations to keep in mind:

- If you don't need near real-time accuracy on your search results, consider dropping the `index.refresh_interval` of each index to `30s`. If you are doing a large import, you can disable refreshes by setting this value to `-1` for the duration of the import. Don't forget to reenable it when you are finished!

- If you are doing a large bulk import, consider disabling replicas by setting `index.number_of_replicas: 0`. When documents are replicated, the entire document is sent to the replica node and the indexing process is repeated verbatim. This means each replica will perform the analysis, indexing, and potentially merging process.

  In contrast, if you index with zero replicas and then enable replicas when ingestion is finished, the recovery process is essentially a byte-for-byte network transfer. This is much more efficient than duplicating the indexing process.

- If you don't have a natural ID for each document, use Elasticsearch's auto-ID functionality. It is optimized to avoid version lookups, since the autogenerated ID is unique.

- If you are using your own ID, try to pick an ID that is friendly to Lucene (*http:// bit.ly/1sDiR5t*). Examples include zero-padded sequential IDs, UUID-1, and nanotime; these IDs have consistent, sequential patterns that compress well. In contrast, IDs such as UUID-4 are essentially random, which offer poor compression and slow down Lucene.

Rolling Restarts

There will come a time when you need to perform a rolling restart of your cluster—
keeping the cluster online and operational, but taking nodes offline one at a time.

The common reason is either an Elasticsearch version upgrade, or some kind of
maintenance on the server itself (such as an OS update, or hardware). Whatever the
case, there is a particular method to perform a rolling restart.

By nature, Elasticsearch wants your data to be fully replicated and evenly balanced. If
you shut down a single node for maintenance, the cluster will immediately recognize
the loss of a node and begin rebalancing. This can be irritating if you know the node
maintenance is short term, since the rebalancing of very large shards can take some
time (think of trying to replicate 1TB—even on fast networks this is nontrivial).

What we want to do is tell Elasticsearch to hold off on rebalancing, because we have
more knowledge about the state of the cluster due to external factors. The procedure
is as follows:

1. If possible, stop indexing new data. This is not always possible, but will help
   speed up recovery time.
2. Disable shard allocation. This prevents Elasticsearch from rebalancing missing
   shards until you tell it otherwise. If you know the maintenance window will be
   short, this is a good idea. You can disable allocation as follows:

   ```
   PUT /_cluster/settings
   {
       "transient" : {
           "cluster.routing.allocation.enable" : "none"
       }
   }
   ```

3. Shut down a single node, preferably using the shutdown API on that particular
   machine:

   ```
   POST /_cluster/nodes/_local/_shutdown
   ```

4. Perform a maintenance/upgrade.
5. Restart the node, and confirm that it joins the cluster.
6. Reenable shard allocation as follows:

   ```
   PUT /_cluster/settings
   {
       "transient" : {
           "cluster.routing.allocation.enable" : "all"
       }
   }
   ```

Shard rebalancing may take some time. Wait until the cluster has returned to status green before continuing.

7. Repeat steps 2 through 6 for the rest of your nodes.

8. At this point you are safe to resume indexing (if you had previously stopped), but waiting until the cluster is fully balanced before resuming indexing will help to speed up the process.

Backing Up Your Cluster

As with any software that stores data, it is important to routinely back up your data. Elasticsearch replicas provide high availability during runtime; they allow you to tolerate sporadic node loss without an interruption of service.

Replicas do not provide protection from catastrophic failure, however. For that, you need a real backup of your cluster—a complete copy in case something goes wrong.

To back up your cluster, you can use the snapshot API. This will take the current state and data in your cluster and save it to a shared repository. This backup process is "smart." Your first snapshot will be a complete copy of data, but all subsequent snapshots will save the *delta* between the existing snapshots and the new data. Data is incrementally added and deleted as you snapshot data over time. This means subsequent backups will be substantially faster since they are transmitting far less data.

To use this functionality, you must first create a repository to save data. There are several repository types that you may choose from:

- Shared filesystem, such as a NAS
- Amazon S3
- HDFS (Hadoop Distributed File System)
- Azure Cloud

Creating the Repository

Let's set up a shared filesystem repository:

```
PUT _snapshot/my_backup ❶
{
    "type": "fs", ❷
    "settings": {
        "location": "/mount/backups/my_backup" ❸
    }
}
```

❶ We provide a name for our repository, in this case it is called my_backup.

❷ We specify that the type of the repository should be a shared filesystem.

❸ And finally, we provide a mounted drive as the destination.

 The shared filesystem path must be accessible from all nodes in your cluster!

This will create the repository and required metadata at the mount point. There are also some other options that you may want to configure, depending on the performance profile of your nodes, network, and repository location:

max_snapshot_bytes_per_sec
> When snapshotting data into the repo, this controls the throttling of that process. The default is 20mb per second.

max_restore_bytes_per_sec
> When restoring data from the repo, this controls how much the restore is throttled so that your network is not saturated. The default is 20mb per second.

Let's assume we have a very fast network and are OK with extra traffic, so we can increase the defaults:

```
POST _snapshot/my_backup/ ❶
{
    "type": "fs",
    "settings": {
        "location": "/mount/backups/my_backup",
        "max_snapshot_bytes_per_sec" : "50mb", ❷
        "max_restore_bytes_per_sec" : "50mb"
    }
}
```

❶ Note that we are using a POST instead of PUT. This will update the settings of the existing repository.

❷ Then add our new settings.

Snapshotting All Open Indices

A repository can contain multiple snapshots. Each snapshot is associated with a certain set of indices (for example, all indices, some subset, or a single index). When creating a snapshot, you specify which indices you are interested in and give the snapshot a unique name.

Let's start with the most basic snapshot command:

```
PUT _snapshot/my_backup/snapshot_1
```

This will back up all open indices into a snapshot named `snapshot_1`, under the `my_backup` repository. This call will return immediately, and the snapshot will proceed in the background.

 Usually you'll want your snapshots to proceed as a background process, but occasionally you may want to wait for completion in your script. This can be accomplished by adding a `wait_for_com pletion` flag:

```
PUT _snapshot/my_backup/snapshot_1?wait_for_completion=true
```

This will block the call until the snapshot has completed. Note that large snapshots may take a long time to return!

Snapshotting Particular Indices

The default behavior is to back up all open indices. But say you are using Marvel, and don't really want to back up all the diagnostic `.marvel` indices. You just don't have enough space to back up everything.

In that case, you can specify which indices to back up when snapshotting your cluster:

```
PUT _snapshot/my_backup/snapshot_2
{
    "indices": "index_1,index_2"
}
```

This snapshot command will now back up only `index1` and `index2`.

Listing Information About Snapshots

Once you start accumulating snapshots in your repository, you may forget the details relating to each—particularly when the snapshots are named based on time demarcations (for example, `backup_2014_10_28`).

To obtain information about a single snapshot, simply issue a `GET` request against the repo and snapshot name:

```
GET _snapshot/my_backup/snapshot_2
```

This will return a small response with various pieces of information regarding the snapshot:

```
{
    "snapshots": [
        {
            "snapshot": "snapshot_1",
            "indices": [
                ".marvel_2014_28_10",
                "index1",
                "index2"
            ],
            "state": "SUCCESS",
            "start_time": "2014-09-02T13:01:43.115Z",
            "start_time_in_millis": 1409662903115,
            "end_time": "2014-09-02T13:01:43.439Z",
            "end_time_in_millis": 1409662903439,
            "duration_in_millis": 324,
            "failures": [],
            "shards": {
                "total": 10,
                "failed": 0,
                "successful": 10
            }
        }
    ]
}
```

For a complete listing of all snapshots in a repository, use the _all placeholder instead of a snapshot name:

```
GET _snapshot/my_backup/_all
```

Deleting Snapshots

Finally, we need a command to delete old snapshots that are no longer useful. This is simply a DELETE HTTP call to the repo/snapshot name:

```
DELETE _snapshot/my_backup/snapshot_2
```

It is important to use the API to delete snapshots, and not some other mechanism (such as deleting by hand, or using automated cleanup tools on S3). Because snapshots are incremental, it is possible that many snapshots are relying on old segments. The delete API understands what data is still in use by more recent snapshots, and will delete only unused segments.

If you do a manual file delete, however, you are at risk of seriously corrupting your backups because you are deleting data that is still in use.

Monitoring Snapshot Progress

The wait_for_completion flag provides a rudimentary form of monitoring, but really isn't sufficient when snapshotting or restoring even moderately sized clusters.

Two other APIs will give you more-detailed status about the state of the snapshotting. First you can execute a GET to the snapshot ID, just as we did earlier get information about a particular snapshot:

```
GET _snapshot/my_backup/snapshot_3
```

If the snapshot is still in progress when you call this, you'll see information about when it was started, how long it has been running, and so forth. Note, however, that this API uses the same threadpool as the snapshot mechanism. If you are snapshotting very large shards, the time between status updates can be quite large, since the API is competing for the same threadpool resources.

A better option is to poll the _status API:

```
GET _snapshot/my_backup/snapshot_3/_status
```

The _status API returns immediately and gives a much more verbose output of statistics:

```
{
   "snapshots": [
      {
         "snapshot": "snapshot_3",
         "repository": "my_backup",
         "state": "IN_PROGRESS", ❶
         "shards_stats": {
            "initializing": 0,
            "started": 1, ❷
            "finalizing": 0,
            "done": 4,
            "failed": 0,
            "total": 5
         },
         "stats": {
            "number_of_files": 5,
            "processed_files": 5,
            "total_size_in_bytes": 1792,
            "processed_size_in_bytes": 1792,
            "start_time_in_millis": 1409663054859,
            "time_in_millis": 64
         },
         "indices": {
            "index_3": {
               "shards_stats": {
                  "initializing": 0,
                  "started": 0,
                  "finalizing": 0,
                  "done": 5,
                  "failed": 0,
                  "total": 5
               },
               "stats": {
```

```
                    "number_of_files": 5,
                    "processed_files": 5,
                    "total_size_in_bytes": 1792,
                    "processed_size_in_bytes": 1792,
                    "start_time_in_millis": 1409663054859,
                    "time_in_millis": 64
                },
                "shards": {
                    "0": {
                        "stage": "DONE",
                        "stats": {
                            "number_of_files": 1,
                            "processed_files": 1,
                            "total_size_in_bytes": 514,
                            "processed_size_in_bytes": 514,
                            "start_time_in_millis": 1409663054862,
                            "time_in_millis": 22
                        }
                    },
                    ...
```

❶ A snapshot that is currently running will show IN_PROGRESS as its status.

❷ This particular snapshot has one shard still transferring (the other four have already completed).

The response includes the overall status of the snapshot, but also drills down into per-index and per-shard statistics. This gives you an incredibly detailed view of how the snapshot is progressing. Shards can be in various states of completion:

INITIALIZING
: The shard is checking with the cluster state to see whether it can be snapshotted. This is usually very fast.

STARTED
: Data is being transferred to the repository.

FINALIZING
: Data transfer is complete; the shard is now sending snapshot metadata.

DONE
: Snapshot complete!

FAILED
: An error was encountered during the snapshot process, and this shard/index/ snapshot could not be completed. Check your logs for more information.

Canceling a Snapshot

Finally, you may want to cancel a snapshot or restore. Since these are long-running processes, a typo or mistake when executing the operation could take a long time to resolve—and use up valuable resources at the same time.

To cancel a snapshot, simply delete the snapshot while it is in progress:

```
DELETE _snapshot/my_backup/snapshot_3
```

This will halt the snapshot process. Then proceed to delete the half-completed snapshot from the repository.

Restoring from a Snapshot

Once you've backed up some data, restoring it is easy: simply add `_restore` to the ID of the snapshot you wish to restore into your cluster:

```
POST _snapshot/my_backup/snapshot_1/_restore
```

The default behavior is to restore all indices that exist in that snapshot. If `snapshot_1` contains five indices, all five will be restored into our cluster. As with the `snapshot` API, it is possible to select which indices we want to restore.

There are also additional options for renaming indices. This allows you to match index names with a pattern, and then provide a new name during the restore process. This is useful if you want to restore old data to verify its contents, or perform some other processing, without replacing existing data. Let's restore a single index from the snapshot and provide a replacement name:

```
POST /_snapshot/my_backup/snapshot_1/_restore
{
    "indices": "index_1", ❶
    "rename_pattern": "index_(.+)", ❷
    "rename_replacement": "restored_index_$1" ❸
}
```

❶ Restore only the `index_1` index, ignoring the rest that are present in the snapshot.

❷ Find any indices being restored that match the provided pattern.

❸ Then rename them with the replacement pattern.

This will restore `index_1` into your cluster, but rename it to `restored_index_1`.

Similar to snapshotting, the `restore` command will return immediately, and the restoration process will happen in the background. If you would prefer your HTTP call to block until the restore is finished, simply add the `wait_for_completion` flag:

```
POST _snapshot/my_backup/snapshot_1/_restore?wait_for_completion=true
```

Monitoring Restore Operations

The restoration of data from a repository piggybacks on the existing recovery mechanisms already in place in Elasticsearch. Internally, recovering shards from a repository is identical to recovering from another node.

If you wish to monitor the progress of a restore, you can use the `recovery` API. This is a general-purpose API that shows the status of shards moving around your cluster.

The API can be invoked for the specific indices that you are recovering:

```
GET /_recovery/restored_index_3
```

Or for all indices in your cluster, which may include other shards moving around, unrelated to your restore process:

```
GET /_recovery/
```

The output will look similar to this (and note, it can become very verbose depending on the activity of your clsuter!):

```
{
  "restored_index_3" : {
    "shards" : [ {
      "id" : 0,
      "type" : "snapshot", ❶
      "stage" : "index",
      "primary" : true,
      "start_time" : "2014-02-24T12:15:59.716",
      "stop_time" : 0,
      "total_time_in_millis" : 175576,
      "source" : { ❷
        "repository" : "my_backup",
        "snapshot" : "snapshot_3",
        "index" : "restored_index_3"
      },
      "target" : {
        "id" : "ryqJ5lO5S4-lSFbGntkEkg",
        "hostname" : "my.fqdn",
        "ip" : "10.0.1.7",
        "name" : "my_es_node"
      },
      "index" : {
        "files" : {
          "total" : 73,
```

```
          "reused" : 0,
          "recovered" : 69,
          "percent" : "94.5%" ❸
        },
        "bytes" : {
          "total" : 79063092,
          "reused" : 0,
          "recovered" : 68891939,
          "percent" : "87.1%"
        },
        "total_time_in_millis" : 0
      },
      "translog" : {
        "recovered" : 0,
        "total_time_in_millis" : 0
      },
      "start" : {
        "check_index_time" : 0,
        "total_time_in_millis" : 0
      }
    } ]
  }
}
```

❶ The type field tells you the nature of the recovery; this shard is being recovered from a snapshot.

❷ The source hash describes the particular snapshot and repository that is being recovered from.

❸ The percent field gives you an idea about the status of the recovery. This particular shard has recovered 94% of the files so far; it is almost complete.

The output will list all indices currently undergoing a recovery, and then list all shards in each of those indices. Each shard will have stats about start/stop time, duration, recover percentage, bytes transferred, and more.

Canceling a Restore

To cancel a restore, you need to delete the indices being restored. Because a restore process is really just shard recovery, issuing a delete-index API alters the cluster state, which will in turn halt recovery. For example:

```
DELETE /restored_index_3
```

If restored_index_3 was actively being restored, this delete command would halt the restoration as well as deleting any data that had already been restored into the cluster.

Clusters Are Living, Breathing Creatures

Once you get a cluster into production, you'll find that it takes on a life of its own. Elasticsearch works hard to make clusters self-sufficient and *just work*. But a cluster still requires routine care and feeding, such as routine backups and upgrades.

Elasticsearch releases new versions with bug fixes and performance enhancements at a very fast pace, and it is always a good idea to keep your cluster current. Similarly, Lucene continues to find new and exciting bugs in the JVM itself, which means you should always try to keep your JVM up-to-date.

This means it is a good idea to have a standardized, routine way to perform rolling restarts and upgrades in your cluster. Upgrading should be a routine process, rather than a once-yearly fiasco that requires countless hours of precise planning.

Similarly, it is important to have disaster recovery plans in place. Take frequent snapshots of your cluster—and periodically *test* those snapshots by performing a real recovery! It is all too common for organizations to make routine backups but never test their recovery strategy. Often you'll find a glaring deficiency the first time you perform a real recovery (such as users being unaware of which drive to mount). It's better to work these bugs out of your process with routine testing, rather than at 3 a.m. when there is a crisis.

Index

Symbols
32gb Heap boundary, 646

A
ACID transactions, 547, 558
action, in bulk requests, 59, 71
ad hoc searches, 16
aggregations, 21, 419
  aggs parameter, 426
  and analysis, 485
  approximate, 459
    cardinality, 460
    percentiles, 464
  basic example
    adding a metric, 428
    adding extra metrics, 431
    buckets nested in other buckets, 429
  building bar charts from, 435
  building date histograms from, 439
  children aggregation, 580
  doc values, 495
  extended example, 443
  field collapsing, 551
  fielddata
    datastructure overview, 503
    filtering, 493, 515
    using instead of inverted index, 484
  filtering just aggregations, 452
  geo, 529
  geohash_grid, 532
  geo_bounds, 534
  geo_distance, 529
  hierarchical rollups in, 22
  high-level concepts, 421

  buckets, 421
    combining buckets and metrics, 422
    metrics, 422
  limiting memory usage, 489
    fielddata circuit breaker, 492
    fielddata size, 490
    moitoring fielddata, 491
  managing efficient memory usage, 509
  nested, 571
    reverse_nested aggregation, 573
  operating alongside search requests, 420
  preventing combinatorial explosions, 502
    depth-first versus breadth-first, 504
  returning empty buckets, 441
  scoping, 447
    global bucket, 449
  Significant Terms, 473
  significant_terms
    demonstration of, 474
  sorting multivalue buckets, 455
aliases, index, 153, 595, 597, 604
_all field, 79, 82, 144, 151, 237
alphabetical order, 353
analysis, 199
  aggregations and, 485
  controlling, 211
  defined, 86
  high-cardinality fields, memory use issues, 488
  in single term match query, 202
  synonyms and the analysis chain, 403
analytics, 21
  over time, 439
analytics systems, 1

About the Authors

Clinton Gormley was the first user of Elasticsearch and wrote the Perl API back in 2010. When Elasticsearch formed a company in 2012, he joined as a developer and the maintainer of the Perl modules. Now Clinton spends a lot of his time designing the user interfaces and speaking and writing about Elasticsearch. He studied medicine at the University of Cape Town and lives in Barcelona.

Zachary Tong has been working with Elasticsearch since 2011. During that time, he has written a number of tutorials to help beginners start using Elasticsearch. Zach is now a developer at Elasticsearch and maintains the PHP client, gives trainings, and helps customers manage clusters in production. He studied biology at Rensselaer Polytechnic Institute and now lives in South Carolina.

Colophon

The animal on the cover of *Elasticsearch: The Definitive Guide* is an Elegant Snail-eater (Dipsas Elegans). This snake is native to Ecuador, in the Pacific slopes of the Andes. As the name suggests, the diet of the elegant snail-eater consists primarily of snails and slugs, which they find by slowly navigating the forest floor or low-lying shrubs.

The male of this snake species range between 636 and 919 mm in length, while females range between 560 and 782 mm. The whole body includes various brown hues, with alternating dark and light vertical bars throughout.

The elegant snail-eater is non-venomous and very docile. They prefer moist surroundings during the daytime, such as under leaves or in rotting logs and come out to forage at night. They lay an average of seven eggs per clutch. The current, moist habitat in which these snakes thrive is becoming smaller due to human encroachment and destruction, which may lead to their extinction.

Many of the animals on O'Reilly covers are endangered; all of them are important to the world. To learn more about how you can help, go to *animals.oreilly.com*.

The cover image is from *Johnson's Natural History*. The cover fonts are URW Typewriter and Guardian Sans. The text font is Adobe Minion Pro; the heading font is Adobe Myriad Condensed; and the code font is Dalton Maag's Ubuntu Mono.

Get even more for your money.

Join the O'Reilly Community, and register the O'Reilly books you own. It's free, and you'll get:

- $4.99 ebook upgrade offer
- 40% upgrade offer on O'Reilly print books
- Membership discounts on books and events
- Free lifetime updates to ebooks and videos
- Multiple ebook formats, DRM FREE
- Participation in the O'Reilly community
- Newsletters
- Account management
- 100% Satisfaction Guarantee

Signing up is easy:

1. Go to: oreilly.com/go/register
2. Create an O'Reilly login.
3. Provide your address.
4. Register your books.

Note: English-language books only

To order books online:
oreilly.com/store

For questions about products or an order:
orders@oreilly.com

To sign up to get topic-specific email announcements and/or news about upcoming books, conferences, special offers, and new technologies:
elists@oreilly.com

For technical questions about book content:
booktech@oreilly.com

To submit new book proposals to our editors:
proposals@oreilly.com

O'Reilly books are available in multiple DRM-free ebook formats. For more information:
oreilly.com/ebooks

Have it your way.

CPSIA information can be obtained at www.ICGtesting.com
Printed in the USA
BVOW10s1418231015

423904BV00002B/7/P